THE BEST OF *No Depression*

D1245294

BRAD AND MICHELE MOORE
ROOTS MUSIC SERIES

THE BEST OF
NO DEPRESSION

Writing About American Music

Edited by Grant Alden & Peter Blackstock

University of Texas Press
Austin

Copyright © 2005 by No Depression, Inc.
All rights reserved
Printed in the United States of America
First edition, 2005

Requests for permission to reproduce material from this work should be sent to:
    Permissions
    University of Texas Press
    P.O. Box 7819
    Austin, TX 78713-7819
    www.utexas.edu/utpress/about/bpermission.html

♾ The paper used in this book meets the minimum requirements of ANSI/NISO Z39.48-1992 (R1997) (Permanence of Paper).

Library of Congress Cataloging-in-Publication Data
The best of No depression : writing about American music / edited by Grant Alden and Peter Blackstock.—1st ed.
    p.   cm.— (Brad and Michele Moore roots music series)
  ISBN 0-292-70989-7 (pbk. : alk. paper)
    1. Country music—Biography.   I. Alden, Grant.   II. Blackstock, Peter.   III. No depression.   IV. Series.
  ML3524. B47   2005
  781.64'0973—dc22
                                                2005007630

Contents

Preface

Grant Alden and Peter Blackstock

For most of the ten years we have published *No Depression,* each issue has appeared with a subtitle that constantly changes but usually promises a bimonthly alt-country magazine (whatever that is). For most of those ten years, too much attention has been paid to the alt-country half of that phrase, and too little to its parenthetical companion.

First suggested by Peter's father as he sought to explain to a family friend what his son was doing, "whatever that is" has always been the best explanation for what *No Depression* is, or might yet become. As we have often reminded readers, alt-country was meant ironically, for we were two music critics living in Seattle, the citadel of grunge, when *ND* first appeared; the whole idea that editors so far from Nashville might be interested in writing about country music, or would dare to do so, was curious at best and arrogant at worst.

Guilty as charged.

Over the intervening years, alt-country came to mean several things. To the mainstream music industry (*O Brother* notwithstanding), it became code for "doesn't sell"; to fans, it came to describe a network of hardworking bands that fused punk rock's DIY spirit to country music's working-class honesty. Most of those initial groups, indeed, didn't sell all that many records and sought greener pastures of one kind or another, or settled into day jobs.

It was their misfortune to be powerful nightclub acts at a time when major labels prized the perfection of the studio and the arena stage; to write compelling and complicated songs for adults when juvenile slogans sold best; and to engage the music industry when it was no longer interested in (or capable of) nurturing talent for the long haul. Modest critical success and sales in the tens of thousands hardly outweighed the imperatives of corporate consolidation, when established artists were dropped for delivering albums that sold only in the hundreds of thousands.

And yet our magazine not only survived, but grew (as has a fragile but sustainable infrastructure of other small businesses that nurture this music . . . these musics). Not because we are especially astute publishers, but because "whatever that is" was meant as a blunt reminder that *ND* was the creation of two editors who remain endlessly curious about—and enchanted by—music.

We are not biologists. It is not our purpose to identify, quantify, and codify a subgenus called alt-country, or to limit ourselves to its study. We are writers, minor-league historians, fans; musicians bridle at being categorized, as do we. It *is* our purpose to write and assign articles about artists whose work is of enduring merit. And, yes, those artists have some tangential relationship (at least to our ears) to whatever country music may have been—even to what it may now be. Or, rather, to the musics of our country, these United States.

The book at hand is our second anthology. The first summarized articles that appeared during our first three years, ending with *ND* #13. In the interest of actually publishing a second volume on the occasion of our tenth anniversary, we limited this anthology to articles that appeared in issues #14 (March–April 1998) through #51 (May–June 2004). Even so, the book could have been twice as long, had we been allowed. We gave the authors a chance to make minor corrections or adjustments to their text; we recognize that much has changed since these pieces originally appeared.

Looking back at that first anthology through the eyes of this one reveals some distinct developments in the nature of *No Depression*. Most immediately obvious, our articles grew longer and more in-depth as the magazine's reputation spread and its circulation expanded. In the beginning, our role was, perhaps, more introductory. As *ND* has grown, we have sought to cultivate and present profiles of major artists that could purport to be definitive journalistic works. It is our hope that these collected pieces have contributed, in some way, to the historical record of the music and its makers.

Our scope also has broadened a bit from those early days, as has the nature of the music we have covered. We are more apt to address a range of American roots-music forms today; this seems an inevitable outgrowth of any publication focusing on the common ground between country and rock 'n' roll, given that both forms owe considerable debts to bluegrass, blues, folk, jazz, rockabilly, and any number of related genres or subgenres.

Indeed, foremost among our regrets about the space limitations inherent to anthologies is that *No Depression* today covers more territory than we are able to reflect here. Which is not to say that there isn't still plenty of variety among the twenty-five artists represented here. Perhaps more to the point, nearly all of these artists are models of the diversity that is *No Depression*—whether in the form of Los Lobos' multilayered Latino-tinged hybrid, or Johnny Gimble's western-swing blending of hillbilly and jazz, or Buddy & Julie Miller's enchanting combination of country, soul, folk, and rock, or the Drive-By Truckers' head-on collision of classic Southern rock with contemporary punk.

It is, ultimately, impossible to boil down to any simple phrase of a few hyphen-bound words. Conversely, though—and happily so—this music is quite easy to write about at length and in depth, and with both passion and intelligence. These are the qualities we have sought to bring to the pages of *No Depression* in our first ten years. Take a look at how the story has unfolded so far . . . and join us for the next ten years, and beyond.

None of this would be possible without the forbearance of our wives, Susan Thomas and Lisa Whittington. Less than none of this would be possible but for the less glamorous work of our third partner, Kyla Fairchild, who tends to the business concerns of our hobby run amok. Special thanks go to our longtime friend, one-time landlord, and office manager, Mary Schuh, and to the brave handful of souls who have sold advertising for *ND:* Trish Wagner, Tom Monday, Kay Clary, and Jenni Sperandeo. We are indebted beyond the power of mere words to all who have written, photographed, and illustrated for *ND,* and to the many who have read our words over the years.

We dedicate this volume to the late Roxy Gordon, editor and publisher of the 1970s outlaw-country newspaper *Picking Up The Tempo.* Though neither of us were aware of Roxy's publication during its heyday, the dog-eared copies he sent to us a couple years after we had started *No Depression* served as a signpost of sorts, a reminder that we were not so much exploring new territory as we were picking up a lost trail in our efforts to cover this music—whatever it is, or was, or will be.

■ ■ ■

(To subscribe to *No Depression,* visit www.nodepression.net or write to No Depression, P.O. Box 31332, Seattle, WA 98103.)

THE BEST OF *No Depression*

Not Just Another Band from East L.A.

Rock 'n' Roll Rebellion and Mexican Tradition Combined to Change the World for Los Lobos

ND #30, November–December 2000

Geoffrey Himes

> I'm going to write about East L.A. I'm going to write about the fruit vendors, the sewing women in the sweatshops, the smell of the tortilleria, the sounds that waft through the air on Saturdays from backyard parties, the Mexican music that was played, the dresser-top altars in Catholic homes.
>
> Louie Perez, Los Lobos

If you had visited East Los Angeles on an autumn Saturday in 1978, you might have stumbled across a social gathering at a senior-citizens home in the morning, a wedding reception in a parish hall in the afternoon, and a backyard barbecue roast in the evening. And at every function you might have seen the same four scruffy musicians, their dark beards barely disguising their youthful, early-1920s faces.

They called themselves Los Lobos del Este de Los Angeles—the Wolves of East Los Angeles. Whether performing beneath crepe paper sagging from masking tape or party lights strung between palm trees, these neighborhood pickers strummed acoustic guitars and harmonized sweetly on the Mexican American folk songs of their parents' generation.

You might not have recognized that this folkloric quartet would go on to win Grammys, score a #1 single, and become one of the best rock bands of the 1980s and '90s. But everything that happened later had its roots in those days in 1978. And every chapter of that story—from 1978 through the present—is told on Rhino Records' new four-CD, eighty-six-track box set, *El Cancionero—Mas y Mas: A History of the Band from East L.A.* (due out November 7).

At the end of those 1978 gigs, Los Lobos would announce that they had copies of their new album, *Just Another Band from East L.A.,* for sale. If you were smart enough to buy one for ten bucks, you could have resold it for $50 ten years later, for only a thousand copies of the vinyl record with the bright yellow cactus cover were ever pressed. Only now, twenty-two years later, has the album been available on CD (Hollywood Records reissued it in September).

If you took that album home in 1978 and dropped a needle on it, you would soon realize it wasn't a typical Mexican folk album. Yes, all the vocals were in Spanish and all the guitars were acoustic, but the songs came not just from the heartland of central Mexico but from everywhere—Cuba, Bolivia, northern Mexico—and there was even an original from the lead guitarist. Moreover, the tunes were played not with the patient fatalism of real folk music, but with the impatient, rhythmic push of North American rock 'n' roll, despite the absence of drums and amplifiers.

Consider, for example, "Cielito Lindo," a staple of Mexican tourist bands. The Los Lobos version begins with the clinking beer bottles, party chatter, and drunken sing-along that typify the loose informality of the session. It starts out as a very traditional folk number, but halfway through, David Hidalgo leaps in with a slashing fiddle solo; the guitars stiffen, and the song becomes more urgent, more modern.

The whole disc is reminiscent of another unheralded debut folk album, one from an elfin refugee from northern Minnesota, 1962's *Bob Dylan*. That, too, was an all-acoustic affair with mostly traditional material, but Dylan banged from his hollow guitar the rock 'n' roll rhythms he had learned from playing piano with Bobby Vee and from singing Little Richard songs with his high school band, the Golden Chords. That rare combination of deep folk roots and rock 'n' roll immediacy would serve Dylan well for the rest of his career. It would do the same for Los Lobos.

■ ■ ■

They hadn't started out as folk musicians. Like most children of immigrants, David Hidalgo, Cesar Rosas, Louie Perez, and Conrad Lozano had been eager to put the Old World behind and to embrace the New. While students at Garfield High School, they had listened to the same kind of music as any other Southern Californian teen: Ray Charles, the Beatles, James Brown, Marvin Gaye, the Grateful Dead. In fact, you can hear songs by all five of those artists on Los Lobos' new box set.

By the early 1970s, they were all in local rock bands. Rosas led the eleven-piece, horn-and-B3 R&B ensemble Fast Company; Lozano anchored the hard-rock combo Tierra; Hidalgo and Perez helmed a group called Checkers. They all dreamed of resurrecting that late-'50s, early-'60s era when East L.A. produced such rock stars at Ritchie Valens, the Premiers, Cannibal & the Headhunters, and Thee Midnighters. Instead they ended up fielding requests for songs by Cream and Sam & Dave.

Frustrated with being stuck in bar bands doing covers, the four friends sought an escape valve and found it in the old Mexican songs their parents loved. The young men discovered they could pick up albums by old Mexican stars for 99 cents apiece in local department stores, and vintage acoustic instruments such as the requinto romantico (a small guitar) or the guitarron (a giant strap-on bass) for $30 a pop in local pawnshops.

They started learning the songs as a lark, something to do between real gigs. "It started out just as a hobby," Rosas remembers. "We were rock 'n' roll musicians—we weren't getting rich, but we were making a living. But the Mexican music was all around us; my mom had those records, and the old folks used to listen to them on the radio. And the sheer beauty of that music drew us in.

"This guy Frank Gonzalez who lived near me was infatuated with Mexican folk music; he would learn the violin parts on mandolin because they're in the same range. He'd play these songs for me, and I'd say, 'Hey, I know that song.' I had an acoustic guitar, and over a couple of beers, we'd sing the songs. I had known David since seventh-grade shop class; I invited him to join us, and he brought along Louie. After a few months, it snowballed."

It is not an uncommon pattern, whether you are in north Dublin, eastern Kentucky, or East L.A. As a teenager, you want nothing to do with the jigs, reels, waltzes, ballads, breakdowns, polkas, corridas, jarochas, and rancheras you hear at the wedding receptions and church dances your parents drag you to. Then you get a little older and discover that those old tunes have a depth and dignity that is missing from your Black Sabbath, Bee Gees, and Eminem records. Suddenly, your parents don't seem so dumb after all.

This dynamic is amplified in immigrant communities, where teenagers reject not just an older generation but a whole culture that was left behind. And just as the rejection cuts deeper, the thrill of rediscovery is more euphoric.

"Homogenization is such a heavy pressure," Perez says. "Immigrant families come to another world—almost another universe—to find a better life, and they want to leave behind all the struggles that propelled them into this new existence. As a result, a lot of Mexican people call themselves Spanish; a lot of people change their last names. When we were young, we were excited by rock 'n' roll radio like any other American kids. We wanted to be part of what was going on, and as a result we turned our backs on what made us different.

"When we were a little older, we learned a couple of songs just to make our folks happy. There had been a big generation gap, but we erased that when we played these songs, and that made us happy. We soon discovered that embracing our own culture gave us tremendous energy. It was more exciting than any other music we had been playing. So we put away our electric instruments for nine years."

■ ■ ■

3

Los Lobos del Este de Los Angeles (a pun on a famous Mexican band called Los Lobos del Norte) played their first gig in 1973 at a senior-citizen center in the neighborhood. They played the old songs with lots of enthusiasm and just enough competence to bring tears to the eyes of the gray-haired grandmothers. The gig paid just $50, but it provided much more emotional satisfaction than playing for chattering drunks.

The lineup eventually settled on Hidalgo, Rosas, Perez, and Lozano, who gradually gave up their ties to other bands. Lozano got a them-or-us ultimatum from Tierra, which later scored a Top 20 pop hit in 1980 with "Together." The bassist chose the lower wages and more congenial camaraderie. Soon the band was playing weddings, dances, restaurants, and backyard parties all over the area. And they were rehearsing a lot in Rosas's living room.

"That music was really fucking hard," he notes. "We were all used to playing simple blues-based rock, and this was much more complicated than that. If you're not used to those cross-rhythms—that three against two—you're nowhere. You have to develop a feel for that or else you fall out of time. We all learned it by doing it over and over."

Those were the days of the Chicano Pride movement. Cesar Chavez led the farm workers on strikes in the Central Valley. Demonstrations led by activists in brown berets filled the streets of East L.A. Murals depicting heroic grape pickers and Aztec gods splashed across empty walls.

It was inevitable that a young band that specialized in traditional Mexican folk songs would get caught up in this movement. Los Lobos played several benefit concerts for Chavez, and even contributed several tracks for a United Farm Workers fund-raising album, *Si Se Puede.* During the weeks surrounding the Mexican holiday of Cinco de Mayo, Los Lobos would be hired by the Chicano Studies departments at countless colleges in California.

"Even when I was in high school," Perez recalls, "there were political rallies and a militant attitude, which was necessary at that time. Unfortunately, there was a separatist element, but that's inevitable when any ethnic group tries to find its place in America. At its best, the Chicano movement made us aware of who we were. It told us that there was more to our culture than just the stereotypes. We realized we didn't have to sanitize our culture; we could take pride in it as it was."

"We grew up facing a lot of prejudice," Rosas points out. "People hated Mexican people—the teachers, the cops, the store owners. No one would help you in school if you didn't know English that well. You saw all these smart kids who couldn't get into UCLA or USC just because they were brown. You grew up with a stigma attached. I knew a lot of people who let that prejudice make them negative. Fortunately, I was blessed with music, and I was able to turn a negative into a positive."

"There was pressure on us to become more political," Perez adds, "but we just wanted to play the music. Other people started bands not because they were into the music, but because they wanted to make a political statement. But they didn't play very well. For us to make a statement, we had to perfect the vehicle; we had to play these songs as well as possible. What we did was innately political anyway; we didn't have to browbeat people and carry signs."

■ ■ ■

All four original members of Los Lobos have family roots in central Mexico, but Rosas is the only one who was actually born in Mexico. He didn't come to the United States until 1961, when he was nine years old, and that has given him a different perspective.

"The other guys were Americans with Mexican roots," he explains. "I was a Mexican who became an American. I grew up with a slightly different reality. I had people speaking Spanish all the time around me; my family had different mannerisms, different customs. Even in the few years I lived in Mexico, I learned how hard life can be. I never would have had the opportunity to be an artist if I hadn't come to the U.S.

"Even today I live in two worlds. One is a very Mexican world. To this day I communicate with my parents in Spanish and nothing but Spanish. That's very heavy within me. When I write songs in Spanish, I'm not here; I'm walking around Hermosillo, the capital of Sonora, as a kid, seeing images that I saw then.

"Then of course I had to learn to live another reality, the American world. I had no choice because it was all around me. When I write songs in English, I'm in East L.A. as an adult, seeing images I see now.

"I live in two equal worlds. I can easily slip into either one at any time. And two is better than one. Knowing things about one culture that people in the other culture don't know is an advantage. I understand things I wouldn't understand otherwise."

This ability to live in two worlds at once was crucial to Los Lobos' distinctiveness. Because they were able to view Mexican culture from an American perspective and American culture from a Mexican perspective, they were skeptical of each side's assumptions and could view everything with fresh eyes.

The results were not unlike the Beatles' take on American music. Because they were listening to their Chuck Berry and Carl Perkins 45s far away in Liverpool, the Beatles were free of the racial complications that Americans brought to the songs and could appreciate them with an English music-hall fan's love of melody.

When Lennon and McCartney tried to copy those 45s as closely as possible, they came up with something entirely different. In like fashion, when Los Lobos tried to copy old songs by Fats Domino, Bo Diddley, and Ritchie Valens (examples of which can also be found on the box set), they too came up with something new.

"The same thing happened to us as happened to the Beatles," Rosas agrees. "It was a little different, of course, but both groups grew up with a different, non-American music at home. So when the Beatles played rock 'n' roll, it had a slightly different, English attitude to it. And when we played rock 'n' roll, it had that East L.A. attitude. The big difference is that I grew up listening to the Beatles. That was a group I have a deep respect for; those guys taught me so much."

An analogy can also be made between Los Lobos and The Band. Each group came from a city (East L.A. and Toronto) that was in North America and yet not part of the U.S. mainstream. Both groups encountered regional musics such as Cajun, rockabilly, New Orleans R&B, conjunto, and bluegrass as outsiders, but they embraced them with the unmatchable zeal of converts.

Both groups boasted a brilliant lyricist who didn't sing lead (Louie Perez, Robbie Robertson) and a multi-instrumental whiz (David Hidalgo, Garth Hudson); each contained four cultural outsiders and one Anglo-American ringer (Steve Berlin, Levon Helm). Most importantly, both groups used their outsider/insider duality to turn American myths and archetypes into some of the most personal and enduring story-songs of the rock 'n' roll era.

The Band existed for eight years before they recorded their debut album, *Music from Big Pink,* in 1968. Los Lobos existed for a dozen years before they released their first full-length, nationally distributed album, *How Will the Wolf Survive?* in 1985. And just as The Band's long apprenticeship is documented on its early recordings with Ronnie Hawkins, John Hammond Jr., and Bob Dylan, so are Los Lobos' early years documented by the self-released 1978 album *Just Another Band from East L.A.* In both cases, the freshness of their best-known albums can be directly attributed to their years of obscurity playing roots music.

■ ■ ■

Los Lobos recorded their first album in the winter of 1977–1978 with the help of East L.A. journalist Luis Torres. But soon after the release of that all-folk album, the band began shifting back to rock 'n' roll. They began playing some of their favorite rock and soul songs on acoustic guitars during their local restaurant gigs. And the more they played Tex-Mex music, which featured accordion, bass, and drums on the recordings, they more they saw how Mexican music and rock 'n' roll could be combined.

Eventually they pulled their electric instruments out of the closets. That left them with three guitarists and one bassist. Someone had to become a drummer, and while he was a good guitarist, Perez couldn't compete with Rosas's big sound or Hidalgo's versatility.

During this transitional period, Los Lobos was hired to open the first L.A. show by Public Image Ltd., the new band led by the Sex Pistols'

Johnny "Rotten" Lydon, on May 4, 1980. In the audience was a local horn player named Steve Berlin.

"It was a boxing arena, a concrete pit with the stage in the middle," Berlin remembers, "designed to be as uncomfortable as possible. The opening act was this acoustic quartet I had never heard of playing this beautiful, traditional music in the most evil, vile atmosphere of any show I've ever been to. It was that Orange County phenomenon of all these privileged kids trying to be as punk as possible. The crowd started yelling and throwing shit for twenty minutes, but Los Lobos kept playing. I thought they were as brave as hell."

Berlin had been born and raised in Philadelphia, where he learned how to play every kind of gig imaginable—bebop, rock 'n' roll, Philly soul, and so on. Some of his Philly pals had moved to L.A. to back up Billy Preston, and they invited Berlin out to form a new group called the Beckmeier Brothers, a blue-eyed-soul outfit that eventually cut a record for Casablanca. Berlin stayed put in California and eventually played for such bands as the Plugz and Top Jimmy & the Rhythm Pigs. Through that latter band, a blues act, Berlin met Dave and Phil Alvin.

"One day they called and asked if I played baritone sax," Berlin recalls, "because they were recording Little Willie John's 'I'm Shakin'' for their first Slash album. I went to the music store, got the bari that I still use, and recorded the song the same day. I was basically in the Blasters from that point on. And what an incredible band it was. Back in those days, the coin of the realm was energy, and they put out as much force and energy as anyone. This was before they all turned into geniuses.

"I didn't really know a lot about older music back then, but I would go to these amazing parties at the Alvin brothers' house—they still lived with their parents in Downey [a blue-collar suburb on the east side of L.A.]. They were incredible record collectors—and still are—and I learned a lot just hanging out at their house, drinking beer all night, and listening to these obscure records."

Meanwhile, the four original Los Lobos were intrigued by the punk scene exploding in Hollywood. Bands such as X, Black Flag, the Go-Go's, and the Blasters were all releasing their first albums, and the city seemed to have come out of its musical doldrums. One night Perez went backstage after a Blasters set at the Whisky a Go-Go and introduced himself as being "from East L.A." Phil Alvin replied, "Cool! We're from East L.A., too." The two bands bonded, and in January 1981, the Blasters invited Los Lobos to open a show at the Whisky.

"It didn't even dawn on me that it was the same band I'd seen at the Olympic," Berlin admits, "because they had gone from pure folkloric to totally plugged-in. That weekend at the Whisky, they blew everyone away. Here was this band that all us smarty-pants scenemakers had never heard of, which is such an indictment of L.A.; all these people thought they were groovy, but they would never cross the river to East L.A. It was Los Lobos that crossed the river, and after that weekend they were the talk of the town."

■ ■ ■

The Blasters began lobbying their label, Slash Records, to sign Los Lobos, and months of nagging finally paid off in a chance to cut a seven-song EP, . . . *And a Time to Dance,* with producers T Bone Burnett and Steve Berlin in 1983. By that point, Berlin was playing so regularly with Los Lobos that he was soon added as a fifth, full-time member.

The EP included four originals, plus "Ay Te Dejo En San Antonio" by Don Santiago Jiménez (Flaco's father), and "Come On, Let's Go" by a largely forgotten rock 'n' roller named Ritchie Valens. The seventh song was a seventy-year-old ballad from the Mexican Revolution, "Anselma," which won a Grammy Award for Best Mexican American Performance.

The combination of that award and some rave reviews gave Los Lobos a chance to make a full-length album. Here was the opportunity they had been waiting for. If ever they were going to be more than a folk-revival act, more than a rootsy bar band, it had to be now. All they needed was the right song.

"We were rehearsing songs for the second Slash release at Gary Ibanez's garage," Berlin remembers. "The songs we had were good, but they were still in the vein of the blues-based things we did on the EP. Then Dave said, 'I've got this one, though I don't have the instrumental part worked out yet,' and he played 'Will the Wolf Survive?' It was like a ton of bricks fell on us.

"It was so different from what we had done before. It was so cool and so powerful that I knew we weren't going to be this little roots band anymore; we were going to be something else. It was such a big step forward for both Dave's music and Louie's words; they were both painting on a much broader canvas now. I remember feeling that everything was going to change from that point forward."

Just as "The Weight" provided the anthemic focal point for The Band's breakthrough album, *Music from Big Pink,* so did "Will the Wolf Survive?" become the center of Los Lobos' breakthrough recording, *How Will the Wolf Survive?* Other songs such as "A Matter of Time" and "Evangeline" indicated that Perez was emerging as a lyricist who could fashion new magic out of old materials in the same manner as Dave Alvin and Richard Thompson.

"When it came time to make a full studio record," Perez explains, "we said, 'Here's where it's time to make our move.' We could trivialize our culture and become caricatures, but that's not what our band was about. We decided we needed to be responsible. We had an opportunity to redefine the stereotypes about our culture. David and I had always written songs, but now we started addressing subjects that needed to be addressed.

"Writers always draw on who they are. I'm not going to write about Pocatello, Idaho; I'm going to write about East L.A. I'm going to write about the fruit vendors, the sewing women in the sweatshops, the smell of the tortilleria, the sounds that waft through the air on Saturdays from backyard parties, the Mexican music that was played, the dresser-top altars in Catholic homes. That imagery impressed me as a young boy, and it stays with me when I sit down to write today."

■ ■ ■

Just as The Band followed up *Music from Big Pink* with the even better album, *The Band,* so did Los Lobos follow *How Will the Wolf Survive?* with the best album of their career, 1987's *By the Light of the Moon.* On songs such as "One Time One Night," "Is This All There Is?" "The Hardest Time," and "The Mess We're In," the songwriting team of Hidalgo and Perez addressed the immigrant experience more directly and more powerfully than any rock 'n' roll album before or since.

Los Lobos also released another album in 1987, a collection of oldies, sort of their equivalent of The Band's *Moondog Matinee.* It was the soundtrack to a low-budget film about Ritchie Valens, and the group dashed off the movie tracks between their laborious sessions for *By the Light of the Moon,* which they were recording down the hall at the same studio. They finished both albums and took off for a summer tour of Europe.

"When we came back from Europe," Perez recalls, "Everyone said, 'Congratulations, you've got a hit record.' We said, 'What do you mean?' And they said, '*La Bamba.*' And we said, 'You mean that little film? That's a hit?'" Indeed, *La Bamba* had become a surprise summer smash at the box office, and Los Lobos' cover of the film's title song (originally a #22 hit for Valens in 1959) climbed to #1 on the pop charts.

"*La Bamba* took over our lives for the rest of the year, and *By the Light of the Moon* wound up on some critics' lists and was otherwise forgotten," Perez continues. "But I don't have any regrets about doing the soundtrack; I like those songs, and I'm proud of what we did with them."

"When we got back from Europe, the single was Top 10," Berlin adds. "We were stunned. It seemed so improbable that this movie with no stars and a bunch of knuckleheads playing the music would be a hit. The rest of the summer was this insane ride. *By the Light of the Moon* was sheer torture to make—and I don't think we did the songs justice—but still it was good work, and it was weird to see it eclipsed by this thing we sort of tossed off."

"Here we were on a certain musical path," Rosas chimes in, "and all of a sudden it got pushed aside by a big hit, which was just a side project we agreed to do. We'd come onstage, and there'd be all these moms up by the front of the stage with their kids, and you could tell they wanted to hear 'Donna,' 'Come On, Let's Go,' and 'La Bamba.'

"It was hard for us to explain that's not what we wanted to do. We could see the disappointment in their eyes, because they had brought their children to hear those songs. It was disappointing and hilarious at the same time; it was bittersweet. At the same time, I loved the *La Bamba* soundtrack. I loved working on it, but it was a period piece."

"We were close to Ritchie's family," Berlin says, "because they still live near Santa Cruz, and whenever we played there at the Catalyst, they'd all come out to see us. They'd even feed us and take care of us. They told us that they sold the rights to Ritchie's story on the condition that we had to play the music. Which was very nice of them. When I first read the script, though, I remember thinking, 'Oh, this will go right to cable.' But they kept working on it and rewriting it, and it gradually came together."

■ ■ ■

Nothing throws a band off its stride quite like a fluke hit. "People would ask us if we were going to do another 'La Bamba,'" Berlin recalls, "and I'd say, 'What would another 'La Bamba' be? We've recorded nearly every song this guy ever wrote.'" There were, however, lots of suggestions about other vintage rock songs the band could remake. There were pressures to keep touring behind the soundtrack.

Los Lobos put an end to all such foolishness by returning to where they had started: acoustic Mexican folk songs. They followed up their #1 soundtrack success with *La Pistola y el Corazon,* a hard-core traditional album they supported with an all-acoustic tour. It was a brave, sacrificial gesture, but it prevented the industry from defining the band. They would define themselves, and they did so as musicians from East Los Angeles' Mexican American community.

"Reporters would ask, 'How do you feel about having a big hit with 'La Bamba'?" Rosas recalls, "and we'd say, 'Well, it's fun. The money is good, but it's not who we are.'

"Any other band would have jumped on that opportunity, but we were songwriters. We could have become an oldies-revival group, but it would have damaged the band. It could have pushed us into a place we might not have been able to get out of. We avoided it by not going there. We shrugged it off.

"The only reason we survived all that craziness was the years we spent as a folk band. It enabled us to appreciate all kinds of good music and not get hung up by prejudices. That's why we've been around so long, because we learned what's important and what's not. When 'La Bamba' came around, it could have damaged our career, but we knew what to do. We changed like chameleons."

La Pistola is a gorgeous, powerful album, far more accomplished musically than *Just Another Band from East L.A.,* far less schmaltzy than Linda

Ronstadt's Mexican-folk albums, and far less conservative than folkloric albums coming from Mexico itself. It, too, won a Grammy Award for Best Mexican-American Performance.

"A lot of people thought we were committing commercial suicide," Perez reveals. "They thought we should cash in all our chips. But all the work we had done, everything we had accomplished up to that point had been eclipsed by this pop hit. Suddenly we were only known for this hit song we didn't write. We were confused, and when you get confused, it's often best to go back to your roots."

By returning to their roots, Los Lobos was able to clear the decks and relaunch a career that shows no signs of slowing down. While they have never matched the sheer brilliance of *How Will the Wolf Survive?* and *By the Light of the Moon,* the group has released a series of flawed but fascinating records (much like The Band's later albums): the 1990 garage-rock exercise *The Neighborhood* (with terrific songs but underwhelming sound); the 1992 art-rock experiment *Kiko* (with terrific sound textures but underwhelming songs); the 1995 children's album *Papa's Dream* (with narrator Lalo Guerrero); the 1996 *Colossal Head* (an uneven compromise between *The Neighborhood* and *Kiko*); and the 1999 *This Time* (a better compromise).

In addition, there have been numerous side projects. Perez and Hidalgo joined producer Mitchell Froom and engineer Tchad Blake to form the Latin Playboys, a quartet that took the fragmentary, improvisatory studio experiments of *Kiko* even further on a 1994 self-titled disc and 1999's *Dose.* Hidalgo and Rosas joined Joe Ely, Flaco Jimenez, Rick Trevino, Ruben Ramos, and Freddy Fender on 1998's *Los Super Seven,* which Berlin produced. Berlin is now working on a sequel, *Los Super Seven II,* featuring Hidalgo, Rosas, Ramos, Susana Baca, Raul Malo, and others. It is tentatively scheduled for release in April.

Rosas got songwriting help from Asleep at the Wheel's Leroy Preston for a 1999 solo album, *Soul Disguise.* Hidalgo joined late-period Canned Heat guitarist Mike Halby as the duo Houndog, which released a self-titled album in 1999. As a group, Los Lobos has cut tracks for tribute albums to the Beatles, Richard Thompson, Walt Disney, the Grateful Dead, Buddy Holly, Doc Pomus, and Johnny Thunders, and for the movie soundtracks of *The Mambo Kings, Desperado, The End of Violence, Untamed Heart, Alamo Bay,* and *A Fine Mess.*

Sample tracks from every one of these projects are included in the ambitious new box set from Rhino. The eighty-six cuts were drawn from thirty-five different sources, including the ten official Los Lobos albums. More than fifty of the tracks were not included on the Slash/Warner Bros. 1993 two-CD anthology, *Just Another Band from East L.A.: A Collection.*

■ ■ ■

Tying all those far-flung recordings together is the same interplay of Mexican folk and American rock, ancestral roots and adolescent hunger, emi-grant memories and immigrant dreams, that have informed Los Lobos' music since the beginning. It enabled them to create a sound that has inspired some of the best roots-rock acts of the 1990s—most notably Alejandro Escovedo, the Mollys, the Blazers, and Ozomatli.

"Our nine years as an acoustic band affected everything that happened later," Perez observes. "We went off on this nine-year field trip; we explored not only our own culture but also music from all over the world. We discovered that bands like Fairport Convention were doing the same thing with their cultures as we were doing with ours. Rock 'n' roll informed the way we played Mexican music because we played the old songs with a rock 'n' roll sense of urgency. And when we returned to rock 'n' roll, Mexican folk music became part of the rock stuff."

"When we returned to rock 'n' roll," Rosas concurs, "we felt like we had just graduated from school. I basically hadn't played electric guitar in eight years, so when we got our amplifiers back out of the closet and plugged in again, it felt fresh and new. And that made us feel like we could write our own stuff, because we had been singing all these old folk songs that have lasted for generations. We had absorbed all the elements of a great song, and now we had this energy to put those elements to work."

"When we came back to rock 'n' roll," Perez adds, "we'd already been a band for nine years. We used to joke that we're the only band that decided to become rock stars as adults. But we didn't look at rock 'n' roll and American culture as something foreign to us. It's not like we were on a remote island watching this culture on television; we felt a part of it.

"That's what's important about this band: We define what it means to be Mexican American because we're part of both cultures. That's what's made us interesting to our fans and to the rock press. I think we've changed rock 'n' roll as a result."

The True Believer

Alejandro Escovedo Takes a Long Look Back at a Life of More Miles than Money

ND #14, March–April 1998

Peter Blackstock

For all the stories he could tell—all the adventures he actively sought out or accidentally stumbled upon, all the characters he has known and loved along the way, all the highs and lows flowing through five decades of dreams chased in glory or in vain, and all the memories that remain—Alejandro Escovedo's music finally boils down to the simplest, most direct connection between the artist and any one person who might be out there listening.

When I close my eyes, I can see myself sitting there in the dark, cozy confines of Chicago House, a late, great acoustic music haven in downtown Austin that played host to several Alejandro Escovedo shows around 1989. The previous year, Escovedo's long-struggling, hard-rocking band the True Believers had gradually crumbled into dust, leaving him to redefine himself as a solo artist. Nobody, least of all Escovedo, quite knew how he would respond to the challenge.

But those evenings evolved into pure magic, Escovedo's eloquent passion pouring out of his voice on songs such as "One More Time," "Broken Bottle," and, most of all, "Five Hearts Breaking": "He hears the pain, roaring in his head / He'll close his eyes and the world turns red," Escovedo sang, and it did. "She held his hand, looked him in the eye / And said believe, believe and everything will be fine," the muse of his song answered. And it was.

All three of those tunes, which appeared on Escovedo's 1992 solo debut *Gravity*, are featured on *More Miles than Money: Live 1994–96*, along with eight other tracks recorded at various venues across the country during a three-year span. The album, released February 24 by Bloodshot Records, gathers material from Escovedo's three solo albums plus two covers that have been longtime staples of his live shows (the Rolling

Stones' "Sway" and the Stooges' "I Wanna Be Your Dog"). As an abbreviat-ed sampling of several years spent writing songs from the heart and per-forming them powerfully in nightclubs across the country (and beyond), *More Miles than Money* serves as a solid closing statement for those who would contend that Escovedo's accomplishments in the 1990s made him the decade's most significant musical artist.

Not a live album in the traditional sense of the term—there is essen-tially no crowd noise, and no intros or between-song banter—*More Miles than Money* wasn't even intended to be an album at all when the record-ings were made. Co-producers Erik Flannigan and Bob Whitfield, both fans of Escovedo's music who owned high-fidelity portable DAT recorders, had taped several of his shows during the mid-'90s, usually straight off the mixing board (with Escovedo's permission). When Escovedo's record deal with Rykodisc came to an unexpectedly rapid demise less than a year after the label released his 1996 album *With These Hands,* Flannigan and Whitfield approached Escovedo with the idea of compiling an album from their accumulated archives.

Preliminary plans with one independent label fizzled last fall, but Bloodshot quickly picked up the ball, scoring their highest-profile act to date (with the arguable exception of the label's cornerstone artist, Mekons/Waco Brothers ringleader Jon Langford). And while *More Miles than Money* doesn't introduce any new entries in the Escovedo catalogue, it is a remarkably consistent, beautiful and valuable document of how his repertoire has developed over the years.

Captured at shows in five cities (two separate dates in Davis, Califor-nia, and one each in Austin, Seattle, San Diego, and Paris, France), the recordings stress the more acoustic side of Escovedo's multiple musical personality, with cello and violin frequently playing important roles in the texture and tone of the renditions. "One More Time," delivered as a rave-up rocker on *Gravity,* is restored to the graceful, yearning ballad I remem-ber from those Chicago House shows. The emphasis on strings doesn't necessarily preclude Escovedo from rocking out, as evidenced by the final track, in which the band stretches out the suite of "Gravity/Falling Down Again" to include a stomping snippet of Lou Reed's "Street Hassle."

Such musical transgressions are an accurate reflection of Escovedo's approach to his live performances, which often involve reworking, if not completely reinventing, both his own songs and those of other artists. Part of this stems from the fact that he has played with a constantly revolving and diverse supporting cast throughout the '90s. The ever-changing Ale-jandro Escovedo Orchestra has ranged from three to more than a dozen musicians, depending on the situation, while his side-project band, Buick MacKane, has provided an outlet for his flat-out garage-rock urges. *More Miles than Money,* despite retaining a relatively unified feel from track to track, features six different combinations of musicians.

"The songs get mutated and abused by so many different bands and configurations that they're never the same night to night. Which I like," Escovedo says. "It makes it interesting for us as a band, as musicians. I've always felt like I've given those guys a lot of freedom to express themselves—within the confines of the song, of course. I mean, the song comes first, but I'm not against stretching them out to give them some room to really say something."

The most blatant example of such stretching out on *More Miles than Money* is the first thirty-five seconds of "I Wanna Be Your Dog," which opens as a virtual free-form noisefest of classical strings, clashical guitars, and a crashing rhythm section before finally fading into form as Escovedo screeches out, "So messed up, I want you here . . ." over three gloriously crunching power chords delivered in thundering unison.

Still, perhaps the most memorable moment on the album is the other cover selection, "Sway," which features a lilting violin pushing and pulling against ringing, shimmering guitar leads as Escovedo recites, with a weary but poignant sense of resignation, words that clearly mean the world to him. Indeed, he admits, when it comes to choosing cover songs, "it's all about lyrics for me. Like 'Sway'—just that chorus, 'It's just that demon life that's got you in its sway'—it says so much about my life and the way that I know a lot of us feel, who fall in love with this thing called music."

■ ■ ■

Alejandro Escovedo probably had no choice but to fall in love with music. Born January 10, 1951, in San Antonio, Texas, he was "in the lower third" of a group of twelve siblings and half-siblings. His best-known older brothers, Pete and Coke, became fixtures on the West Coast Latin jazz and rock scenes, playing with such bands as Santana, Azteca, and Malo. (Coke died in 1986; Pete remains a well-known name in jazz circles, while Pete's daughter Sheila became a pop star in the 1980s under the name Sheila E.) Two other older brothers, Phillip and Bobby, played bass and drums, respectively. His younger brothers Javier and Mario are guitarists in Southern California hard-rock bands; Javier and Alejandro spent most of the '80s playing together in the True Believers. (But more on that later.)

Alejandro's father, who was born in Saltillo, Mexico, in 1907, was a musician as well. "He sang in mariachi bands for a while, and he also sang in swing bands, just kind of sitting in with some bands in the Bay Area," Alejandro says. "But I don't think he ever pursued it as a career; it was just something he did. He always sang; he was always an entertainer. And he still is."

Coke and Pete are actually Alejandro's half-brothers, from their father's first marriage; there is enough of an age gap between them and Alejandro that they didn't really grow up together. "But I remember they used to come visit us, and stay with us," Alejandro says. "And they were very different—because we were country kids, living out in the country, north of

San Antonio. And they'd be dressed up like city guys, kinda jazz guys; they'd have skinny ties and nice shirts and suits. They were living in California, in the Bay Area. So they really stuck out when they came to Texas. I think I have a picture of Pete and Coke trying to get on a horse, but they've got, like, pointed black shoes and straight-legged pants and stuff. It's pretty funny."

California is also where Escovedo ended up in the late 1950s. "I was seven or eight years old," he recalls. "We went first to Orange, California, in Orange County, a beautiful little town. When we got there, it was basically all avocado orchards and orange groves. My father got a house with nothing down, just a handshake.... From Orange, we moved to Santa Ana, and I went to school there up until the seventh grade. And then we moved to Huntington Beach. And we lived in Huntington Beach from seventh grade on, through high school."

Music wasn't really in Escovedo's plans at that point, though. "I wanted to be a ballplayer, that was my first ambition—to be a pitcher. I played all through high school and then played some American Legion ball."

The first flirtation with his future career came courtesy his father, who was working as a plumber at the time. "He was doing this job for this guy who used to make guitars for these country-western stars. And so he traded a job for a guitar. He brought me home the guitar and this beautiful little Fender Champ amp. He taught me a couple chords, but I took the guitar apart because I wanted to paint it, like, a much cooler color. And I never painted it. Javier ended up putting the guitar back together. That was his first guitar, and he really went on to learn to play it."

Despite that misfire, Escovedo couldn't help but absorb all the musical influences that were around him. "My parents were very prominent in my musical education, in that they bought us all our first Beatles records, and they would always make a point to let us know when the Beatles or the Stones were on TV," he remembers. "My mom was really into swing, so we heard a lot of big-band stuff: Ellington, and even Benny Goodman, all that kind of stuff. And my father loved the rancheras, you know, Mexican music. My mom and dad also loved this style of music called trio music, which is usually three guitar players and beautiful harmonies—real romantic stuff.

"I remember my aunt would come, and she'd sing in the backyard, and they'd start drinking, and playing these records really loud. And we'd try to go to sleep over the din of laughter and jokes and dancing and singing. And she would start singing, and eventually it would turn into crying. And then consoling. And then singing again. And then crying again."

Eventually, the burgeoning live-music scene in late 1960s Southern California started to catch Escovedo's ear. "There was a great club in Huntington Beach called the Golden Bear," he says. "And there was this whole chain of clubs up and down the coast. The first time I saw the Paul

Butterfield Blues Band, I was in high school, and I went to Golden Bear to see them play, and I'd never seen a band like that before. . . . And then a lot of the black blues guys, too, would come through all those small clubs.

"And then the rock clubs—every beach town had a pier, and at every pier there was usually a skating rink that became these ballrooms, like the Rendezvous Ballroom and the Skate Rink in Huntington Beach. And they would have bands play. So I got to see, like, Love, and I got to see the Buffalo Springfield in a teen club that was right next to the Golden Bear. I got to see the Doors. And then, also, all these cool garage bands, like Limey & the Yanks, the East Side Kids, Mouse & the Traps—all those bands, you'd see them up and down the circuit."

Country music was making an impression on Escovedo around this time as well. "Cal Worthington would have his own show from his car lot, and he would have people like Buck Owens and all these country stars," he recalls. "We'd go down there sometimes and check out the bands. And when I was in high school, we started a little paper. I think the first review that I ever wrote was for *Sweetheart of the Rodeo.* Either that or the Burrito Brothers. And I remember I wrote one for *The Fantastic Expedition of Dillard & Clark,* which is a great album. So I was always interested. I mean, being from Texas—and my father loved country music too. So when the first wave of this country-rock stuff came, I really took to it."

While all this was happening around him, Escovedo's life was in a considerable state of turmoil. He had left home early ("I was about fifteen or sixteen"), dropped out of high school, got married, and had two kids (who are old enough today that they've made Escovedo a grandfather). The marriage lasted only a couple years, and in 1972 he took off for Washington, working for several months as an apple picker in the Yakima Valley. In 1973, he moved back to Huntington Beach; soon after, he relocated to Hollywood.

A whole new musical adventure awaited him in the belly of the beast. It seems he had arrived in town right about the time that the New York Dolls and the Stooges had begun performing frequently in Los Angeles. "I used to listen to the Stooges practice every day," Escovedo recalls. "And we always used to hang out at this place called Rodney Bingenheimer's English Disco. It was kind of the place to go and hang out and meet girls."

One of the girls he met around that time was Bobbi Levie, whom he actually had gone to high school with back in Huntington Beach. He distinctly remembers hooking up with her at Patti Smith's first show at the Whisky a Go-Go—"the only people in the audience were the Stooges, and about four or five of us." Escovedo and Levie got together after the show, and soon became constant companions and lovers, eventually moving to San Francisco together in 1975.

"I got a job at a local junior college up there that had a great film teacher, so I started taking classes with him," Escovedo continues. "And we started to do this little movie called *Eighteen and a Half.* It was loosely based on this kind of Iggy Pop character who's about to turn nineteen and feels that if he turns twenty and he hasn't made it, that he's over the hill. . . . And he finds this band, which was kind of like the Dum Dum Boys—that Iggy Pop song, 'The Dum Dum Boys,' it's the story of the Stooges, you know.

"And we figured, well, we don't know how to play, but Alejandro can maybe hit an E chord or something, so let's be the band [in the movie]. So we went to go film a show. We had a bass player by the name of Nola, and he was pretty out there. He could sit in a room for eight hours and not say one word. And he'd wear this beautiful leopard-skin suit, with leopard-skin platform boots. And the drummer didn't know how to play. And then I was the guitar player, and I didn't know how to play."

This motley crew grew into the Nuns, who became one of the linchpins of the embryonic West Coast punk scene. "We were just there at the right time," Escovedo says. "We started playing this place called the Mabuhay Gardens. We told them that we had a huge following, and we didn't have any following. Our following was basically transvestites and drug dealers. In fact, the first show was with the Dils."

The band's first single, "The Decadent Jew"/"Wild," was released by fledgling independent label 415 Records, the province of future major-label honcho Howie Klein. In January 1978, the Nuns and the Avengers opened for the Sex Pistols at their last show ever (well, not counting the 1996 reunion tour), at the hallowed San Francisco venue Winterland.

Escovedo's thoughts about that historic night are intriguing. "I remember it being quite a spectacle," he begins. "I remember that I had always loved music so much; when I listened to the Kinks' lyrics, and The Who's lyrics, and the Stones, at the time, it seemed like we were going to change the world through this powerful medium. And then to see it turned into a circus, and basically a farce—I realized that the Sex Pistols had nothing to do with music, really. It was important in that it really screwed the musical establishment at the time. But at the same time, there wasn't anything constructive that came out of it, really. It was kind of nihilistic. . . . It was weird to see the whole thing crumble before your very eyes."

■ ■ ■

"Shortly after that, we went to New York to tour," Escovedo picks up the story. "We toured the East Coast by train—'Amtrak and ain't comin' back.'"

That sly slogan turned into truth for Escovedo, who was so enamored with what he saw in Manhattan that he decided to stay there rather than return to San Francisco. "The first night we were there, we went to Max's Kansas City to see the Heartbreakers play, and we sat at a table with Andy Warhol, and George Clinton was there, and Richard Hell."

All of which must have been an exciting, eye-opening experience for a young musician who had never traveled to the East Coast before. "Oh man, for me, it was amazing," Escovedo affirms. "Because that's what I had always dreamed of doing, was going to New York. I never really wanted to go to London or any place like that. I wanted to go to New York. It was very exotic to me. So it was great—and I stayed. The Nuns went back to San Francisco without me."

Levie moved out to New York shortly thereafter, and the young couple took up residency in the Chelsea Hotel, whose residents at the time included another young couple, Sid Vicious and Nancy Spungen. "We had a lot of great friends in the Chelsea," he remembers. "We had good times, and met some incredible people. There was this guy Neon Leon, there was a band called the Spiders from Philly that were living there. All these guys were pretty prominent in the New York scene at the time.

"And then Nancy got killed," he continues, referring to the death of Spungen at the hands of Vicious, who himself died of a heroin overdose a short time later, in February 1979. "When she was killed, that's when we decided to leave. Everyone decided to leave—this whole group of people who kind of hung out."

Escovedo and Levie stayed in New York, however, moving to a place on the Lower East Side. Escovedo had begun playing with a singer named Judy Nylon, but soon received a call from Chip Kinman of the Dils, the band that had opened for the Nuns at their first show at Mabuhay Gardens in San Francisco a few years earlier.

"The Dils had finally broken up, and Chip gave me a call in New York. He said, 'Hey, I broke up the band, do you wanna start a band?' And I said, 'Sure man, come on out.' . . . I'd been playing with Kevin Foley, who had also been playing in Judy's band. We were practicing in the basement of Giorgio Gomelsky's studio. Giorgio was one of the Rolling Stones' first managers, and had managed the Yardbirds. He's this Russian beatnik. This rehearsal studio was amazing because it was, like, us, Ornette Coleman's band, David Johansen's band, and Judy's band.

"And then Chip came out, so we got together with Kevin on drums, and this guy Barry 'Scratchy' Meyers, who was the Clash DJ, and he was also in Rude Boy. And we became Rank and File. We started to play these songs, mostly Chip's songs, and we practiced for a while and played around New York, and got a really good following and response."

Eventually the band decided to take their show on the road. "We went on tour for seven weeks; we had seven dates in those seven weeks," Escovedo recalls with a laugh. "We played Dayton, Dallas, Austin, San Francisco, Portland, Seattle, Vancouver." The Portland date was particularly significant because Tony Kinman, Chip's brother and former Dils band-mate, was living there; he hopped aboard the van at that show and eventually became Rank and File's bassist and co-leader.

"And, of course, the trip to Austin was significant because that was my first trip to Austin since I'd been a little kid," Escovedo adds. The band played at Raul's, the center of the Austin punk scene circa 1978–1980, and they quickly became enamored with the city. The Kinman brothers hooked up with their childhood pal Steve Chaney (later a member of the South by Southwest Music Fest's executive staff), and Escovedo ran into one of his friends from New York, the critic Lester Bangs, who had just moved there (shortly before his death in 1982). "We had a great experience in Austin. I remember calling Bobbi from a phone booth and I said, 'Man, this place is cool, we should move here.' And she goes, 'No way. I don't wanna leave New York.'"

The rhythm section departed after the tour, leaving the Kinman brothers and Escovedo looking for a new drummer back in New York. "We'd put an ad in the paper saying, 'We're trying to play country music,' and we'd get guys who said, you know, 'I'm into New Riders of the Purple Sage.' And we'd go, 'Uh, that's not what we had in mind.'"

Escovedo eventually convinced Levie to move to Austin, where the band assumed their country-leaning aspirations would be greeted with greater understanding. "We found Slim Evans; he became our drummer. And that's when the whole thing really started for us, once we moved to Austin. And at that time, also, you've got remember that we'd get to see Billy Joe Shaver, Townes Van Zandt, Butch Hancock, Jimmie Dale Gilmore, Joe Ely, Lucinda Williams, and Nanci Griffith playing all the same little clubs."

Around that time Escovedo also became acquainted with Sterling Morrison, the former guitarist for the Velvet Underground. Escovedo had taken a job in a library at the University of Texas, where Morrison was a postdoctoral scholar. "One of the very first days I was working there, this guy starts walking toward me with two big carts just packed with books. And I thought, 'Oh great, here I am, one of my first days, I'm gonna have to deal with all these books.' And he walks up and he hands me his ID card, and it's Sterling Morrison. And I just flipped out. I asked him something really stupid, like, 'Are you still playing?' And he goes, 'Yeah, sometimes,' and he kind of laughed." (Over the years, the two became friends; "Tugboat," the final track on Escovedo's 1996 solo album *With These Hands,* was written in memory of Morrison shortly after his passing a couple years ago.)

Despite the artist-friendly environment of Austin, Rank and File still found themselves to be a bit of a square peg in the city's music scene. "At the time, punk rock was still very strong there, and that whole roots-rock Leroi Brothers type stuff was real strong. So, we were too country for a rock club, and the country clubs wouldn't book us because we were too rock for the country clubs. So we didn't have a home anywhere; we were in no-man's-land."

Eventually, Steve Chaney, who had begun managing the band, got them a regular gig on Sundays at the Shorthorn, an off-the-beaten-path beer joint in north Austin. That led to bookings at the Alamo Lounge, a downtown venue that was a vital cog in the city's acoustic scene at the time (Butch Hancock recorded a live album there). "It was this great hotel, and this bar downstairs was all glass and brick," Escovedo says. "You could see all these great people play acoustically, but you couldn't talk. And if you did get loud, you'd get kicked out.

"So we played acoustically, which we'd never done before—I never really even played an acoustic guitar before. And that's when our popularity changed in Austin, playing the Alamo Lounge. It got us into another crowd, and also we learned from those guys, Butch and Jimmie and all those people. I learned a lot from them. But we also had something that they didn't have because we were more like the Bobby Fuller Four or something. We were a little more rockin', a little more like Buddy Holly with, like, the Everly Brothers singing, because the [Kinman] brothers did the harmonies."

Though Escovedo hardly sang at all in those days, he does distinctly remember one tune on which he took a lead vocal. "One significant event for me during that period was that people kept saying, 'Why don't you sing a song?' I'd never sung a song in public before. But I chose this Jimmie Rodgers song called 'I Love the Women' . . . and I used to do that. So that was the first song I sang in public. It got a good response, so I kept doing it ever since." (Indeed, a September 1997 show in Cleveland found Escovedo singing that tune at a star-studded Rock and Roll Hall of Fame tribute to Jimmie Rodgers.)

With their popularity growing locally, the band decided to do a West Coast tour, a move that ended up netting them a record deal with Slash/Warner Bros. "In San Francisco, we played at the American Indian Center, and this guy David Kahne came to see us. We got signed to Slash, and he ended up producing our *Sundown* record. . . . He went on to produce Fishbone and the Bangles, and he just did that band Sugar Ray."

Sundown was a modest seller, but became a very influential record in the ensuing years, when no shortage of roots-rock and alt-country bands began referencing Rank and File's cowpunk sound as one of their primary inspirations and influences. Still, this wasn't really Escovedo's band; though he co-wrote one of the tracks on *Sundown,* as time went on the spotlight was becoming more and more focused (somewhat naturally) on the Kinman brothers.

His decision to leave the band, which came during a West Coast tour to support *Sundown* with a promising young L.A. band called Lone Justice, was a difficult one. "The guys had gotten really down on me about what I was playing, and I just said, 'You know what, I don't want this anymore. It's not fun for me. I don't think that I deserve it, and I just don't want it.' So I called up Bobbi, and it was pretty traumatic, really. Because once again, here I am, having put such an emotional investment into this band, and it meant a lot to me, and we were making progress all the time. And there was this whole movement being built around bands like the Blasters and Rank and File and the Long Ryders and all those bands that were starting to come out."

But Escovedo wasn't walking away without a plan. Back in Los Angeles, his brother Javier had been in the notorious punk band the Zeros in the mid to late 1970s, but at the time wasn't playing with anyone. "So I called him and said, 'Javier, what do you think about starting a band together?' He said, 'Man, that'd be great.' . . . And so we're calling each other, Jav and I, from Austin to L.A., going, 'You know, I wanna be the new Mott the Hoople—I wanna have a band that has good rockin' songs, but I want it to be literate, and I want it to be great songs and stories.'

"So he finally came out; he took a Greyhound bus. He got off with one bag of luggage and a guitar, and that was it. And then we started the True Believers."

■ ■ ■

The aggressive Austin punk scene of the late 1970s and early '80s, dominated by such bands as the Skunks and the Big Boys, was beginning to segue into something somewhat different by the early to mid-'80s. The Wild Seeds were a scruffy, soulful garage-rock outfit destined to make some great records before the decade's end. Zeitgeist, the most melodic and probably most accessible band of the bunch, started out on DB Records and eventually made two albums for Capitol after changing their name to the Reivers. Doctors' Mob was Austin's answer to the Replacements, boasting the T-shirt logo, "Show up drunk, show up late, or don't show up at all." Glass Eye was the most original-sounding band of the bunch, bending Kathy McCarty's classically beautiful voice against the twisted melodic and rhythmic turns of brainy bassist Brian Beattie.

Exactly how the True Believers fit into this so-called "New Sincerity" scene was hard to figure. "We couldn't sing, man; we were, like, the worst singers, but it didn't stop us, because we had this really cool sound," Escovedo says. "I was playing a real kind of Santo & Johnny–like surf guitar, playing a Strat through a Fender amp, high on the reverb, real clean sounding. And then Jav had his guitar a little more distorted and more rockin'. We had these real spacious songs that sounded like traveling from Austin to El Paso. It sounded like West Texas to me. And yet, somehow, our Latin roots were coming in, too—maybe in the way the voices sounded, the way we phrased certain words."

It didn't take long before others in Austin also began to sense that something special was going on here. The first time they played Club Foot, the premier local venue for underground rock acts at that time, they opened for Los Lobos. "David [Hidalgo] came out and played accordion on 'Just like Tom Thumb's Blues' with us," Escovedo says. "And I remember after that show, Joe Nick Patoski came up and said, keep it up man, you're doing great." Before long, Patoski—later a senior editor at *Texas Monthly* magazine—became the True Believers' manager.

After an aborted attempt at a demo for Columbia— the label tried to pair the brothers with an L.A. rhythm section—Escovedo started mulling over the idea of toughening up the sound by adding a third axeman to the band's guitar army.

Enter Jon Dee Graham, who had been in a band called the Lift, which Escovedo said he "couldn't stand; I hated them." But he was intrigued by the talents of Graham, who also wrote songs and was learning to play lap steel as well. Around the same time he also was recruiting Rey Washam, formerly of the Big Boys and later of Scratch Acid, to replace original drummer Keith Carnes.

"I called Jon Dee and Rey up and said, 'Listen, we want you to play on this record, so let's go and rehearse and maybe do a gig or two, and then we'll make this record.' Well, really, there was no record to be made; I was lying to them. But I got them in the band. . . . Our coming-out party was a great success, and then we just started touring, and touring, and touring. One thing I had learned from the old punk days was that you get in the van and you work. We were booking our own gigs, and we were doing that whole circuit—Athens, Oklahoma City, Dallas, Houston, the Carolinas."

The next step, a record deal, came about largely because of Waterloo Records, long Austin's premier independent record store. "When we weren't getting a record deal, they [Waterloo co-owners John Kunz and Louis Karp] finally said, 'We'll put up the money for you guys to do a tape,'" Escovedo says. Another Austin pal, Kent Benjamin, hooked them up with Jim Dickinson, the Memphis underground semi-legend who had produced or performed with Big Star, Ry Cooder, the Rolling Stones, and others.

Washam presently departed to join Scratch Acid, so Escovedo called upon his old New York pal Kevin Foley to anchor the rhythm section, with bassist Denny DeGorio, for the recording sessions. The quintet spent three days in 1985 at Arlyn Studios in Austin with Dickinson, and emerged with what eventually became their self-titled debut record for Rounder/EMI. "Rounder had just gotten a distribution deal with EMI, so that looked real attractive to a certain majority of the band," Escovedo says, noting that they turned down an offer from the English label Demon/Zippo.

A record-release party in the Waterloo Records parking lot was one of the most memorable musical moments of the summer of 1986 in Austin. "It was right during rush-hour traffic, and so John Kunz went out there and fake-stalled his car right in the middle of Lamar Boulevard. So there was this enormous traffic jam. And there were hundreds of people there anyway. And we didn't play one song off the album. We played all covers. It was great. Yeah, we did 'Neat Neat Neat' by the Damned, we did 'Queen Bitch' by Bowie."

Another high-profile show that summer, however, became an omen for the hard road ahead of the band. The True Believers and several other Austin bands were in New York City to play a showcase at the Lone Star during the New Music Seminar, "and we found out that morning that my brother Coke had died," Escovedo recalls. Coke's death was caused by internal bleeding after a recent hospital stay involving a tumor, Escovedo explained, though he adds that "Coke had thoroughly enjoyed himself, kind of in excess.

"It was very, very devastating. It was the first time I'd ever really been faced with death in my family. But my mom and dad, and brothers and sisters, supported us and said, 'You need to go ahead and do what you set out to do.' So we did interviews all that morning with European press, and with VH1, which was just starting up at the time. And of course the first question they asked was, 'You come from a musical family . . .'

"And then, to add insult to injury, that night, Denny, our bass player, got busted [for marijuana possession]. So Tim Swingle [of Doctors' Mob, another Austin band on the bill] came on and played bass. I think that was a sign of what was to come for the Believers; our life on the road was pretty precarious."

Heavy touring behind the record, much of it spent opening for Los Lobos, provided Escovedo with some of his fondest memories of the True Believers days, but the road also took its toll. "We wiped ourselves out touring behind that record," he admits.

A feature story in *Spin* by Pat Blashill, who had been their roadie on the tour, provided major exposure, but not exactly the kind the band wanted: Its insider tales of debauchery and decadence on the road had serious repercussions on band members' marital relationships, Alejandro says, including his own.

Even so, by mid-1987 the band seemed ready to roll behind its second album, recorded in Atlanta with Georgia Satellites producer Jeff Glixman and packing the harder punch of the band's live sound, which had been missing from the first record. Two weeks before the album's scheduled release that summer, however, the band was dropped amid a merger between EMI and Manhattan Records, which also saw such acts as the Del Lords, Brian Setzer, and the Neville Brothers cast by the wayside.

The band kept going for another year, and in some ways its lineup was stronger than ever. Former Dwight Yoakam bassist J. D. Foster had been brought aboard, along with drummer Hector Muñoz (who continued to play with Escovedo throughout the 1990s). But in a more fundamental way, things were never the same. "The spirit was gone," Escovedo admits.

"And there was starting to be a lot of infighting between Jon Dee and Jav, and me in the middle of all of it. We were losing it."

The final blow came in the fall of 1988 when an Austin newspaper quoted Javier, on tour with Will Sexton at the time, as saying he was no longer a member of the True Believers. That was the first Alejandro had heard of his brother's decision to leave.

■ ■ ■

Those acoustic gigs at Chicago House in 1989 were Escovedo's first steps in redefining himself as a solo artist. Gradually, the Alejandro Escovedo Orchestra developed—first with bassist Foster and keyboardist Chris Knight, who worked with Escovedo at a record store, and then with a host of musicians from all over the map of the Austin music scene: horn players Alex Coke and Bill Averbach, accomplished and respected members of the jazz community; Danny Barnes and Mark Rubin, who were just beginning to create the Bad Livers; Muñoz and fellow Latin percussionists Henry Martinez and Espiritu Espinoza; viola and clarinet player Spot, famed producer of early Hüsker Dü and Minutemen albums; singer-songwriter Lisa Mednick, who played saxophone rather than her usual keyboards and accordion; and others. It was quite a sight, and sound, to behold.

On the other end of the spectrum was Buick MacKane, which featured former Doctors' Mob drummer Glen Benavides from the very start to the very end (Benavides quit the band in December 1997, apparently signaling the dissolution of the group). Various guitarists and bassists along the way included French expatriate Thierry LeCoz; Miles Zuniga, later co-leader of the hit-making pop band Fastball; and even Escovedo's brother Javier, who played bass on a 1997 tour. But most often, the lead guitar and bass slots were filled, respectively, by Joe Eddy Hines and David Fairchild, both of whom played on the Buick MacKane record *The Pawn Shop Years* released by Rykodisc last year.

Though many Austinites felt Buick's garage-band basics paled in comparison to the wide-open possibilities of the Orchestra, Escovedo points out that there was more going on behind Buick's slaphappy mask than people may have realized. "I wrote a lot of songs with those guys," he explains. "A lot of the songs you hear on my first solo album were written with Buick. And I really missed the camaraderie I had had with my brother and Denny and those guys in the early days of the Believers, before things got weird. Buick was a place for me to get away from the seriousness of the Orchestra—and of my life at home."

The problems at home eventually led to a separation from Bobbi Levie, his wife since the mid-1970s and for whom he had written the song "Thirteen Years," about the all the time they had spent together since then—and, more tellingly, apart: "From San Francisco to New York / All I seem to do is work / My feet hurt and it's not from dancing / Close to you." Levie gave birth to the couple's second daughter, Paloma, in 1990 while they were separated, but the new child didn't bring them closer. On April 24, 1991, Levie committed suicide.

Escovedo spent much of the next several years dealing with that tragedy in the public eye, to the point that there is little left to say or to dwell on, as he sees it. Part of *Gravity* and most of *Thirteen Years,* his second solo album, dealt with Levie's death, but at some point, in the midst of all the interviews and articles, "the story became bigger than the songs themselves," he suggests. "I talked about it so much for about three years, and I was kind of spent after that. I was drained. I felt like I exposed myself way too much, and that the story became bigger than the records, and bigger than me. It wasn't really about me anymore, it was just about this kind of tragedy....And I think that, for a while, I felt like I was almost capitalizing on it myself, by writing about it, by talking about it. I felt like I was being disrespectful to her. But it was the only way I could express all these things."

In the end, those first two solo records told pretty much everything about that period of his life that needed to be said. That they even saw the light of day was a statement in itself, given that Escovedo had backed away from trying to make a living as a musician in the aftermath of the True Believers' breakup. He was working at Waterloo Records while the Orchestra and Buick were developing, content to play music for reasons unrelated to career objectives. But that changed after Levie's death—partly because of friends such as Stephen Bruton.

Bruton had recently moved to Austin from Los Angeles, where he had spent several years as the guitarist in Bonnie Raitt's band and occasionally had toured with Bob Dylan. He produced Jimmie Dale Gilmore's 1991 debut for Elektra, and began talking to Escovedo about doing a record with him as well. "When Bruton jumped on board, Watermelon got really interested," Escovedo says. Appropriately enough, Watermelon was co-owned by Waterloo Records boss John Kunz, who had been so instrumental in making the True Believers' first album happen—though Escovedo says Kunz's Watermelon partner, Heinz Geissler, was the main force behind the solo deal.

Gravity and *Thirteen Years* proved beneficial for both parties, providing a rebirth of Escovedo's career and helping establish Watermelon as a respectable new roots-rock label. He toured frequently in the early to mid-1990s to support the records, earning reams of positive press and adding several precious memories along the way—such as a house party after a Sunday-evening gig in Athens, Georgia, in November 1993, swapping songs late into the night with Kevn Kinney, Vic Chesnutt, Syd Straw, and others while Michael Stipe sat and listened. In 1994, he produced an album for Pork, a garage-rock trio of Austin women that includes Dana Lee Smith, whom Alejandro married that year.

By the time he was ready to make his third album, it seemed clear that Escovedo was due for a jump to a bigger label. Rykodisc, one of the three or four biggest independent labels in the business, signed him and issued *With These Hands* in 1996. It featured a somewhat more rocking and diverse musical approach and sported some high-profile special guests, including Willie Nelson dueting on "Nickel and a Spoon," Jennifer Warnes adding backing vocals to two cuts, and his musical kin Pete Escovedo and Sheila E. (as well as Pete's wife and two sons) contributing percussion to the title track.

As if on cue, however, the up-and-down nature of Escovedo's career cycled back around again with a double whammy in the fall of 1996. Rykodisc, disappointed with the sales of *With These Hands,* wanted to renegotiate the record deal with significantly smaller budgets; Escovedo scoffed at that, choosing to leave the label instead. "I think that they just lost faith a little early in the game," Escovedo says. "I was under the impression that they understood it wasn't going to be an overnight sensation, that it was going to be maybe be two or three records down the road."

Around the same time, he was diagnosed with hepatitis C, a chronic disease that slowly destroys the liver and has necessitated significant changes in Escovedo's diet and lifestyle. "I don't drink nearly as much as I used to. I try not to drink, but I do from time to time. For a while, I was just out of commission. I couldn't do anything but sleep; I slept for weeks. And I looked like I was about to die. I went through a real depressed time. . . . But I feel a whole lot better now. It's been more than a year now since I was diagnosed with it, and I feel much better. I've had a lot of friends who have helped me, just trying to get me off the couch and saying, 'Hey, get up and start doing stuff again.'"

■ ■ ■

The new *More Miles than Money* may mark the beginning of yet another comeback trail for Escovedo, but in one intriguing respect he has already come full circle, right back where his musical career started.

The disc's closing suite, "Gravity/Falling Down Again/Street Hassle," is but one example of how he often weaves one song into another at his live shows. "We'll segue the '13 Years' theme into, like, noise, into 'I Wanna Be Your Dog,' and then back out to maybe something like 'She Towers Above.' I like those contrasts, you know? Dissonance, and beauty, and melody, and dissonance. We used to do one that would go from 'Hard Road' to 'Pale Blue Eyes' to 'Bury Me' to 'Falling Down Again,' and then throwing 'Street Hassle' in there too. The whole thing was, like, twenty-five minutes long."

If there is a goal to all those segues, Escovedo says, it is this: "Without trying to sound too pretentious, you can make it like a short film. There's all these different images, and then moments where the songs are bridged by little passages of just instrumental pieces, and then words, and so you see something there. And then maybe the emotion becomes angry, and just out of control. And then maybe we see something floating—something floats out of all this barrage of noise."

The irony is inescapable: His musical career began when an attempt to make a movie turned into a band, and now it has evolved into a band that is trying to turn music into a movie. And while those twenty-five-minute moments of inspiration may be testing the audience a bit—"A lot of times they just kind of shake their heads and go, 'All right, this is ridiculous,'" he admits—there's always the chance that one person out there will feel the connection, will understand the emotion, will see something floating out of that barrage of noise. And sometimes it's worth it just to get through to that one person.

"After all the touring I've done," Escovedo says, "I've found that there is an audience out there, however large or small, that wants to hear my songs. And I'm willing to go out there and play them."

Ain't Life Grand

Jon Dee Graham's Borderless Vista Is the Culmination of a Journey from One Moment to Another

ND #37, JANUARY–FEBRUARY 2002

Peter Blackstock

The most lasting impression of Jon Dee Graham is his laugh. His is not a lighthearted chuckle, but a full-bellied bellow, a roar of approval and amusement unleashed with an infectious enthusiasm that leaves no doubt about the way he approaches the world. Graham has seen his share of dark days, to be sure—but his big sweet laugh squarely reaffirms what he once rapturously declared in song: It's a big sweet life.

Sweetness for Graham today seems a fairly clear-cut pursuit of happiness. He lives with his wife and two-and-a-half-year-old son William in a friendly South Austin neighborhood, their house flanked by the storybook white picket fence. A few blocks west is the Continental Club, where Graham has performed every Wednesday night for the past couple years, continually sharpening his skills as a songwriter, singer, guitarist, and bandleader.

After nearly two decades as a sideman or secondary tunesmith with an impressive succession of artists, Graham finally struck out on his own in 1997, releasing his debut album *Escape from Monster Island* on Freedom Records to widespread acclaim. *Summerland* followed in 1999 on New West, furthering his reputation as a wise lyricist equally adept with forceful rockers and poignant ballads.

Hooray for the Moon, due in January on New West, is a triumphant culmination of Graham's gradually growing momentum. Produced by Don Smith and featuring his regular bandmates Mike Hardwick (guitar/Dobro/pedal steel) and Mark Andes (bass), plus ace-in-the-hole drummer Jim Keltner, it is a powerful recording of eleven songs that Graham deems "the best I could bring to the table." They sound like nothing less.

The album's first two tracks have been around a while. "One

Moment" is a chestnut from his years with the True Believers that brought a modest windfall when Patty Smyth covered it in 1992; the half-jokingly-titled "Restraining Order Song" predates the Believers days. The middle of the record spotlights two telling covers—"Way Down in the Hole" by Tom Waits (whose gruff singing is clearly a touchstone for Graham) and the Spanish-language anthem "Volver," a staple of every Latin band that played the Texas-Mexico border circuit where Graham grew up.

Those geographical roots also run deep in "Laredo," a raging, harrowing rocker that Graham aptly terms "as dark as anything I've ever done, if not darker." Striking a balance are softer songs such as "I Go Too," a beautiful promise from father to son ("Climb up on my shoulders, you can see the parade"); and the closing "Tamale House #1," a lingering memory of a faded romance painted across a dying-dawn sky of "post office gray and cantaloupe orange."

"Tamale House #1" traces its narrator's tracks across the Congress Avenue Bridge in downtown Austin, which is about as far as Graham ventured in support of his first two albums. Road-weary from countless years of touring and eager to stay home with his family, Graham seemed content to simply play his weekly gig at the Continental. To be fair, he did play occasional out-of-town dates, but he admits that "it was commando runs. We would get an anchor date somewhere that I really wanted to play, and we'd play there, and do three dates around it, and come home. It was enough to maintain a presence, but not enough to really build anything."

The result is that Graham's profile remains lower on the radar than the quality of his records would suggest he deserves—something he seems determined to address with *Hooray for the Moon*. "I think this record really demands that I take it out," he acknowledges. "And I think in the past I've really compartmentalized my life—you know, now I'm playing rock 'n' roll guitar; now I'm a daddy. And I think that I've gotten to the point with it now where I can go out and feel right about it. Because this is what I do."

■ ■ ■

Jon Dee Graham has been doing this since he was thirteen years old, when he got his first gig playing bass in a country band in his hometown of Quemado, a town of about three hundred on the Mexican border in southwest Texas. "This strange pair of guys show up from nowhere, and they're living in a rented trailer house down on the river road," Graham recalls.

"There was obviously a limited pool of talent for them to draw from. So I borrowed a bass guitar from someone to play with these guys. It only lasted about a month because at one of the shows, a federal marshal showed up and arrested these guys for being AWOL from the air force."

Though that inauspicious beginning was Graham's initial band gig, it wasn't his first musical endeavor. "I played the piano in the Methodist church from when I was ten to about thirteen," he explains. "I think what happened was, when I was ten, I asked for a guitar, and [my parents] were like, 'Well, let's try piano first.' So I was playing piano in church, but every couple of months I was still asking for the guitar. And after a couple years, I won, and got the guitar—a Sears Silvertone."

Later, Graham played tuba in the high school band. He graduated early and headed to Austin—ostensibly to attend honors classes at the University of Texas (where he had been accepted into UT's prestigious Plan II program), but with dreams of playing music looming in his mind, against his family's wishes.

"When I was twelve, right about when I got my first guitar, I remember having a talk with my older brother and telling him that what I wanted to do was be a musician—and him delineating for me all of the reasons why that was the most foolish idea on earth. So I knew even then that this is what I wanted to do," Graham says. "And when I left home to go to college, I remember having a big talk with my dad about how, you know, now it was time to put all of that stuff behind me and to get on with the business of my life. But there was just no escaping it."

Graham's destiny was perhaps divined much earlier, judging from an early childhood experience that he still recounts with vivid clarity. His formative years were spent in Whiteface, a tiny town near Lubbock in the Texas Panhandle, and one of his oldest memories involves a visit from "Uncle Budge," who had been adopted by Graham's grandfather in the 1930s after Budge's parents were killed in an auto accident.

"Budge was like the colorful guy in the family," Graham relates. "And when I was four and a half or five, I remember everyone talking about Uncle Budge comin' to town. So, he shows up, and he's wearing a western shirt with gold threads spun into it, he's got a bottle of whiskey tucked in his back pocket, and he's got a mandolin. And all the men were outside with Uncle Budge, passing this bottle around, and he's playing mandolin, and they're all singing. And I remember looking and seeing the women in the house looking out the kitchen door and shaking their heads.

"I remember his hair smelled like Lucky Tiger, and a cigarette dangling outta the corner of his mouth, and just playing the hell outta this mandolin. . . . He wasn't a professional musician; in fact, he was a roughneck, just traveled around working oil wells. But I remember that mandolin—it had the ornate carved little horn on the top, and this real deep red sunburst.

"It just all blends together somehow: the sunburst, the brilliantine in the hair, the bottle of whiskey in the back pocket. It was the most exciting thing I'd ever seen."

■ ■ ■

The Graham family's move to Quemado shortly thereafter—spurred by crashing prices in the cotton industry that had been their trade in the Panhandle—opened up other opportunities for music-related excitement to the impressionable young Jon Dee.

"We spent so much time over in Mexico growing up," he relates. "There was no drinking age in Mexico, so we would go over there to drink. And in the spring, every weekend there would be dozens of quinceañeras—it's like a Mexican debutante ball, when a girl turns fifteen, they have this big coming-out party for her. So every weekend in the spring, we'd go across and crash whatever party it was. And they always had live bands.

"There were young girls, there was alcohol, there was live music—it was fantastic," he continues. "I still remember these bands sort of banging out phonetic versions of 'She's About a Mover.' And with clearly no idea what was going on—but they completely related to the Farfisa [organ], and the sort of obviously weird San Antonio–Latin bent of that Doug Sahm stuff.

"And then the big bands that would come through, the Latin soul bands—that was, like, my junior year, I started really getting into that. We would go to see Sunny & the Sunliners, and Little Joe. And these guys would show up with, like, eight-piece horn sections, and traveling with a B3, a drummer, and a percussionist. These nine- or twelve-piece bands, just blazing."

Pulling Graham in another direction was the hard-rock radio station in San Antonio with a signal that carried to the Rio Grande Valley. Though the station's bread and butter consisted of such obvious mid-1970s staples as Aerosmith and Led Zeppelin, they also occasionally veered into much more adventurous territory.

"I was driving around late one night and they played something off of that first Patti Smith record," Graham says. "And I was like, 'What the hell is this?' It was sandwiched in between, like, 'Black Diamond' and some Aerosmith song. . . . And then a couple months later, they started playing stuff from [the Heartbreakers' debut] *L.A.M.F.* They had completely blended, somehow, these two things. And they saw no contradiction in it whatsoever, because to them it was just more loud rock."

It is not hard to figure, then, how Graham's own music has come to express the connections, rather than the contradictions, between seemingly disparate styles. "You take those three bases—playing in a country band at thirteen, and then going to these Latin dances, and then getting that [hard-rock and punk] stuff when I was probably sixteen—I don't know how, but it makes sense. . . . There's some kind of thread that loops all of those together."

■ ■ ■

Not surprisingly, Graham's high school years also included occasional journeys to San Antonio for big rock shows. His first, he recalls, was Johnny Winter, with Peter Frampton opening (pre–*Frampton Comes Alive*). It is natural to inquire if Graham also attended the notorious San Antonio appearance of the Sex Pistols.

"I didn't," he answers. "You know, I remember wanting to go, but somehow, something came up, and I didn't make it. But Jesse went."

"Jesse" is Jesse Sublett, who would soon ask Graham to play guitar in the Skunks, one of the primordial punk bands of Austin's late-1970s underground. Graham was playing with a group called the Whip-Its, but hooked up with Sublett after the departure of the Skunks' original guitarist, Eddie Muñoz (who moved to Los Angeles and ended up in the Plimsouls). The Skunks' seven-inch single "Can't Get Loose"/"Earthquake Shake" became the stuff of local legend, akin to the status of Superchunk's "Slack Motherfucker" or Mudhoney's "Touch Me, I'm Sick" in their respective communities a decade later.

When he joined the band, Graham had just turned nineteen and had completed three semesters at UT, but he didn't make it through the fourth. "By that time, I'd been touring some with the Skunks, and I was missing classes, and I was making really good money," he recalls. "And, you know, once you've opened for the Clash, it's kind of hard to go back to class."

Graham's tenure with the Skunks lasted about a year and a half; he left in 1980 "in a huff," he says, partly because he felt a need to start working more on his own songs. "In the Skunks, I really didn't write that much; I think maybe I wrote two songs in two years," he explains. "And that was one of the reasons why I left— I just felt that there wasn't anything I could do in that band except play guitar, and I wanted more than that."

Nevertheless, his next venture was also a guitarist-only role—but one with considerable intrigue. Fiery Austin blues singer Lou Ann Barton, who had just made a record for Asylum with legendary producer Jerry Wexler, hired Graham to play guitar in her band. It was a bold and controversial move, since the local blues scene (built around Antone's nightclub) and punk scene (centered on Raul's) were light-years apart in those days, aesthetically and ideologically.

"It seemed like a really good move, but I think it pissed a lot of people off in the blues mafia, and pissed a bunch of people off in the Raul's scene," Graham says. "That whole purist attitude was pretty strong back then; not much crossover was allowed. But being the way I am, I kinda liked that. Because it was completely in the face of both camps."

In retrospect, however, Graham admits that it never really worked. "It was a horrible move, and it didn't last that long; I think it was less than a year, maybe nine months."

The problems apparently were related more to business concerns than musical ones. "That was a great record, and, god, that woman can sing," he says. "But I think she also suffered from that 'velvet rut' syndrome of Austin, where it's like, 'Why would I wanna go further than a three-hour drive?' We played regularly in Dallas and Houston and San Antonio, just regional stuff."

A brief spell with the Gator Family (which included Graham's soon-to-be wife, Sally Norvell; they divorced in the mid-1990s) was followed by what Graham calls "the dark time of the Lift." Though the Lift was one of Austin's most popular club acts in the early '80s, Graham now feels the band's music didn't measure up to his own increasingly demanding standards.

"Musically and creatively, I was wanting to do something that meant something, rather than being the big band that the college kids would come out and see," he explains. "We were drawing like crazy; it was a really good living. But it was unsubstantial. It didn't mean anything."

Still, his days in the Lift served a purpose. "It was writing school for me," he admits. "I ended up writing a lot of the lyrics. And I'm not particularly proud of the stuff that I was doing, but it was making me write all the time. It was real unreflective, un-thought-out—'Here's a piece of music, the words need to go something like this'—and I'd just crank something out, and it'd be a song.

"And, toward the end of that, I sort of started realizing that this could be done better," he concludes, with a hearty laugh.

■ ■ ■

"So I left that band, and for about six months I didn't do anything. I just lived by myself, and played guitar, and was writing—but I didn't like anything that I was seeing. I would go out and see bands, and everything just seemed stupid.

"Then one night I went to see Los Lobos at Club Foot, and the True Believers were opening. And I was like—this is it. This is the best thing I've seen to date.

"And I couldn't pin it down—I still can't pin it down. I couldn't say what it was about it that was so powerful or so cool, but I knew there was something going on here that nobody else was doing, and nobody else could even touch."

The True Believers at the time were a four-piece led by brothers Alejandro and Javier Escovedo, both of whom wrote and sang and played guitar. In a 1997 interview, Alejandro said of his initial relationship with Jon Dee: "We were kind of enemies because he had been in the Lift when I was in Rank and File. The Lift was kind of this new romantic band, and I couldn't stand them."

Escovedo did, however, admire Graham's musicianship, and eventually decided to recruit him for the True Believers, along with drummer Rey Washam. "Alejandro and I had a bunch of common friends, so we'd talk, and one time they were opening for the Long Ryders at Liberty Lunch, and he said, 'Come out and bring your guitar, and just sit in with us.' And I did, and that was it."

The end result transformed the True Believers into one of the great rock bands of the 1980s, though the magic went largely undocumented at the time. A 1986 debut disc for Rounder/EMI featured solid songwriting but failed to capture the band's sonic power; the stronger follow-up was shelved shortly before its release and didn't surface until Ryko issued both records on one CD, *Hard Road,* in 1994.

Much of what made the Believers special was the breadth of styles represented in the songs of the Escovedo brothers and Graham. On the first record, for example, Alejandro's enduring folk-rock anthem "The Rain Won't Help You When It's Over" contrasted with Javier's full-throttle attack "I Get Excited," while Graham cast a whole different mood with the brooding, bluesy "Lucky Moon."

Somewhat surprisingly, Graham initially didn't harbor any expectations of contributing to the True Believers' repertoire. "I came into it thinking that I would just be another guitar player," he says. "My first instinct was, OK, I'll just shift back into the sideman mode, and I can play all this different stuff and do the lap steel stuff, and I'll be a support element in here.

"But Alejandro wouldn't let me. He was like, 'Well, what about that song you were playing the other day at sound check?' And we'd do that, and then it was in the set. Or I'd be playing a riff at sound check, and he'd go, 'You oughta finish that.' So he kinda pushed me into it, or wouldn't let me hide behind being just a guitar player again. And I really owe him a lot for that."

Graham didn't write a lot with the Believers—he wound up with two cuts on each record—but the quality was considerably greater than anything he had done before. "One Moment," from the ill-fated second album, earned him notice from other artists; Austin singer Kris McKay covered it on her 1990 Arista Records debut.

By then, though, the True Believers were already long gone, a victim of record-company abandonment compounded by infighting and various diverging interests. Javier took a gig with Austin teen upstart Will Sexton; Graham moved to Los Angeles with his wife when her career as a rock-video director was taking off, though he returned for occasional acoustic gigs billed under the name Blue Retrievers.

"I've heard so many different versions of why the band broke up," Graham reminisces. "Basically, what I remember is that the record not coming out sort of dealt a death blow, and then, like the steer that's already been shot in the head, we stumbled around stunned for a little while longer, until we actually died."

■ ■ ■

It didn't take long for Graham to start getting serious gigs after his move to Los Angeles. He played guitar with Michelle Shocked on the tour for her 1989 album *Captain Swing.* "It was the first time I'd ever played with a horn section," he says. "We were playing these almost jump-blues, big-band arrangements."

Shortly thereafter, he hooked up with X's John Doe, who was about to record his solo debut for Geffen, *Meet John Doe*. Graham played on the album, co-wrote a couple of its songs, and hit the road with Doe's touring band (which also included former Television guitarist Richard Lloyd). Musically, it was a solid success. The record remains Doe's best solo effort to date, and the live shows were incendiary.

It also turned out to be a good lesson in the workings of the music industry. "Geffen spent all this money on him; it was like, this is gonna be John's big shot," Graham says. "But the record wasn't really doing very much, and three weeks into the tour, we run into this Geffen field rep at a gig, and we're all drinking with him, and he gets drunk enough to go, 'I like you guys, and I gotta tell you, the word came down from the office that we're supposed to sit down behind this record,'" meaning the label would no longer aggressively promote it.

In the midst of those gigs, plus some work with former Lone Justice guitarist Ryan Hedgecock and Doe's X ex Exene Cervenka, Graham gradually started to assert himself as a solo singer-songwriter. "Tremendously unsuccessfully," he chortles, recalling his early efforts at such L.A. haunts as Genghis Cohen and the Ash Grove. "The 'career' side of it [as a guitarist] was going really well. But the 'hobbyist' side, as a solo performer, was just dead-ass. There was nothing happening with it."

On the other hand, Patty Smyth's cover of "One Moment to Another" ended up earning him a cut on a gold record, as a result of her album also featuring a hit-single duet with Don Henley. That success led Graham to try his hand at being a songwriter in trade. "I was like, OK, I can do this. And I got my little garage studio set up, a little demo thing, and I set out to write songs that other people would cover. And it was just the most godawful experiment in crap."

The revelation for Graham was that his best writing came from a much deeper well. "When you pull back and you look at it, the song I've made the most money off of . . . is way out there," he says of "One Moment," which opens with the lines: "In the name of the fifty-three saints / I will go search he says / Seek out the hurting says / Where comes this pain?"

"It makes no lyrical linear sense," he admits. "But it was written from a really personal place. When I set out to write for someone, or for something, or to some end, it's a disaster, every single time. Because the craft emerges, and the artifice is all over it. The only songs of mine that end up being worth a damn are the ones that demand to be written."

■ ■ ■

A solo show at Cactus Cafe in Austin during the 1992 South by Southwest festival was a minor revelation for Graham. Mixing his True Believers highlights with some promising new tunes, he flat-out slayed a packed house at the classic acoustic venue. "Obviously it was a stacked deck because it was back in Austin," he says, "but that show made me feel like I might actually be able to do this. I remember feeling like I did a good job, and then I listened back to the tape of it, and was like, yeah, this might work!"

There was still one more significant detour for Graham to wander down, though. "Around the end of '93, beginning of '94, my marriage was falling apart, and it was a pretty dark time," he says. "And I had this offer to go on tour with Calvin Russell."

It is necessary at this point to explain the unfathomable story of Calvin Russell. A grizzled ex-con lurking in the lower ranks of the Austin songwriter strata—he rarely ventured beyond the Austin Outhouse, a funky dive that was home to many of the city's most interesting misfits—Russell somehow had become a sensation in Europe, where his hard-boiled American roots-rock was accepted as rough, raw, and real.

And real he was. "Basically, he's an ex-con, a fifty-year-old felon," Graham says. "You hear about all the sort of outlaw-country stuff—Calvin was for real. He really was the *Drugstore Cowboy* guy."

His overseas popularity was equally genuine. "My first European show with him was in the Netherlands, and he sells out this place of maybe eight hundred, and people are singing along. And he's paying me better than John [Doe] and Michelle [Shocked] ever did."

Graham recorded an album, 1995's *Dreaming the Dog,* with Russell, and toured with him extensively behind it. "By then my marriage was official-ly over, so I basically toured Europe for eleven months. We went to the Bataclan in Paris, that holds, like, 2,500 people, and sold out three nights. And this is Calvin, who lived in a fuckin' trailer house in Pflugerville [a small town just north of Austin]. People would go, 'Where does Calvin live?' Well, he owns a little island in the canals in Rotterdam; he has an old stone house built in the 1700s on this island. He owns an apartment in Paris. And he has a trailer in Pflugerville.

"It was hilarious because I would have people say, 'What have you been doing?' And I'd go, 'Well, I was out with Calvin Russell.' And there'd be this little chuckle, and, you know, 'Really? Good work.' And the truth of the matter is, I was making more money with Calvin than I'd ever made with any other band, anywhere."

■ ■ ■

After the tour with Russell, Graham moved back to Austin with Roy, his son from his first marriage. He didn't have any designs on reintegrating himself back into the local music scene, though.

"I kind of moved back here under cover of night," he says. "I didn't call anybody, I didn't tell anyone I was back. I was framing, and doing some carpentry work, and taking care of Roy. He was three and a half then. That went on for about six months. I was totally hiding out, and I wasn't gonna play."

But a chance encounter at a grocery store with multi-instrumentalist Mike Hardwick, who had worked with Texas songwriters Jerry Jeff Walker, David Halley, and Michael Fracasso, resulted in Graham getting lured back into the music. Hardwick invited Graham to play on a session he was producing, and they wound up doing some picking together on the side.

"I started going over to his house about two or three times a week, just drinking coffee and playing guitar," Graham says. "We started playing the Cactus and Flipnotics, and people were really interested and were starting to come out."

When they appeared on the KUT-FM radio program *Live Set,* Freedom Records owner Matt Eskey contacted them about releasing a tape of their performance on the show. Hardwick and Graham instead talked Eskey into letting them record a low-budget studio album, which became Graham's 1997 solo debut, *Escape from Monster Island.*

Both that record and its 1999 follow-up on New West, *Summerland,* mixed older songs from the True Believers days and his L.A. period with newer tunes written since his return to Austin. That is true of *Hooray for the Moon* as well, but there was one major difference this time around. Instead of self-producing the record with Hardwick in Austin, Graham and his band traveled to Los Angeles to work with Don Smith, who has produced albums for John Hiatt, Cracker, and many others, in addition to engineering discs for the Rolling Stones, Tom Petty, Bob Dylan, et al.

Though Smith was actually the fourth in a series of producers who were at one point slated to do the album, he turned out to be an excellent choice. Graham appreciated his sense for both mainstream and left-of-center projects: "He mixed [the Stones'] *Voodoo Lounge,* and he was mixing the Jon Spencer Blues Explosion, and he mixed *Full Moon Fever* for Petty," he says. "It was this weird blend of kind of outside stuff and just real right-smack-in-the-middle-of-the-road big radio records."

One of Smith's main contributions resulted from what initially was a major snag in the recording plans. Graham and his band booked time with Smith in late July and early August, but drummer Rafael Gayol was already booked on a summer tour with the Flatlanders during that window. "So I called Don and said, 'The drummer's gonna be gone, we're gonna have to either move the date, or find another drummer.' And he goes, 'Well, let me make a couple of phone calls and I'll call you back.' So he calls back in twenty minutes and goes, 'What do you think about Keltner?'"

Jim Keltner is, of course, one of the most accomplished drummers in rock 'n' roll history, with credits far too extensive to list (start with John Lennon, Dolly Parton, and B. B. King, and continue on for hours). "I was like, you know, you're pulling my leg. This is a cruel joke, don't be doing this.

"And then the other part of me is thinking, this is so manipulative, he can't get Keltner. It's gonna be a bait and switch. He's gonna tell me Keltner, and then he's gonna show up with, you know, the guy that's touring with the Up with People revival or something. So I said, 'Well, yeah, I'd love that, but, can you really get him?' And he's like, 'Oh, Jimmy's an old friend of mine, and he's available, and he's more than happy to do it.'"

The expertise and experience both Keltner and Smith brought to the table proved invaluable. "I had this feeling that there was nothing that could be done in the studio that either I couldn't do, or I couldn't figure out how it was done—and Don just proved me totally wrong," Graham says with a laugh.

"I learned that there's all kinds of stuff you can do in the studio that I just have no idea about. I'm proud of the stuff that I've done on my own, and I'm very chauvinistic about the Austin thing. But you listen to this record and you know it's not made in Austin."

Which isn't to say it was heavily produced. "Easily seven-tenths of this record was live," Graham says. "What was cut when we were doing the basics, that was it—that's what you hear on the records."

Among the few things that were added later was a classic cameo by Little Joe, leader of legendary Tejano group Little Joe y La Familia—one of the bands Graham used to go see during his childhood days on the Texas border. Joe was brought in to sing a backing vocal track on "Volver," which Graham describes as "the 'Yesterday' of Mexico. You hear it everywhere—in elevators, on the street; you ask any kid to sing it and he can."

Graham had actually already returned to Austin when Little Joe's part was added, late one night after La Familia had played a show in Los Angeles. 'They showed up at the studio in their bus at, like, three in the morning, all tanked outta their minds, and came into the studio and just sorta burned it down," Graham relates. "And, those 'gritos' and stuff you hear—it's like, Little Joe's singing, and the band is kind of wandering around yelling and talking. I would have given anything to see it."

■ ■ ■

What remains, then, is the road. Sometime in early 2002, Jon Dee Graham and his band will head out on tour behind *Hooray for the Moon*, determined to show the rest of the country what they've been delivering every Wednesday at the Continental Club in Austin for the past couple of years.

"There's a big element of 'prove it'-ism," he acknowledges, "because at least half the touring that I've done behind the first two records has been either an acoustic duo or just me with an acoustic guitar. So I wanna take out the band—just to prove it."

When the Fallen Angels Fly

In Two Years, Billy Joe Shaver Lost His Mother, His Wife, and His Son; His Songs Live On

ND #32, MARCH–APRIL 2001

Grant Alden

> There's a race of men that don't fit in,
>   A race that can't stay still;
> So they break the hearts of kith and kin,
>   And they roam the world at will.
> They range the field and they rove the flood,
>   And they climb the mountain's crest;
> Theirs is the curse of the gypsy blood,
>   And they don't know how to rest.
>
> ROBERT SERVICE, 1907

White-haired now, and probably the last great cowboy poet, Billy Joe Shaver drives a long white van that is partly home, partly tour bus, and mostly jumbled with stuff. He is careful to lock a red club across the steering wheel because, he says, some of his former bandmates have kept their keys, and their drug habits.

Two guitars rest in the back, a battered black Strat and a Gibson 335, long-ago gifts to his only son, Eddy, from friends Duane Allman and Dickey Betts. Eddy—John Edwin Shaver—was buried in Waco on January 4. He died early New Year's Eve of a heroin overdose. He was thirty-eight, had married in October, and was to have begun recording his second solo album on January 2.

His grave, Shaver says, is still covered with flowers. Grass already grows on the graves of Billy Joe's mother, Victory Odessa Watson, and Eddy's mother, Brenda Tindell Shaver, both of whom succumbed to cancer within a month of each other in 1999.

Today, Eddy's father has driven his guitars through freezing rain south to Austin. After lunch, we carry them in the back door of Willie Nelson's studio and leave them with a friend who will lock the instruments up in Willie's vault. And there they will stay.

We have come to talk about what is now the Shavers' final album together, a resilient, fierce, proud masterpiece titled *The Earth Rolls On,* set for release April 10 on New West Records. We have met only once before, on Waylon Jennings's tour bus in July 1996, for a conversation between Shaver and Jennings that appeared in *ND #5.* I do not presume he remembers that half-hour encounter.

Nevertheless, I ended up carrying one of Eddy's guitars because I was there, and it needed carrying.

■ ■ ■

The last cowboy poet has never been a household name, but Billy Joe Shaver is a stunning songwriter—has been for a long, long time. When he finally found an audience in the early 1970s, it was comprised principally of his peers. Tom T. Hall and Kris Kristofferson, neither of whom suffered fools gladly or commonly recorded other people's material, both cut his songs. Then Kristofferson produced Shaver's 1973 debut, *Old Five and Dimers Like Me,* and Tom T. wrote the liner notes.

That same year, just before Austin would be anointed a musical mecca and the notion of outlaw country would acquire marketing currency, Waylon Jennings cut an album of all-but-one Shaver songs, *Honky Tonk Heroes* (reissued in 1999 by Buddha). That record pretty much cemented Shaver's role as the outlaw poet laureate. Even though many of the labels he recorded for are no longer in business, much of Shaver's music is back in print, and the rest of it ought to be.

Today, most of what Shaver owns fits in that white van, and the IRS has been on his tail for years, trying to get the rest of it. "I've got lawyers on that stuff," he says. "I don't know why I thought I was exempt. Because I never voted and I never owned no land, I didn't think I'd have to pay taxes." Guess they can't figure out why he is not a rich man, either.

Then again, maybe he is. Over lunch, he mentions that George Jones has promised to cut one of his songs for his next album. "That's like an award to me," Shaver says.

■ ■ ■

George Jones was born in Saratoga, Texas, on September 12, 1931, and was singing on the streets of Beaumont by the time he was twelve. Billy Joe Shaver was born in Corsicana, Texas, on August 16, 1939, and began singing for spare change at an even more tender age. Pretty much everything one might ask about his life after that can be found in his songs, beginning with "Georgia on a Fast Train." Much of that history has been covered in detail by Michael McCall's fine two-part series in the *Journal of Country Music.*

Billy Joe had an older sister, Patricia, but his father had another family. Before Billy Joe was born, his dad left. His mother took the best work she could find, in a Waco honky-tonk called the Green Gables, and left her kids back in Corsicana with her mother, Birdie Lee Watson.

We sit to talk at a table in a back room of Willie Nelson's studio, just a few paces from where Eddy's guitars rest. I have brought a present, a copy of Robert Service's 1907 book *The Spell of the Yukon*. Service immigrated to Canada from the UK, and alternated between being a tramp and a poet and a bank teller. *The Spell of the Yukon* was meant as a vanity project, just some stories he had collected in verse form, but it became a best seller. It is not exactly high art, but I treasure my grandfather's copy, and I love those poems.

It proves a very lucky guess. Shaver holds the old red-leather volume to his heart, thumbs through it, and considers it often during the next hour and a half. "You can't know how much this little book means to me," he says softly. "I love poetry, man, I really love it. This guy here was my favorite, Robert Service. Out of all of them. I reckon it's because he lived a lot of it and knew what he was talking about. We all like to hear things and know that the guy saying them is the one that lived 'em."

Looking at the book, he began to remember his own life in that same quiet voice, beginning with the teacher who introduced him to Service. "Mrs. Leff. She's a hundred years old, still alive, bright as ever," he says. "She turned me onto this stuff. I got so interested in it, guess that's when I started writing. Oh, I been writing a little of this and that ever since I was a kid.

"I hid it so long, back when I was young, coming up. If you wrote poetry or you sang, you was called a sissy. And it was hard. I had enough trouble as it was, but then I had this English teacher that kinda led me along, showed me, brought it out of me. And she instilled in me that I actually have talent.

"We didn't have a radio. My grandmother raised me and my sister, actually on her old-age pension. She took in quilting, she made lye soap, stuff. We was real, real poor. I'd hear something on somebody's radio somewhere—there was a general store down the road. I'd pick up what little I could, just make up the rest of it, and sing, tap my foot, didn't have no instruments. My first guitar my grandmother bought when I was about eleven years old. She passed away about a year later.

"Yeah, we was on the welfare line. My grandmother, I never heard her say a discouraging word, though. She was always real positive. Of course, she told us right away there wasn't no Santa Claus, no matter what the other kids said. Said to go along with it, you know, but there wasn't none."

Each summer, Shaver would go visit his mom in Waco, end up singing in the Green Gables, spending soldier's tips on the jukebox. Each fall he would go back east to Corsicana. After his grandmother died, Shaver moved to Waco with his mother and her new husband. Maybe football seemed like a way out. Certainly he had the size for it, and he dabbled in school long enough to stay eligible.

Then his best friend, Larry Smith, convinced Shaver to enlist in the navy on a buddy program, said they would both serve together. Thing was, Smith didn't enlist with Shaver, because he wanted the starting job at wide receiver on the football team. Shaver wasn't cut out for military life, but they stayed friends; Shaver even went AWOL a few times to meet up with Smith (who ultimately joined the army).

That is where the rest of "I Been to Georgia on a Fast Train" came from. Caught AWOL, he was chained to a black soldier. They spent most of the trip trying to hurt each other, but it changed Shaver's life.

"We turned out to be pretty good friends at the end of that. But, boy, was it rough; he was a bigot, and I was too. But that was back when I thought that was the way things were supposed to be. I was only seventeen. You know, we got talked at when we were kids, we did down here. It was all stupid. Don't make no sense, now. But it did then, some reason or another. All that different-colored skin things, used to be such a big deal, ain't nothin' to it, really. Just different-colored skin, that's all."

■ ■ ■

Shaver's military career ended over a fight with an out-of-uniform officer; a few things got broken, and he was thrown out of the service. As he sings it, Shaver came home with an eighth-grade education and a good Christian raising. And a bad conduct discharge that he later got upgraded. He was twenty years old, and soon in love. Brenda Tindell was seventeen, married to Billy Joe, and pregnant with Eddy—without her father knowing—but managed to finish high school.

It worked out, more or less, although they were married and divorced three times over the years. Her father had a ranch, and taught Shaver to be a cowboy. "I never was dedicated enough to be a rodeo cowboy," he says. "It takes a special person to do that. You've got to really want it, and go through all that misery and stuff. I was married, too, and my wife, she wouldn't let me do that. 'Stay off those bulls and things.' I'd sneak around and get hurt every now and then. About all I wound up with was a cowboy attitude. You can't get rid of that. Still wear boots; got to where I don't wear hats anymore, my neck's so messed up."

Mr. and Mrs. Shaver made a handsome pair when they went listening to music, which they often did, and Shaver ended up with a reputation as a brawler.

"I think a lot of people built that up a little," he says with maybe a little twinkle. "If I had a fight down an alley somewhere, it'd be two or three guys I beat up instead of just one. Something like that. I don't know why I had that reputation for fighting. Just did. Just did. Course it mighta helped I didn't lose many fights. Mighta helped. But I didn't fight that much. Cain't now. I guess that's what they made guns for, though," and he laughs.

"Most of 'em's in beer joints, where those situations arise. You're young and full of piss and vinegar and think you can do anything, and most of the time it's over a woman," he sighs. "Something like that. I used to take my wife out when we lived in Waco, and I had to quit taking her out because every damn time we went somewhere there'd be some . . . Of course, she was a looker, and there'd be somebody would mumble something. And I just hated people that mumbled. I'd say, 'Well what the hell did you say? Why don't you speak up?' And then the fight'd break out."

Despite the fights, Shaver had never abandoned his Christian faith. He was working in a sawmill when he received what he took to be a message from God. It was delivered in the form of a very large saw that took off most of the fingers on his right hand. A local doctor managed to reattach two of them, though Shaver nearly lost his arm in the bargain.

The family moved to Houston, where Shaver made the acquaintance of another struggling songwriter, named Willie Nelson. Pretty much as soon as he had figured out how to hold a pick in his right hand, Shaver took off for Nashville. "I wasn't thinking very good," he allows. "Well, I was thinking I shoulda went to L.A., but I couldn't get a ride going that way. I went on the other side of the road, got a ride first time, all the way to Memphis.

"This guy gave me ten bucks when I got out of the car. And I said, 'No, man, I can't take your money.' He said, 'Take it. Somebody did the same thing for me. Just do it for somebody else.' And I said, 'All right.' Of course I did the same thing many times after that.

"I'd divorced my wife—run off, actually, I guess you'd call it. She didn't think I could do it, so I set out to prove her wrong, I guess." He pauses. "No, just something made me do that. I knew I could do it because I'd been writing poetry all my life. Always knew I could do that. Actually, that's what I fell back on, to tell you the truth. [When] I cut these fingers off in a sawmill, I remember sending a real short prayer. I said, 'God, if you'll let me get outta this mess, I'll go to doing what I'm supposed to do.' And sure enough, he helped me and I got through it."

Nashville wasn't quite ready for Shaver in 1966, and he had a wife and kid home in Waco. So he ended up working construction back in Texas until he fell off a piece of scaffolding carrying two bundles of shingles. He kept working for six more weeks before a chiropractor told him he had crushed a vertebra.

"It just happened there was an old doctor there, from Germany, named Dr. Hipps. And he knew how to do that fusion stuff. I've not had much trouble from it until just recently. He died right after that, too, and I thought, good God, how lucky I am, that man fixed my back up like that."

The message seemed clear enough, so he healed and headed back to Nashville.

■ ■ ■

"I knew [songwriting would] always be something I could fall back on," he says. "Eventually I had to because of all these things that happened to me. It should've been the first thing I went for; it should've been just the opposite. Most people it is. Most people have something to fall back on from music. But it went the other way with me. And I actually fell back on the music because I was so beat up," he laughs some.

"I couldn't do much else. Been chunked off, banged up, beat up, knocked around, pieces and parts of me missing." He sighs. "But I did get to live a lot of it, so it was pretty easy for me to write it.

"I had a wife and kid, and you know how it is, family. Actually, they didn't think that was a real job. And back then, in country music it really wasn't. You couldn't make much. If you was looking for money, then you was in the wrong town, Nashville, Tennessee. Unless you was Harlan Howard or somebody, and even he wasn't making that much. God, what a writer! Guy's damn near as good as me," and though Shaver is laughing, he is not quite joking.

Kris Kristofferson once landed a helicopter on Johnny Cash's property to get his music heard. Shaver took a characteristically direct approach to meet the dean of Nashville songwriters, Harlan Howard.

"I had a motorcycle then, and I ran up to his publishing company's front porch, hit the door with it and backed off. He come out and said, 'What the hell's going on out here?' I said, 'Are you Harlan Howard?' He said, 'Yes, I am.' I said, 'Well, I'm Billy Joe Shaver. I'm the greatest songwriter ever lived.' And he says, 'Well, hell, I thought I was!' And we became good friends from then on. He listened to a few of my tunes, and sent me over to Bobby Bare."

He pauses, then chuckles. "Actually, he sent me over, and he didn't give me no recommendation." Bare was a pretty hot country singer in the 1960s, and had gotten into music publishing. Shaver had a truck his mother-in-law had given him, that motorcycle, a beat-up guitar, no place to sleep, and a head full of songs.

Their meeting is an oft-told legend. "Bobby had a six-pack up on his desk, like most people did back then," Shaver says. "And he's about two or three sheets in the wind, I guess. I said, 'I got these songs.' He said, 'Just leave the tape.'" Well, Shaver didn't have any money to cut demos, and he carried his songs in his head, not on paper. But he is a hard man to say no to.

Finally Bare struck a deal with the tall Texan. "I don't know, mighta been the way I slouched out, hat in my hand. I guess he felt sorry for me or something. He said, 'C'mon back. You got a guitar? I'll tell you what I'll do. You sit down there and start singing a song. If I don't like it, now, I'm going to stop you, and that's going to be it.' I think the first song I sang him was 'Evergreen,' of all things." "Evergreen," retitled "Evergreen Fields," is one of two old songs on his new album. (In Michael McCall's

JCM piece, Shaver remembers it having been "Restless Wind," the other old song on his new album; both tunes originally appeared on 1976's *When I Get My Wings*.)

Sure enough, Bare had ears, offered Shaver $50 a week to write for his company, Return Music, and let him sleep in the office. Bare ended up having a hit with Shaver's "Ride Me Down Easy."

That is as much of the story as usually gets into print, but there is a little more to it. A rumor floating around Nashville claims Shaver was once told by an unnamed publisher that if he brought in a lawyer, the deal was off.

"Yeah, they did," he says, very softly. "They said, 'If you get a lawyer, forget it.' And we needed money at the time, they knew it. And they did it, and I lost out on a lot of stuff. Bobby did well. But I didn't. I got credit, but as far as money . . . but that's all right, too. My family had to suffer a lot for it; I hate that. Might have been a different story if . . . I'd had a little more money out of my music. Bought some shit we didn't need, something like that. It's one of those things; it happens to a lot of people."

Shaver wrote a number of songs for Bare's company that neither he nor anybody else ever recorded. A few years later Bare sold the company, and somehow along the way Shaver's work ended up bundled with Paul McCartney's songs in Michael Jackson's empire, and . . . they got lost.

"I don't know exactly how all that shit happened, but it wound up around '77 or so that it all went to SBK," Shaver says. "Some reason or other, they said they lost all my songs. They never did pitch 'em anymore. There were other writers writing for them that were real big, and I assumed that they didn't want to mess with me because I wasn't signed to them anymore."

Perhaps that means he could resell those songs to another publishing company (he is not presently signed). "I know 'em all," he chuckles. "That's one good thing about my songwriting. I live with them enough that I never forget any of the words. I can see the title and I can sing the whole song for you. Sure can."

But he won't worry about it.

"It didn't matter to me, because I always knew I could write some more songs," he says. "And I did. And it's just as well that it happened that way because if I'd have been real popular, more than likely the kinda songs that came out of me now wouldn't have come out. So I'm happy, pretty happy, really. And I never was one that had any need for a lot of money."

■ ■ ■

Shaver spent much of the 1970s at the edge of the inner circle of country music's hottest subculture, a motley crew of roguish Texans who insisted on recording their music with their own bands, and had the audacity to be commercially successful doing so.

He had driven down to the second of Willie Nelson's Fourth of July picnics—called Dripping Springs Reunions back then—with one of Harlan Howard's future ex-wives. Shaver ended up in a trailer, with a guitar, playing "Willy the Wandering Gypsy and Me," which was how Waylon Jennings first heard the song written about his friend.

"It was kind of about me, too," Shaver says. "I spelled it like I do my name, because I actually was kinda in awe of him, and scared of him, too. I didn't know if he'd like me writing a song about him, because I really didn't know him that well. I knew well enough, I guess, to write that song."

Waylon promised to cut an album of Shaver's songs, though it took Shaver six months of stalking Jennings across Nashville, and a physical confrontation, to turn what may have been a partier's promise into *Honky Tonk Heroes.*

Shaver sat in the studio and watched, learned, and stirred up some trouble defending his work. "I actually had to sing the songs first, and then he'd overdub, 'cause the way that I did my lyrics was a little bit different from him. Not much, because I'd actually been influenced by him a little bit, so it all came from him. It was just—I was doing that old Texas shit. And he'd gotten away from Texas for a while, and he was up in Nashville doing that Nashville stuff."

Shaver had cut a single ("Chicken on the Ground") for Mercury in 1970, but it went nowhere. Three years later he got a deal with Monument, for whom he recorded *Old Five and Dimers.* Monument went out of business shortly thereafter. He roared around town for a while, then had another religious experience, at the end of which he came home singing the beginning of "I'm Just an Old Chunk of Coal (But I'm Gonna Be a Diamond Someday)," a huge hit for John Anderson in 1980.

He cut a single for MGM in 1974, just before they went out of business, then moved his family to Houston and quit smoking, drinking, and drugging. Later, through his friendship with Dickey Betts, Shaver landed on the Allman Brothers' label, Capricorn. (The Allmans also cut his song "Sweet Mama.") Capricorn released *When I Get My Wings* and *Gypsy Boy,* and then it, too, went out of business.

Columbia released 1981's *I'm Just an Old Chunk of Coal* and 1982's *Billy Joe Shaver,* and didn't go out of business. They also didn't sell too many of his records.

Once again, Shaver was tempted to find other work. "Well, I've yelled and whined and whimpered around and said I was gonna quit and stuff, but who in the world do you go to to quit?" he laughs. "Who do you go to and say, 'Here, take this watch and pension and stuff and stick it up your ass?' There's nobody there. There's nobody to go to.

"You actually, personally have to decide in your mind that you're just done with it, and you'll never be done with it, never will quit. Because you don't know who to go to to quit. Nobody's running the show.

Nobody. And you get fans; you get real caught up in it. And you'd do it, God forbid that the promoters know, but you'd do it for nothing."

Shaver teamed up with his son, Eddy, who had proved to be a guitar prodigy. The two co-produced 1987's *Salt of the Earth* and convinced Columbia to release the album (it was reissued in 2001 as part of the Lucky Dog "Pick of the Litter" series). It didn't make Columbia much money, either, but did cement a musical partnership that pulled Shaver further away from country and toward roadhouse honky-tonk. And Shaver, the band name that embraced their partnership, became road warriors.

"I've spent all my money that I made off writing going down the road, paying people," Shaver says. "My wife used to just have a fit about it. She said, 'You take all our money and spend it on these damn guys going up and down the road.' I said, 'Well, I like doing that, you know. I like singing and stuff.' 'But you ain't no good at it.' And I said, 'Well, I do the best I can, just like the writing,'" and he is laughing pretty good by now.

"She'd say, 'You're no good at that, either.' And dancing. She used to tell me, 'You ain't got an ounce of rhythm in your body.' And she mighta been right about the dancing. But the rest of it, I don't guess so. But I sure miss her. I miss Eddy, too. But, there ain't nothing bring 'em back. Just try to get with 'em later on."

Don't be in a hurry.

"Well, it doesn't matter. Doesn't seem like I can. I'd be losing all I ever worked for if I tried to do myself in. My words wouldn't mean nothing if I don't practice what I preached. Not that I'm that important, but I'm just as important as anybody else."

■ ■ ■

Eddy Shaver left his father for a time in the late 1980s to tour with Dwight Yoakam, and played on records by Guy Clark, Willie, Waylon, and friends. But mostly he worked with his father. By the time Praxis, a Nashville indie label, had linked up with Zoo, a short-lived BMG imprint, the Shaver sound had moved far from country radio. It made them perfect labelmates for Jason & the Scorchers.

Tramp on Your Street, produced by R. S. Field and released in 1993, was and is a masterpiece. It also sold well, something like 150,000 copies. The 1995 sequel, *Unshaven: Shaver Live at Smith's Olde Bar,* produced by Brendan O'Brien (Pearl Jam, Stone Temple Pilots), was a pretty fair representation of a blazing live band. Predictably, Praxis ceased to function.

By 1996, Shaver had joined old friends Waylon, Willie, and Kris Kristofferson at Houston-based Justice Records, for whom he recorded a wonderful suite of songs called *Highway of Life.* Unable to secure adequate distribution, owner and producer Randall Jamail released Shaver.

Shaver responds to the suggestion that he has not had much luck with record labels with characteristic humor: "Well, they haven't had much luck with me, either."

The Earth Rolls On will be the band's third release for New West. It follows 1998's graceful acoustic tribute to Shaver's mother, *Victory,* and 1999's *Electric Shaver,* produced by Ray Kennedy, who often co-produces with Steve Earle under the nom-de-knob Twangtrust.

Throughout those albums, Shaver has often re-recorded his own songs. "Leanin' Toward the Blues," for example, one of the tracks he cut for MGM, reappeared on *Electric Shaver.* "Black Rose" shows up in three different forms.

"A lot of my records got stopped. You know, when they get stopped, and there's songs on there that I think everybody oughta hear, I'll do 'em over again," he says. "Now that they're out [reissued], it seems like I did a lot of things over, but actually what happened was the records got stopped, and I thought, that song needs to be heard, and I'll do it over again. And then a lot of times I'll do 'em better."

■ ■ ■

Two issues surrounding Eddy Shaver apparently came to a head during the making of *The Earth Rolls On.* First, Eddy had a drug problem. Second, a number of critics and fans had never much cared for the intersection of Eddy's guitar virtuosity with his father's lyrics.

Sometimes I've agreed with that second part, but listening again to *Highway of Life, Victory,* and *Electric Shaver,* it is hard to find fault with Eddy's increasingly sympathetic and supportive work. The bombast for which he was justly famous as a live player was tempered. It sometimes takes players with serious chops a long time to learn to settle back into the textures of the song, and Eddy's work on *The Earth Rolls On* suggests how subtle a player he had become.

He was also infinitely important to his father, not simply as a son and guitar star. "Eddy did a lot of stuff. He didn't get a lot of credit for anything, but he sure did do a lot," Billy Joe says. "He arranged all my songs and pretty much put 'em all together. Didn't get much credit. Sure gonna be missed. We kinda grew up together, me and him. He was like Jimi Hendrix, Johnny Winter, Dickey Betts, and all that bunch. He brought that with him to the table with my music, and it came out a glorious thing.

"I used to have so much trouble when we first started. People said, 'That ain't country,' you know? We was always in the middle of neither one, that kind of no-man's-land, and then we decided we didn't care, because we liked it that way, and so we kept it. But this last record got away from it a little bit, and we didn't have quite as much control on it as we did the other ones. But it's good. It's a good record."

Somewhere along the line, Eddy's drug problem flared up, and New West tried to help. "I had many one-on-one conversations with Eddy himself," New West president Cameron Strang wrote in a letter to *No Depression.* "I encouraged other musicians that knew Eddy, who'd gone through drug problems of their own, to talk to him. At one point, New

West (with the help of Peyton Wimmer of the SIMS Foundation and the Musicians Assistance Program in Los Angeles) got Eddy into a treatment program in California."

Billy Joe says the label offered to pay his rent for a year, anywhere he might choose to live, so long as it wasn't near Eddy in Waco. "They were trying to get me away from Eddy so he could hit the bottom and maybe make it," he said. "I think everybody really tried to help, and it's too sad that it didn't work. But me being blood, I couldn't turn my back to him, so that's the way it was."

The way it was, a lot of people guessed that Billy Joe's interracial love song "Black Rose" was about heroin. "I didn't meant for it to be about that," he says. "I've done just about everything there is to do, but it never did do nothing for me, so I didn't mess with it. But I tried everything. I'm ashamed of it, but I did. I can't see that it helped anybody. That's an illusion that a lot of people—they may not have quite as much talent as other people—they think they can do that shit, catch up. That's just completely wrong. The greatest songs I ever wrote and the best stuff I ever did was on a natural."

Those tensions swirl throughout the resulting album. The opening "Love Is So Sweet" will play quite nicely as a love song written by a wise old songwriter, but much of it is written to his son, and its message is directed at another man Shaver would prefer not be identified.

By the eighth track, a father-and-son collaboration titled "Blood Is Thicker than Water," everything is on the table. "You come dancing in here with the devil's daughter," Shaver snarls in the opening, and he doesn't much care for the woman who became his son's wife a month after the album was finished: "Now she's stealing rings off the hands of your dying mother / If that witch don't leave, I believe I'm going to have to help her." His son comes in on the chorus line: "Blood is thicker than water."

Eddy responds in the third verse, after a brief solo: "Can't you see I'm down to the ground, I can't get no lower / I've seen you puking out your guts and running with sluts when you was married to my mother / Now the powers that be are leading you and me like two lambs to the slaughter / I need a friend, I'm your son, and you're always going to be my father." Their voices join again in the chorus, and the song closes with a stanza about heaven and redemption.

"I feel like blood's going to have to help blood," Billy Joe says, "because that's the way that stuff is. There's nobody like your family. Your blood kin, there's nobody like that. There's friends, sometimes there's some real good friends, but when you're blood kin to somebody, you're blood kin to them. That's all there is to it."

The thing to remember is that "Blood Is Thicker than Water" was not a spontaneous moment in the studio. No, Billy Joe, Eddy, and Ray

Kennedy worked it over some to make it come out right. The other thing is, the refrain really asks to be sung along with.

The whole album is not that hard, couldn't be. "Leaving Amarillo" is an almost giddy musician's revenge on crooked club owners, and "New York City Girl" is a joyous love song. But it is a powerful record, just the same.

The title track concludes things, and runs just over six minutes. Most of the last half is devoted to one of Eddy's most gentle, most revealing solos, and, yes, it sounds like goodbye.

■ ■ ■

"If I were going to choose one person that I was going to be stuck with, say, on a ship out on the ocean or some remote island or whatever," Ray Kennedy says over the phone, while mixing a new Nanci Griffith album, "Billy Joe would be my first choice. Definitely. If it wasn't a woman.

"I find him deeply interesting as a person. He's like an onion: He's got so many deep layers inside of him that he doesn't reveal very easily. But once you get to know him, he's full of brilliant thoughts and he cuts right to the chase. He's very poetic, but he's very precise in his view of the world. What lies behind that is a lot of wisdom. I think if Jesus came back into this world, I think he'd come back in a form like Billy Joe Shaver, something like that.

"I lost my dad a couple years ago. He was the one person who made a phone call that made all the difference in the world."

Kennedy knew the Shavers pretty well from *Electric Shaver* and before. "Basically, as a record producer, you have to deal with the artist's vision, and then you have the record label's vision," Kennedy says. "And then you have the selection of songs that you have to choose from. Well, at *Electric Shaver* time, Billy and Eddy were still into trying to keep that *Tramp on Your Street* kinda thing going, the thing that really was quite successful for them.

"So we leaned more heavily into the rock and blues thing, and Eddy played a lot more solos. I look at it as a three-piece rock band with a hillbilly singer. And the one cool thing about the first record I discovered: Billy had this really cool baritone voice that he didn't use very much. I found out the reason he didn't use it is because he couldn't ever hear himself very well when he sang in a lower register, so he started pitching everything up, especially in the studio. He's such a polite guy, he wouldn't ask the engineer to turn him up in the mix."

Kennedy assembled two all-star bands in Nashville last September for *The Earth Rolls On,* one acoustic and one electric, seeking to create fresh contexts and new sounds to go with Shaver's words. Greg Morrow (a Shaver alum from *Salt of the Earth*) and Ken Coomer (Wilco) played drums, Garry Tallent (E Street Band) handled bass, and Eddy Shaver was joined on guitar by Doug Lancio, Kenny Vaughan, and Kennedy.

While Shaver is proud of the record, he is not happy with how it got made. "It got outta my hands," he says. "We were closely involved with it, and it got took away. Maybe that's what people want to hear, I don't know, but I think it coulda been better. Actually, my band was supposed to do it. We recorded the record first, and they promised that it was coming out. And then it got changed around. I had to go do pre-production work with Ray during the time that we were supposed to record, and then it got changed around to where we had to have different players; we needed Nashville players, which, to me, just sucks. Not that I have anything against them; it's just that it got away from the reality of the stuff that I was doing."

A moment later, he lightens up. "It probably is the best one I've made," he says. "Probably because it got out of my hands. More than likely it's the best thing that way, but it still hurts, you know?"

As for "Blood Is Thicker than Water," Kennedy says, "It was 90 percent finished, and it just got altered a bit in the studio. We had to come up with an arrangement where Eddy had his part to sing that really meant something, you know, and then we had to sort out who should sing what. In the process of that, a few lines got changed, and then there was a few syncopation problems with some of the lines [that] were longer than others.

"In other words, the form of it was a little unusual, and we started to straighten it out, and I said, 'Wait a minute, Billy, there's something really cool about having the structure of this be a little bit weird, where there's an extra bar here and there. I think it's kinda cool, and you don't really notice it.' And he goes, 'Oh! Great.' He's such a trusting person, once you get to know him, and if you've worked with him . . . He does have pretty strong opinions about things, but musically when you get in a situation with him, once he trusts you, that's it."

Kennedy also had nothing but praise for Eddy. "When we were doing this record, he was in great form. He was totally straight and really on top of it. He's got those old guitars that Duane Allman gave him, an old Strat, and Dickey Betts gave him an old 335, very valuable guitars. Those have been his main guitars. Well, I got him into playing my Gretsches, and he just was having a blast with that, playing Duane Eddy kinda stuff."

■ ■ ■

Eddy Shaver was pronounced dead at 2:58 a.m. on December 31, 2000. That night, Billy Joe was booked to play the Hilltop Bar and Grill, a club owned by Poodie Locke, Willie Nelson's longtime manager, in Spicewood, just outside of Austin. Billy Joe showed up for the gig, and Willie Nelson filled in on guitar.

Two weeks later, Shaver has no clear idea what he'll do next. Nor should he. He seems committed to the notion that this will be his final record for New West, but he is as proud of the album as he is frustrated by how it was made.

"I'm going to work my ass off on this record," he says. "Mainly because it's the last one me and Eddy did together, that he had something to do with. It's something that I gave my word I'd do, and I'll keep my word. And I'll enjoy it, too. I'll enjoy doing it."

Maybe he'll finally publish a book of poetry. "A friend of mine's been after me to publish some of my poems. I've got a lot of poems. I've got trunks full of 'em. I might do it. Might do it. Might do it. I thought I'd leave them things, you know, for my folks—shoot, ain't no more folks left now. I thought I'd leave it for them, so they could make a little money off it. But everybody's gone."

Meanwhile, he is left to ponder the hard message his God now seeks to convey. His voice turns impossibly sad. "He's got something else for me, I guess. Or I'm fixing to go see them, one or the other. We always loaded me up with insurance because we just knew I was gonna die. The whole family—my mother, her mother, Brenda, my son, all of them—knew I was going to die first. I'll be danged if I ain't here. I'm the only one left. I kinda wish I hadda, but, then again, I don't know if they'da been able to take that, if it's as hard as it is on me. It's hard. 'Course we mourn for ourselves, that's true.

"But, hey, I ain't through. I'm not through yet. I ain't through mourning. Don't know if I ever will be. I just wish to God that I could go back and use what I know now and do it all over again and make up for my shortcomings and my stupidities and things like that. I wish it did work that way, but I know it doesn't."

■ ■ ■

Evening falls across Austin, it is still raining, and the radio is calling for snow the next day. Billy Joe's van is pulled in front of the Continental Club, across the street from the Austin Motel, where I will sleep. Dale Watson has an early show there, and one of Billy Joe's friends is playing with him. Not wishing to intrude, I drive on.

Later, I walk across the street to see Jon Dee Graham's set and to stare at some ice cubes. A big hand falls on my shoulder, and Billy Joe asks if I'm alone, takes the seat next to me, and buys the next round. A few people, more than a few, including Jon Dee, come by to hug Billy Joe, say a few words.

Somehow they were playing "Blood Is Thicker than Water" when he walked into the lobby of the Austin Motel to get a room, so he went up the street instead. The room reminds him of Paris, he says.

Mostly there is nothing to do but talk about things that hurt, and I end up asking something about Kurt Cobain and Nirvana. Billy Joe says, yeah, he knew about Nirvana. In fact, he says, he'll send me a four-track recording of "The Earth Rolls On" that he and Eddy put together, a version that ends with a shotgun blast.

Fortunately Jon Dee comes onstage about then, and dedicates his first song to Billy Joe. A few minutes later, Billy Joe gets up, wishes me well, and leaves a ten-dollar bill on the table.

Outlaw Blues

Ray Wylie Hubbard Felt the Heat of Texas's Country-Rock Heyday, but Rose from Its Ashes to Find a Cooler Groove

ND #45, MAY–JUNE 2003

John T. Davis

They say there's two kinds of people in the world:
The day people and the night people
And it's the night people's job to get the day people's money.

"NIGHTTIME," RAY WYLIE HUBBARD

Hey, hippie, why don't you get a job?"

Ray Wylie Hubbard paused in the crosswalk and peered out from under a tousled mare's nest of hair, searching for the sound of the vaguely familiar voice. "I'm tryin'," he said as he spotted his inquisitor, a journalist who had coincidentally pulled up to the light as Hubbard was crossing Fifth Street in downtown Austin.

Hubbard did, in fact, have a job. He was preparing to go onstage at Antone's as part of the Americana Music Association's Thursday night South by Southwest showcase. But first he had to get a clean shirt. Which meant he had to go to the garage across from Antone's and change into his gig clothes beside his car. Well into his fourth decade as a performer, and Hubbard was using a parking garage as a dressing room.

If I had some black cat's bones
I'd take the things down to Antone's

"KNIVES OF SPAIN"

A short time later, he was onstage with guitarist Gurf Morlix and the rest of his ensemble. Hubbard was premiering material from his new album, *Growl* (released in April on Rounder Records), and Morlix was particularly pivotal to the proceedings—he produced the record and was integral in shaping its dark and turbulent sound. Morlix's name is a much-coveted credit in some circles, given his swampy, deep-dish guitar style and his previous production of much-lauded albums by Lucinda Williams and Robert Earl Keen.

For their second collaboration—the first was 2001's *Eternal and Low-down*—Morlix and Hubbard not only descended into the blues, but also seem to have delved beneath them into some sort of subterranean realm—the indigos, perhaps. The songs on *Growl* are as gritty and lowdown and elemental as its title suggests. The silvery razor of Hubbard's bottleneck resonator slide guitar (a glittering counterpoint to his rumbling voice) flashes across a landscape that seems to have been crafted by Mississippi Fred McDowell and Flannery O'Connor working in tandem.

"We ain't been nowhere at all since the Fairlane threw a rod," Hubbard sings in "Purgatory Road." "Whatever it is, is being damned to hell / By my Daddy and God." The song ends with an extraordinary image of a blind boy playing guitar, oblivious of the desolation around him.

The same haunted figures wander in and out of different songs on the album: A preacher and a back-porch skeptic reenact the wrestling match between Saint Michael and the Devil; a father's idea of bonding with his son is to take him to an all-night dice game; the rise and fall of a young band on the road concludes that all stars ultimately wind up fallen; a sinner, very far from heaven, dreams of an afterlife where horses run free and unfettered.

Then there is "Screw You, We're from Texas," which bids to become an "Up Against the Wall, Redneck Mother" for the twenty-first century. A raucous singalong extolling the virtues of Lone Star musical chauvinism, the song nevertheless runs the risk of being misinterpreted in the currently volatile political climate (one wag said the title sounded like George Bush addressing the United Nations).

Hubbard just shrugs. "The problem with irony is, not everyone gets it," he says. "I wrote the song over a year ago, so it's not like it's a reaction to anything going on now. The way I was trying to write it was as if the Ramones were from Texas. . . . If they want to burn my records in the other forty-nine states, well, first they're gonna have to buy 'em."

Hubbard knows all too well the perils of writing anthems. As a young long-haired singer in Red River, New Mexico in the early 1970s, he dashed off the lyrics to "Up Against the Wall, Redneck Mother" after a bouffant-haired woman pinned him in a corner and asked just when, exactly, he was going to straighten up and fly right.

Hubbard's friend Bob Livingston, a charter member of Jerry Jeff Walker's Lost Gonzo Band, taught the song to Jerry Jeff. The first time Walker sang it at a show, Livingston recalled, "You could tell people loved it. They climbed up on tables and punched each other in the face. Jerry Jeff wasn't a fool . . ."

Indeed not. He included the song on his landmark 1973 album *Viva*

Terlingua; thirty years later, Hubbard is still obliged to trot it out at nearly every gig.

Especially in college towns. "I'll get onstage and people will scream right off, 'Play "Redneck Mother"!'" he says, shaking his head with bemused resignation. "So I'll play it and say, well, now what would you like to hear? And they'll shout, 'Play "Redneck Mother" AGAIN!!' What are you gonna do?"

> Drinkin' with my lowlife companions
> Dancing with a woman who's not my wife
> Laughin' at a joke that I've heard before
> Welcome to a night in my life
>
> "LOWLIFE COMPANIONS"

The night before his Antone's showcase, Hubbard was onstage at the Austin Music Hall, performing at the Austin Music Awards in a segment billed as "The Improbable Return of Redneck Rock." The loosely knit session found Hubbard reunited with 1970s-era Austin progressive-country founding fathers such as Rusty Weir, Steven Fromholz, Asleep at the Wheel's Ray Benson, Billy Joe Shaver, and Bob Livingston.

Graying hair and reading glasses were the norm among the group now, and priorities had, let us say, changed. Hubbard stepped up to the microphone with alacrity to sing "Redneck Mother," explaining off-mike to Ray Benson, who was ramrodding the session, "I've got a babysitter at home that I'm paying six dollars an hour. I'm gonna go ahead and sing now."

"It was nice to see those guys," he said after the show. "I don't want to be a nostalgia act, but I did 'Redneck Mother' because they asked me to. I would have preferred to go on and do a more dirty rock 'n' roll thing like I'm doing now, but it was a lot of fun. B. W. Stevenson popped into my head, you know? I sensed that loss of B. W., and it was kind of . . . god, we're all mortal, we're gonna die!" Hubbard laughed, a trademark wheezing cackle.

Hubbard and Stevenson, the honey-voiced presence behind the 1973 Top 10 hit "My Maria" and other country-rock classics, were both Dallas boys. Hubbard was born in Hugo, Oklahoma, in 1946, but grew up in the Dallas suburb of Oak Cliff, a funky, blue-collar district that also served as an incubator for Jimmie and Stevie Ray Vaughan. Dallas lay north across the Trinity River, glittering in the distance like Oz.

First at Oak Cliff's Adamson High School and later as an English major at North Texas State University [now the University of North Texas] in nearby Denton, he ran across kindred spirits such as Stevenson, Fromholz, Michael Martin Murphey, and others who would one day help spark a renaissance in Texas songwriting. He hung around Dallas joints such as the Rubaiyat and Mother Blues, soaking up lore and licks from the likes of Jerry Jeff Walker and Townes Van Zandt.

He gypsied up to Red River, New Mexico, for an extended residency, and came back to Dallas in time to find hippies commencing an improbable love affair with honky-tonk music, Tony Lama boots, and a Texas culture previously all too easy to scorn. The resulting yeasty mixture of country, rock, folk, and blues was an irresistible lure for a lot of incipient musicians, Hubbard not the least of them.

"I played Willie Nelson's Picnics," he said, trying to explain the allure of those days: "There was pot, mud, naked women, and beer. Why would you want to do anything else?"

> There are these bridges from the past to the present
> There are these bridges from now until dawn
> There are these rivers that flow on forever
> We are like rivers on our way home
>
> "AFTER THE HARVEST"

Today, Hubbard finds himself a pivotal transitional figure between generations of Lone Star musicians. At the Austin Music Awards, he was ranked with the other graybeards of Texas country-rock. On the other hand, Compadre Records, an indie label out of Houston, just released a Texas music sampler that places a Hubbard track alongside contributions by downy-cheeked upstarts such as Pat Green, Cory Morrow, Kevin Fowler, and Jack Ingram.

A week after South by Southwest, Hubbard found himself onstage at an auditorium at Southwest Texas State [now Texas State University] in nearby San Marcos, swapping songs with a diverse lineup that included Tish Hinojosa, Marcia Ball, Flaco Jimenez, and Ruthie Foster, under the auspices of the SWT-administered Center for Texas Music History.

Because Hubbard came into his prime relatively late in life (more on that later), he is regarded in some respects as a "new" artist, although his chronology places him in the same generation as Willie and Waylon and the boys. He has a chameleon-like ability to segue between the two eras. The common denominator is the songwriter's pen.

"Billy Joe and Fromholz and myself are all still writing, and that's the important thing," he says. "Maybe we're not selling out stadiums like Willie, but we're still creating.

"It's important for me to bring something to the table. A lot of these young guys today, like Pat and Cory and Hayes Carll, they acknowledge the fact that the writers they like are guys like Guy Clark, and Townes Van Zandt, Billy Joe, me, and Willie, you know? Cory and Pat have nailed down the contemporary college market, but they are very aware of the fact that the writers they like are these guys—they're not singing Nashville staff-writer stuff."

Hubbard pauses and grins a grin that Huck Finn would have recognized: mischief leavened with just a dollop of malice.

"For some reason," he continues, "Pat and Cory and these guys kind of like me, which is definitely new to me. Back in the old days, Rusty [Weir] and Gary P. Nunn and those guys just put up with me—I don't think they liked me at all." The grin evolves into Hubbard's trademark rumbling, wheezing laugh, usually reserved for some manifestation of the absurdity of life its ownself.

"But I feel very fortunate, in a way. I mean, I got to see Lightnin' Hopkins and Mance Lipscomb and Freddy King play. I saw Ernest Tubb play. The first time I met Willie, he was climbing through a window. It was some band house in Dallas, and Willie was playing the 57 Doors club. I was in the back room with some dancer, and he came crawling through the window saying, 'I forgot my keys.' And I said, 'That's Willie Nelson!' Nobody can ever take those things away from me. It was very cool to have seen those guys play. And when finally I met them, they were all very giving and gracious. Well, Lightnin' was a little drunk, but then so was I.

"So now, the whole thing for me, getting older, is not what I can get, it's what I can contribute. Cory and Hayes came out to the house, and I showed them some fingerpicking patterns. I showed Hayes how to make a rock 'n' roll E chord, rather than a country E chord—you got to put a little bite on it.

"I'm not wealthy, but I feel like I'm prosperous."

He also has that ace up his sleeve, which helps. As he waited to go on after Pat Green in some enormous venue one night, a backstage observer wondered how Hubbard was ever going to follow the yee-hawing, beer-slinging frenzy Green had just induced. "Hey, what do I have to worry about?" he answered without missing a beat. "I'm the guy that wrote 'Redneck Mother'!"

> Now there's little demons on the
>   Hindu temples
> Above the door and all around
> What that says is we get past what
>   scares us
> And we can stand on sacred ground
>
> "STOLEN HORSES"

Robert Johnson went down to the crossroads at midnight and sold his soul to the Devil so he could play the guitar. Hubbard sold his soul to Buddha. Or perhaps Rainer Maria Rilke, the poet who wrote, "Our fears are like dragons guarding our most precious treasures." Johnson received his dark gift, though at what some say was a terrible cost. Hubbard's gifts, which continue to manifest themselves, came at the cost of his fears, his self-doubts, and his addictions.

For years—decades, really—it is possible that Hubbard thought doubt and fear were for suckers and losers. Who had time for introspection? There was always another drink, another gig, another pill, and another girl waiting.

"We used to have a rider in our contract that just called for beer and electricity," Hubbard recalled. "Just plug in and go. What we lacked in talent, we made up for in attitude, you know?"

"We" was the Cowboy Twinkies, Hubbard's first band of note; they embraced excess like it was kinfolk. Onstage with the Twinkies, Merle Haggard's "Silver Wings" would segue into "Communication Breakdown"; the guitar player would leave his guitar howling feedback onstage while he went to the bar for a pick-me-up; the bass player would play surf music, no matter what everyone else was playing; Hubbard, in leather pants, shoulder-length hair and a Lone Star Beer football jersey, would hang onto his Telecaster and let the madness wash over him.

He sang songs about fringe dwellers such as roadside preachers, ne'er-do-wells driving $60 Fords, South Dallas stickup artists, sloe-eyed femme fatales ("I used to date a woman that stole cars. I told her that was terrible. She said, I only steal Lincolns. Oh, I said, well . . . OK.") . . . lots of what cowboy singer Ian Tyson calls "whore and knife songs." Some tunes from that era, among them "Bordertown Girl," "Compromise," and "Portales," still hold up today.

Hubbard seemed fully formed in the mid to late 1970s, with a river-bottom baritone, a mordant and irreverent sense of humor, a touch for vividly lyrical storytelling, and the sort of booze-fueled romantic fatalism that made reaching thirty look no better than an even-money proposition. He was a lot of fun to watch and get to know, but hanging out with him wasn't for sissies.

Sound check in the afternoon started with gin and grapefruit and progressed to whiskey and cocaine by showtime. Then it was back to the motel, or someone's house, for more pills, booze, and music until dawn. A few hours sleep, and then it was time to move the circus on down the road. "We were young," Hubbard recalled. "I thought you could close down a bar in Austin and just take a couple of white crosses and drive straight through to Colorado." (The first verse of "No Lie," a song from *Growl,* is a literal play-by-play of those lost weekends.)

It went on that way for years: come to town, take their money, drink their whiskey, screw their women, and ride on.

Bystanders tried to keep up at their peril. One New Year's Day, a lifetime ago, stumbling home at dawn after seeing Hubbard and the band at some forgotten Hill Country dance hall, I lay curled up and shivering under a crepe myrtle bush, throwing up a stomach full of cheap bar whiskey and strange chemicals and thinking, Jesus, 364 more days of this?

It got to where it wasn't much more fun than that for Hubbard. He was scared to drink more and too scared to stop. A bout of pancreatitis in the 1980s put him in the hospital and on the wagon for a while, but it didn't stick. He got married, sired a son, got divorced.

> I'm going down to the police station
> Just go on and turn myself in
> For all the bad things I been doing
> Maybe I won't do 'em again
>
> "THREE DAYS STRAIGHT"

By the time he finally got sober for keeps, on his forty-first birthday in 1988, things had reached an intolerable impasse: "It was like drinking poison and hoping the other guy dies," he said.

He met his second wife, Judy, at an AA meeting, and that helped. She was a smart, funny, good-looking Texas blonde with a full quota of sass (Fort Worth writer Dan Jenkins has a term of endearment for women like Judy: "Just fuckin' lights-out."). When she was sixteen years old and working the door at the old Mother Blues club in Dallas, Judy was the one Lightnin' Hopkins would send to the bar to fetch him just another little sip of gin. Hubbard found this infinitely endearing.

One night, the soon-to-be-ex–Judy Stone told Hubbard something about herself that resonated inside him like a tuning fork: "Some get spiritual 'cause they see the light," she said, "and some, 'cause they feel the heat."

Hubbard's appetite for spiritual nourishment became both eclectic and voracious. Besides Rilke's poetry and Buddhist and Hindu philosophy, he plucked bits and pieces from half a dozen cultures and disciplines to fashion a rough-and-ready order out of the random cosmos. His songs began to reverberate with richly embroidered allegory and imagery from biblical prophets and Delta bluesmen alike. God and the Devil both showed up often in his lyrics, though neither seemed to have a corner on the enlightenment market.

Hubbard and Judy formed an independent record label in 1992 (roughly coincident with another collaboration, their son, Lucas) and released *Lost Train of Thought,* Hubbard's first album of original material in nearly a decade. It marked the tentative beginning of a torrent of music that shows no signs of diminishing. Judy also took over managing her husband's career, a role she retains today.

In 1994 Hubbard released *Loco Gringo's Lament* on Dejadisc, then moved to Philo/Rounder for a nearly annual succession of albums: *Dan-*

gerous Spirits, Crusades of the Restless Knights, Live at Cibolo Creek (self-released), *Eternal and Lowdown,* and, now, *Growl.*

At the same time the albums began to gestate, Hubbard took what he calls "my first guitar lesson"—at age forty-three. He found his way back into music by teaching himself to fingerpick, circling back around to become an apprentice of his craft once more.

By that time, he and Judy had moved to Wimberley, a fashionably bohemian little burg in the Hill Country outside of Austin. Their house is on a hill, with a breathtaking view of the Twin Sisters mountains to the west. But the place was a wreck when they took possession. There were no appliances in the kitchen, and the swimming pool was a swamp.

Judy issued a decree: Fix the pool first. "We can order out for pizza while we're floating in the pool," she reasoned. "We can't swim in the kitchen."

For his part, Hubbard discovered a tiny loft—almost a cloister—overlooking the beamed living room. It became what he called "my dark little kingdom." Late at night he would climb up into the loft and surrender to the humility of learning to play guitar all over again. He labored to create a conduit for the music he felt stirring inside of him—meditation, sit-ups, running scales over and over, whatever it took.

Slowly, night after night, he learned to slip past the dragons of his fears and, as Rilke promised, there were treasures waiting: "On the other side were these songs."

The creative process has evolved—he also taught himself mandolin and bottleneck slide guitar, and the songs on *Growl* were mostly written downstairs, at the kitchen table—but it hasn't abated.

The songs on *Growl* are another product of humility. Hubbard played rough versions of the tunes for Gurf Morlix just before the latter left for a three-month sojourn to Canada. The pair planned to go into the studio upon Morlix's return.

"What do I do while you're gone?" Hubbard asked him. The response: Play each song fifty times.

One can easily imagine the eruption from Certain Other Artists upon receiving such plebeian instructions.

"You're kidding!" was Hubbard's not unexpected response. Au contraire, bubba. "Gurf said he wasn't kidding . . . so I actually did that. I was keeping track of all the times I played the songs in a little book that I was gonna show him when he came back. I blew that off, but I kept playing. So when it came time to record, we just nailed 'em."

"Gurf is the bodhisattva of grit and grease and groove," proclaims Hubbard, in accounting for the subterranean funk that permeates *Growl.* "When we did this record, he just made it sound so cool. Gurf would say, 'Let's put some growl on it,' meaning, let's not worry about getting it clear or sweet or correct, [but] where it sounds like Slim Harpo.

"Me and him and Rick Richards, the drummer, were the band. We called ourselves the Delirium Tremolos. Rick would get in there and beat on stuff, and Gurf would say, 'OK, Rick, that sounds really good—now fuck it up.' And Rick would start loosening his heads and playing on old, cracked cymbals, just to get a really cool, gritty sound.

"If everybody else hates this record, I don't care, because Gurf Morlix likes it."

> There's a preacher out spreadin' the word
> There's a blonde in a Thunderbird
> One of them tells me to kneel and pray
> One of them gets to me in a real bad way
>
> "LAST TRAIN TO AMSTERDAM"

Judy Hubbard has a rival for her husband's affections. His name is Tony Nobles, and he makes guitars in Wimberley. He has already built three beautifully filigreed acoustic guitars for Hubbard, to join the electrics already in the house, and there is every sign of more to come.

The first step, as they say at Whiskey School, is to admit you have a problem. Hubbard is still in your basic denial; Judy considerably less so.

Just the other day, he came in with a small-bodied electric guitar, ostensibly for his son. With, as it happens, a neck that is just the right size for a bottleneck slide. "Look!" he told Lucas, "I bought you a guitar, and we can share it!"

"Tony built the first guitar for me," said Hubbard. "And when I came walking in to the house, Judy said, 'What the hell is that?' And I go, 'This is Judy Girl!' Yeah, I designed this guitar, and Tony built it, and it's called Judy Girl. And that was OK until I brought home Judy Girl II . . . and Judy Girl III.

"So I walked in the other day and said, 'This is Lucas Boy I.' Maybe I can get away with it."

He shook his head ruefully. "I swear to God, sometimes we make the Osbournes look like Pat Robertson . . ."

■ ■ ■

These days, Hubbard is a vegetarian who wears a Tibetan bracelet around one wrist. The nails on his right hand are long and vaguely sinister looking, the better to pluck guitar strings. But one would mistake him for a rarefied PC aesthete at one's peril.

For one thing, he remains a compulsive smart-ass. Talking to a famous novelist profiling him for *Esquire* many years ago, he responded to a question about his career path by saying: "When I was a kid in Oklahoma, I used to throw rocks at chickens . . . I liked it, but you know, I never had the arm to go to the top."

Today, he'll often introduce himself onstage with gently mocking self-deprecation: "Since you've seen me last, I have four new songs I sing and three new funny things I say."

Maybe that appreciation for irony and irreverence is why he can still appreciate trotting out "Redneck Mother," even after its references to hippies and rednecks have passed into antiquity.

Hubbard sometimes refers to the song as his "jacket," alluding to the official file that follows police characters around. The throwaway item he dashed off in a Red River bar a couple of epochs ago has proven as improbably durable as, well, Hubbard himself.

And it has lent him perspective.

"I've had Jerry Jeff cut 'Redneck Mother,'" he begins, "and then I found out a little while ago that Cracker just cut 'Redneck Mother'! It's just phenomenal. So among the people who have recorded my songs are Jerry Jeff Walker . . . and Cracker. But that's good enough for me. Because I don't write songs to see if someone will cut them.

"A long time ago, Waylon Jennings and I were talking, and he said, 'Why don't you write me some songs?' And I said, 'What kind of songs?' And he said, 'Waylon-Goddam-Jennings songs, what kind do you think?'

"But I never could write for other people, not like those Nashville briefcase writers who go to work every morning. I just wrote because I got inspired or because I couldn't help myself.

"But for me," he says, standing his ground and staking his claim, "that's good enough. It's very gratifying that thirty years ago Jerry Jeff recorded my song, and a month ago, Cracker did it." He laughs a wheezing laugh of pure, befuddled delight. "Tell me that's not cool!"

One Road More

Three Decades after Their Debut, the Flatlanders Are Finally More a Band than a Legend

ND #39, May–June 2002

Don McLeese

It is a star-studded event with a uniquely Austin twist, this second annual induction ceremony for the Texas Film Hall of Fame. Only Austin would expect the unlikely assemblage of Dennis Hopper, Cyd Charisse, Willie Nelson, Sissy Spacek, Lyle Lovett, and former (forever, to this crowd) governor Ann Richards to convene on the grounds of an abandoned airport in the middle of Austin's nowhere. Joining them on this Friday evening in early March are hundreds of folks who love to rub shoulders with luminaries, and who are willing to pay $5,000 for a banquet table of ten for the privilege.

Now that Robert S. Mueller Airport on the city's underdeveloped northeast side has given way to the larger Austin-Bergstrom International on the southeastern outskirts of town, the old airport's huge Hangar 4 has been transformed into Austin Studios. The football-field-sized production facility is home base for the likes of Richard Linklater and Robert Rodriguez (who opens the Hall of Fame proceedings with some sneak footage of his forthcoming *Spy Kids 2,* shot here). On these grounds, adjacent to the parking lot for military vehicles of the Texas National Guard, this evening's assemblage includes even the notoriously reclusive Terrence Malick, the brilliant director (*Badlands, Days of Heaven, The Thin Red Line*) whose induction climaxes the ceremony.

Then it is time for the hangar to transform itself into the world's largest honky-tonk, featuring a group that, like Malick, has previously been more heard about than heard, more written about than seen. It has been more than thirty years since Joe Ely, Butch Hancock, and Jimmie Dale Gilmore combined for their first recording, one that wouldn't be widely distributed in the United States until 1990, when it bore the recast title *More a Legend than a Band.* The album had previously resurfaced on vinyl (as *One Road More*) a decade earlier in England, where Ely's raucous roadhouse music—though categorized as country in the States—was finding favor among roots rockers and punk rockers alike.

Without Ely's ascendance, those Flatlanders tapes might still be languishing in a Nashville vault, all but unheard. It was Ely's recording career that introduced the world at large to the songs of his Lubbock buddies Hancock and Gilmore, paving the way for both of them to enjoy (or at least endure) recording careers of their own. In stories about each of them, the Flatlanders' myth has grown ever larger, as if the band were some sort of long-lost Rosetta stone of alternative country, a curiously time-warped amalgam of Texas traditionalism and hippie radicalism. Now that their lives have brought the interrelationship of Ely, Hancock, and Gilmore full circle, the Flatlanders are threatening finally to become more a band than a legend.

"Remember when we used to be here now? / Living in the moment / For days and days and nights and days on end?" Ely sings on "Now It's Now Again" from *Now Again,* an album that sounds less like a revival of former glories than a fresh start. Due out May 21 on New West Records, it is a follow-up album that has been thirty years in coming. Ely calls "Now It's Now Again" one of the disc's "déjà vu" songs, a lyric that conjures memories of that brief period in the early 1970s when the three found themselves back home in Lubbock after some far-flung travels.

By 1971, Ely had been bumming around the country, hopping trains and hitching rides, working in a traveling circus and hustling pool games. (If this music thing doesn't work out, he still keeps his cue stick chalked.) Hancock, who had dropped out of Lubbock's Texas Tech just a couple credits short of his degree in architecture, had been working as an architect's assistant and shooting photographs in San Francisco before deciding to return to Texas. With Hancock, it has always been impossible to tell which are the hobbies and which the livelihood—is he a photographer who dabbles in songwriting, or a river-rafting guide with a minor in metaphysics?

As for Gilmore, he had made the obligatory 1960s West Coast "summer of love" pilgrimage, and by the early 1970s, had already retired from music for the first time. Since returning to Texas, he had been in a band of Lubbock transplants in Austin called the Hub City Movers (Lubbock bills itself the "hub city" of the Texas plains), playing on the opening night's bill at the legendary Armadillo World Headquarters. But, in the tug-of-war between this world and the spiritual world that has continued to define his artistry, he had decided to concentrate on his studies of Eastern religion, away from the distractions of Austin, and had moved back home with his parents. In line with his detachment from the material world, he was working as a janitor.

It was Gilmore who provided the early link between Hancock and

Ely, two friends of his who didn't really know each other. One day Gilmore would go bicycle riding with Ely; on another he would be hanging with Hancock. Gilmore eventually told Ely that his friend Hancock was writing some amazing songs that he should hear.

Though country traditionalism was hardly in fashion at the time among younger Lubbockites, this was a period when the cultural vanguard was retreating from the excesses of psychedelia for the comforts of homespun tradition, when albums such as the Byrds' *Sweetheart of the Rodeo* and Dylan's *Nashville Skyline* were turning down the decibels while the war in Vietnam continued to roar. Though Ely was more the rocker of the three, he, Gilmore, and Hancock recognized that they shared an affinity for the rootsier strains of blues, folk, and country, along with a disdain for the conventions of straightlaced Lubbock.

"We just happened to bump into each other at a strange time in history and started playing together," says Ely, as we visit behind the makeshift stage at the Hall of Fame sound check. "We had a few common influences, and we knew some songs together, but then we each had a whole category of songs that we knew separately. We were reading a lot of the same books."

"And we were disgusted by a lot of the same things," says Hancock. "Those were the days when there was a lot of disgust over the way things were going in the country."

"Basically, the source of my greatest entertainment was hanging around with these guys," says Gilmore.

It is prophetic that the first major bonding incident Gilmore remembers came from a joke taken to ridiculous extremes. He had heard the local country station play a novelty flip side by Ray Price that claimed to be "the shortest song in the world." Just "dee-deedling-ding-ding-ding." When he told his friends, Ely started playing a really slow, draggy blues riff and singing, "This . . . is . . . the . . . longest . . . song . . . in . . . the . . . world . . ."

They stretched it out for hours on end, rolling on the floor, laughing hysterically. Other friends would come by, get the joke, tire of it, and leave. Gilmore, Ely, and Hancock just kept going: "We're . . . almost . . . positive . . . that . . . this . . . is . . . the . . . longest . . ."

"It was like this recognition passed among us that we are all equally insane," Gilmore remembers, claiming this was the start of the band that would be the Flatlanders. "It was one of the magical moments of my life."

Bonded in slapstick surrealism, they wound up sharing a house together on Lubbock's Fourteenth Street. It was more of a crash pad than a commune—folks coming in and out, someone awake at every hour— just as the musical interplay they shared was more like a song-swap than a band. Rent was $85 a month, and they often had to scramble to make it. Some people suspected this was a drug house, but the three of them hardly required such substance enhancement. They were way out there on their own.

"We were all outsiders who showed up inside a house one day," says Hancock with a laugh. Once Gilmore put down his janitorial mop, Hancock was the only one then working for a living—driving a tractor for his dad, an experience that he has since credited as a formative songwriting influence (you've got to fill those hours somehow, he says, and the tractor provides a steady rhythm).

In retrospect, the rise of the Flatlanders has raised the question of just how it was that culturally isolated Lubbock was able to spark such a creative surge of songwriting. Explanations range from DDT trucks (Hancock says they spent their boyhoods on bicycles following the insecticide trucks, inhaling the toxic clouds) to UFOs to the inspiration of the flatland horizon that seems to extend forever—where all roads lead from Lubbock. Maybe it was just the simple fact that when you live in a place where there is nothing to do, you have to amuse yourself. Though none of them still lives in Lubbock, Lubbock lives inside them.

"In an odd kind of way, you've got to go a long ways to get away from Lubbock," says Hancock, who ran a combination art gallery/tape duplication service/performance space through much of the 1990s in downtown Austin called Lubbock or Leave It (a scaled-down version continues without him in a north Austin location). "There's no place on earth that's really far away from Lubbock, Texas."

Fellow traveler Terry Allen would later title an album *Lubbock (on Everything)*. He was an inspiration to the three, a guy just a little older than Gilmore and Hancock (who are two years older than Ely), who had been writing some very original material since high school. When someone you knew was doing it, it kind of demystified the whole songwriting process, made it seem within the realm of possibility.

"He was the impetus for me to become a songwriter," says Gilmore. "It wasn't his style that affected me, just the pure fact that he was so brazenly creative."

Further impetus would come from a hitchhiker who caught a ride with Ely. He introduced himself as Townes Van Zandt and pulled a copy of his recently released *Our Mother the Mountain* album from his knapsack to give to Ely. Here, they discovered, was a fellow Texan about their own age who had his own album, one that sounded almost as good to them as Dylan. And then, of course, there was the example of Lubbock's patron saint of rock 'n' roll, local hero Buddy Holly, whose brief life offered proof that such magic wasn't an impossible dream—it could strike the boy next door.

Taking their music outside the house seemed like a logical next step for the three, though their transition into a band didn't involve much beyond introducing songs to a wider circle of listeners that they had enjoyed sharing among themselves. When they needed a name for the billing, they decided to call themselves the Super Natural Playboys—"Super Natural" after the health food store that was their local hangout, "Playboys" from Tommy (no relation) Hancock's Roadside Playboys, by way of homage to Bob Wills's Texas Playboys.

These self-styled Playboys soon discovered that their mix of country standards and original material played as well to the older crowd at the Elks Lodge as it did at their own generation's more natural habitat, the local Aunt Maudie's Fun Garden coffeehouse. Some radio folks recognized the cross-generational appeal of the music and put in a word with Nashville's Shelby Singleton, who owned Plantation Records (and would subsequently revive the legendary Sun label). Singleton and staff producer Royce Clayton had recently scored big with Jeannie C. Riley's Grammy-winning rendition of Tom T. Hall's "Harper Valley P.T.A.," and they thought maybe these twangy young Texans had a similarly unlikely hit in them.

It wasn't until a circuitous route took these high-spirited amateurs from the Elks Lodge to Nashville that questions were raised about the aspersions that might be cast in conservative country circles by the "Playboys" moniker. While they were trying to decide on a name that wouldn't give Hefner-ish offense to God-fearing two-steppers, staff producer Clayton said something about how strange it was to "have a bunch of flatlanders come to town and show Nashville how to play hillbilly music."

"Flatlanders! That's it!" said Steve Wesson, whose musical saw would provide a signature element in the arrangements (and resurfaces on *Now Again*). The sessions spawned the first recording of Gilmore's "Dallas," released on a single credited to Jimmie Dale and the Flatlanders. When the single didn't make any waves, the album was all but shelved, though there were rumors of a few eight-tracks distributed to some truck stops. ("My dad had one," insists Gilmore, though I've yet to see one.)

In an article previewing the Texas Film Hall of Fame bash, the *Austin Chronicle* claims that the Flatlanders were "laughed out of Nashville in the early Seventies," a line that gets a snort of derision from Ely. If only they had made enough of an impression on Nashville to be laughed out of town. "Nashville never even knew we were there," he says.

"We made a record that we still love, but it somehow got projected onto us that we'd been trying to make it big or something," says Gilmore.

Turning tail from Tennessee, the Flatlanders played a few dates back home in Texas—the very first Kerrville Folk Festival (with former president Lyndon Johnson in attendance, less than a year before his death), and a week at the beer garden of Austin's Armadillo World Headquarters—but soon the young men went their separate ways. Gilmore followed his spiritual pursuits briefly to New Orleans and then moved to Colorado, where he retreated for the better part of the 1970s, living among followers of the teenage guru Maharaji.

"We'd already been reading all this Zen and Krishnamurti, and we were never going to have that sort of deep attachment that drives so many career ambitions," says Gilmore, of the Flatlanders. "But there was definitely an element of disappointment because our hopes really did soar for a while. We were too young to realize what a long shot it had been."

Not that the Flatlanders' experience discouraged Ely. He proceeded to form a supercharged band, recruiting the likes of steel virtuoso Lloyd Maines, bluesy guitarist Jesse Taylor, and accordionist Ponty Bone to inject considerable octane into many of the songs he had played with the folkier Hancock and Gilmore. "Even in junior high, I'd always been leaning toward having a loud band," Ely once told me. "There was something I liked about having the neighbors slam the door and call the cops. . . . When my band got signed to MCA, I thought it would be a great chance to get all of our songs—Butch's and Jimmie's and mine—that got everybody on the dance floor and started the most fights, put 'em on tape and it'd be a country record."

While Ely was finding a wider audience for Hancock's and Gilmore's songs, Hancock did whatever Hancock does. It is hard to monitor his activities for a given week, let alone track them for a decade. Whenever the mood struck, he released cassettes of new material on his own Rainlight label, selling them wherever he felt like performing. He always had at least a couple brainstorms going, diversions that distracted from a full-time focus on music.

"I've had a real good career," he once explained to me. "It just hasn't been a mass-consumption career. If people are really interested, they'll seek it out and find it. I could say it's my duty to get those songs out to the world, but the real experience for me was in writing the song, or having the experience whether I wrote about it or not."

Though the Flatlanders lasted less than two years, and each of the three proceeded to make very different music on his own, the legend would endure for decades. Particularly around Austin, it was no surprise when a concert by any of them would encore with an impromptu Flatlanders reunion. A lot of bands pretend to be friends; these were friends who had once pretended to be a band.

"With some bands, they make a record, they break up, and that's it," explains Ely as we continue to visit backstage before the Hall of Fame performance.

"But we weren't trying to have a band when we got together," says Gilmore. "We were just friends."

"We never really thought of that record as being any more than a chronicle of a certain period of our lives," continues Ely. "Just like now these songs we've been writing kind of define this period of time. And then all the songs that we've recorded individually between then and now are part of the same chronicle."

In other words, once a Flatlander, always a Flatlander. Even if it has taken three decades and three dramatically different career trajectories for these three fast and free-spirited friends to regroup for a follow-up album. Even if they have long since forsaken the flatlands of Lubbock for the hillier environs of Austin, where Ely and Gilmore enjoy spreads in the countryside, while the ever-restless Hancock has moved to the desert ghost town of Terlingua, where the former architecture student has been building a house most often described as more of an "art project."

"We're now officially the Hill Country Flatlanders," says Ely with a laugh.

While this evening's gala Hall of Fame occasion finds the Flatlanders very much in their element, whatever that element may be, Hancock's guitar is severely underdressed for such a glamorous event. Whereas Austin's glitterati have shopped expensively for this see-and-be-seen night, Hancock's instrument sports basic black duct tape holding together its splinters from a sound check mishap—it slipped from the shoulder of the band's guitarist, Robbie Gjersoe. The ever-smiling Robbie apologized profusely to Hancock, who explained that the guitar previously had been a casualty of airline baggage handlers, and that it was now broken where it had formerly been glued. Though, Hancock being Hancock, he couldn't resist giving Robbie a little something to think about.

"I told Butch I'd pay for it," explains Gjersoe. "And he said, 'Oh, you'll pay for it all right. You'll pay for it when you least expect it.'"

To Ely, Hancock says with a laugh, "Another fine mess you've gotten us into," a line likely recycled from the days of Cisco and Pancho or the Lone Ranger and Tonto. "I have a feeling this isn't going to be much of a listening crowd," responds Ely, surveying the vast expanse of almost one hundred banquet tables. "It'll be more like a dance, a drunken brawl."

Ely's sound check finds him giving a Tex-Mex spin to the opening verses of Bob Dylan's "Desolation Row"—"They're selling postcards of the hangin' . . ." (Later he will mention that there has been some talk of another incarnation of Los Super Seven, including Dylan and Joe Strummer.) Hancock keeps mumbling what seems to be his mantra for the weekend: "The things we go through to go through the things we go through."

In the midst of such philosophizing, a backstage film crew shooting some documentary footage of the event starts asking Ely about the band. The guy with the microphone is vaguely familiar with each of their music individually, but isn't aware of their convoluted history together and apart.

"How long have you all been playing together?" he asks.

"Well . . ." Ely responds, and then takes a long pause.

The story doesn't reduce itself easily to a sound bite, and, in typical

Flatlanders fashion, fails to follow a linear progression. What is fascinating about the Flatlanders and their surprising *Now Again* album is the way the music presages a future, one that has come as a collaborative revelation to each of them. Where the Flatlanders previously had been a signpost in the rearview mirrors of three very different singer-songwriters, the band now has a creative impetus all its own, a body of material that each insists could never have come from any one of them individually.

"Just the way the songs came about, rhythmically, melodically, and lyrically," says Ely. "We were surprised by the whole damn deal, the way it came together and everything."

While each of them has put his imprint on the material of the others—as if the Flatlanders catalog, individually and collectively, was a shared body of work—writing together wasn't something that came naturally to them. Laughing together, yes. Hanging together, whenever. Serving as each other's biggest fans, always, but keeping the songwriting process of each of them something separate from their friendship.

"I think we just never took it seriously," says Ely, as if the three of them had too much fun when they got together, so often with family and other friends, to spoil it with work. "A lot of people write songs together for a specific reason."

"We'd always threaten to write songs together and we'd never do it," Hancock says with a laugh. "Jimmie and I wrote one song together, called 'See the Way,' and this was, like, fifteen and twenty years ago. He showed me a verse and part of a chorus, and then a year later I said, 'Hey, Jimmie, remember that song you showed me? I wrote another verse to it.' And then after another five years or so, 'cause he'd moved to Colorado, he came down to Austin and we wrote a third verse together."

Given that collaborative pace, it is amazing that it took only thirty years for a Flatlanders follow-up. Even the three were surprised at how organically the music developed once they committed themselves to working together. The springboard was 1998's soundtrack to *The Horse Whisperer* for MCA, where Ely was then under contract (his second go-round with the label). The three of them convened at Ely's studio to see if they could come up with anything.

Though only one Flatlanders song was earmarked for the soundtrack, they amazed themselves by coming up with three. All of them ended up on *Now Again:* the bluesy shuffle of "My Wildest Dreams" and the old-timey balladry of "Filbert's Rise," along with an album-closing reprise of "South Wind of Summer" (slower and statelier than the sound-track rendition, before breaking into a string-band gallop of a coda).

"This was the first time we'd actually planned to meet together for the purpose of writing a song," says Ely.

"Or almost for any purpose," jokes Hancock.

"Except for Mexican food," says Gilmore.

"I don't think we had any preconceived notions that we were going to come up with anything," Ely continues. "It was almost like an experiment to see if this works. And we were kind of surprised that it actually did."

"And not just that we did it, but that the songs were actually good," says Gilmore.

"And had nothing whatsoever to do with *The Horse Whisperer,*" Ely says with a laugh.

The collaborative element proved crucial, for otherwise the Flat-landers may well have seemed like less than the sum of their parts. It could have been Crosby, Stills & Nash for folks who don't care much for Crosby, Stills & Nash. For all that Ely, Hancock & Gilmore share as friends and fans of each other, their musical strengths wouldn't automatically appear to mesh. None of them is known as much of a harmony singer, though the radiance of the vocal blend on Hancock's "Julia" reinforces the spirit of revelation. While reports of the work in progress continued to circulate, you had to wonder: Why would a third of an album from each of these distinctive singer-songwriters be preferable to a whole album from any one of them?

Even the body of material they've shared bears individual stamps rather than a collective brand, with Hancock's "(If You Were a) Bluebird" somehow becoming a signature song for the very different musical signa-tures of Gilmore and Ely. Such stylistic differences extend to Ely's full-throttle transformations of Hancock's "Boxcars" and Gilmore's "Dallas," taking those songs where the writers wouldn't or couldn't. (For his part, Gilmore claims the transcendent "Because of the Wind" as "a Jimmie Dale Gilmore song that Joe Ely happened to write.")

Once the Flatlanders disbanded—or went on their Rip Van Wink-lesque hiatus—Ely built a reputation as one of the most dynamic rockers this side of Bruce Springsteen; Gilmore emerged as a songbird in contem-porary country; and Hancock convinced a smaller but equally devoted following that he is the most inspired songwriter this side of Bob Dylan. Whatever their musical relationship, no category seemed large enough to contain it. "It's like we've all lived inside each other's songs for thirty years," says Ely.

The seriously playful *Now Again* finds a common denominator in the qualities that first bonded the three: an absurdist sense of humor, an intu-itive spirit of serendipity, and the inspiration of musical roots that blur the distinctions among country, folk, blues, rock, even jug-band music. The creative interplay sounds like a natural progression beyond the reach of time or trends, just as, back in the early 1970s, the Flatlanders could sound twenty years behind the times but prove to be twenty years ahead of them.

"I'm not sure what I expected it to sound like, but this is so much bet-ter than I could have imagined," says Jay Woods, New West's senior vice president and general manager. He had been a fan of the three growing up in Lubbock, and had been trying to persuade the Flatlanders to record a twenty-fifth-anniversary reunion album when he was with Houston-based Justice Records in the mid-1990s. "The songs have evolved so much since we saw them outdoors at Stubb's a year ago, when New West made a serious offer to sign them. Back then, they sort of traded vocals, but now those three-part harmonies are magical."

"Working on harmonies was something we'd never done in our lives," says Ely. "We knew we wanted to come together as voices on this, where each voice is almost like an instrument. When you put Butch and Jimmie together, it's almost like a bassoon and a clarinet, the most uncanny combination of voices I've ever heard in my life."

And when you put the three songwriters together, the creative interplay takes them places they would never have explored on their own. Take "Pay the Alligator," arguably the goofiest song that any of them has ever put his name to. Filled with whimsy yet played for keeps, the song somehow reminds of material as diverse as Dylan's "Gotta Serve Somebody," Chuck Berry's "Brown-Eyed Handsome Man," the Lovin' Spoonful's "Did You Ever Have to Make Up Your Mind?" and any number of Coasters novelties.

"It might be sooner and it might be later / But one thing's for sure, you gotta pay the alligator," the song insists.

Huh?

It turns out they had been listening to playbacks of another song at Ely's studio when Gilmore emerged from the bathroom and said something about the radiator. "Did you just say, 'Pay the alligator?'" asked Hancock. "No," responded Gilmore, "but that sounds like a good idea for a song." "It sounds like something you'd hear your grandfather say," said Ely. "'If you don't watch out, you're gonna have to pay the alligator.'"

With the three sharing songwriting credits on twelve of the album's fourteen tracks (the album-opening "Goin' Away" by Bruce "U. Utah" Phillips and Hancock's "Julia" are the only exceptions), such a sense of anything-goes possibility pervades *Now Again*. Whether swapping verses, sharing harmonies, or coaxing each other toward a higher sense of nonsense, the trio exudes a spirit of camaraderie that suggests no one could have as much fun listening to the music as these guys had recording it.

"There's a lot more gut-wrenching laughter that went into the making of the album than actually shows up on the album," says Hancock.

"We kind of realized that we could write songs that were larger than any of us," says Ely. "Usually with three people, the songs get smaller because you have to compromise with everything. From the time we first started writing to when we finished mixing, it seems like the songs just got larger in perspective."

"What really amazed me is that it was exactly like one person writing," says Hancock. "Because I know myself when I'm trying to write, it's like at least three people inside my head, arguing back and forth, with one part of me testing it against the others."

"We have a shared sensibility and sense of humor that is absolutely indefinable, though Butch and I in particular have tried to define it," says Gilmore.

The best material ranks with the most inspired that any of these three have recorded on their own—from the call-and-response spiritual "Yesterday Was Judgment Day" to the loping Waylonesque homage of "I Thought the Wreck Was Over" to the dance hall shuffle of "My Wildest Dreams" to the luminous surrealism of "Down in the Light of the Melon Moon," the album's stunner. Sung by Hancock, with the others harmonizing on the hypnotic chorus, the elliptical narrative somehow channels the spirit of both Marty Robbins's gunfighter ballads and Ennio Morricone's spaghetti-western themes.

The song had its seeds in a tune Ely had begun writing back in the Lubbock days, a story that would carry a hint of mystery, the quality he admired in Bobbie Gentry's "Ode to Billie Joe." Back home, he had seen a tree carved as if somebody had started writing something and then stopped. The lyric languished in his notebook until he happened to mention it to Hancock decades later during the Flatlanders sessions. Hancock said he had also been working on a mysterious musical narrative, one where the only witness is the watchful eye of the "Melon Moon." Jimmie added the real life story of Lubbock friends who had claimed they saw a UFO at the airport, flipped out, and not been the same since.

"So we started a new story combining elements from the ground up," says Joe. "We didn't want to say too much, and the song left you to fill in the story yourself. I think the worst thing we could possibly do would be to make a music video of this."

Over the course of almost three years, the trio got together whenever they had the chance—a couple of days here, a week there, maybe just two of them working while Ely or Gilmore was touring, or Hancock was off in the desert. They recorded as they wrote, road-tested the preliminary results on three national tours, and then recorded the songs again (and again) to reflect what they had discovered about the musical dynamics in concert. Since they wouldn't shop for a label until the album was all but done, they didn't have to meet a schedule or please a record company. They just kept recording until they were satisfied.

"On my own albums, there've been very few times when I've had the luxury of going out on the road, playing the new songs for a few months, and then recording," says Ely.

"Usually, you don't really learn the song until after you've recorded it, and you start singing it a lot better," says Gilmore. "Everything is so backward because of the end product driving the music. It's such an artificial process, and it shows up in the quality."

"Look at Nashville today," continues Ely. "Nobody's going out and playing those songs before they record 'em and put 'em on the radio. And then you listen and go, 'What made anybody think that was worth singing?' Music goes through all those phases, where sometimes it's just a product, and then sometimes it becomes so vital to the whole society that you can't imagine it could be any other way."

Where the Flatlanders' 1971 sessions in Nashville cast Gilmore as front man, highlighted Hancock's songs, and relegated Ely to sideman, the balance of power has plainly shifted over the course of decades. Not that there are any power struggles among these three, but Ely is clearly the driving force behind the Flatlanders' reunion. It was his MCA deal that brought the Flatlanders back together for the cut on the film soundtrack, his studio that served as the music's clubhouse, his tireless tweaking of the tapes that turned good times into great music.

"Joe is such a workaholic and an amazing producer," says Gilmore. "I think he only sleeps four hours a night, and I'm just not like that. . . . He always had a better idea about how this music business worked than Butch or I did. The funny thing is, I think I started out as Joe's music mentor, and he ended up as mine."

"We're all kind of perfectionists in certain ways, and then each of us is sort of lax in different ways," says Ely. "We worked hard, but when the songs were done they didn't feel like a lot of work had been put into them. We worked at eliminating stuff; we threw away a lot. We filed 'em down and polished 'em. Each of them was like a little carving, and we left a lot of wood shavings on the floor."

Despite Ely's expectation that the Hall of Fame crowd would be more interested in drinking and dancing than listening (not that there is anything wrong with that), their set serves as a triumphant coming-out party for a crowd that has been paying attention to these guys, individually and collectively, for years. New material from the album blends easily with old favorites from the songbooks of Townes Van Zandt and the Carter Family, while vocal trade-offs turn the likes of "I Had My Hopes Up High" and "Dallas" into exuberant romps.

"We've got a brand new song that sounds like a real old one," says Gilmore, introducing "Wavin' My Heart Goodbye." It was that kind of night.

Though Ely and Gilmore remain committed to solo recording deals—and Hancock remains committed to being uncommitted—you can't help thinking that a follow-up to *Now Again* will come a lot sooner than thirty years. All three have cleared their calendars to take the Flatlanders on the road, making the band their top priority for 2002.

"We're not looking any further ahead, just like we didn't last time, but

I wish we could start on another album before this one even comes out," says Ely. "We have a lot more resources and a lot more patience than we did back in the Lubbock days."

"Even though we still have problems with set lists," says Hancock with a laugh.

Before the Flatlanders even take the stage at the Hall of Fame bash, they discover an unlikely fan. Terrence Malick, whose aversion to attention is legendary, who refuses to talk for public consumption even to promote his films, goes out of his way to tell these guys how much he appreciates their music.

"It was a real thrill to meet him," says Joe. "He said he was a big fan, and I had no idea. *Badlands* is one of my favorite movies, and *Days of Heaven* just might be my favorite. It's almost like 'Melon Moon,' just the things that are left unsaid and all that space to be filled up. We were surprised he even knew who we were, and when I said maybe we could get together and play songs all night, he said that would be wonderful.

"I'd love to get the Flatlanders and Terrence Malick together and have him hear 'Melon Moon,'" Joe continues. "I don't know if anybody else could make a movie out of it, but he could."

Burning Memories

Ray Price Forged the Bridge from Hank to Bing

ND #27, MAY–JUNE 2000

David Cantwell

> There's no difference between singing a country song in a west-
> ern suit and then going around behind the curtain and walking
> out the other side with a tux on and singing the same country
> song with a pop arrangement. It's the same thing.
>
> RAY PRICE

Before he took the stage of Central Missouri State University's Hen-
dricks Hall on November 15, 1997, Ray Price had proved he could
still sell out the house. The old building was packed to the last row
of the highest balcony, mainly with the forty-, fifty-, and sixty-
something fans forgotten by contemporary country radio.

Onstage, Price proved he is still a singer's singer. Wearing a tuxedo and
backed by his legendary band, the Cherokee Cowboys—featuring his
longtime pianist and bandleader Moses Calderon, as well as the great (and
now late) Jimmy Day on pedal steel guitar—Price moved through a
remarkable twenty-one-song set of "old country songs."

He focused primarily on his greatest hits: a medley of "Crazy Arms"
and "Heartaches by the Number," a bluesy "Night Life," beautifully gentle
readings of "Burning Memories" and "A Way to Survive," and glorious,
string-backed versions of two of Price's biggest smashes, "Make the World
Go Away" and "For the Good Times." Each of these was crooned with
commanding, thoughtful, flawless phrasing; he expressed nearly as much
with the pauses as with the lyrics themselves. Even on the version of his
controversial 1967 recording of "Danny Boy" that ended the evening,
Price was still able to belt it out, not once backing off the mike or taking
the easier, lower note in a song that demands perfection.

On numbers like these, the small string section Price had for the date—two of Price's own veteran players, augmented by a pair of CMSU students who read their parts from music stands—lent the performances a dramatic urgency. Critics today praise Price for his great honky-tonk sides, while his later countrypolitan work is dealt with in disappointed dependent clauses. But the majority of the country audience, if record sales and concert draws reveal anything, hasn't cottoned to such distinctions. Like Price, they just like what they like.

So it was with typical brashness that Price paused during "For the Good Times" to address his fans. "I've been fighting for these things for years," he said, raising his arm extravagantly like a magician once again pulling a rabbit from his hat. "Ladies and gentlemen . . . strings." On cue, four violins sent the melody soaring. The audience applauded with conviction as Price nodded and smiled in approval.

■ ■ ■

Just months after that Central Missouri State concert, Price was in a Los Angeles recording studio, cutting his new album. Now, after two years of searching for a label willing to support it, *Prisoner of Love* is about to be released on Buddha/Justice. The news angle is going to be that Price, seventy-four-year-old honky-tonk hero and country music legend, has made a flat-out pop record. As if he hasn't been doing that for thirty-five years.

Actually, the record, produced by Justice head Randall Jamail, brings together the pop and country sides of Price's art as well as anything the singer has ever done. On the country side, most obviously, is Price's country croon, close kin to Hank Williams's, Eddy Arnold's, and Tommy Duncan's. There are backing vocals by Mandy Barnett, guest shots by guitarists Jesse Dayton and Junior Brown, and, as always, fantastic country songs: a version of his classic hit "I've Got a New Heartache," a recording of his own composition "Soft Rain," a new Hank Cochran tune called "The Only Bridge You Haven't Burned," and a song that could serve as the theme song to Price's entire country-pop career, Harlan Howard's "Uptown Downtown (Misery's All the Same)."

On the pop side, most obviously, is Price's pop croon, a dear relative of Bing Crosby's, Frank Sinatra's, and Tony Bennett's. The album's swinging, jazzy arrangements, featuring strings and, on a couple of tracks, brass, are courtesy of David Campbell, whose work has appeared on recent albums by everyone from Linda Ronstadt, Elton John, and Aerosmith to Beck (Campbell's son), Counting Crows, and Green Day. And for the first time in his career, Price has recorded an album of classic pop compositions: standards such as "Prisoner of Love" and "Body and Soul," an absolutely devastating version of Lennon and McCartney's "In My Life," and a "Fly Me to the Moon" that very nearly matches the famous versions by Bennett and Sinatra.

Price has heard that one before. "People say, 'Are you trying to be like Sinatra?' No! I'm trying to be like me," he laughs. "Well, 'Why'd you do

"Fly Me to the Moon"?' 'Cause it's a good song! Man, I just try to sing it the way I feel it. I don't try to be like anybody else; if I try that, it don't work.

"Everybody, all my fans, love the old songs, and nobody's recording them anymore, so we thought we'd take a swing at giving them something they want to hear. What we're doing now is a little something different. But," he adds, dropping the clue that is the key to making sense of his seemingly divided career, "the truth is it's something I did years and years ago before I first started."

■ ■ ■

In *The Encyclopedia of Country Music,* Daniel Cooper writes: "When Ray Noble Price was inducted into the Country Music Hall of Fame in 1996, many noted that the honor was long overdue." One of them was Price. "Thank you," he said, accepting the award from Kris Kristofferson in front of a national television audience. "It's about time."

Can't argue with that. No one in the post-Hank era, except maybe Elvis Presley, has had a greater impact on country music than Price. He is, to borrow from Kristofferson's Hall of Fame introduction, "the living link between the music of Hank Williams and the country music of today." In fact, Price's early Columbia recordings were often little more than Hank imitations, a predictable development. Price used Hank's Drifting Cowboys for most of his early recording dates, and when the two men toured together, Price would sometimes stand in for Williams when Hank was too drunk to perform. It was partly upon the strength of Price's recording of "Weary Blues (from Waiting)," a song Williams wrote specifically for his protégé, that Price first appeared on the Grand Ole Opry in 1952. When Hank's wife, Audrey, left him for good, the two men even became housemates for a time.

Despite these enviable connections, Price's initial recording career was a bust. As the 1950s began, he released four unremarkable singles, none of which charted. Then his recordings of "Talk to Your Heart," which at least had the virtue of sounding merely influenced by Hank rather than wholly imitative of him, and "Don't Let the Stars Get in Your Eyes," which was a nearly note-for-note (yet sloppier) copy of Skeets McDonald's smash from the previous year, each cracked the Top 5 in 1952. These records were derivative, but in hindsight, their success may have saved Price's career long enough for him to have one: His next five singles, released in the months following Hank's death and sounding as Hank-like as ever, did no better than his first four.

As Price emphasizes in a story he has told repeatedly through the years, it was at this point that a fan's compliment—"You sound more like ol' Hank every day"—prompted Price to decide he needed to be more than a clone of someone else's legend. Of course, since he had for several years sung Hank's songs at Hank's gigs and had toured with Hank's band, all the while singing in Hank's style—even hunching over the mike in mimicry of his mentor—this was surely not the first time Price had heard such a comment. Perhaps it wasn't the comparison that troubled Price, but the way five failed singles told him the comparison was becoming a liability. "It hit me at the right time," he now says. "I finally heard it."

Whatever the reason, when Price next entered the studio at the tail end of 1953, he took his first serious step toward a sound of his own. Though still recording with a core group of Drifting Cowboys, Price now highlighted guitarist Grady Martin and the other session musicians, encouraging the band to decorate their honky-tonk with touches of western swing. Martin joined Jerry Rivers on twin fiddles to kick it off, then quickly switched instruments to join Don Helms and Sammy Pruett for the Texas Playboys–inspired guitar attack at the break. Also, for the first time on a Price session, there were drums in the mix.

Price also sang "Release Me" differently. Like legendary western-swing vocalist Tommy Duncan, he was more likely here to croon, to hold a note rather than to twist it, even hinting in a couple of spots at the vibrato that would soon become a calling card. His voice sounded fuller and looser all around, less pinched. "Release Me," a two-sided Top 10 hit with the more traditional-sounding Cajun romp "I'll Be There (If You Ever Want Me)," dangled a possible future in front of Price, though it took him awhile to take the bait. Over the next two years, Price released eight singles (three hits, five flops), and for the most part they were all variations, again, on the classic Williams theme.

Still, even as he hedged his bets in the studio, Price continued to inch toward a distinctive sound on the road. The crucial decision was when Price decided to let the Drifting Cowboys go. He replaced them with the remnants of Lefty Frizzell's band and dubbed them the Cherokee Cowboys. Over the course of various lineup changes, the mainstays of a new sound began to emerge: Van Howard provided guitar and high harmonies; Jimmy Day signed up on pedal steel; Pete Wade played lead guitar; and in the studio, the single-string-style fiddle of Tommy Jackson was earning more and more of the spotlight. When the group entered Bradley Studios on March 1, 1956, a full two years since "Release Me" had charted, nearly all the elements of the classic Price sound were finally in place.

"Crazy Arms," learned from a demo tape provided by songwriters Ralph Mooney and Charles Seals, was the record that elevated Price from footnote to legend. The contrast between the out-of-control lyric (his arms are crazy) and Price's tightly wound delivery (the vibrato is back, and it makes the record feel as if Price is battling his own quaking form) is what sells the song emotionally. It was the music, though, that got people to crank their car radios and rush the dance floor. Jackson's fiddle is the star of the single's first half, and Day's steel shines in the second, at least until the piano of Floyd Cramer joins in at the close. But what made

"Crazy Arms" a great leap forward was the crazy rhythm—in 4/4, not the 2/4 then expected of country songs—put down by session bassist Buddy Killen and company. "Back then it was hard to get the bass to pick up," Price told the *Journal of Country Music* in 1992, "so I thought it might be a good idea to have an acoustic and electric bass double on the same note."

It was a very good idea. The new rhythm, soon to be known as the Ray Price Beat, made the singer's career. "Crazy Arms" bumped Carl Perkins's "Blue Suede Shoes"—another of those rockabilly records that had been exploding ever since Elvis burst on the scene the year before—from the top of the country charts, and parked itself there for five months. In the decades since, Price and "Crazy Arms," and the hits that followed, have been credited with saving traditional country music from the rockabilly onslaught. "I've Got a New Heartache," "Wasted Words," "My Shoes Keep Walking Back to You" (with drummer Buddy Harman nailing the "hard" onto Price's hard shuffle), "City Lights," "Invitation to the Blues," "Heart over Mind," "Pride," "Night Life," and on and on—these hits were the very template for honky-tonk in the years between the rise of Elvis and Beatlemania.

Price shaped the direction of country music in other ways, too. He recorded the breakthrough hits for some of country's greatest songwriters—Roger Miller, Harlan Howard, Bill Anderson—and his support played a crucial role in the careers of Miller, Charlie Walker, Willie Nelson, Johnny Paycheck, Johnny Bush, Darrell McCall, and Buddy Emmons. (All of those but Walker gained invaluable experience as members of the Cherokee Cowboys.) Price's early-1960s albums, particularly *San Antonio Rose, Night Life,* and *The Other Woman,* further solidified his reputation.

In retrospect, it is easy to see how the Bakersfield sound, outlaw country, and the New Traditionalist movement, as well as significant segments of today's broad alternative-country community, all owe a heavy debt to the Ray Price sound. That was what Kristofferson meant when he said that Price is the bridge from yesterday to today. In truth, even much of contemporary radio's Hot New Country can be traced back to Price's simple yet profound tinkering with country rhythm. Not that Price wants to hear this. "I may have started something," he laughs, "but I'm not taking the blame." He made the point even more succinctly during a 1995 radio interview with a Wichita DJ. Informed that all the young stars cite him as an influence, Price grumbled, "God, I hope not."

Regardless of where country music has wound up, Price's place in country music history is as rock-solid as the decade-and-a-half's worth of classic honky-tonk sides it is based upon. But then, as the story goes, he threw it all away. In 1967, Price released a pop version of the folk song "Danny Boy," backed not by twin fiddles but by an entire string section. For more than thirty years now, Price has persisted, more or less, in this supper-club pop vein. The approach produced many artistic and commercial successes for Price—his 1970 crossover hit with Kristofferson's "For the Good Times" is the most obvious example—but his later pop work is routinely dismissed in country music annals with harsh words such as "schmaltz" or even "betrayal." The hits kept coming, and even today Price sells out more than 100 dates a year—but some folks, it appears, have never forgiven him for those strings.

■ ■ ■

Price was born in 1926 in a tiny East Texas town called Perryville, about a hundred miles due east of Dallas. After his folks split up when he was three, he divided his time between his dad's farm and his mom's place in Dallas. Today he still resides with his wife of thirty years in the Perryville area, on a ranch with his horses and her poodles. "Perryville's got two churches and a grocery store, and most of the time they're broke," he jokes. "It's rolling hills, like in Kentucky, and lots of evergreens. It's beautiful."

Growing up, Price enjoyed honky-tonk and western swing, particularly by legends such as Ernest Tubb, Floyd Tillman, and Bob Wills, just as you would expect of an East Texas youth. The young Price never got a chance to see those men in person, though: "The one time I tried to see Wills, there was so many people I couldn't get in." His access to their music was provided mainly by the occasional record ("My dad had a few records of Jimmie Rodgers. That was about it.") and by radio. Besides broadcasting country music, the radio exposed Price to the wide world of Depression-era and WWII-era pop music. Price paid particular attention to the shows of Bing Crosby, the period's superstar. "Crosby was the big thing," he remembers. "I used to love to hear him sing."

Near the end of the war, Price served a stint with the marines in San Diego, then in Oklahoma. "At that time, Sinatra was big—the swoon tunes, you know. Everything I was exposed to in the marines was pop music." When he returned to Texas he began veterinary studies at North Texas Agricultural College [now the University of Texas at Arlington]. Just for fun, he began singing with friends at little joints such as Roy's House Cafe, mainly doing versions of his favorite entries on *Your Hit Parade*.

"I was doing a lot of pop singing then," he remembers. "I wasn't in the business; I was just doing it in college. We had a little group, and then we'd sing in different little places, some of the free venues and things like that, just to be doing it. I was enjoying it 'cause I never thought about being on records. Most of all it was just slow love ballads, 'Prisoner of Love' and things like that. I was a fan of a lot of the pop cats. Like the Ink Spots, of all things, and the Mills Brothers. And of course Nat King Cole was a great singer, and Louis Armstrong, and a lot of the other singers. Bing Crosby especially. That's the kind of music I like to sing."

He liked singing it so much that, with the encouragement of friends, he quit school to pursue a singing career in 1948. There wasn't a lot of call for pop singers in North Texas, though, so it is hardly surprising he wound up pursuing his new vocation on radio shows such as the *Hillbilly Circus* and the *Big D Jamboree.*

In 1949, a friend hoping to get his songs published asked Price if he would be willing to sing the demos, and the pair headed to the studio of Jim Beck, an engineer in Dallas. Beck liked the singer more than the songs, and soon he signed Price to record the two sides that, when sold to a Nashville independent in 1950, became his first single. The record, "Jealous Lies" with "Your Wedding Corsage" on the flip, did so poorly in the marketplace that it may as well never have been released—except that it solidified Price's ambitions. "After I got the contract and recorded, it lit the fire," he says.

"Jealous Lies" is a bad record. Price croons the unremarkable song in a style obviously inspired by pop-country singer George Morgan's smash hit of the previous year, "Candy Kisses," but his voice is high and thin and, at this early date, too far beyond his control for such a subtle approach. To employ vibrato, for instance, you must be able not only to hit a note but also to sustain it, and the twenty-four-year-old Price could not.

But viewing this first single, in conjunction with the young singer's attraction to midcentury pop music in general, as the literal and aesthetic starting point of the Ray Price story provides a new shape to that story. It is a different perspective from beginning a couple of years later with Price as a Hank Williams wannabe, as most accounts of his history have done. Seen through a pop lens, evolutions in the Price sound can be heard not as betrayals but as fulfillments; seeming innovations can also be understood as savvy compromises; once-clear distinctions begin to blur. The details of the story remain the same, but they build to different crescendos.

■ ■ ■

"Jealous Lies" was released on Bullet Records. The label's greatest success was "Near You," a swingy, piano-driven number by Francis Craig and His Orchestra that had been the nation's biggest pop hit in 1947. (Thirty years later, George Jones and Tammy Wynette would top the country charts with the song.) Price's debut single, delivered in an unimpressive, pop-derived croon, went nowhere, but that didn't stop him from sticking with the style. Price signed with Columbia Records in 1951, and of the first three singles he released that year, all six sides could fairly be said to continue this crooning pop style.

Then Price received "Weary Blues" from his new friend Hank Williams. Soon he was also borrowing Williams's band in the studio. Over the next two years, virtually everything Price released—some twenty sides—closely followed the Hank blueprint. "I don't care if Bing Crosby was singing in front of that band, he'd sound like Hank Williams," Price says today, and while this is certainly overstatement, his choice of example is telling.

At any rate, sounding like ol' Hank didn't generate much more chart success than his original country-pop approach. One of the few diversions from the Hank form was Price's second charting single, "Don't Let the Stars Get in Your Eyes," which featured a rousing saloon-style piano. A few months later, Perry Como topped the pop charts with a big, brassy version of the song.

In fact, country songs on the pop charts were a significant trend at the dawn of Price's career. Former Oklahoma country singer Patti Page had scored 1951's biggest pop hit with a cover of Pee Wee King's "Tennessee Waltz." Tony Bennett hit with a soaring-strings rendition of Hank's own "Cold, Cold Heart." And so on. "I noticed years ago the pop people would come in and get the great country songs and sell millions of them, as pop songs," Price remembers. "So there's no difference in my opinion. It's the way they're, you might say, portrayed."

"Release Me," hitting the country charts in the spring of 1954, began the process of returning Price to the pop crooning that was his first love. His voice had deepened since "Jealous Lies," and it would now do what he wanted. There was still a good deal of Hank in his delivery, but there were also moments in the phrasing and inflection where he sounded more like a twangy Bing Crosby—that is, more like Tommy Duncan—than Hank Williams. Musically, the arrangement also leans toward western swing, itself a country form with more than a little connection to big-band jazz.

As time passed, Price refined his new pop-influenced delivery. In 1955, he cut for the first time a song called "Let Me Talk to You," which he sang in a big, nearly bel canto style; his vibrato here and elsewhere hints at the way Tony Bennett sang Hank's "Cold, Cold Heart" or, in 1953, "There'll Be No Teardrops Tonight." By the time Price recorded his signature number, "Crazy Arms," in 1956, his Crosby-and-Bennett by way of Williams-and-Duncan vocal style was nearing perfection.

Rock 'n' roll had invaded country by then, too. So, in a canny maneuver, Price borrowed the 4/4 time already associated on country radio with the rockin' pop attack of Presley, Perkins, and Johnny Cash. "Crazy Arms" topped the country charts all summer, climbing to #27 on the Honor Roll of Hits pop chart and leading Jerry Lee Lewis to release the song as his first single. It was finally knocked out of the top country spot by a big, swooning love ballad, Elvis Presley's "I Want You, I Need You, I Love You."

Over the next decade, Price released hit after hit with his new brand of post-Elvis, pop-influenced honky-tonk. However, with rock 'n' roll pressing in on the left, and the Nashville Sound pushing back on the right, Price's modern, pop-influenced sound was received by many country fans not as pop at all, or even as very modern, but as downright traditional.

Still, Price's country recordings, fiddles and all, somehow managed to break into the lower reaches of the pop charts: "My Shoes Keep Walking Back to You" made it to #63 in 1957, and "City Lights" went nearly as high the following year.

Occasionally, pop performers would release versions of these singles—Debbie Reynolds had a minor hit with "City Lights" in 1960, for instance—that climbed not much higher on the pop charts than Price's had, despite all their violins. In 1959, Guy Mitchell scored a #1 pop hit with an insipid cover of "Heartaches by the Number," then just missed the Top 40 the following year with versions of "The Same Old Me" and "My Shoes Keep Walking Back to You."

Almost as soon as Price had achieved consistent success on the country charts, he began experimenting with poppier sounds. On various 1957 recordings, Price was a Nashville Sound star, a singing cowboy, a jazz singer. On a second try at "Let Me Talk to You," he employed a fiddle that sounded suspiciously like a violin, and was more indebted to the early dramatic style of Tony Bennett than ever. "Tony Bennett is a great, great singer," Price says. "I've loved him for years and years."

At first, these variations from the Ray Price Beat remained secrets of the studio. But when he released "I'll Be There (When You Get Lonely)" later in the year—the song was a fairly generic stab at post-Elvis pop balladry, but he nails the thing—it climbed to #12 on the country charts.

A few months later, Price released *Four Hits by Ray Price,* an EP of Nashville Sound covers: Ferlin Husky's "Gone," the Everly Brothers' "Bye Bye Love," Jim Reeves's "Four Walls," and Jimmy C. Newman's "A Falling Star," each a major country-to-pop crossover hit. "That's What It's Like to Be Lonesome," a Top 10 hit, featured the Anita Kerr Singers. The grand "City Lights" was, in the words of historian Daniel Cooper, "a fusion of the Nashville Sound with the Ray Price Beat." By this point, the pop side of Price wasn't a secret anymore.

■ ■ ■

"I think strings are beautiful," Price says. "They're the closest thing to the human voice for me. Singing in front of them is like being lifted in an elevator. And if the strings can turn me on, I'm able to turn them on, and it becomes a good night."

Strings had been used on a country-music session at least as early as 1955, when Eddy Arnold re-recorded "The Cattle Call" in New York. But by the time Price included strings on sessions half a decade later, they were still nearly unheard-of in country music, a few years of the Nashville Sound notwithstanding.

The result, 1960's *Faith,* was a reverent, often dramatic affair and Price's most explicitly pop recording to date. Throughout, Price's tenor soars in a way that harks back to the WWII-era pop music of his youth, while the hushed arrangements anticipate, somewhat, Elvis' gospel album, *His Hand in Mine,* released later in the year. (Not surprisingly, either, since Price's and Presley's recordings often shared a cadre of musicians: guitarist Hank Garland, bassist Bob Moore, drummer Buddy Harman, and pianist Floyd Cramer.)

"I wanted strings," Price remembers, "and Columbia wanted me to do a faith album. So . . . I asked Don Law, who is gone now and who was a great producer for me . . . 'Can I do these things different?' He says, 'What do you want to do?' I said, 'Well, to tell you the truth, I want to sing these religious songs like love songs. 'Cause to me, that's what they are. I'd like to get a lot of violins behind it and get some arrangements made.' So we got Anita Kerr to make the arrangements, and I used seventeen strings."

Country historian Rich Kienzle, in his liner notes to the Bear Family collection *Ray Price and the Cherokee Cowboys*, disputes Price's claim of a seventeen-piece string section. "Aural evidence and Columbia recording session ledgers show only four present," Kienzle writes. The issue is further confused because the discography for the same set lists neither four nor seventeen string players, but six. Whatever the number, strings are featured on *Faith*, and Price sings these old hymns like love songs. Those two tactics, the strings and the singing, seemed to sum up where Price had been headed all along.

Over the next few years, he released a number of hits in his classic shuffle style—"Heart over Mind" and "Pride" are the best-known—and also paid tribute to western-swing legend Bob Wills on the album *San Antonio Rose*. In hindsight, these years can seem as if Price was momentarily treading water, hesitant to get in over his head with the country-pop blend he had been building toward for a decade. But after the hard shuffle "Walk Me to the Door" and the slow ballad "Take Her off My Hands," each with orchestra-enhanced arrangements, became a two-sided hit in early 1963, Price's inner pop singer surfaced as never before.

The album he set it loose upon was *Night Life*, revered today as a honky-tonk classic. There can be no doubt that it is. But within the context of Price's career, it should also be remembered as one of his earliest and most cohesive arguments that country and pop are, in some important sense, "the same thing."

Price accorded "Lonely Street," a pop hit for Andy Williams in 1959, a prominent position on the album; he belted "Bright Lights and Blonde Haired Women" as if he had been studying Louis Prima; and on yet another version of "Let Me Talk to You"—this time with a string section to help persuade his lover to "fall in love again"—Price was as pop, and as seductive, as at any moment in his career. The title track, with Buddy Emmons's bluesy, horn-like pedal steel swapping sad tales with Pig Robbins's morose piano, feels like a honky-tonk version of Sinatra's saloon classic "Only the Lonely."

In the wake of *Night Life*, four of Price's next six chart entries included prominent string arrangements. The most significant and successful of these was his recording of the Hank Cochran classic "Make the World Go Away," which went to #2 in 1964. Price originally recorded the song as a shuffle, but he rearranged and re-recorded it, ultimately releasing a version with overdubbed strings and a backing chorus.

In striking contrast to the strings swirling extravagantly about him, Price sings his first line, "And get it off my shoulders," quietly, subdued, just as he had begun so many of those *Night Life* sides. Because he opens close to a whisper, he can build to a scream. By the time he unleashes the line again at the choruses—"just get it off, off of my shoulders!"—we can feel just how dangerously the world is pressing down upon this man and how much power he has granted to the woman he believes can relieve the weight.

"Make the World Go Away" is vulnerable, desperate, beautiful pop music. Price's version squeezed onto *Billboard*'s Hot 100; just two years later, a similar but considerably less impassioned version of the song by Eddy Arnold rose to #6 on the pop charts.

And then, after one final burst of *Night Life*–styled honky-tonk in 1965 and '66—or one final period of foot-dragging, depending upon your view—he cut "Danny Boy," the record that had been crying to come out of him for years.

■ ■ ■

"Danny Boy," based upon an old Irish folk tune given the title "London-derry Air" in the nineteenth century, is one of those songs that draws great big voices to it like a moth to a flame, often with similarly fatal results. Through the years, everyone from Bing Crosby to Conway Twitty (in a rockabilly version) to Elvis Presley to Jackie Wilson has taken a turn. Price had known the song for years, but it came to his attention at this point in his career because his pedal steel player, Buddy Emmons, had been including an instrumental version of the song during the Cherokee Cowboys' opening sets, and had encouraged Price to sing it.

"Every year at the disc jockey convention," Price recalls, "Columbia and all the record labels would have their shows each night for the disc jockeys to showcase their talent. And always I closed the Columbia show . . . with 'San Antonio Rose.' But I went out and closed the show, and stopped it, with 'Danny Boy.' And for three years I would close the show with 'Danny Boy,' and all of the disc jockeys said, 'Come on, man, record that song, record the song.' And I finally did. Clive Davis [then a Columbia executive] was the one who let me do 'Danny Boy.' And after I did it, they ostracized my butt right out of the business."

Well, not out of the business exactly. "Danny Boy" was a #9 country hit, far more successful on radio than, say, "Night Life" had been, and the subsequent album went to #3. But it definitely met resistance at country radio. The fact that the record was nearly five minutes long probably didn't help much, and, what is more, the music backing Price's vocal was nothing like what he had killed the house with at the DJ convention. The

Ray Price Beat was gone, replaced with an arrangement that, in the quietest spots, was nothing more than bass and piano. In the loud spots, an enormous wall of strings bursts out of the silence with all the emotional power of sunlight breaking through clouds to shift and shimmer across a dark meadow. It was beautiful, like so much of Price's music, but in a new way. And despite all the clues, it was not what people had expected. Characteristically, Price dug in his heels at the objections, pushing forward with the sound he knew had been in him all along.

"Some of the jockeys that had wanted me to record the damn song got on my case," Price remembers. "Like in Houston, over the air, they swore they'd never play another Ray Price record." For a time Price toured less, partly because he was so hurt that some fans had turned on him, partly because it is tough to tour with an orchestra. And when he did play out, some fans stayed away because, as it turns out, it is tough to two-step to an orchestra, too. But Price stuck stubbornly, admirably, to the pop sound he adored.

On his terms, it paid off. "Danny Boy" was hardly a failure on the country charts, and on the pop side it climbed all the way to #60, his biggest crossover success so far. Appropriately enough, it was even possible during this period, on some Top 40 stations, to hear Price sing "Danny Boy" back-to-back with Engelbert Humperdinck's hit version of "Release Me," the very song that had begun Price's journey back to pop nearly fifteen years before.

Price sings "Danny Boy" with both restraint and exuberance. His voice starts low and tentative, soars to a place he had been taking us for years, and then beyond that to a place he had only dreamed of. His voice sighs and cracks, and as he rises up to the final lines, he grants this hoary old tale of love beyond the grave a dignity and power that can't be denied.

"You will call and tell me that you love me / And I shall sleep in peace till you come," he cries. In that moment, you can hear a singer gripping the limits of his very own legend, then letting it go for something he loves more.

■　■　■

"Danny Boy" did not conclude the Ray Price story, but it signaled the beginning of the second volume. During the fallout from the song, Price left Nashville and moved back to Texas, where he remains today. In the same period, he hired Moses "Blondie" Calderon, the pianist, bandleader, and musical director who ever since has functioned for Price somewhat as Ralph Sharon functions for Tony Bennett. In 1969, he married the woman to whom he remains married today. And, some three decades later, he is still a pop singer.

To Price, though, he always was, and still is, simply a singer of good songs, no matter their origin. "It's hard for me to make the distinction between country and pop," he has said consistently to anyone who has asked, "because music is music." Certainly his post–"Danny Boy" career has supported this point of view. Despite having been accused in some quarters of betraying country music for pop, Price had country hits in the two years following "Danny Boy" at only a slightly less successful rate (three Top 10 records and four more in the Top 20) than in the years immediately preceding the switch. The three albums released after "Danny Boy" all went Top 10.

And this was before he recorded "For the Good Times," the country chart-topper and #11 crossover smash from 1970 that has defined him ever since. "I would say 'Danny Boy' and 'For the Good Times' are the best songs I've ever got to sing," he says. "For the Good Times" ushered in perhaps his career's most successful period; in its aftermath, Price ruled the country charts, scoring four #1 country hits and two #2s in just over three years.

The eight albums he released after "Danny Boy" but before he left Columbia in 1975 deserve an essay of their own. Stunning strings, arranged by countrypolitan fixture Cam Mullins, provide the primary background on these records, though acoustic guitar and pedal steel still get their licks in now and then. Price's voice is the center of attention, though, along with his choice of material, which remained impeccable and undeniably country. A list of the folks who provided the songs for these albums reads like a roll call for a country songwriters hall of fame— Bryant, Clement, Cochran, Gibson, Hall, Howard, Kristofferson, Nelson, Newbury, Payne, Putnam, Robbins, Rose, Russell, Weatherly, Webb, Williams.

"For the Good Times" is representative of the era, in both its stunning sound and its expression of complex adult emotion. Mullins's strings intensify the melancholy mood, assisting in the seduction and cushioning the inevitable blow. The clopping, pulsing drum and tic-tac are clearly country in feel, ticking away the final moments of the love story at the heart of the song. Like nearly everything Price recorded in these years, "For the Good Times" sounds like a man is speaking to you, commanding and ultimately earning your emotional commitment.

After Price left Columbia, he continued to chart in the 1970s and throughout the '80s, even as he bounced from label to label—from Myrrh to ABC/Dot to Monument to Dimension to Viva to Step One. He even had a brief return to the spotlight, and to straight-up honky-tonk, on a Columbia duet album with Willie Nelson in 1980. The singles were less frequent and successful, though the quality of these records, particularly his singing, was as impressive as ever.

All in all, Price's post–"Danny Boy" years add up to a thirty-five-year legacy of masterful country-pop crooning. And still, still, he is asked to justify his abandonment of honky-tonk. "Why must you always try to make me over," Price wonders aloud on the very first track to his first post–"Danny Boy" album. He could be singing to a lover, but the question could also be aimed at the country-music world itself. "You're trying to reshape me like your old love, in the image of someone you used to know . . . Take me as I am or let me go."

■ ■ ■

"The whole thing of this album [is] I'm looking back at my career," Price says of his new release, *Prisoner of Love.* He is referring, specifically, to the new album's moving version of "Eighteen Again," a song that has been a staple of his live shows for a few years. "I am about three-quarters home. I wish I was eighteen again . . . Damn right! You better believe it, but only if I could keep my knowledge. Then I'd know where all the traps were before I got in them."

Prisoner of Love gazes over a career brimming with soulful music, and not a few traps. Yet what is perhaps most amazing at this late date is that it actually demands that Price's career be heard with fresh ears. The seamless way with which he moves from pop standard to country classic and then back again underlines the point that, to him, the music remains the same. It is the way the songs are portrayed that is different. A song's portrayal is no small thing, of course, but Price's remarkable singing still manages to make a wide-ranging body of work seem entirely of a piece. "I want to be remembered as a real nice person," he says, then adds, "and a hell-ay-cious singer."

"When I sing, I want it to sound like I'm just talking to you," he explains. "I'm not singing it; it's just something that I've come up with. That makes the song more real, a better reading. . . . Every song I sing, I feel. Sometimes it gets pretty strong. It depends on what kind of mood I'm in or what's gone down or something. Sometimes it gets so emotional you kinda just have to back out for just a minute, get your head collected so you won't mess up and sound like something you're not supposed to. I like to make it sound real. That's what I work for."

You can hear this approach at work all through *Prisoner of Love.* In the way he invests "In My Life" with a lifetime's worth of devotion. ("It was hard for me to learn from the old Beatles record, just listening to it, and then singing it the way I wanted to sing it, but we finally got it," he says.) In the way he makes "Prisoner of Love"—a pop hit in 1946 for Perry Como, just about the time Price began singing it out with friends— embrace a trap he knows he can't escape. In the longing he pours into "Ramblin' Rose," a Nat King Cole hit that was the title track to a country-themed album by Cole in 1962. In the way Price devotes himself to every stubbornly romantic word of "If It's Love," a new song by Hank Cochran's son, J. R. ("Only on my opinion now," Price attests, "but I think it's one of the greatest songs I've ever recorded.") And maybe most of all in the way "Eighteen Again" and "What a Wonderful World"—one dreaming of what is past and will never be, the other completely invested in the moment—conclude the album, doubling each other's power by arriving back-to-back.

Each of these songs is surrounded by David Campbell's exceedingly lush and sympathetic string arrangements. "Now the reaction I get from the strings is: more, more, more!" Price says, sounding like a man whose vision has been vindicated. Still, as always, Price's voice provides meaning to all the pomp and circumstance.

"This is my fiftieth year in the business, and if I'm ever going to expand and try new things, I got to do it now. I just want to expand and maybe get some new fans and please old fans. . . . You can [rest on your laurels] if your head stops, but I can't do that.

"I'm still searching for that place. I'm still trying to master my craft. . . . [I want] the best sound that could ever be. That's it."

The Music Came Up from His Soul

From Western Swing to Classic Nashville Sessions, Johnny Gimble Has Fiddled His Way through the History of Country

ND #42, MAY–JUNE 2002

Bill C. Malone

The title of Johnny Gimble's newest CD, *Just for Fun,* goes a long way toward explaining the man and his music. It would be naive to say that the money hasn't been important to him; Gimble, after all, has been an extraordinarily commercial musician. But his sheer passion for music and his compulsion to share it with others have done the most to sustain him through his long and varied career.

Gimble has been making consistently good music for over sixty years. Mention his name, and many people immediately remember him as the award-winning session musician who, along with Buddy Spicher and a few others, brought the fiddle back into prominence in Nashville in the 1970s, after it had been virtually abandoned by mainstream artists. But that was more than twenty years ago. Others will think of his tenure as a Texas Playboy with Bob Wills. That was fifty years ago.

When he joined Wills in California in 1949, Gimble had already been making music in Texas and Louisiana for more than a decade. He hasn't stopped. A stroke on Christmas Eve in 1999 has slowed the master fiddler a little bit, but he is still playing an occasional gig, making records, and teaching fiddling workshops in Texas and New Mexico. The satisfaction of seeing, as Gimble terms it, "the light bulb go off" when a young musician masters a difficult chord or, better yet, puts an original spin on a tune, is more than enough to keep Gimble busy teaching the apprentices who make the trek to Taos.

■ ■ ■

When Gimble entered the world on May 30, 1926, in the Chapel Hill community near Tyler, Texas, he could scarcely have avoided the sound of the fiddle. In many ways, East Texas remained a cultural outpost of the Old

South. Confederate statues still guarded courthouses in virtually every county seat, and a biracial population, Democratic political leanings (with a strong populist flavor), and evangelical Protestant religious preferences provided evidence of the region's kinship with Dixie.

Although young men in this part of Texas typically wear cowboy hats, boots, and jeans, their society is a product of the mid-nineteenth-century migration that brought the Gimbles and people like them from Georgia and other southeastern states. Marked by heavily wooded rolling hills and red dirt (except for the sandy lands where Tyler's famous rose fields flourish), the region still knelt before the throne of King Cotton.

Fiddle contests, such as the yet-thriving affairs held in Athens and Crockett, convened regularly in East Texas, as expressions of civic spirit or as celebrations of old-time traditions. When Gimble was born, a few veteran fiddlers, such as James Knox Polk Harris, from nearby Longview, could still speak of their experiences in the Confederate army. People still met frequently in their neighbors' homes to dance to "Tennessee Wagoner," "Hell Among the Yearlings," and other lively fiddle tunes that were already old before they were transported from Tennessee, Alabama, and other southern climes.

The domino game "42" was all the rage at that time, and often families would invite their neighbors in for a series of matches that might be going on simultaneously at four or five tables. Fiddlers were frequently invited to provide relief between contests or to play for the dances that sometimes concluded the evening.

It wasn't hard for budding young musicians to find role models, and Gimble found his in the performances of his paternal uncles, John and Paul, who played fiddle, "tater bug" mandolin, and guitar at the house parties, or simply on the back porch. They played many of the old hoedowns, but occasionally a tune like "Washington and Lee March," probably learned from a Milton Brown recording, or a pop number like "Redwing," from the turn of the century, would creep into their repertoire.

Most Texas fiddlers, in fact, probably did not "swing" their tunes the way Gimble does, but they were always receptive to a broad range of musical styles, from ragtime to pop. Gimble didn't have to go very far—only a scant fifteen miles to Lindale—to find an example of these eclectic inclinations and a link to the early-radio string bands. This was Huggins "Lefty" Williams, at one time the mainstay of the famous East Texas Serenaders, but now living with his invalid mother, not far from where Uncle John Gimble lived.

Like many of the fiddlers and string bands in Texas, Williams and the Serenaders had been receptive to new tunes and styles, and had shown a particular fondness for ragtime melodies. Gimble remembers learning "Beaumont Rag" from Williams and being fascinated by the infectious bow shuffle with which the old fiddler invested the tune. He sat enthralled as he watched Williams play, but it wasn't easy to learn from a left-handed fiddler.

Intriguing as Williams's playing style may have been, the evidence of his show-business experience may have been more thrilling to young Gimble and his brothers. He recalls that "we saw a stack of records, and that really impressed me." These were the recordings that the Serenaders had made for Brunswick, Columbia, and Decca in the late 1920s and early 1930s, and were evidence of the seemingly glamorous world that beckoned professional musicians. (Lefty Williams lived long enough to learn of Gimble's awesome fiddling talent, and as an old man, he was once quoted as saying of his protégé, "Johnny can beat me playing hot fiddle.")

■ ■ ■

Music was a constant diversion in the Gimble household. Johnny's father, James Frank Gimble, had a small farm, but made his living as a telegrapher for the Cotton Belt Railroad. He worked at his job all night long, and slept only a few hours before managing a few hours of farm work alongside his sons. He played no instrument, but he encouraged the music preferences of his six sons and three daughters, mainly by bringing fiddles, guitars, and mandolins into the household. All of the Gimbles played or sang, and soon the Gimble boys were in business as a family band. Johnny was about ten years old when he developed a love for both the mandolin and the fiddle and discovered they were tuned the same way.

Johnny's first professional experience came in about 1937, when he and brothers Jack, Gene, and Jerry went to work for a flour salesman named Big Boy Green, who enrolled them into a group known as the Peacemaker Boys, named for a local flour brand. Big Boy installed a speaker on his car and advertised their appearances with a recording of Bob Wills's "Black and Blue Rag." Performing on flatbed trucks, the boys played music and sold flour in towns all over East Texas.

Big Boy was a promoter from the old school who drummed up interest in his product by holding concerts and using corny gimmicks that seemed straight out of blackface minstrelsy or vaudeville. Sometimes, a little African American boy would tap dance and play tunes with his teeth. Occasionally, after a layer of flour was spread on the makeshift stage, local boys were encouraged to root for hidden coins with their hands tied behind their backs.

About two years later, in 1939, Jack having departed for the navy (he volunteered prior to the bombing of Pearl Harbor, and was there when the Japanese made their attack), the three youngest Gimble boys (Gene, Johnny, and Jerry) and good friend James Ivy attained sponsorship from Howard Dodd Grocers and became the Rose City Swingsters (inspired by Tyler's claim to be the "Rose Capital of America"). Clearly profiting from the influence of seminal Fort Worth band the Light Crust Doughboys, the

Swingsters played a mixture of pop, hillbilly, and cowboy tunes while advertising their sponsor's product, Rose Queen Flour, all over East Texas.

The Swingsters often performed from flatbed trucks, but they also appeared on radio broadcasts in Tyler and Kilgore, and in the dance halls and honky-tonks that had emerged in the wake of Prohibition's repeal. Gimble and his brothers knew the hoedowns and folk ballads inherited from the Old South, but they and their audiences were also increasingly receptive to the current dance tunes that marked the repertory of early western swing.

Cotton and its folkways may have dominated the lives of most East Texans as the 1930s drew to a close, but the booming oil fields of nearby Van, Kilgore, Gladewater, and Longview forecast the region's future. Few people got rich from the oil discoveries, but they put a little bit of money in circulation, inspired a quest for diversion and recreation, and made it possible for such "fighting-and-dancing" joints as Tyler's Ambassador Club, Longview's Mattie's Ballroom, and a dive in Lufkin remembered only as "the hammer and hatchet" club to thrive. The Gimble boys recalled these clubs with amusement and little affection, noting, for example, that people went to the Ambassador Club mainly to fight.

Gimble didn't hear much big-band jazz in those days, nor does he recall having heard the music of the great gypsy musicians Django Reinhart and Stephane Grappelli. Sometime in 1938, though, he heard the recorded music of Cliff Bruner and the Texas Wanderers, a discovery that changed his life.

Bruner had joined Milton Brown's Musical Brownies in 1935, when he was only twenty, and after Brown's death in April 1936, he embarked on an influential career as a fiddler and bandleader. His name became known and revered throughout southeast Texas and southwest Louisiana. Working mainly out of Beaumont, Bruner virtually inaugurated a revolution in nearby Cajun country, where fiddlers such as Harry Choates and Leo Soileau added songs and styles learned from the Texas musician to their traditional French mix. Gimble declares, for example, "You can hear Cliff when you hear Harry Choates play 'Dragging the Bow.'"

Gimble was fascinated not only by the hot, improvisatory fiddling of Bruner, but also by the jazz licks laid down by steel guitarist Bob Dunn (probably the first country musician to electrify his instrument) and mandolin player Leo Raley. Gimble described Raley's style as "rinky tinky ragtime," but he was impressed by his early attempts at electrification. Hearing these examples of "hillbilly jazz" (which Bruner described as "hokum"), Gimble realized that, as talented as he already was with his fiddle, many musical worlds remained unexplored, and his fiddle was capable of seemingly limitless possibilities. He is still fond of quoting Cliff Bruner, who told him that "if you can hum it, you can play it, if you'll practice until your fingers do what your mind thinks."

■ ■ ■

Gimble's career apart from his brothers began in about 1943, right after his graduation from high school, when he joined the locally famous Shelton brothers (Bob and Joe), who, with their Sunshine Boys, presented an odd mixture of "brother duet" singing and western swing instrumentation. Gimble was hired to play tenor banjo and fiddle, but was permitted to play only one or two tunes on the latter instrument during their schoolhouse shows, the venues where most prewar hillbilly bands played.

After Gimble expressed his frustration one day when another fiddler was employed to play at one of their gigs in a Texarkana nightclub, Joe Shelton clumsily tried to console the teenager by saying his banjo was indispensable for the rhythm the band was trying to achieve. Shelton also tried to console Gimble by telling him, "I don't think you'll ever be a fiddle player"—a prediction that fortunately went unfulfilled.

Working out of Shreveport, Gimble continued to play the tenor banjo as he toured with the Sheltons in Texas and Louisiana, and through their influence, he became part of the band that accompanied Jimmie Davis in 1944 in his successful campaign for the Louisiana governorship. The stage experience gained through his involvement with the Sheltons was invaluable, but Gimble's most cherished memory is the tutelage received from fiddler Jimmy Thomasson, who became a lifelong friend and "taught me how to hold a fiddle," Gimble claims.

The Gimble boys certainly contributed more than their share to the campaign against fascism in World War II. Three of them served in the navy, and Johnny did a stint with the army. His induction into military service came toward the end of 1945, but he arrived in Germany too late for combat. He therefore spent much of his time playing music in officers' clubs and absorbing the big-band jazz heard on the Armed Forces Network.

Listening to Benny Goodman and bass player Slam Stewart, Gimble was introduced to a host of jazz and blues improvisations, and received further confirmation of the wisdom imparted earlier by his mentor, Bruner. Gimble argues that he learned as much from Goodman's swinging clarinet style as from any other source, and he still speaks with wonderment at the antics of Stewart, who bowed his bass while he hummed the notes.

In the immediate postwar years, during country music's first great commercial boom, Gimble began putting those ideas to use in a succession of Texas bands, beginning in 1947 with Jesse James and His Gang in Austin (where he first electrified his mandolin). Next, he joined his brothers in a band called the Blues Rustlers in Kilgore and Goose Creek, and then moved on to Buck Roberts's Rhythmairs in Corpus Christi.

The Corpus Christi stint was particularly fortuitous because one night when Bob Wills and the Texas Playboys played a gig in the city, Playboys mandolinist Tiny Moore heard the Rhythmairs play and was impressed by Gimble's scat singing, fiddling, and electric-mandolin playing. Moore quickly mentioned Gimble's name to Wills, who was looking for a replacement for fiddler Jesse Ashlock. Gimble didn't hesitate when the invitation was made to join the Texas Playboys, even though the affiliation promised a grueling life on the road. Gimble is still fond of saying, "Would a sandlot baseball player turn down the opportunity to play for the New York Yankees?"

The three years he spent with Bob Wills, from 1949 to 1951, were the most exciting in Gimble's career. He exulted in the freedom he found with the Texas Playboys, eagerly accepting Wills's challenge to "play everything you know." Executing the swinging improvisations that Wills heard but could not play, and sometimes joining Tiny Moore on scorching mandolin duet pieces, Gimble set a standard that other swing musicians could hope to emulate but would never surpass. He participated in three recording sessions for MGM that included such classics as "Warm Red Wine," "Remington Ride," "Boot Heel Drag," and "Faded Love."

Recalling those exciting days, and the exhilarating music that issued from them, Gimble said, "Playing a swing chorus is like being a surfer. You just ride the wave if you have a good rhythm section. You don't have to think. Turn on and it comes out."

■ ■ ■

Life as a Texas Playboy was exhilarating and challenging, and Gimble insists that, despite the rigors of a demanding schedule, he and the other Playboys "couldn't wait to get on the bandstand." This life, however, soon proved exhausting for a man who loved his home and family. By 1951 he had "settled down" in Dallas, playing music there with the bands of Al Dexter and Dewey Groom and working for producer Don Law, a talent scout for Columbia Records who was recording many of that label's acts at Jim Beck's local studio.

Gimble, therefore, has the distinction of having been part of western swing in its waning days and of being an active participant in the burgeoning honky-tonk scene that edged Wills-style music aside in the early 1950s.

He never felt comfortable playing in honky-tonks (even though he has done so quite frequently), but he contributed directly to the shaping of the honky-tonk sound, chiefly through his performances in Beck's studio. This experience marked Gimble's first stint as a session musician, and he became a sideman for a remarkable group of singers, including Ray Price, Marty Robbins, and Lefty Frizzell, who, in the early 1950s, made their first important recordings, in Dallas.

The Dallas–Fort Worth area was rife with musicians who found eager and receptive audiences among the local aircraft and automobile-industry employees and other blue-collar workers who sought relief and diversion in the local clubs or at weekend variety radio shows such as Fort Worth's *Saturday Night Shindig* or Dallas's *Big D Jamboree*. Nevertheless, most country musicians still had to supplement their musical habits with outside employment.

Gimble was no exception. He worked a host of jobs to support both his musical passion and his family's needs. At one point he was employed as a carpenter during the day while playing music four nights a week at Rosa's Ballroom and appearing frequently on KRLD's *Big D Jamboree*. Gimble brought a measure of security into his life, however, when he obtained a license at a local barber college—a route followed, not by coincidence, by several of his musical colleagues. Three of his old buddies from the Rhythmairs had already decided to go to school there, and they received good deals because one of the owners was a brother of club proprietor Rosa (who was married to singer and bandleader Al Dexter). Until Gimble moved to Nashville in 1968, his professional life revolved around cutting hair and making music.

In 1955, Gimble moved to Waco and became the host of a noon television show on KWTX, *Home Folks,* inherited from his old friend and mentor Jimmy Thomasson. Playing music mostly on weekends, he supported his family as a barber, including a stint at the VA hospital from 1961 to 1968. Except for a brief period when he and his family lived in Alaska (1959–1960), Gimble spent most of these years playing music in his off-hours or on weekends, and generally using Waco as his home base. He sometimes ventured to Dallas to play for square dances, and occasionally provided entertainment for rodeos when someone like cowboy actor Rex Allen passed through the area.

Gimble's participation in the 1964–1965 tour of the Aunt Jemima Band Wagon was one of his most significant musical adventures of these years, primarily because it marked the beginning of his talented bass-playing son's professional career. Along with fifteen-year-old Dick Gimble, Johnny joined a group headed by longtime Dallas musician Jim Boyd that advertised flour and pancake mix at grocery stores throughout East Texas. This interlude could not help but bring back memories of the Rose City Swingsters.

■ ■ ■

Gimble made his first foray into the world of big-time commercial country music in 1968 when he moved to Nashville and entered, arguably, the most productive—certainly the busiest—period of his life. Averaging about eight sessions a week, each stint running about three hours, he recorded with most of the city's leading musical lights, from Porter Wagoner and Dolly Parton early on to George Strait and Keith Whitley a couple of decades later, and just about everyone in between. (An undoubtedly incomplete discography on the All Music Guide Web site notes Gimble appearances on 225 albums.)

Since recording sessions were built around the individual needs of singers or writers, Nashville's producers were reluctant to let Gimble "play everything he knew," but he soon became one of the most valued members of the industry's A-Team of session musicians, a distinction few fiddlers had known since the days of Tommy Jackson in the mid-1950s.

"The thing I enjoyed most was the camaraderie," he explains, and he still marvels at the ease with which the local producers and musicians adjusted to the widely differing styles of singers.

Gimble credits producer Bob Ferguson and singer Connie Smith with the recognition he received throughout the industry. On Smith's 1972 recording of "If It Ain't Love (Let's Leave It Alone)," Ferguson told him to play what he wanted to, telling him, "Just jump in there and play me some Johnny Gimble." Smith was so impressed with his contributions that she sent out a handwritten note to DJs all over the country to let them know that Gimble was the man who executed all those heart-stopping improvisations.

Despite the crucial role he played in shaping the sound of the recordings made in Nashville, Gimble never felt comfortable with the mass-produced artifacts of Top 40 country music. He simply wanted to play swing, the music closest to his heart. Thus he was more than eager and willing when Merle Haggard asked him into the studio in 1970 to be part of the album *A Tribute to the Best Damn Fiddle Player in the World (Or, My Salute to Bob Wills)*.

Gimble's presence on that album, and on a collection in 1972 devoted to a reunion of the Texas Playboys, *For the Last Time,* made his name known and revered among a new generation of young fans and musicians who were discovering western swing for the first time. He participated only briefly in Leon McAuliffe's revival of the Texas Playboys, but otherwise made vital contributions to the renewed popularity of the music he loved.

The most satisfying moments of his venture into western swing revivalism were not only his frequent collaborations with such veterans as Herb Remington, but also the opportunities to play with and tutor such young and influential enthusiasts as Alvin Crow and Asleep at the Wheel. Such exposure had contributed to his selection in 1975 as the Country Music Association's Instrumentalist of the Year. He eventually won four more of these awards, as well as nine awards from the Academy of Country Music (between 1978 and 1987) for Best Fiddler of the Year.

Gimble also was a ubiquitous presence during the mid-1970s "outlaw country" breakthrough, appearing on dozens of records by Willie Nelson, Waylon Jennings, Jerry Jeff Walker, Guy Clark, Jessi Colter, and countless others. In addition, he branched into pop realms far from the reaches of the country charts; you'll find his name on the Manhattan Transfer's *Pastiche* and Paul McCartney's *Wings at the Speed of Sound,* to cite two examples from 1976.

■ ■ ■

Nashville was good to Gimble, but the insistent and regimented routine of session playing became "work," and he longed to go back to Texas to do "his kind of music." His own sense of nostalgia dovetailed perfectly with the realization that the longing for the good old days sells a lot of records in country music, and probably explains why he wrote the popular tune "Under the X in Texas" (best known through the performances of Red Steagall).

Bolstered by a good pension supported by money invested in the musicians' union fund, Gimble moved back to Texas in July 1978. In an environment that was much more accepting of his free-spirited style of music, he immediately became one of the kingpins of the state's thriving music scene. He had already achieved almost iconic status in his native state as the virtual embodiment of western swing, largely through his association with Willie Nelson since 1975, and because of a series of albums with groups such as Asleep at the Wheel.

Increasingly, however, solo performances gave free reign to his virtuosity. Gimble's first solo album, *Fiddling Around,* recorded in Nashville for Capitol in 1974, had been co-produced by Haggard. In 1975, chiefly through the influence of Nelson, he issued the widely circulated *Texas Dance Party* (for Columbia), which received extensive exposure from the "progressive" programming of Austin's KOKE and other Texas radio stations.

These early solo recording ventures were popular, but quickly went out of print. Consequently, Gimble decided to issue his own recordings or to work with smaller labels such as Delta in Nacogdoches, Texas. Around 1978 he produced his first independent recording, *My Kind of Music.* The next year he was part of a particularly satisfying project, released by CMH Records in Los Angeles, called *The Swing Pioneers.* On the latter record he played alongside some of the founding fathers of western swing, including his hero Cliff Bruner, Fred "Papa" Calhoun (piano player for the legendary Musical Brownies), Deacon Anderson (the lap steel guitarist who had played with Bruner), Muryel "Zeke" Campbell (the hot guitarist for the Light Crust Doughboys), and J. R. Chatwell (the legendary fiddler, who sang on the LP but could not play because of an incapacitating stroke).

Gimble's identification with western swing became so strong that he even played the role of Bob Wills in the 1982 Clint Eastwood movie *Honkytonk Man.* (He had previously appeared in Willie Nelson's 1980 film *Honeysuckle Rose.*) Gimble never stopped making music, but he had attained the kind of legendary status that now allowed him to do it on his own terms. Residing first in the Austin suburb of Round Rock, Gimble and his wife Barbara lived in a succession of homes, but by 1991 had settled down in Dripping Springs, just west of Austin.

From this convenient vantage point, Gimble could make frequent trips into the capital city to play with and lend encouragement to the young musicians there who idolized him. He toured with Willie Nelson for about a year, and he occasionally teamed with steel guitarist Herb Remington, his old friend and fellow Texas Playboy from their West Coast days, to pay homage to vintage western swing in a group called Playboys II.

In the midst of Gimble's reunion with his Texas roots, national attention beckoned once again, courtesy an innocently made home recording that produced unforeseen but fortuitous results. One early morning he had ventured on to his front porch to record the singing of a mockingbird, and had playfully "mocked" the bird with his fiddle. The bird then saucily imitated the fiddle licks.

Gimble sent the recording of this spirited interchange between bird and fiddle on to his friend Chet Atkins, who in turn gave the tape to Garrison Keillor, longtime host of NPR's *Prairie Home Companion*. Keillor declared, "I've gotta get that guy on my show."

Playing his music, and sometimes appearing in humorous skits, Gimble found a new audience. He says that when he mentions Garrison Keillor or *A Prairie Home Companion* in his concerts, audiences invariably break into applause. Keillor in turn paid tribute to Gimble in a short poem:

> He smiled as he played
> Some old serenade
> And the music came up from his soul.
> You could hear the stars falling
> Whenever he picked up his bow.
> And the shuffling and sliding
> Of ghost dancers gliding
> On kitchen floors long ago.

Since the early 1990s, awards have come frequently. In August 2001, Gimble was the featured act at the new Country Music Hall of Fame's first special exhibit, Nashville Salutes Texas! Country from the Lone Star State. Texas Folklife Resources, located in Austin, often has invited him to appear in Texas classrooms as part of its campaign to present "master folk musicians" to the state's schoolchildren. In 1994 he received his most prestigious honor when the National Endowment for the Arts presented him a National Heritage Fellowship.

Special as these acts of recognition may have been, the experience of making music with his bass-playing son, Dick, has probably been most gratifying. Since at least 1964 he has often played alongside Dick in a band that was first called Home Folks and is now called Texas Swing. His granddaughter Emily, an ardent disciple of Ella Fitzgerald and Peggy Lee, appears on Gimble's newest CD, and a nephew, Jason Roberts, plays the Gimble style as a current member of Asleep at the Wheel. Johnny can be assured that the Gimble name and heritage will remain prominent in Texas music for a long time to come.

The key to understanding Gimble's musical productivity, apart from his remarkable creativity, is simply his passionate love for music. Gimble could just as easily have been referring to himself as he recalled an oft-told story about one of his mentors, J. R. Chatwell: "J. R. didn't seem to go where the money was; he went where the rhythm was good." When Gimble was in the army, and brothers Jack, Bill, and Gene were in the navy, they typically carbon-copied their letters to one another. Looking back on some of that surviving correspondence, Gimble notes that "all we ever talked about was music." His brothers told me that during the peak of Gimble's Nashville days, when he occasionally came back home for a visit after a series of grueling sessions, the first thing he wanted to do was play music.

The stroke of 1999 has made some of his fretwork more difficult, since it attacked the right frontal lobe of his brain, which controls the left side of his body. But it has impaired neither his sense of humor nor his enthusiasm for making music. When informed by an MRI scan that a black hole had appeared in his brain, he said, "I hope that 'Orange Blossom Special' falls through it. I get requests to play the damned thing and have to play it."

Jim Baker, a fiddle-playing friend in Dallas, put a different twist on Gimble's impairment when he asked him how the stroke had affected his playing. Gimble replied that in a recent concert with pianist Floyd Domino, he had tried to reach the notes on one of his tours de force, "Fiddlin' Around," and "couldn't play the son of a gun." Baker ruefully replied, "Now you know how the rest of us feel."

Gimble has striven mightily to pass his heritage on to contemporary generations, through workshops, seminars, and summer camps given under the auspices of Texas Folklife Resources in Austin, and through his annual Swing Week workshop held each July at the Fort Burgwin campus of Southern Methodist University near Taos, New Mexico. (A brochure describes the event as "hot music in the cool mountains.") Recalling the most recent workshop in July 2002, Dick Gimble remembered that his dad was always the first person up each morning, and was already playing his fiddle on the porch of the dining hall as the students gathered for breakfast.

These opportunities to transmit his gifts and preserve his legacy undoubtedly awaken memories of the little boy who thrilled to the discovery of Cliff Bruner's music and who once sat at Lefty Williams's feet in Lindale.

"It was all passed on to me," Gimble declares, "and if I can get people to enjoy the music as much as I do, I'll be satisfied."

The Man in Black and White and Every Shade in Between

*Johnny Cash Is a Complex, Contradictory Character . . .
and "a Pretty Happy Man"*

ND #42, NOVEMBER–DECEMBER 2002

Bill Friskics-Warren

Take I-23 north from Kingsport, Tennessee, or south from Wise, Virginia, and you'll find more or less the same mix of old and new Appalachia: roadside flea markets within sight of Wal-Mart Supercenters, generations-old strip-mining operations alongside latter-day pulp mills, double-wides in hollers overlooked by McMansions on the hill.

That isn't the case once you get off the interstate and the road narrows to two lanes, as it does when you cross the Tennessee-Virginia line and wind northeast on Highway 58 toward the Carter Family homestead in Scott County. It isn't that the landscape suggests a bygone era; the shady blacktop that snakes its way through this corner of southwest Virginia reveals more than its share of late-model pickups, trailers, and prefab homes. It is just that, bereft of billboards and fast-food chains, its rugged recesses have yet to be inundated by the more garish trappings of modernity.

This is even more the case farther up the road in blink-and-miss-it Hiltons (population thirty), where a filling station–cafe with a rabies advisory in its window marks the turnoff to the Carter Family Fold, which lies just three miles down A. P. Carter Highway in Maces Spring.

"Fold" is the name that Joe Carter, A. P. and Sara's only son, gave the barn-like amphitheater he built into the rise just to the left of his father's old grocery store (now a museum) in 1976. Invested with biblical freight, the term could not hardly sound more antediluvian, conjuring either an enclosure for sheep or a congregation, a "flock" bound together by shared values or beliefs. Or, for that matter, a crowd of witnesses like the one that gathers, at the behest of Joe Carter's sister Janette, in the Fold's hodge-podge of chairs, benches, and transplanted school-bus seats every Saturday night to listen and dance to the old-time music that is synonymous with the Carters and the mountains of southern Appalachia.

"Fold" has a broader connotation here, though. It is also an old English term for a small basin or drainage, very much like Poor Valley, the narrow holler bisected by the A. P. Carter Highway that encompasses everything from the log cabin where A. P. was born to Mt. Vernon United Methodist Church, the white clapboard chapel behind which he and Sara are buried. The brooding slabs of pink granite under which they lie are adorned with copper plaques shaped like 78 rpm records, inscribed with the refrain "Keep on the Sunny Side."

Mother Maybelle Carter and her husband, A. P.'s brother Ezra ("Eck"), are buried just outside Nashville, but the modest white cottage with the wraparound porch they built in the early 1940s is here at the Fold as well. The house, which is lined with box elders and Canadian hemlocks and sits a couple hundred yards off the road facing south, now belongs to the couple's only surviving daughter, June Carter, and her husband, Johnny Cash.

The Cashes are there the sunny Friday morning in September I make the trip out to the Fold. The man of the house—dressed only half in black, a white work shirt being his concession to the light—is sitting in the living room where Mother Maybelle and her daughters Helen, Anita, and June used to rehearse. Photos of kin, many of them taken by Cash, including a cherubic shot of a young Rosanne, compete for space among knick-knacks and Carter-Cash memorabilia on every wall and countertop.

His feet elevated to alleviate swelling from water retention brought on by diabetes, Cash has been at the Fold working on June's follow-up to 1999's exquisitely unvarnished *Press On*. The album is scheduled for release on Dualtone early next year. Cash's own *The Man Comes Around*, the fourth installment in his series of recordings with producer Rick Rubin, comes out November 5 on Lost Highway.

It has been a week since the Man in Black made a surprise appearance at the Americana Music Association Awards in Nashville to receive the first-ever Spirit of Americana Free Speech Award for his lifelong commitment to voicing the struggles of those on society's margins. More surprising still, especially given his retirement from public performance, was Cash's return to the stage at the AMAs to sing with his wife and several generations of Carter women. His cameo prompted June, always in fine comedic form, to dub him a "Carter brother."

"June asked me to sing a song or two on her album, and I said, 'OK, I'll be first brother.' Or maybe she called me 'Carter brother' first; anyway, I got a real kick out of singing along with her," says Cash. He looks more frail than imposing, propped up in his black-leather recliner. Yet at seventy, and beset by asthma, diabetes, and glaucoma, it is remarkable just how vital, even unassailable, Cash and his craggy baritone remain.

He and June still maintain three houses, splitting time between their place at the Fold and their homes in Hendersonville, Tennessee, and in Jamaica. Cash continues to seek out and write new material to record, the most striking case of the latter being the title track of his new album, an eschatological wonder seemingly inspired by the biblical book of Revelation. He remains hungry and plugged in, not just spurred on by his renewed popularity among urban hipsters drawn to his dark side, but nurtured as well by the comforts afforded by faith, family, and home. Tellingly, perhaps, he takes his coffee black, but with three sweeteners.

"You see, Mother Maybelle and the Carter Sisters sang all those songs all those years they were on my show," Cash goes on. "I guess it was getting me ready for this because it came so easy, these sessions did. I'm singing songs like 'Sinking in the Lonesome Sea' and 'Keep on the Sunny Side,' all those songs that the Carter Family had. They're so comfortable, so easy for me, that I feel like a brother in there singing with all those girls."

Cash, who has been a Carter-in-law for thirty-four years now, more than qualifies as a member of the fold. Yet at this point he is less a brother than the family's musical patriarch, an inheritor—and then some—of A. P. Carter's prodigious musical legacy, as well as those of Sara and Mother Maybelle.

The young John R. Cash (Sam Phillips later re-christened him "Johnny") listened often to the Carters when, growing up the son of Arkansas sharecroppers, he tuned in the group's broadcasts on Mexican border station XERA. The way that Cash, after the manner of A. P., was "bassin' in" with the Carter women at the AMAs in September suggests he was particularly attuned to the male voice in the trio.

A case can likewise be made for the influence of Mother Maybelle's driving thumb-brush rhythms on the amped-up boom-chuck that Cash—and guitarist Luther Perkins and doghouse bass player Marshall Grant—patented at Sun Records during the 1950s. Cash has also devoted himself to collecting songs and tracing their genealogies, much as A. P. Carter did in his day.

"I've always been impressed with A. P.'s work in collecting and writing these songs for the Carter Family," says Cash. "His contribution was momentous. Of course, so was Maybelle's contribution, so far as writing and collecting. And Sara's.

"A. P., he went out there and was selling fruit trees sometimes, and he'd trade a fruit tree for a song. He was a prolific collector. He went all over these hills and these mountains and these valleys around here, listening to songs and collecting different verses, and different songs from different people.

"I've followed in that tradition of collecting and writing," continues Cash, who has a voluminous catalog of recordings, covers as well as originals, to show for it. "You never know where you'll find a good song, and I've always got my ears open, now more so than ever.

"Someone will say, 'I've got this old song,' and immediately I'll think, 'I bet I know every word of it.' They'll start in, maybe on a verse I'm familiar with, but then they'll go southwest, or then they'll go a different direction than I thought they would have gone. There'll be lyrics I never heard before, and I'll say, 'Where'd that come from?' Sometimes they can explain it to my satisfaction, and sometimes they can't."

The influence of the Carter Family extended not just to Cash's music, but to his moral and spiritual development as well. "June and her family have kept me steadily on course at times when the rudder was shaky," Cash told me in 1999. "Maybelle was a great friend, she and Pop Carter both. They were like parents to me.

"My parents were living in California at the time," continued Cash, referring to the mid-1960s, when he and June were first getting together. "[My parents] were happy, after they got to know a little about them, that I was spending a lot of time with the Carters because they were people who truly cared for me, as did June. They knew she did. So it was their love and care for me, and the musical influence, and the musical sharing, eventually, with all of them, that was very binding. And we're all still kind of bound up that way."

Indeed, much as the Carters did, Cash has long been committed to preserving and nurturing the family fold. "June and I have six daughters and one son, and neither of us have ever used the term 'stepdaughter,'" he says, his tired yet searching eyes filled with pride.

"Talking about family relationships and harmony in the house, you put your arm around your stepdaughter and say, 'This is my daughter' when introducing her to somebody, and it makes her day. It makes mine too. I don't understand this 'step' junk. I know people do it, as a matter of course, but I don't. I just don't do it. I never have gotten any flak for it from anybody, not even their mothers." (Not even, one suspects, for maintaining ties to his singing ex-sons-in-law Marty Stuart, Nick Lowe, and Rodney Crowell.)

"I'm a family man," Cash adds. "I'm a home man. I love my home. I love my peace and quiet more than anything in the world."

Somewhat vexing, then, is the extent to which Cash's commitment to home and kin has been eclipsed by the solitary and decidedly gothic image he has projected since he started working on his bracing series of American Recordings with Rick Rubin. Then again, maybe it is less the persona that Cash has cultivated these past few years than the one that the marketing and publicity departments of his record companies, and the press, have projected onto him.

First came the sepia-toned cover of his 1994 *American Recordings* album, which pictured Cash, draped in a billowing black duster and framed by a brooding sky, scowling like someone's idea of the grim reaper (and seemingly willing to oblige). Then there was the record's kickoff track, a remake of "Delia's Gone," the grisly murder ballad Cash first cut for Columbia in 1962.

Rock critics, of course, ate it up, as they did Cash's subsequent covers of songs by the likes of Soundgarden and Beck. The mainstream press soon began lionizing the Man in Black as an avatar of darkness—equal parts proto-punk and forerunner of the modern gangsta MC. It certainly came as no surprise when the *Murder* volume of Cash's tripartite retrospective *Love God Murder* received lots more attention in print than—and out-sold—the volumes in the series that spoke to the romantic and devotional sides of his persona.

None of which is to deny that Cash's dark side—his addictions, his hell-raising, his bouts of illness and emotional turbulence—defines a big part of his myth. Or, for that matter, that many people identify with the outlaw-hero tradition of which that myth is an extension.

"I understand them obsessing on the dark side," Cash says. "Every-body's got a dark side. In the nineteenth century, the biggest ballad of all, of the whole century, was 'The Ballad of Jesse James,' and it didn't come along until the 1880s. And that's up against Stephen Foster and the rest of them, you know? Americans have a history of upholding their outlaw heroes, of holding them up as people to be admired and emulated. Jesse James brought down the establishment, at least in his own mind he did."

Despite Cash's appreciation for—and embodiment of—the outlaw-hero mystique, he also admits that he has, in some ways, contributed to this increasingly narrow perception of his image and legacy. "I pigeonholed myself a lot," he says. "It's true that maybe I'm defining myself more as an artist, and maybe as a person, in these latter years. I don't know. But look-ing back at myself, and at what I projected out there, there seems to be a hardness and a bitterness and a coldness . . . and I'm not sure I'm too happy with that. I'm not sure that's the image I want to project, because I'm a pretty happy man."

It is almost impossible, hearing these comments at the Carter Fold, not to be reminded of the melioristic admonition of the Carters' signature song, "Keep on the Sunny Side," especially the tension between darkness and light it recognizes. Cash has struggled to embrace that dialectic at least since he cut "I Walk the Line" for Sun in 1956. He has said that he wrote the song as a pledge of fidelity to his first wife, Vivian Liberto, and no doubt that is the case. But over the years "I Walk the Line" took on much greater significance as Cash—the first person elected to both the country and rock 'n' roll halls of fame—emerged as one of the most iconic and complex figures of the second half of the twentieth century.

A mass of contradictions, he was a doper and a lay evangelist; a pro-tester of the Vietnam War who palled around with Richard Nixon's pet preacher, Billy Graham; a singer of grim odes to murder like "Cocaine Blues" and an aficionado of clodhopper cornpone who once released an

LP called *Everybody Loves a Nut*. Cash is truly one of the few who, with Walt Whitman, can say, "Do I contradict myself? / Very well then I contradict myself, / (I am large, I contain multitudes.)"

Above all, this hard-won multiplicity, this struggle—not nearly as easy as "I Walk the Line" claims—to remain true to that unruly heart of his, is what makes Cash so heroic. Witness how, over the obdurate beat of the Tennessee Two, he sings of keeping the ends out for the tie that binds. Like a down-home dialectician—and in a baritone that is somehow both tender and unyielding—Cash is confessing just how desperately he wants to unite the disparate strands of his gloriously conflicted self in hopes of subduing the beast within.

The Man Comes Around, Cash's new album with Rick Rubin, reflects this dialectical sensibility better than any of its three predecessors. This isn't to say it is a better record than, say, *American Recordings* or *Unchained* (it isn't; among other things, it is too reliant on covers of overexposed rock and pop material); but it offers a more complete picture of the man—more or less equal complements of love, God, and murder.

Covers of Ewan MacColl's "The First Time Ever I Saw Your Face," the Eagles' "Desperado," and Hank Williams's "I'm So Lonesome I Could Cry" (a duet with Nick Cave) give love its due. Versions of "We'll Meet Again," "Bridge over Troubled Water," and the apocalyptic title track (a recent Cash composition) speak to issues of transcendence, while stabs at "The Streets of Laredo," Sting's "I Hung My Head," and Cash's own "Sam Hall" do murder proud.

The arrangements on the album are also richer and more evocative—less monochromatic—than Cash's other records with Rubin. The prevalence of piano is of particular note, as is the ambient cast of many of the album's tracks. "It's not so much production as kind of a cushioning for my ragged voice," Cash says. "I think that's why Rick added some of those things. There's much more instrumentation on this one, but it fits. It works."

Indeed, and while Cash's stentorian vocals may sound tattered, they still convey an almost biblical authority, a reverberant mix of judgment, hope, and, above all, steadfastness.

The flood of reissues—and a pair of tribute albums—that have greeted the seventieth anniversary of Cash's birth have likewise done justice to the complexity of his seemingly inexhaustible persona and legacy. Long-out-of-print collections of devotional, patriotic, historical, protest, and humorous numbers that Cash made for Columbia during the 1960s and '70s have resurfaced as part of the ongoing repackaging (by the label's Legacy division) of his back catalogue. Also included in this series is *Songs of Our Soil,* a concept LP from 1959 in which Cash looks back on his hard-knock childhood in the cotton camps of the Arkansas Delta, and *The Fabulous Johnny Cash,* also from '59 and the best single album of his career.

Three concert recordings are newly available as well—not just Cash's famous dates at Folsom Prison and San Quentin, but also a previously unreleased document of a show at Madison Square Garden in December 1969. Most revealing about the last of these is the range of material and emotion it encompasses. Alongside serious signature numbers "I Walk the Line" and "I Still Miss Someone" are the seriously funny "A Boy Named Sue" and knotty political statements such as "Last Night I Had the Strangest Dream," a more dialectical than polemical number—a dove with claws, indeed—about the war in Vietnam.

Nor was there a lack of gospel and sentimental fare on the program at Madison Square Garden that night. With contributions from the Carter Family, Cash's brother Tommy (their father, Ray Cash, was in the front row of the audience for the show), old pal Carl Perkins, and the Statler Brothers (whom Cash discovered), the set finds the Man in Black gathering unto himself virtually everything he holds dear. All that is really missing are the comedy sketches of his wife June, who was at home, soon to give birth to the couple's son, John Carter Cash.

Columbia's release of the Madison Square Garden concert also serves as a reminder of the pivotal variety show Cash hosted on ABC from 1969 to 1971. More than any broadcast before it, and maybe since, *The Johnny Cash Show* made hillbilly culture "cool" with mainstream and even countercultural audiences.

"A big deal was going down all right; I could tell by how the crowds were swelling and the press kept getting bigger and bigger," Cash recalls of the show, which ABC broadcast from the Ryman Auditorium, at that time still the home of the Grand Ole Opry. With guests ranging from country stalwarts Roy Acuff and Minnie Pearl to cross-cultural icons Mahalia Jackson, Louis Armstrong, and The Who, *The Johnny Cash Show* offered further evidence of Cash's commitment to seeking out the ties that bind, rather than the walls that divide, people.

Indicative of where Cash's head and heart were during this era was "A Boy Named Sue," a wry talking-blues that *Playboy* cartoonist Shel Silverstein wrote about the generation gap. Whereas "Okie from Muskogee," one of Merle Haggard's singles from the same year (1969), was a joke-turned-fightin'-words, "A Boy Named Sue" was a joke that rang out like an anthem. Communication, even to the point of conflict, Cash was saying, is the best way to breed the tolerance and mutual understanding needed to bridge any gap.

Things come to a head on the record during its final scene, in which the character played by Cash, happening upon his father dealing poker in a dingy saloon, thunders across the room: "My name is Sue! How do you do! Now you gonna die!" (And how he manages to make those lines sound scary, after all the punch lines that have preceded them, is an honest-to-goodness marvel.)

A brawl of Rabelaisian proportions ensues, the two men kicking, gouging, and bloodying each other beyond recognition as the Tennessee Three's jabbing rhythms and Carl Perkins's guitar provide rollicking ringside commentary. It is not until the son pulls his gun that the old man finally explains why he named him Sue (although not why he ditched him and his mother in the first place).

"Son, this world is rough, / And if a man's gonna make it, he's gotta be tough . . . And it's that name that helped to make you strong," his father tells him, the implication being that by giving him a name like Sue—its "sissy" connotations just the sort implied in the gibes at hippies in "Okie"—he made his son the man he had become. The kid relents after the old man says his piece, and the two reconcile, but it isn't so much because the son believes his father made him who he is. No, it is that after mixing it up with him and hearing him out, he finally knows, right or wrong, where the man he now calls Pa is coming from.

Speaking not only to the silent majority who presumably tuned in country radio, but also to the longhairs who listened to rock stations, "A Boy Named Sue" nearly topped both the country (#1) and pop (#2) charts in 1969. (By contrast, "Okie" spoke only to one side of the debate, going #1 country but stalling just outside the pop Top 40.)

Nevertheless, apart from scattered singles and his prison albums, many historians and critics, particularly those of a revisionist bent, view the music Cash made after leaving Sun as less emblematic of who he is than the more elemental sessions he did with Sam Phillips and, four decades later, Rick Rubin. More expansive and often more produced records such as "Ring of Fire" and "Sunday Morning Coming Down" that Cash made for Columbia with producers Don Law and Bob Johnston—or those he did with old Sun cohort Jack Clement later on—apparently didn't fit the picture some critics had of the "rough cut" Cash.

"Look at the years that I spent on each body of work, and you'll see that I put in a lot more years on the Jack Clement and Don Law kind of productions that don't get touted as much lately by the press," says Cash, countering the prevailing rockist perspective. That said, Cash admits that he got "off-track record-wise" as the 1970s gave way to the '80s.

"I was not interested in the records I was making," he says. "I was grinding them out just because I had a record deal. And the less interest I showed in my work, the worse my records sounded, until I came to the point I was totally disinterested, and at that time [1985], CBS dropped me.

"Which was fine with me," he adds. "A lot of people really got upset over that, but I didn't, not in the least. I knew it was coming. I was kind of hoping it was coming because I wanted out of there. I wanted an excuse to get away. I wanted to escape. Trouble was, I didn't know where I was going when I did get out of there. It would still be seven or eight years [after a brief, and fairly inspired, stint with Mercury] before I would have a record deal with Rick Rubin.

"It was like déjà vu with my Sun days when Rick said, 'Just come in, sit down with your guitar, and sing me the songs you want to record,'" Cash remembers. "That's what Sam Phillips said. Sam Phillips said, 'Come in and play anything that you like.' So I started singing my songs, Hank Snow songs, Carter Family songs, a little bit of everything."

Cash still recalls his days at Sun with relish (a denim shirt embroidered with the Sun logo was hanging on the line to dry the day I visited the house at the Fold). "Those were very heady times," he says. "[In] '55, I was at Sun Records and there was Elvis Presley, Carl Perkins, Jerry Lee Lewis, and myself, and we went out on tour and we had a party.

"We loved what we were doing. We hoped and prayed that it would never end. Of course, when it's going like that, you don't think it ever will. But Elvis left, and then the whole bunch of us kind of fell apart at Sun Records and we all went our separate ways. That was a sad time for all of us.

"At Sun Records, Sam Phillips was always the boss," Cash continues. "He was always Mr. Phillips. We all called him Mr. Phillips. I still have a hard time calling him Sam, because we all had so much respect for him. He was a man who knew what he was about. We all believed in Sam Phillips. We always believed if Sam said it, it had to be right. Even if he told you that's all the money you made in royalties, you tried to believe him."

Even then, though, Cash was holding disparate strands in tension, playing the "devil's music" while thanking heaven for blessing him with the gifts to do so. "Sam Phillips would call me to come in and record, but there might be someone else there, too, recording," Cash explains. "So I would go in, and I'd wait my turn, and if things were going good, he'd keep going with me. Nobody else would take over the time. I don't think I ever had anybody take my time. Elvis could have, but he didn't; he never did come in and take over my time. Jerry Lee Lewis did once, but he did-n't take it for very long. Nobody follows the Killer.

"The Killer was always the Killer," Cash adds. "Jerry Lee Lewis was always the same back then as he is today. He never has changed, and he never will. I never will forget going on the tour the first time with him in a car. He'd start in preaching to us. See, he hadn't been out of seminary long. He started in preaching to us telling us we were all going to hell. And I said, 'Well, what about you?' And he said, 'Well, I'm going to hell too. We're all out here doing the devil's work.' I said, 'I'm not doing the devil's work. I'm doing it by the grace of God because it's what I want to do.'"

One of the reasons Cash left Sun in 1958 was to record what became *Hymns by Johnny Cash,* the gospel album Phillips wouldn't let him make.

This dialectical sensibility, this drive to unite putatively conflicting musical and cultural threads, is writ large in the way Cash reached out to Bob Dylan in the early 1960s. The relationship the two men forged not only shaped their lives and music, it transformed the country and pop worlds as well—especially after Dylan recorded in Nashville, a move that anointed country music (and the laid-back, less-is-more approach to playing that defined the Nashville Sound) as hip for the rock crowd.

Dylan, of course, was singing Cash's songs long before he left Hibbing, Minnesota, for New York in 1960. "I used to sing this before I ever wrote a song," Dylan says on the Cash tribute *Kindred Spirits,* by way of introducing "Train of Love." In fact, it is arguable, at least in part, that Dylan picked up aspects of his vocal phrasing—as well as his penchant for surrealism—from the likes of "Big River."

Cash would later return the favor, cutting Dylan's "Don't Think Twice, It's All Right," "Mama, You Been on My Mind," and "It Ain't Me, Babe" (a Top 5 country duet with June in 1964) for his *Orange Blossom Special* LP. Cash and Dylan teamed up to record "Girl from the North Country" for Dylan's 1969 album *Nashville Skyline,* which featured liner notes by Cash. The duo reprised "Girl from the North Country" on the premier episode of Cash's TV show later that year. Bootlegs of the recordings they made in Nashville after the *Skyline* sessions, including versions of "Blue Yodel," "Guess Things Happen That Way," and a chugging take of "Mountain Dew" with Carl Perkins on guitar, have been circulating ever since.

Cash first sought out Dylan in Greenwich Village in late 1963 or early 1964. "I had his record called *Bob Dylan,* and then *The Freewheelin' Bob Dylan,* so I went down to the Village looking for Bob one night," recalls Cash, who has always been something of a folksinger at heart. "They said that he had been there but he had gone. So I said to myself, 'If I hang out here in the Village long enough, I'll run into him.'

"June and I were working together then, and I'd go onstage in those little places, and I'd sing my songs and call them folk songs, waiting for Bob to show up. He never did show up in the Village, but I was booked at the Newport Folk Festival in Newport, Rhode Island [in 1964], and that's where I met him. And Joan Baez, too. Bob came in my room with Joan Baez and started jumping up and down on my bed and hollering 'Johnny Cash! Johnny Cash! It's really you!' He was laughing and just acting the fool, you know? It was a lot of fun. And June was there—June, Joan, and Bob."

According to Dylan biographer Robert Shelton, following Cash's performance at Newport Friday night, the four of them retreated to Baez's room at the Viking Motor Inn, where the two men committed a bunch of songs to tape. As a token of thanks, Cash gave Dylan one of his guitars.

"I always admired Bob so much for his writing," Cash says. "What I admired about him too was his delivery. I loved his singing. I thought he was the best hillbilly singer I ever heard. When I first heard him, I told

June, 'That's the best hillbilly singer you've ever heard. He don't think he is, but he is. The very best.'

"Boy, and he sang those songs with conviction too. 'The Lonesome Death of Hattie Carroll.'

"'Lone Ranger and Tonto headin' down the line,'" Cash sings, just above a whisper. "'Fixin' up everybody's trouble, / Everybody's but mine / Somebody musta told 'em / I was doin' fine.'"

The Newport Folk Festival also proved a crucial point of convergence for Cash and Kris Kristofferson, another Nashville outsider the Man in Black befriended. In the process, Cash helped introduce country music to a new breed of songwriter who, with the likes of Mickey Newbury and Tom T. Hall, would infuse Music Row with a plainspoken existentialism derived as much from Hank Williams as from Bob Dylan and the Beats.

"Kris was at my house for a dinner party one night," Cash says. "This was 1967. I told him, 'June and I are going to Newport to do the Folk Festival again. I'd love for you to do a song on the show if you can get up there.' He said, 'I'll be there,' and he hitchhiked up there.

"When it came time for him to go onstage, I said, 'Kris, you go out and do whatever you feel like doing, then call me back out and I'll come back on.' So it came time for him to go on, and he stood there frozen. He couldn't move. I said, 'Kris, the emcee's calling you,' and he still couldn't move. He couldn't speak. He was petrified. Well, finally, June walked up to him, kicked him in the seat of the pants, and said, 'Get out there.'

"So he went out and he did 'Sunday Morning Coming Down' and 'Me and Bobby McGee.' I forget what else he did, but the next day on the front page of the *New York Times*, it said, 'Kris Kristofferson Takes Newport.' I was really proud of that for Kris. He really needed that break; it was a great leap forward, and he got a really good one there."

The most fortunate convergence of Cash's life, however, wasn't primarily musical, but romantic: his acquaintance with his future second wife, June Carter. The couple first met backstage at the Grand Ole Opry during the late 1950s, a good ten years before they were married in 1968. June had been on tour with Elvis Presley, with whom she also shared a manager, Colonel Tom Parker.

June remembers Cash coming up to her at the Opry (she was a regular on the Prince Albert segment of the show) and saying, "I want to meet you. I'm Johnny Cash." June's response: "Well, I ought to know who you are. Elvis can't even tune his guitar unless he goes, 'Everybody knows where you go when the sun goes down.'" The line was from "Cry, Cry, Cry," Cash's first hit for Sun; when June was touring the South with Elvis, she recalls the King dragging her into cafes along the way to play Cash's records on the jukebox.

Mother Maybelle and her daughters didn't join Cash's road show until the early 1960s, but it wasn't long afterward that June found herself falling for Cash—and dreading it—after discovering he was in the throes of a wicked addiction to pills and booze. She captured the mix of foreboding and desire she felt in "Ring of Fire," a song she co-wrote with Hank Williams cohort Merle Kilgore and that Cash took to the top of the country charts for seven weeks (#17 pop) in 1963.

June's "Ring of Fire," which her sister Anita had recorded as "Love's Burning Ring of Fire" in 1962, was the confession of a woman terrified of her passion burning out of control lest it, or its object, consume her. Cash's swaggering interpretation of the song could not hardly be more different; spurred on by the galloping rhythms of the Tennessee Three, he sounds as if he couldn't wait to jump into the flames. "I fell into a burning ring of fire / I went down, down, down / And the flames went higher," he sings, as the mariachi trumpets of Karl Garvin and Bill McElhiney fan the blaze.

Cash says he knew what lay behind the lines he was singing; he certainly inhabited them as if he did, abandoning himself to the purifying love he somehow knew would eventually save him from himself. Which, of course, it did. And thus was born one of the most indelible love stories of the past forty years, one that will be given the big-screen treatment in *Cash*, a forthcoming biopic to be directed by James Mangold (*Girl Interrupted*, *Heavy*) and not, as rumored, by Quentin Tarantino.

"As of right now," says Cash, "the number one contender to play me is Joaquin Phoenix. He's agreed to do the part, and if he and the studio can work it out, I suppose he will. There's a major draft that needs to be done on the screenplay. The version that I have, I didn't approve of at all. There's too much Hollywood junk in it, too much sex and violence for no reason at all—unwanted, unneeded things that just don't work for June and I. So we've got a major rewrite on the screenplay, then if Joaquin Phoenix is still interested, and he can work it out with the studio, he'll play the lead. The girl they're talking about playing June is this girl [Reese] Witherspoon. They say she's perfect for the part."

Indeed, Witherspoon's comedic gifts are likely to do June justice. But perhaps even more crucial than casting the movie will be the ability of the screenwriters to depict the Man in Black as the righteous, irascible, conflicted, utterly complex soul that he is. It would no doubt be tempting, when making concessions to the market, to collapse the tensions that have hounded and driven Cash into a one- or two-dimensional variant of the persona we have seen during the Rick Rubin era. Again, this isn't to say that the latter-day emphasis on Cash's dark side is mistaken (or that Cash hasn't made worthy records with Rubin)—just that it is incomplete and, as a portrait of so rich a character, woefully inadequate.

Any rendering of Cash needs to account not just for his pill-popping years, the time he flipped off the camera, and his line about shooting a man in Reno just to watch him die (a line he hadn't lived but adapted—

doubtless from Jimmie Rodgers). It also must address his love of God and family, as well as his fondness for the likes of "Arkansas Traveler"–style hijinks and sentimental weepers—his embrace, as the Carter Family put it, of life's dark and sunny sides.

Any treatment of Cash's legacy also must acknowledge how attuned he is to issues of social class. And not just at arm's length, but how he has for decades sustained a vision of justice that compels him to side with all who struggle on the margins—the very thing, in other words, that makes him the Man in Black.

"Those are my heroes: the poor, the downtrodden, the sick, the disenfranchised," Cash says. "I just heard a new song by Guy Clark called 'Homeless.' It's really a good song. I'm going to record it. 'Homeless, get out of here,'" Cash intones, his energy flagging. "'Don't give 'em no money, they just spend it on beer.'

"Ain't no end to street people," he adds. "There's no end to the people of the margins. There's no end to the people who can relate to that. People on the margins of economic situations, and of the law. How many people have we got in prison in the USA now—1,300,000?" [The figure is more like 2 million.]

It is precisely this prophetic voice—Cash's ability, in "Folsom Prison Blues," to connect the dots between poverty and incarceration, or, in "The Ballad of Ira Hayes," between racism and disenfranchisement—to which the Americana Music Association and the Nashville-based First Amendment Center paid tribute in September.

Cash said he particularly appreciated the chance "to say a word or two at a time when everyone was waving flags and speaking out for America." Yet, in lieu of making an acceptance speech, Cash surprised everyone in the audience that night, when, in a weakened yet commanding baritone, he recited an updated version of his 1974 poem "Ragged Old Flag."

Those in the audience who leaned to the left politically, myself included, might have wished Cash had spoken out against the Bush administration's talk of attacking Iraq. Folks on the right probably didn't find the image of a ragged old flag patriotic enough. But, as his comments at the Carter Fold a week later attested, the matter was, very much like Cash himself, more complicated than that, particularly given the way the aggression and injustices perpetrated by the United States have contributed to the sometimes shabby state of our nation's flag.

"You're absolutely right about that," Cash said, when I asked him as much. "The raggedness of the flag is due to a lot of things that we've brought onto it ourselves. The fires that we've put it through."

On this day at the Carter Fold, however, it is Cash and his wife who are feeling ragged. "We're a little busted down today," says June, after poking her head into the room to play us a rough mix of the version of the

Carter Family's timely "Storms Are on the Ocean" she had recorded the day before.

"We're just tired," Cash adds.

No doubt, and not just from recording fourteen songs in two days, but, in Cash's case, from a lifetime of trying to come to grips with his own conflicted self—amid a world of people who, much like his latter-day mythologizers, are too rarely drawn to the light.

■ ■ ■

Postscript: June Carter Cash died on May 15, 2003. Johnny Cash followed a few months later, on September 12.

The Long Journey Home

Rosanne Cash's Path from Nashville to New York Has Taken Her beyond Country Stardom

ND #44, MARCH–APRIL 2003

Lloyd Sachs

f looks could kill, the cover shot of Rosanne Cash's 1985 album *Rhythm & Romance* would have landed her on somebody's most-wanted list. Staring hard into the camera, a country-rock femme fatale in boudoir white, she dared you to crack wise about her shoulder-padded jacket, orangey spiked hair (coif by Rique, credits the LP sleeve), and dangling earrings. Was this the same woman who, on her previous album, *Somewhere in the Stars,* took a schoolgirl's path to sultry in a gold-trimmed black top, a heavyweight-championship-wide gold belt, and a mop of purple-tinted dark curls?

Looking back through the years at such fashion statements, another artist might be overcome by self-consciousness or a case of the giggles. But Cash, who has evolved into a stylish boho-sophisticate, is nonplussed by the aggressive stylings of yesteryear. "Look," she says with a quick laugh, "I had a profound streak of rebellion, and I let that play out. I liked to take chances. I had a lot of internal freedom. I didn't worry about fitting in."

The problem was, a lot of people did worry about her fitting in during her years in Nashville. Even when she was littering the country charts with #1 hits and playing next-wave queen to Rodney Crowell's next-wave king, she was considered an outsider by industry types who wished she would act more like a country star by taking her act on the road—and keeping it there—and toning down her non-country leanings. "Musically, *Rhythm & Romance* was seen as rebellious back then," she says. "Now, it's a safe, overdone pop record."

By the time her ardently gossiped-about marriage to Crowell hit the rocks several years down the road, she had hit the rocks with Music City. If she couldn't make it there, even after having Made It, she would make it in New York, New York.

"I moved here in 1991," Cash says, having momentarily found a pocket of calm in the 1855 brownstone she shares on the Lower West Side with her second husband—and second producer-husband—John Leventhal and their family. "But I was a New Yorker before that, probably starting when I longed for the city, like you long for a person, when I was in my teens."

Which brings us to the revealing cover shot of *Rules of Travel,* her first album in seven years and quite possibly her best. Shot by her friend, the famous photographer Annie Leibovitz, in subzero December weather on the rocky, wave-whipped shore of Maine, it features her in a *French Lieutenant's Woman* getup, standing before a shipwreck and contemplating her next move.

Cash will detail the tidal incidents she has survived in her life and career. She will name names. But as tough edged as she still is, she has evolved into a person who prefers to believe that living well is the best rebellion.

■ ■ ■

The Big Apple has been very, very good to Cash. Mixing there with literary and media types as well as musicians, she has added to her reputation by scoring as the author of a well-received story collection, *Bodies of Water,* and a children's book, *Penelope Jane: A Fairy's Tale.* As a magazine writer, she made it into the 2000 edition of *Da Capo Best Music Writing* as well as the *Best of the Oxford American,* where she rubs prose with such luminaries as Tony Earley, Susan Sontag, and Walker Percy. She is now writing a memoir of her Nashville years for Viking, has curated a book of songwriters' musings on their favorite tunes (*Songs without Rhyme*), and holds forth as an all-purpose pop-cult tipster on www.rosannecash.com. Her recent recommendations include Francine Prose's *The Lives of the Muses* ("which made me wonder if Alfred Stieglitz was Georgia O'Keefe's muse"), the movie *Adaptation* ("I liked the pace and the free association"), and "Norah Jones, Norah Jones, Norah Jones: What a beautiful voice."

All this while playing mother, in her home and from afar, to her newborn son (now four), three daughters, and a stepdaughter.

And, oh yes, much of this while dealing with the disheartening setback of not being able to sing.

Well, you knew there had to be a little black magic stirred into her cup of contentment. There always is.

As the result of a rare hormone-related condition brought on by her pregnancy with Jake, Cash developed a large polyp on her vocal cords. When her voice grew raspy at four and a half months, she assumed it was an allergy, but the condition wouldn't go away. "When a voice doctor put a camera down my throat and saw the picture, he literally stepped back," she says. "He had never seen such an enormous polyp on anyone unless they had been smoking for forty-five years."

Not only could Cash not sing for her supper, she also couldn't sing her son to sleep. Some songwriters don't need the conduit of their voices to get what they hear in their heads onto the page. She does.

"If I can't sing, I can't find the words and notes that move me, the melodies that pull me," she says. "It made me ache. I grew incredibly depressed. I couldn't even pick up a guitar, because it upset me so much. I didn't know who I was anymore."

A specialist told her that her voice would come back after she gave birth and her hormones normalized, and after an agonizing wait for his words to come true, they did. But that ushered in a new set of fears. Working with a vocal therapist, she was assured that her voice was not damaged. She was out of shape as a singer, but slowly and surely, singing two songs a day, then four, then a full set at six months, she was back. Not only that, but as those radiant high notes on *Rules of Travel* attest, she was singing better than ever.

"I didn't realize how much a part of my self-image it was," she says. "But I have to say that the time away was a revelation. I was secretly relieved that I had lost my voice. I felt all this pressure drain away. I had always felt anxious about being a singer, and to be able to let that go for a while did me a world of good. I feel more freedom about it now. I don't have anxiety. I'm able to let go and get lost in the moment more. I'm not constantly monitoring myself the way I used to."

What young singer wouldn't monitor herself if she was the offspring of Johnny Cash—if, as Crowell put it, she was faced with the daily challenge of "crawling out from the shadow of global enormity of her father"? And if, as she wrote to her father as a young girl, she was determined "to do something great"?

"When I first met Rosanne, she was very shy, almost crippled in her shyness," Crowell says. "She didn't have a lot of confidence in her musical abilities. There was a melancholy quality in her sound that was like what John Lennon had in his middle period, with 'Hide Your Love Away' and 'Help.' It was compelling, but removed, like a warm fire you'd want to stand next to, but not want to get in."

"The main impact Rodney had on me was one of confidence," Cash says. "I was so insecure and ambivalent about being a singer, and he was steadfast in his admiration and conviction about my voice, which he took a lot of care to record right. I would never have continued as a singer, past the first record, if it weren't for him. He held the belief when I couldn't."

"And I learned how to make records with him. We developed a working method in the studio that was quite disciplined and focused, and I go by that still today. He taught me how to listen to drums. I had no idea about drums before I met him."

■ ■ ■

It makes sense that *Rules of Travel,* which features backing vocals by Steve

Earle, Sheryl Crow, and Teddy Thompson as well as a stirring duet with her father, has a recurring road theme. Cash has roots in the South (she was born in 1955 in Memphis) and grew up in the West (she moved to Southern California with her parents when she was three, and lived there with her mother, Vivian Liberto, after their divorce when she was eleven).

She went back to Tennessee after high school to work in her father's traveling show, and then studied drama at Vanderbilt, later continuing at the Lee Strasberg Institute in Los Angeles. Stung by a bad case of un-requited love, she escaped in 1976 to London, where she worked for CBS, then her father's label. After her career-making years in Nashville— roughly a decade-long stretch from the late 1970s to the late '80s—she gravitated north.

In conceptualizing the cover shot of the new album, Cash and Lei-bovitz talked long and hard about metaphors and myths, about the charac-ter of the album and all her travel and where it leads—which, ultimately, is home. In touching on various aspects of her career, the album itself leads home as well, though not as literally as Cash's 1996 *10 Song Demo,* a spare self-made effort that wasn't intended for release until Capitol head Gary Gersh cottoned to the idea of an unadorned Cash. (Gersh subsequently was deposed, and his successors largely let the album wither on the vine.)

Marked by a real sense of renewal after her split with Columbia on the heels of her 1993 album *The Wheel*—"I was starting to feel like furniture; no one got what I was doing," she says of her latter days at Columbia—*10 Song Demo* compensated for its lack of radio-friendliness with brilliant reflective pieces, including the bouncy "The Summer I Read Colette," which gloriously rejects being "blinded to the beauty in our own lives," and the moody "Just Don't Talk About It," which captures Cash's deep hurt after losing a baby four months into another pregnancy.

Rules of Travel—blessed with smart finishing strokes such as cleanly lay-ered guitars, electronic effects, Beatlesque touches, dashes of organ, and wonderfully restrained contributions from the guest singers—is a kind of extension of *10 Song Demo.* With the gifted Leventhal again playing most of the instruments, it provides an elegant backdrop for Cash's fetching vocals, which have never been more winningly relaxed in tapping into her obsessions with fate and fulfillment.

On 1990's *Interiors,* her breakthrough effort as a songwriter, Cash's closed-in intensity had a way of keeping the listener at bay. On the new recording, her easy mastery draws you into the heart of originals such as the hook-enhanced title cut and the dreamy-hopeful "Will You Remember Me," as well as commissioned tunes such as "Hope Against Hope," by the tag team of Joe Henry and Jakob Dylan. ("I was so sick of my own thoughts and feelings," says Cash. "I asked, couldn't we ask others to write songs?")

It was Leventhal's idea to ask Johnny Cash to sing on "September When It Comes," a hauntingly lovely tune about pain, rebirth, and rest written by Cash and Leventhal. "Rose was hesitant to ask," said Leventhal. "She doesn't like to impose. But listening to what the song was about, how the texture of the music resonated, I said, 'This is kinda your dad.' When we put it together, it was shocking how powerful the results were. He felt he didn't sing it that well, maybe because he revealed a vulnerability you don't normally associate with him."

Laid low by asthma, glaucoma, and diabetes—at this writing, he was back in the hospital with a foot infection—the seventy-year-old legend has battled respiratory problems that have made singing a test of will for him. But that only adds to the emotional impact of "September." Even as he sings, "I cannot move a mountain now / I can no longer run / I cannot be who I was then / In a way, I never was," you are in the grip of his powerful spiritual presence.

In sheltering her father on the song with the warmth and openness of her voice, Cash embodies the shift that has taken place lately in how they relate to each other. He is no longer the caretaker, the man in charge who ordered her to not go back to London when she came home for a visit, insisting she have someone send her belongings, thinking she might never return home. Nor is he the object of her anger or disappointment for being out of her life so much when she was a child. The harsh psychic noise of his split with her mother, which culminated in a period when he was fighting drugs and booze and demons and wreaking havoc in his public life, has faded.

"As I have felt more protective toward him, my adult self surfaced a bit more," says Rosanne, who pays sweet tribute to her father with her cover of his classic "I Still Miss Someone" on *Kindred Spirits,* one of two recent Johnny Cash tribute albums. "I don't have compelling 'issues' with him anymore. I've pretty much accepted that he belongs to the world as much, or more, than his family, that he has a great heart, and that whatever I missed in my childhood was partly what made me who I am, and I don't complain about that.

"He's not much for phone conversations, especially now that he doesn't feel well much of the time, so we don't talk as much as we used to about books or politics or films or music. We used to have great conversations about those things. He's quieter now. When I go to see him, a lot of times we will just sit without talking, as he conserves his energy."

Crowell has spoken with awe about how much his life was changed the first time he heard Johnny's 1956 classic "I Walk the Line" (which Crowell remade with the help of his former father-in-law on his 2001 album *The Houston Kid*). For Rosanne, it was a recently reissued 1965 album of her father's, *Johnny Cash Sings the Ballads of the True West,* with a picture of him as an ornery gunslinger on the cover, that held deep significance. "It was an escape for me," she says. "I liked listening to my dad in character."

The recording provides a panoramic look at an age gone by with songs such as "Sam Hall," "Hiawatha's Vision," and "The Ballad of Boot Hill," as well as Cash's spoken narration. Says Rosanne, "It made me become obsessed with the idea of a concept record, where all the songs were about one thing. I thought, and still do think, that concept records were the ultimate in record making, and I have always wanted to do that as well as *Ballads of the True West* was done."

But her old man had serious competition in a foursome of future conceptualists from England. "I was in second grade when 'I Want to Hold Your Hand' was released in America," Cash recalls, "and I remember very clearly sitting in the back seat of a car, next to my friend Gretchen, whose older sister was driving. She turned on the radio and the Beatles came on and Gretchen was talking in my ear but I didn't hear a word. And after it was over, I kept thinking, 'How do I get that back on the radio?' That memory is singed in my brain. I came alive to a life outside the anxiety and tension in my house, to a world I wanted to live in."

■ ■ ■

Cash's mother, Vivian Liberto, also had an influence on her daughter's musical sensibility. "She played Ray Charles's *Modern Sounds in Country and Western Music* album over and over, and I memorized it, by osmosis. I didn't realize until I was in my thirties how important a prototype it was for me.

"As I got into my teens, I was a California girl through and through, meaning I hated the Beach Boys. My friends and I thought they were a fabrication for Midwesterners. Later, of course, I came to deeply respect Brian Wilson, but most of the records still make my skin crawl. I loved the Beatles, and then loved Blind Faith, Crosby, Stills, Nash & Young, Traffic, Elton John, Janis Joplin, and then songwriters like Joni Mitchell and Jackson Browne. Joni, particularly with *Blue,* made me wake up to the fact that a woman could write her life through songs and have it be meaningful and singular and edgy and personal without collapsing in on herself."

Cash's first album, never released domestically, was a folk–poppish affair issued on a German label in 1978. Though it documents her maiden efforts with Crowell, who produced three tracks, she dismisses it out of hand. "I was a kid," she says, laughing at how the German producer insisted on correcting her English pronunciation.

She had met Crowell, who was playing guitar in Emmylou Harris's Hot Band, at a party thrown by Waylon Jennings. They both arrived on the scene at a time when the old image of country music was being shot full of holes. The outlaw movement had hit, and hit hard, shifting attention to Austin, Texas. Alt-country, whatever that would be, was taking its baby steps. Crowell, like Harris, appealed to the rock audience by drawing on rock and roots styles. Cash was on the same page. Her interests ranged, increasingly, from what she calls "post-feminist pagan rock" to Appalachian folk.

Signed to Columbia, she enjoyed an auspicious start in 1979 with *Right or Wrong* (recently reissued on Australia's Raven Records as a single-disc twofer paired with her 1981 smash *Seven Year Ache*). Boosting and encouraging her feisty vocal attack with his demonstrative production, Crowell, whom Cash married the same year, introduced a formula that worked well throughout the 1980s. He provided first-rate original songs and brought in top-notch cover material from unsung pros such as Keith Sykes, while Cash chipped in a song or three of her own.

Though Columbia was happy to have Johnny Cash's daughter on its roster, and happier to have a new hitmaker, the label's execs didn't understand her in the early days all that much better than they did during her final, introspective phase with the label. The country establishment wanted her to accept its standards and practices—which did not include stretching her musical sensibilities, prioritizing motherhood over career, and, in her own more controlled way, taking as independent a stance as her father had.

Her employers had to be talked into releasing the Cash-penned title track from *Seven Year Ache* as a single. The song, which she has said was influenced by Rickie Lee Jones's street-minded concerns (as reflected in lines such as "You act like you were just born tonight / Face down in a memory but feelin' all right"), became the first of her eleven #1 hits on the *Billboard* country chart.

For all her success, she repeatedly failed to win awards at the annual music-industry soirees. "I Don't Know Why You Don't Want Me," written with Crowell, was about failing to win a Grammy—which she finally did for that very song, taking home the award for best female vocal country performance in 1985.

"The Nashville establishment not only didn't embrace me, it vilified me," says Cash. "I thought people would accept me, that they would want something fresh, but a lot of people were turned off by the choices I made."

"Rosanne was a recording artist," said Crowell. "Superstardom was not of interest to her. She had grown up in a household with a superstar and seen what that was about. She didn't go on the road or kowtow to the powers that be to become a household name. These days, it would be impossible to have #1 hits without going on the road. That speaks volumes about what the times were like then."

Cash and Crowell succeeded as artistic collaborators in spite of, or maybe fueled by, stormy exchanges in the studio and at home. The cracks in their marriage, perhaps tweaked by Crowell's lack of commercial success when Cash was enjoying lots of it, grew wider when he began staying out on the road to feed his own string of hits in the mid to late 1980s.

Working for the first time with an outside producer, David Malloy, on *Rhythm & Romance,* Cash suffered a bit. With a cushy synthesizer–electric keyboard sound, the songs failed to resonate with her essential character. Distracted by the demands of caring for a new baby, she didn't have the wherewithal to correct the situation.

Riding in on a white horse, Crowell produced three tracks—Cash's "Hold On," John Hiatt's "Pink Bedroom," and the Benmont Tench/Tom Petty number "Never Be You"—that he regards as highlights of their partnership, but about which she has reservations. *King's Record Shop,* a Crowell production released in 1987, was a strong return to form that spawned several hits and won Cash some awards. It includes a nice cover of her father's "Tennessee Flat-Top Box," and pointed the way to her increased involvement with social causes with "Rosie Strike Back," an Eliza Gilkyson tune about a battered wife. But after having dominated *Rhythm & Romance* as a songwriter, Cash had a reduced profile here. "A lot of that album was Rodney channeling his ideas," she says.

With 1990's *Interiors,* she shed her Svengali—or tried to—in order to have a go at concept-album making, and producing. She says she was "stunned" when *Village Voice* rock critic Robert Christgau (who, in his *'80s Record Guide,* proclaimed her "the decade's premier interpretive singer") tagged the album her "divorce record." While the end of her marriage certainly informs the songs, which more often than not trade in feminist-streaked disillusionment and bitter disappointment (the fetchingly bittersweet "What We Really Want" is a notable exception), they were not straight-up autobiography.

"There's this syndrome in Nashville where personal lives are supposed to be on public display," says Cash. "I mean, Barbara Mandrell had an exact replica of her bedroom in her museum on Music Row. I don't like the idea of confessional songwriting. It diminishes song as art. Everyone latched onto 'Paralyzed,' but it didn't have anything to do with my marriage. It was about overhearing my parents' marriage break up. It was about me, but in a completely different context."

However personally revealing *Interiors* was or wasn't, it was embraced as an act of courage and conviction by her female peers. "She broke down the stereotype of a country artist for me," says Mary Chapin Carpenter, who has been friends with Cash since touring Australia in 1990 with her and Lucinda Williams. "That's how I first noticed her. She was making fresh, honest, personal art, and with such an exquisite sense of control."

"I didn't intend to produce *Interiors* myself," says Cash. "I was looking around for producers, I felt I needed to work away from Rodney, and I asked Malcolm Burn to meet with me. I played him my demos, and he listened to all the songs without saying anything, and at the end he said, 'Why aren't you producing this yourself?' I said, 'I don't know.' When he left, I was on fire.

"I knew what to do. So I called [top-flight session guitarist] Steuart Smith to help me with arrangements, and I decided that it was going to be an acoustic record, that I didn't want to use a full drum kit on anything. I hired Roger Nichols, the best engineer I knew, and Steuart and I hung a sign over the door to the control room which said, 'Abandon thought, all ye who enter here,' a take on Dante's 'Abandon hope . . .' We wanted to just be intuitive, to let it unfold without too much analysis.

"In the end, I played it for Rodney, and he said, 'It's not finished.' I freaked out. He persuaded me that I needed more balance, and we cut 'Real Woman' and 'On the Inside.' I hate the first song, love the second. So he was half right."

"Rosanne had reached a point where she really didn't need me anymore," said Crowell. "I helped frame her as a vocalist, and I was a good source of bringing in extra material. But she had really come into her own as a songwriter. A lot of young artists think they're songwriters long before they are, and the first song she brought in for *Right or Wrong,* 'This Has Happened Before,' told you she had this obvious gift. But having grown up in the shadow of great artistry and being a particularly intelligent person, she allowed herself to develop her talent as a songwriter alongside her artistry."

■ ■ ■

Living in Nashville had done a world of good for Cash. "Settling down there saved my life," she says. "I was headed for a hard life in California— a life of drugs and bad attitude. Nashville softened me. It made me more reflective. I bought a log house in the woods, got off drugs, had children, and became more nurturing." But eventually she felt isolated, artistically as well as geographically. "The core of who I was as a writer was getting muddled by self-absorption and by spending a bit too much time in the underworld of my own psyche. I hadn't lost my way completely, but I was losing my edge in increments.

"It's a damn good thing I met John Leventhal," she continues. "I was in danger of emotional implosion and artistic dilution and spiritual fascism. Really, I was getting soft and New Age-y in my thinking, I was veering toward a narcissism in my writing that would be intolerable to me now. John gave me back my focus, just by being around him. He also has a fierce discipline—more discipline than me, actually, far more. And he has a native New Yorker's world view, which is to say somewhat cynical, but at the same time passionate."

Their partnership began with her 1993 release *The Wheel,* recorded in New York. "I feel like I overproduced it," says Leventhal, who attained Grammy-winning success producing Shawn Colvin and also has worked with Kelly Willis, Kim Richey, and Joan Osborne. "I wish I had made it simpler." But with coolly evocative songs such as "Sleeping in Paris" and "Seventh Avenue," *The Wheel* had the feeling of rising to the surface following the submersion of *Interiors.*

As much comfort and joy as Cash has found in her marriage to Leventhal and her culturally enriching life in New York, she has had to deal with the drug addiction of one of her daughters (who is in recovery) and a recurring invasion of her privacy by a stepsister. According to Cash, she has been impersonated to invasive effect over the past two decades by one of the daughters of her famed stepmother, singer June Carter (whom Johnny Cash married in 1968). Cash claims the woman has exploited the similarity of her given name, Rozanna, and nickname, Rosey.

"The reason I have not done anything about it, beyond asking her to stop, is that it is so painful to June, and I respect June," explained Cash, who says that she is finally planning to pursue a cease and desist order. "Both her daughters have done horrible, unspeakable things to me and to the whole family." June's other daughter, Carlene Carter, whose star as a new-breed country singer once rose in a parallel trajectory to Rosanne's, has spiraled sadly out of the picture amid recent arrests for drugs and identity theft.

Nothing can slow Cash's rediscovered momentum, though. In November, she shared the stage of Nashville's Ryman Auditorium with Crowell, with whom she says she is on good terms ("*Houston Kid* just brought me to my knees—it's so powerful"). The concert, which also featured Mary Chapin Carpenter and John Hiatt, was a benefit for a rehab center that Hiatt sponsors.

Cash went to this year's Sundance Film Festival in the guise of music supervisor for a film in the making based on *Big Stone Gap,* a best-selling novel by her friend Adri Trigiani, and as a participant in a Songwriters' Snow Ball that also featured Grant Lee Phillips, John Doe, and Lou Barlow. Two versions of "Three Steps Down," a song from *Rules of Travel,* were used on the since-canceled HBO series *Mind of the Married Man*— Cash's version and one by Marc Cohn, who wrote the song with Leventhal. And she continues to enjoy the presence of cultural luminaries such as humorist Fran Lebowitz. "I think I have unwittingly borrowed my current sense of humor from her," she says.

With Capitol championing *Rules of Travel* at a time when such personal, non-niche projects are routinely sold short, Cash is sitting especially pretty. "I never felt this kind of support, ever, in twenty-five years," she says. "I'm being treated like a new artist."

Whatever you think she is thinking as she gazes at you as the country-rock-pop-whatever French lieutenant's woman, know that there is a smile under that pose. Surf's up.

Happy Woman Blues

Lucinda Williams Attracts the Opposite Sects of Artistic Respect and Commercial Success

ND #33, May–June 2001

Silas House

It probably won't surprise anybody to learn that Lucinda Williams drives a truck. A big ol' truck—Chevy Silverado with a king cab and hard-shell bed-cover. She doesn't take up much of the wide bench seat and sits close to the steering wheel. Magazine photographs make her look like a tall, gangly woman made up of all legs and arms, but in truth she is no bigger than a breath.

Tonight, cruising the streets of Nashville in her truck with that fine, brand-new-car scent, she seems completely at ease. She weaves in and out of racing traffic without half-thinking about it. She holds onto the wheel with one hand and navigates the streets as if she were born here.

That's the thing about Lucinda—she is surprising. After all the media attention she received for *Car Wheels on a Gravel Road,* some journalists felt compelled to paint a picture of Lucinda as an out-of-control diva. It is obvious tonight that she has it together, but on the other hand, she wouldn't be too upset if she didn't. She is a country boy's dream: a smart-as-hell woman driving a cool truck.

Check this out: She's happy, too.

Before we ever pile into her Chevy and hit the road, I arrive at Lucinda's house to find a note on the door: "Come on in. I'm running late. Make yourself at home." When I enter, a Big Mouth Billy Bass greets me, sitting alone on a long foyer table. Over it hangs a clock encircled by these words: "Bless the Lord at All Times."

Lucinda is running up the stairs. "I'm sorry!" she hollers. "Just come on in and be at home." It is easy to feel at home here. Though stunning folk art graces the walls, it doesn't feel like one of those homes where you are afraid to sit down. It isn't a museum. A sad fiddle and an Irish-sounding voice pour from the stereo. She has left me a bottle of cabernet sauvignon on the coffee table, along with a lone glass and a bowl of goldfish crackers.

The room will either make you feel intimidated or safe. There is a wall of crosses and religious art. Day of the Dead skeleton figures play guitars on the fireplace mantle. A wooden snake stretches the length of one wall over a sofa. A screened-in porch connects to the living room, and on its railing sit eight tall candles, each of them labeled for a different use. There is one that is to be burned for the Spirit of Writing, one for the Spirit of Music, another for Protection from Bad Hairdressers, even one to invoke a Peaceful Home. The candles to conjure music and writing have been burned the most.

Apparently, the fire gods blessed Lucinda. Her new album, *Essence,* was written in record time (by her notoriously deliberate standards) and is due out June 5. A mix of good grooves and typically lyrical narrative, *Essence* is something new for Lucinda: This is the record where her confidence comes across loud and clear.

Lucinda comes down the stairs apologizing for being late, as she has gotten a reputation for it. Some of it unfairly—she is quick to argue with the *New Yorker* article that claimed she was routinely three or four hours late for interviews. "I was never that late. I wasn't raised that way," she says quickly. "And I don't mean to be late. I'm trying to do better."

Over the course of the night, it will become clear that this is what Lucinda is always doing: trying to do better.

"I was raised with real high standards," she says. Her father, Miller Williams, a renowned poet who has published twenty-nine books and read at Clinton's 1996 inauguration, always encouraged her to do her best. "I was taught to constantly ask myself, 'How can I make this better?'" Her respect for her father is palpable.

I read aloud from the poem "The Caterpillar," which her father wrote about her:

> In bed again
> re-covered and re-kissed
> she locked her arms and mumbling love to mine
> until turning she slipped
> into the deep bone-bottomed dish
> of sleep

A sense of wistfulness seems to settle over the space between us. "Yeah, that's about me," she says quietly. "That's one of my favorites." It is a subtle, powerful expression of a father's love for his daughter, as represented by the little girl's discovery of a dead caterpillar. "That's the key right there," she says. "Subtlety. That's the challenge in writing."

Being exposed to some of the South's great literary minds taught her a lot about challenges and writing. Widely considered one of the best song-writers of her time, Lucinda says her upbringing naturally had a great deal to do with that. "A love and respect for language is the thing," she says. "And I learned that from literature." As a child, she devoured the work of Flannery O'Connor and Eudora Welty. Her favorite book is *Wise Blood,* her favorite film the John Huston adaptation of that O'Connor novel.

And there was the music as well. She remembers loving to sit and lis-ten to her mother, Lucille Morgan, play the piano. Lucille was a music major at Louisiana State and introduced Lucinda to many forms of music, but perhaps most importantly, Lucille "was into folk songs." Many friends say Lucinda inherited not only musical talent from her mother, but also her personality and spirit. "Just having the piano there as an outlet had a major impact on me," she says. "I got the music from my mother and the words from my dad. I got the best of both worlds."

The best of both worlds is something that comes up again and again. It is something Lucinda admires, especially in people. "It's so hard to find dualistic people, people who crave intellectualism but also know how to have a good time. My fantasy man has always been a poet on a motorcy-cle," she says with a laugh. Her laugh is full of joy, a delightful scratch on the air. She says that she always loved everything: books and films and music, but also singing and dancing and living with passion. "Those dual-istic personalities—those are the best kind of people. No doubt, hands down the best combination."

This passionate duality becomes obvious once we hit the town. At dinner, Lucinda is quiet and eyes her menu from behind stylish glasses. "I can't see anything anymore," she says. "It's horrible." She looks like every-body's favorite ultra-hip college professor in her glasses, black jacket, tank top, and funky pants. Her eyes are intelligent and analytical. Like all great writers, she seems to be taking everything in at the crowded restaurant. "I'm always observing," she says. "Even when I'm not sitting down and writing, I'm taking notes and stashing them away."

When Lucinda leads us across the street to the club at 12th and Porter, she seems to stroll with determination, walking like a woman who steps quickly and carefully over rows in a garden. Inside the club, there is that other Lucinda, the one who likes to have a big time. A Knoxville band led by John Paul Keith (formerly of the Nevers) is playing, and Lucinda is tak-ing in every lick of the guitar, every word of the song. She sways to the music, lost in it for a moment. "I love getting out in the clubs and hearing the bands," she says.

Other people sit at tables and smoke cigarettes. They tilt back their heads and blow their smoke toward the ceiling, then look around to see if anyone has noticed this much-rehearsed move. They scan the crowd instead of watching the band. Lucinda just closes her eyes and listens.

People are leaning into one another, whispering, their eyes locked on us. A couple of people approach her, offer their hand to be shaken, and tell her how wonderful she is, what an impact her music has had on them. She is gracious and nods as they ask her questions, but she is also not exactly sure of what to make of being recognized like this.

Her close friend Dub Cornett, a documentary filmmaker whom Lucinda calls "the Will Rogers of Nashville," has seen more and more people recognize Lucinda in the fourteen or so years that he has known her. And he says the success of *Car Wheels* (a Grammy, gold record, the top of numerous 1998 Top 10 lists) hasn't changed her a bit.

"The difference with Lucinda is that she's an artist, not an entertainer," Cornett says. "She never wanted to be a star, she just wanted to sing, to make art. She does it because it feels good."

When Lucinda and Dub take me on a tour of East Nashville—"the cool part of the city, the places people should really see when they come here"—we pass places like the God Almighty Café and the Hair of Sensation Beauty Salon. Finally, we pull into a twenty-four-hour barbecue joint. It is one in the morning, and we are hungry again. Since the restaurant is a take-out place where you order at the window, we eat in the truck. Lucinda unwraps her chicken sandwich only to find that it is a whole chicken breast—bone and all—between two pieces of white bread. "In my forty-eight years, I've never had a sandwich that had bone in it," she says, holding up a sauce-soaked piece of bread. She eats it anyway, tearing the meat off the bone with her hands. "It's good, though."

When one of us comments on how hilarious it seems for a celebrity to be sitting in her truck, eating a chicken-with-bone sandwich, Lucinda looks genuinely surprised. "I'm not a celebrity," she says, holding shreds of chicken up to her mouth. "Am I?"

The wild success of *Car Wheels* was hard to get used to for her, and she admits that she is hesitant to be seen as a star. "I'm real resistant to that; I hate all that. I'm so brazenly honest about everything in my life, so I don't know how to do that 'star' thing." She relates a story in which Tom T. Hall gets out of bed one day and is told that he is a star now. In response, Hall says, "OK, what do I do now?" Lucinda can relate.

"Being a star is just other people's perception of me," she says. "There's no difference in me as a person. Maybe you're selling more records and more people know your name. So? I'm still the same person I was before people knew who I was."

Of course, being more well-known means being misquoted by leading national publications, having an unofficial Internet site with weekly updates (this particular week there was even a news flash that Lucinda's hair is "blonde and shoulder-length again"), and having her love life examined regularly. To set the record straight, she has recently parted ways with her boyfriend and bass player, Richard "Hombre" Price, but they are still "really good friends. There is no dirt to dig for."

Like most things in her life these days, she is dealing patiently with the spotlight. "There's a lot of things I don't like about the music industry, so that's just one more thing to dislike," she says.

There is another thing that success brings, however: the pressure to live up to the last record. "It's terrifying," she says. "There's a safety in people not knowing who you are because you can just do whatever you want to and it doesn't matter. I'm trying to learn to not worry about what other people think, but that's hard. The main thing is that I want my fans to like it first. That's what counts. And if the critics like it, that just adds to it."

Among the recent critical accolades: VH1 selected her as one of the one hundred most important women in rock, and a book called *Shout, Sister, Shout!* named her the most influential female artist of the 1990s. "Oh my God. That blew my mind," she says. "To tell the truth, I don't know if I feel deserving of that."

Lucinda is loyal to her label, Lost Highway, a new branch of Island/Def Jam. "My label is a real blessing. It has all the backing of a major label with the creative freedom of an indie label. It's the best of both worlds." She has always had a soft spot for independent labels. "Indie labels are the wave of the future. Everything is so corporate that it all has to stop eventually. That applies to everything in this country . . . look at all the mergers. The mom-and-mop operations are just going out of business."

Lucinda is one of the few successful rebels of the music industry. She decries the lack of artistry in Nashville's mainstream scene: "There's so much great country music, but I just don't even listen to country radio."

Her insistence on remaining a rebel and her continued refusals to "sell out" have led to her being labeled "hard to market." This is the woman who once recorded a demo for CBS Records only to have its Los Angeles division call her "too country," while the Nashville division found her "too rock 'n' roll." She is fine with this. "I'm not just about folk-angst-narrative-singer-songwriter. I listen to a lot of different stuff," she says. "I listen to Chet Baker and John Coltrane and all that. I mean, why can't I love Loretta Lynn, but also the Doors and Buffalo Springfield?"

Essence is certainly a reflection of that eclectic nature. The record is a bit of a departure for her, but one that has been coming for a long while. Before and during the recording of the album, she was listening to such artists as Nina Simone, Dusty Springfield, and Sade. "I feel like it's a woman's record, a more mature record," she says. "It's been liberating for me."

Part of that liberation may be in her willingness to rely more on the music this time. "Some of the songs on this one are not as narrative driven," she says. "I allowed myself to lean on the groove as much as on the lyrics. I've always loved that kind of music, and it was just a matter of time before it showed itself in my music."

The title track, "Essence," a sexy, breathy call for a lover, contains lyrics that are already getting attention. "Yeah, there's that one little word," Lucinda says with a mischievous grin, referring to a verse in which she sings, "Baby, sweet baby, can't get enough / Please come find me and help me get fucked up."

"When I'm writing, I don't think about the music industry," she says. "It does not enter into my world of art."

"Essence" is also the first single, and to appease radio stations, Lucinda created her own edited version before she could be forced to do so by higher-ups. "When I say that line, we just take the guitar and pump it up a bit. It gets really loud there, and you just don't hear me say it. It's a stupid thing to have to do, but this is a good compromise."

The songs of *Essence* are anything but compromises, covering styles and themes that range from loneliness and nostalgia to pure love and desire to religious ecstasy.

A gospel track, "Get Right with God," is raising even more eyebrows than "Essence." The churning, mesmerizing number is on the surface an ode to serpent handling. Because of lines such as "I would risk the serpent's bite / I would dance around with seven / I would kiss the diamond back / If I knew it would get me to heaven" people have already asked her if she has become a born-again Christian.

"I've been fascinated with snake-handlers a long time," she says. "I'm just an observer, but there is a subliminal connection with it all, and it's my own search within. I mean, I'm just like everybody else. I'm searching. . . . I've always been on a spiritual path. There are different paths, of course. Lately the path has been the Eastern religions, and I've been exploring Christianity."

She has recently taken up reading the Bible. Even though she was "more or less raised an agnostic," she says she was always taught to have respect for religion and the scriptures. Her family's liberal political outlook still accommodated a sense of ritual and tradition. Again, she thinks it was the best of both worlds. She treasures a gift her father recently gave to her: a collection of her Methodist grandfather's notes from his sermons and ministry.

"It's that duality thing again, " Lucinda says. "Religion and questioning. I've always had that in me, always had that curiosity about it all."

Simply enough, she wrote "Get Right with God" after seeing a roadside sign in Mississippi with those very words on it. With music and lyrics that perfectly capture the energy and passion of a Pentecostal church service, the song is in part her tribute to fundamentalist religion.

"I have such a respect for that form of religion," she says. "They're the last rebels in this country. The last true independents. I admire that level of passion and faith. To believe in something that strongly is just an honorable thing to me."

Country music is represented on the new album, too, particularly on the song "Reason to Cry." "I was actually thinking of that song as being a more R&B kind of song," she suggests, "but most of my favorite country songs are almost R&B based."

The album also contains "Out of Touch," which Lucinda calls her commentary on modern life. "It's my anti-computer song," she laughs. She raises a fist in the air and yells, "No e-mail!"

The opening tune is a melancholy, yearning piece that is somewhat light on lyrics (the title, "Lonely Girls," is repeated twenty times through the course of the song) but still manages to paint a devastating picture, especially with its final line, "I oughta know about lonely girls."

The most lyrically satisfying tune is "Bus to Baton Rouge," based on a childhood trip to her maternal grandparents' home. A narrative that Lucinda says is "almost a short story," it includes heartbreaking lines such as "There are other things I remember, as well / But to tell them would just be too hard."

Other songs on the album include "Are You Down," a rousing kiss-off with a vibe recalling the Doors' "Riders on the Storm"; the poetic "I Envy the Wind"; "Broken Butterflies," a dark, gothic narrative; and "Steal Your Love," which proves that Lucinda's voice has never sounded better.

"I do think the vocals sound really great on this record," she says. Although she is almost as well known for her trademark voice—as eclectic as Lucinda herself, her singing can capture everything from stark betrayal to unadulterated joy—she seems to have more faith in her writing abilities. When told that many of the nation's leading novelists and poets look up to her as a literary figure as much as a singer, Lucinda admits that she likes to think of herself that way. "I love words. I have always loved language."

The album was written and produced without a hitch. Lucinda was surprised by how well everything turned out. "I remember actually questioning myself . . . 'Wait a minute, this can't be . . . I can't have all these songs written . . . I haven't been working on them for two years.'" She says the songs dictate to her when they want to come out. "I get in this Zen-like state of mind where I just let things flow through me and open myself up. I spent days in that state, sitting at the kitchen table just writing, writing, writing."

Recorded in a Minneapolis studio, *Essence* was produced in just over five months. Bo Ramsey produced the basic tracks; Lucinda and Charlie Sexton—the former Texas teen sensation who has been Bob Dylan's guitarist the past couple years—ended up producing the final record. "Bo came down and laid out what led up to what the record is," she says, "and Charlie was really instrumental in coming in and helping with the overdubs and everything, taking the songs to the next level. He did little things that just took it over the next level, production-wise. He was so great to work with."

Back at her house, Lucinda is happy with her new album, happy with her producer, happy with life. Most of all, she seems incredibly passionate about everything. She points out various pieces of religious and folk art. "I mean, look at this. How can you deny its power and beauty?" she asks, holding up a devil mask with a snake wound about it. "There's a sense of defiance to it that makes me feel protected. Besides, these things emanate a nice energy to me."

Moving down the hallway, she picks up the Big Mouth Billy Bass and pushes the button so that the rubber fish will raise its head and sing "Don't Worry, Be Happy."

Dub Cornett says Lucinda is as strong as he has ever seen her. "She's healthy and mentally centered. She's in a good place in her life."

Lucinda sits down on her couch and takes in the room for a moment. Throughout the night I have noticed that she seems completely at home, no matter where she is. But here she is different, once more. She looks safe.

"Yeah, I am happy," she says.

But aren't all the great artists the ones who are miserable and in constant hunger? To create these yearning, searching songs, shouldn't she be chugging on a fifth of Jack Daniels, mourning the past, covering her face to cry pitifully into both hands?

"I write from a place of suffering, but in order to write, I have to be centered. I have to have a sense of well-being," she says. "To write a song, I have to go back to that inward place of pain. I go to that place a lot, and I come out of it to write about it. For subject matter, there's nothing better than suffering, but to turn that subject matter into a great song, you just have to have compassion and passion for life and a great imagination."

One look at the stamp of determination and hard work and satisfaction on Lucinda's face, and it is clear. She knows exactly what she is talking about.

Hearts on Fire

The Ties That Bind Buddy and Julie Miller Wind Deep into the Core of Faith and Soul

ND #23, September–October 1999

Bill Friskics-Warren

Our hearts are restless until they find their rest in thee.

ST. AUGUSTINE

How many times have you read a record review with the word "longing" in it? "The longing in her voice was palpable." "Few write with such longing." "On this wrenching ode to longing and loss . . ." The word is among the most shopworn modifiers in the rock-crit lexicon—a workhorse pressed into service anytime a lazy writer, or one with a deadline looming, needs shorthand to talk about the vaguest stirrings of desire.

But this isn't the sort of longing St. Augustine is talking about in the above passage from the *Confessions*. He isn't referring to mere restlessness, to an emotion that ebbs and flows with our moods, much as, say, boredom or wanderlust do. No, he is talking about a basic hunger, about a condition stitched into the fabric of our being, a striving for something more. Much more. Augustine is saying that people are by nature incomplete—broken, even—and that we can't find peace or fulfillment without an abiding connection to what transcends and grounds us. In his view, God.

The 1,600-year-old theology of the Bishop of Hippo doubtless doesn't leap to mind when people hear Buddy and Julie Miller's records. Chances are that most marvel at how no one, not even the couple's close friend and collaborator Emmylou Harris, sings the Millers' songs with the heart-in-throat conviction they do. Others wonder why the couple hasn't received wider recognition. Still others dwell on how much the duo sounds like Gram and Emmylou circa *Grievous Angel,* or, in their more Anglo-Celtic-derived moments, like Richard and Linda Thompson.

These, however, are but passing considerations. Writ large as it is in their music, it is the ontological gnawing that Augustine speaks of that strikes at the heart of who the Millers are—their faith, their relationship with each other, their sense of vocation.

Virtually every song in the couple's catalogue is born of this yearning. "I Call on You," "Take Me Back," "Out in the Rain," "My Love Will Follow You," "Don't Tell Me"—all burn with a seemingly infinite desire to connect. "I need something like a cure for my soul," moans Julie on the strung-out blues-rock of "I Need You," a song from her new album, *Broken Things* (HighTone). This plea turns to desperation when Buddy joins her on the lines "I need something bad and I need it now / I got something wrong with me / You better fix it 'cause I don't know how / I need you."

This craving suffuses more than just the Millers' lyrics. From the couple's ravaged harmonies, to Buddy's fevered guitar playing—his stabbing solo on "I Need You" smacks of the pangs of withdrawal—the Millers abandon themselves to this deep-rooted urge as if their lives depended on it. And to varying degrees, they do. Having no direction home nearly killed Julie. As it was, it literally drove her crazy, and easily could have driven the couple apart.

I Call On You

"All my life, even when I was, like, twelve years old, I was depressed," Julie explains. She is sitting with Buddy on the floor of the studio he built in the couple's turn-of-the-century Nashville home. "A question burned inside me, but I didn't know what it was. I just remember looking at people as if to say, 'Tell me something!' But I didn't know the question, and no one around me seemed restless inside or hungering.

"People at church would sing these songs about Jesus dying on the cross and giving his life, but they'd have this blank look on their faces," Julie continues. "I didn't know how weird it was, because you don't have much to measure things by when you're young. All I knew was that I was lonesome for someone to be inside my head and inside my soul with me."

Julie's heart was restless throughout her adolescence. She was born in Dallas in 1956 and grew up in Austin. "I had this longing, but nothing I did would make it go away," she says. "I tried to be a good Christian—I prayed, I read my Bible, I went to church—but I only got more depressed. Finally, when I was sixteen or seventeen, I said to God, 'You know I believe in you, but I don't know how to do this. So, goodbye. Whatever it takes to bring me back to you, do it.'"

Julie spent the next few years in and out of counseling. At one point she even checked herself into a mental hospital, but her feelings of unrest, which by this time bordered on despair, persisted. "I'm down to nothing but just this heartache √ That I keep carrying around inside," she later wrote on "Out in the Rain." Indeed, many of her songs seem to have come from this barren place.

Julie also met Buddy (born Steven Paul Miller in Fairborn, Ohio, in 1952) during this time—the mid-1970s. Buddy had just moved to Austin from Massachusetts. Fresh from "a little hippie band that traveled around in a school bus," he was auditioning for a spot in a combo called Rick Stein & the Alleycats. "Julie was the chick singer, and I was the almost-not guitar player," Buddy remembers. "She told them not to hire me."

Buddy and Julie later joined another local band, Partners in Crime, while Buddy also played with good friend Gurf Morlix in a country outfit that worked the Texas dance hall circuit. The couple's musical ecumenism was well suited to the easy mix of blues, country, rock, and border music that thrived in Austin at the time. But in 1980, when Buddy appeared to have a lock on a record deal, they moved to New Jersey, just outside New York City. Once there, Julie sank deeper into depression.

"I would stand onstage and pretend to be this sexy, cool chick singer, and about halfway through the set I would switch channels," she says. "I'd wanna go hide in a closet or under a staircase or look for a garbage can to crawl in." Small wonder she went on to write such lines as "When the lie comes down like a kiss on the lips / It's a fragile wire the memory trips / The taste is sweet but the kiss is unkind / There's a crawl space in my head that I find."

One night, when her way seemed unrelentingly dark, Julie cut her body repeatedly with a broken beer bottle, trying to kill herself. The attempt was enough to land her in the psychiatric ward, a place she good-naturedly refers to as "the shop." After raising hell about getting out—she and Buddy had a gig opening for Muddy Waters the following night—Julie got the attention of the hospital's medical director. Their conversation precipitated an epiphany.

"After I talked with the head psychiatrist for a while, he said, 'Julie, if you had three wishes today, what would they be?' Of course he wanted me to say, 'I wanna get out of here,' so that he knew that I really did want to get out. But I thought, 'Three wishes and I can have anything I want?' So I said, 'I really only want one thing. I just want to know what the truth is.'"

It was the question Julie had been asking her entire life. "I didn't recognize it at the time," she says, "but I think God took it as a prayer because he says if you search for the truth with all your heart you'll find it."

Not long after Julie got out of the hospital—just in time, by the way, to open for Waters—Buddy brought home a copy of Emmylou Harris's *Roses in the Snow* LP. "Buddy put on the record," remembers Julie, "and suddenly I heard Emmylou singing the words, 'Those who have strayed were sought by the master / He who once gave his life for the sheep / Out on the mountain still he is searching / Bringing them in, forever to keep.' [From the traditional tune "Green Pastures."]

"Something went through me," Julie continues. "It was like Jesus was this longing friend, father, lover of my soul, just missing and loving and waiting for me. And I just started crying.

"But I didn't say, 'Now I'll become a Christian.' Not yet anyway, because I didn't think I was good enough to be one. I did say I was sorry, though. Then God put my life before me with all those terrible scenes like I was in hell and said, 'You were never alone. I've always been here.' God said that, not audibly, of course, but in my heart."

My Love Will Follow You

Having found a measure of peace—as well as the object of a lifetime's worth of searching—Julie headed back to Texas, leaving Buddy, who had stuck with her all this time, to soldier on alone in New York. "She found a group of Christians one night, or a church or something," Buddy recalls. "We were playing at a club for two nights, and after we played the first night, she never came back. She left everything, including her stupid cat, with me."

"My car, my guitar, everything," blurts Julie, admitting that she wasn't exactly easy to live with at the time. "You have to understand: Buddy is a naturally good person and partner. Me, on the other hand, if it weren't for God, I would be bad news."

Buddy stayed busy in Julie's absence. He not only kept his band together (Shawn Colvin took Julie's place), but started playing with Kinky Friedman as well. Before long, though, he began feeling some unease of his own. "Julie and I kept in touch while she was in Texas, and over the next few weeks, I saw a change in her," Buddy explains. "It got me thinking, and I guess God started working on me a little bit."

In keeping with his more stolid nature, Buddy's conversion was less dramatic than the one undergone by Julie, who, from her infectious laughter to her soft spot for strays, is clearly the more pixilated of the two. "I'm more like the little wind-up toys that go in one direction," Buddy says. "All God had to do was pick me up and put me on another path. I left New York in a year, maybe a year and a half, with a different heart toward things. I tried—and still do try—to be more aware that there's something else going on than just me."

Finding their hearts' rest in God and each other, the Millers married in 1981, shortly after Buddy joined Julie (née Griffin) in Lindale, a small town in East Texas just outside Tyler. There the couple became active in a religious community that eventually took them to Seattle and, toward the end of the decade, the Bay Area. But something was missing: music. The Millers hadn't written songs or performed in public since leaving Texas. Hungering to do so, they struck out on their own and started playing again.

Shortly thereafter, T Bone Burnett heard one of Julie's demo tapes and expressed interest in becoming her producer. When the two met to explore the matter further, Burnett played Julie one of his recent projects, Peter Case's self-titled solo debut. "T Bone played this great song that Peter was singing, 'Three Days Straight,' and Victoria came in singing," recalls Julie, referring to Victoria Williams, who was then married to Case. "T Bone was so proud of his record and of Peter, but all I did was go, 'Who's that girl?' And he said, 'Oh, that's Victoria.' As soon as I heard her singing, I was like, 'I need to know that girl. How do I find her?'"

Julie soon caught up with Williams at Sacred Grounds, a Christian coffeehouse in San Francisco. "She came to hear me play, and we were instantly like soul sisters," says Williams, who had just released her 1987 debut, *Happy Come Home.* "I was like, 'Well, I was gonna do Hank Williams. I thought maybe I'd do a Luke the Drifter song.' And Julie was like, 'I love Luke the Drifter songs.' So we go into the kitchen and learn 'House of Gold' together, and she comes up and sings with me. We've been in close contact ever since. We just love each other."

For his part, Buddy put in a call to Jim Lauderdale, an old friend from his days in New York. Lauderdale had been in Los Angeles for several years, and, along with Lucinda Williams, Rosie Flores, and others, was the toast of the city's then-thriving "Town South of Bakersfield" roots-country scene. "Jim was doing really well," says Buddy. "He'd just finished a record Pete Anderson had produced. It was for CBS. It never came out, but it's great. Anyway, when Julie and I moved down there in '89, Jim took me on as his guitarist."

Lauderdale and Buddy played a lot of duo gigs together, a number of them in Nashville. After several trips east, Buddy suggested to Julie that they move to Music City. (Julie had by this time released a pair of albums for Myrrh, the pop-rock arm of the Christian-music label Word.)

"We were paying so much rent in L.A. that at the end of every month I was looking around for a guitar to sell, to make ends meet," Buddy explains. "And we didn't like it there anyway."

"We had never even talked about moving to Nashville," Julie recalls. "In fact, we always sort of snickered about Nashville. But Buddy said, 'Musically, we can do what we do anywhere, and if we move to Nashville, we could afford to buy a house.'"

Nothing Can Stop Me

When the Millers arrived in Nashville in 1993, they threw themselves into making music. Not exactly restless, they nevertheless had a sense of urgency about them: It was as if they could hardly contain the creativity that had built up inside them over the past decade. Buddy immediately set up Dogtown, the home studio in which he and Julie produced her third and fourth Christian-music albums, *Orphans and Angels* (Myrrh) and *Invisible Girl* (Street Level).

These albums, released in 1993 and '94, feature a number of people who would become the couple's closest friends and collaborators. Emmylou Harris duets with Julie on "All My Tears," a song written in memory of the late singer-songwriter Mark Heard that also appears on Harris's *Wrecking Ball* and again on Julie's new album. On drums is the late Donald Lindley, who also played with Lucinda Williams and Rosie Flores. Also in the credits are Victoria Williams and her husband, former Jayhawk Mark Olson; the two couples, along with Lauderdale, have occasionally toured and recorded together as the Rolling Creek Dippers.

Meanwhile, Buddy signed a deal with HighTone Records, and, in 1995, released his debut album, *Your Love and Other Lies.* Widely touted as the best hard-country record of the year, it established the Millers—Julie wrote or co-wrote seven tracks and sang on three—as one of Nashville's best-kept secrets.

Galvanized by fiddle, steel, and loads of Buddy's gutbucket guitar, *Your Love and Other Lies* compares favorably with such 1970s touchstones as Gary Stewart's *Out of Hand* and Joe Ely's *Honky Tonk Masquerade.* But as Buddy's cover of the Otis Redding hit "That's How Strong My Love Is" on his sterling 1997 album *Poison Love* proved, he is a more soulful singer than either Stewart or Ely. If anything, Buddy's brand of country-soul paints him as his generation's answer to Memphis legend Dan Penn (who, after a chance meeting with Buddy, wound up singing on *Your Love*).

The Penn analogy couldn't be more fitting, says Miller's longtime friend Gurf Morlix, best known for his decade-long tenure as guitarist in Lucinda Williams's band. "When I first started playing with Buddy back in late '75 or early '76, I was just amazed at how steeped in country he was," says Morlix. "I knew some Hank Williams and Jimmie Rodgers and some other stuff, but Buddy came in knowing every country song ever written. Not only that, he knew the R&B stuff as well. He heard it all growing up, and it just got ingrained. I'm sure the same thing happened with Dan Penn, or with Elvis, for that matter. Elvis listened to country music, gospel, and R&B—an amalgam of things. Some people put it all together better than others, and Buddy is definitely one of those people."

"Buddy and I were talking about Ralph Stanley," says Steve Earle, who, like Morlix, has collaborated extensively with the Millers. "I'm more of a Stanley Brothers fan than I am a Ralph Stanley fan. But Buddy's got a real thing about Ralph. He equates Ralph Stanley with Ray Charles. That's a real insight into Buddy and the way he thinks about music.

"I think Buddy Miller might be the best country singer working today," Earle continues. "It's one of my main barometers for how fucked up mainstream country music is right now that Buddy Miller's not automatically on country radio. It just amazes me. Not only that, but he does

R&B tunes amazingly well. I think that the best country singers could have sung Otis Redding songs and pulled it off. All my favorite ones could have anyway, and Buddy is my favorite country singer, period."

Even if nothing on Buddy's debut quite measures up to Dan Penn or Otis Redding at their finest, every song on the disc drips with feeling. "Hold On My Love," a duet with Harris, is particularly wrenching, as is the "River Deep, Mountain High" pledge of "My Love Will Follow You." Listening in retrospect, it is hard not to hear these songs in context of the anguish and hope the Millers must have felt during the separation that preceded their marriage in 1981. Then again, when, on the soaring bridge of the latter song, Buddy vows, "If you should go so far / That you cannot get back / You may not remember / But my heart will not lose track," he could just as easily be assuming the voice of God, in whose steadfast love he and Julie have found a resting place.

A covenant similar to that expressed in "My Love Will Follow You" also animates the Millers' musical partnership. Nowhere is this more evident than when they sing together. Much as family singers have done from the Carter Family on down, the couple's harmonies convey a rarely matched depth of intimacy. Witness "Take Me Back," an Appalachian waltz from *Blue Pony,* Julie's 1997 HighTone disc. When she and Buddy sing, "If my love was fire / It would burn this house down," they do much more than make the notes work. Their voices—his reedy, hers willowy, both exquisitely soulful—modulate much like partners who anticipate each other's moves on the dance floor.

"Buddy and Julie's phrasing is utterly unique," says Emmylou Harris of this unspoken communion. "They do tricky little things that sound so completely natural. I'm not sure if they work them out in advance or whether it's something about the way their phrasing comes together."

"Sometimes when we're at home by ourselves, we sing instead of talk," Julie says. "We jokingly sing about the cats and stuff, about whatever pops into our heads. But when Buddy joins in, he always knows the harmony, even on songs we've never sung before."

"I think it comes from growing up together musically," Buddy adds. "We know each other so well that we have a kind of telepathy going on. Whenever we do something together, it becomes something else. It's kind of like a third thing."

The Buddy System

It might seem strange, given the force of the intangible "third thing" of which Buddy speaks, that the Millers have thus far pursued separate recording careers. The extent to which they contribute to each other's albums, though, is evidence that their musical ties are uncommonly deep.

Consider the evolution of "Don't Tell Me," a heart-stopping ballad from Buddy's *Poison Love*. Julie wrote the song for her widowed uncle upon the death of his wife of some fifty years. "When I came up with that, I was singing into a little tape recorder," she says. "I didn't even like what I heard. But when Buddy was looking for songs for his record, he found it on a tape and liked it. I had written it off, but after hearing him do it, I thought, 'Wow, that is a good song!'"

"Good" understates the matter considerably. Taking the notions of passion and commitment to metaphysical extremes, "Don't Tell Me" updates "That's How Strong My Love Is," rendering palpable the conviction that love conquers all—even the grave.

"I discovered the song while going through some old tapes," Buddy says, shaking his head in amazement. "It was just two verses. Julie probably made them up on the spot. I couldn't believe it. It would have been lost."

"That stuff happens all the time," Julie says. "Just this morning, Buddy's on the phone in the next room, and I'm in here struggling with this little tune that's running through my head. He's only heard me play a few bars, but as soon as he hangs up the phone, he goes, 'What was that?' And he makes me tape it. It's incredible. He's so appreciative of what I'm sitting here having no confidence about. I don't think many people enjoy that kind of relationship."

Victoria Williams agrees, and she should know: Williams and her husband Mark Olson enjoy much the same musical and marital rapport as the Millers do. "Traditionally, people in show business have a hard time being married, at least that's what you hear," Williams observes. "But I think if you keep your priorities in line, it works out really great. Mark is just such a wonderful person. He's so unselfish and caring, and I think Buddy is the same way. It's so funny. When Mark and I finally got together, Julie would say, 'You found your Buddy.'"

That said, the Millers' creative partnership isn't without its share of conflict. "Working together in the studio can get pretty intense," Buddy admits. "Sometimes Julie believes there should be a lot more telepathy going on than there is. And that makes her angry."

"It does. It does," she confesses, letting loose a piercing laugh.

"Our musics are two different things," Buddy adds, contrasting his country-soul approach with Julie's more eclectic sensibility, one that sets the darker hues of country, blues, and Anglo-Celtic folk music against a rock backbeat. "But we really do try to go to each other's place when we're working together. When we're making my records, for example, Julie tries to get as . . ."

"I'll hick up for you anytime, honey," she gibes, finishing Buddy's thought.

"I don't always get Julie's rock and pop stuff," Buddy continues. "I mean I wouldn't be playing it on my records, although my stuff has rocked a bit more lately. But your stuff hasn't gotten any more country," he chides, looking directly at Julie.

Maybe not, but it sounds as though Buddy's sawdust-and-steel proclivities will set the tone for the couple's next studio project, the duo album the Millers have been talking about making for at least two years. "It's gonna be Buddy's choice, so we're gonna country out," concedes Julie. "We've got all the songs ready to go."

The couple's duo record will have to wait, though, until Buddy finishes his third solo album for HighTone, *Cruel Moon* (due in October). Besides a bunch of new originals, the record will include covers of Gene Pitney's "I'm Gonna Be Strong," Paul Kennerley's "Love Match" (with Steve Earle), and the Staple Singers' "It's Been a Change." Buddy also duets with Emmylou Harris on the mandolin-sweetened title cut, while Julie sings on several songs and, on one unearthly track, lays down a jungle groove on drums.

After delivering the *Poison Love* masters to HighTone in early August, Buddy headed straight into rehearsals for a tour with Harris and Linda Ronstadt (supporting their new collaborative album, *Western Wall*). He and Julie will play some East Coast and Midwest dates with Dave Alvin and Rick Shea later this fall.

Such wall-to-wall scheduling is hardly new for the Millers, particularly for Buddy, who has been in demand ever since the couple moved to Nashville six years ago. Buddy has picked and sung in the touring bands of Harris, Lauderdale, and Earle. He has produced albums for Greg Trooper, Spyboy, and the Vigilantes of Love. He also played a pivotal role in the making of Lucinda Williams's *Car Wheels on a Gravel Road*.

Not only that, but at least a dozen acts have recorded the Millers' songs, including Harris and jazz singer Jimmy Scott ("All My Tears"); Brooks & Dunn ("My Love Will Follow You"); Suzy Bogguss and Garth Brooks ("Take Me Back"); Lee Ann Womack ("Don't Tell Me"); George Ducas ("I'm Pretending"); Cry Cry Cry ("By Way of Sorrow"); the Williams Brothers ("Broken Things"); and the Dixie Chicks, who do "Hole In My Head" on their new album, *Fly*.

I Still Cry

As these collaborations attest, the Millers have established a strong sense of community since moving to Nashville. But where Buddy's efforts in this regard tend to be concrete—touring, playing, and producing with a variety of people—Julie's are more mystical and spiritual. Her means of connecting with others—not just people, but all creatures ("Be kind to children and animals," she urges in the notes to her HighTone debut)—is through her singular gift for empathy.

"Dancing Girl," from *Blue Pony,* is about a child who is being sexually abused by her father. "All the Pieces of Mary" portrays a homeless woman who suffers from mental illness. "Letters to Emily" deals with a father who is cut off from his only daughter. These aren't exercises in fiction. Each song vividly sketches someone Julie knows or has met. And in each case, the music, with its prevalence of minor chords and aching arrangements, conveys her anguish over the suffering of the person or persons in question.

The songs on her new album are no different. "Maggie" plumbs the misery, and resiliency, of a woman who was orphaned at six. "Two Soldiers," an adaptation of the traditional ballad "The Boston Boy" (sung with Emmylou Harris), stems from Julie's discovery of all the blood that was once shed in the Millers' neighborhood, the site of several Civil War battles. And the shimmering "I Still Cry" mourns the death of Donald Lindley. Julie dedicates the album to Lindley, his widow, Kathy, and their son Jesse, whose painting of his father as an angel drummer adorns the CD booklet.

So attuned is Julie to the suffering in her midst that, for her, even nature mirrors its presence. "I know why the river runs / To a place somewhere far away / And I know why the sky is cryin' / When there aren't any words to say," she sings, bemoaning the absence of a loved one in "I Know Why the River Runs." At seemingly every turn, Julie's songs achieve a level of catharsis rarely heard in these irony-clad times. It is as if she is channeling her former restlessness, and the heartache it gave her, into compassion for the sorrow of others. And more often than not, her vocals—as gauzy yet piercing in their way as those of Delta bluesman Skip James—make those feelings so real they are scary.

"That's her gift," says Victoria Williams, referring to Julie's seemingly limitless capacity for empathy. "When she wrote 'All My Tears' after Mark Heard died, that came straight from her heart."

"I am blessed with an ability to feel for people," Julie admits. "I do feel it."

Not just for people, Steve Earle says, but for animals as well. "Julie is just this incredible and mysterious creature," Earle explains. "We were late for an airplane, trying to get to a land mine benefit in D.C., and everybody was there except her. It was me, Buddy, Emmy[lou Harris], all her band and crew. Julie was coming into the airport, and there was a bird that had flown into the building and was running into glass and stuff trying to get out. Julie caught the bird and took it outside. There absolutely wasn't any way in her mind that we were gonna get on the airplane until that bird was taken care of. Animals gravitate toward Julie, especially wounded ones and those that are lost. And I think there's a reason for that. She has a connection to things that are intimidated by their surroundings, and she relates to that. She responds to it."

What makes Julie's gift more remarkable is that she lives with fibromyalgia, a disabling condition that afflicts sufferers with chronic pain and fatigue—in Julie's case, often making it agonizing for her to sing.

Which isn't to suggest that suffering is necessarily redemptive, much less that Julie has had to go through hell to be a better person. No, sometimes suffering just makes people bitter—or worse, kills them. Yet as theologian John Mogabgab writes, there remains the possibility "that our hearts, wounded by the boundlessness of human agony, grow tender and alert to the wounds of others. Then our wounds become portals of vulnerability through which the pain of others can enter our lives, awakening us to a more generous sense of our common humanity and discovering in turn refuge, consolation, and healing."

Such is certainly the case with Julie Miller.

"Julie has something to say, and, musically, Buddy helps her say it," Gurf Morlix observes. "She's found a calling. She can write songs that make people weep openly. Not everyone can do that."

As an example, Morlix cites "Broken Things," the song Julie wrote after violence erupted in Northern Ireland in 1993, killing twenty-nine people and injuring hundreds of others.

In the liner notes to her new album, Julie not only dedicates "Broken Things" to the families who live with that loss, but also says the song is for "all whose hearts are broken things." But "Broken Things" could just as easily sum up her own journey to this point, especially the past twenty-plus years with Buddy. It is hard to conclude otherwise when, in a fragile, prayerful voice, she sings, "Well I heard that you make old things new / So I give these pieces all to you / If you want it you can have my heart."

St. Augustine could hardly have said it better.

Sweet Emotion

Rising from Down Under with Her Family's Guidance and Her Heroes' Admiration, Kasey Chambers Is on the Brink of Becoming Alt-Country's Brightest Star

ND #37, JANUARY–FEBRUARY 2002

Geoffrey Himes

"This is a song," Kasey Chambers tells the audience at Wolf Trap, "that I wrote about all the radio stations around the world who play Britney Spears and not me."

She chuckles at her own joke. The very idea of this Australian singer-songwriter competing for airplay and audience with the Pepsi commercial icon is amusing—it is like Steve Earle complaining about Puff Daddy, or Ichiro Suzuki complaining about Tiger Woods. They are playing different ballgames.

Besides, on this night Chambers has achieved something Spears will never enjoy. It is June 1, 2001, just three days before Chambers' twenty-fifth birthday, and she is opening for two of her biggest heroes, Lucinda Williams and Richard Thompson, at the National Park Service's open-sided, cathedral-like pavilion in the Virginia suburbs of Washington, D.C.

Chambers's levity soon fades as she launches into the song, which is the centerpiece of her second solo album, *Barricades and Brickwalls,* to be released January 29 on Warner Bros. Maybe she is addressing radio programmers, maybe she is addressing a would-be lover, but there is a very real ache in her voice when she sings the opening lines:

> Am I not pretty enough?
> Is my heart too broken?
> Do I cry too much?
> Am I too outspoken?
> Don't I make you laugh?
> Should I try it harder?
> Why do you see right through me?

This song, "Not Pretty Enough," will prove the highlight of a long, wonderful evening. As good as Thompson and Williams will be later on, they have little left to prove, sailing through their sets with the assurance and mastery they have earned. For Chambers, though, this is all still very new—playing for thousands of people, sharing the stage with her heroes—and she pushes herself into risks that pay off with breathtaking results.

She is not nearly the songwriter that Thompson and Williams have become, but very few are, and at twenty-five she is a good songwriter with the potential to get much better. Furthermore, she is already a better singer than Thompson or Williams ever have been or ever will be. Not only does she have a lovely, silky soprano, but she also has the same catch-in-the-throat quality as Judy Garland, Dinah Washington, Bonnie Raitt, and Julie Miller. Her voice can be so emotionally transparent that nothing is held back, and so strong that it can survive the consequences.

And Chambers has that rarest of vocal gifts: the ability to convey two contradictory emotions at once. When she sings the line "Am I not pretty enough?" at Wolf Trap, there is a suggestion of doubt, as if she weren't sure if she was attractive enough to hold a man's loyalty. But there is also a suggestion that she knows she is pretty and can't understand why the man can't recognize it.

Standing onstage at Wolf Trap, Chambers is pretty, though in an unconventional, bohemian way. She wears a purple velvet jumper over black denim jeans and under a sheer, long-tailed black blouse. Her long brown hair is stacked in an unstable, off-kilter pile atop her head, a thin silver hoop pierces one eyebrow, and a silver stud juts through her bottom lip. But her round, softened face, with its generous mouth and wide eyes, has the same appealing openness as her voice.

The combination of that face and that question—"Am I not pretty enough?"—makes you wonder what kind of man would be foolish enough to walk away from her. And the heart-grabbing effect of that voice makes you wonder what kind of radio programmer could ignore her. The song works on both levels.

"The two meanings were intentional," she says a few weeks later from her home in Avoca Beach, New South Wales. "I didn't want to write a song where people go, 'Boy, she's a bitter person because her career's not as successful as she'd like.' Because it's not like that. So I wanted to write it so it could be a love song, too. I was aware it was coming out that way as I was writing. It made sense that way, and there's a bit of truth in that approach, too.

"Most importantly, I didn't want it to be a whining song or an 'I'm pissed off at you' song. It's saying, 'I'm proud of who I am.' And that applies to both interpretations. I'm proud that I'm outspoken. I'm proud that I can cry in front of people. If these are the reasons you don't love me—or that you won't play me on the radio—that's OK, because I'm happy with the way I am. If it means I'll lose you as a lover or as a radio station, that's OK, because I don't care.

"It doesn't bother me so much when it happens to me," she adds, "but I can't stand it when I see it happen to other people. So many talented people don't get the respect they deserve, and so many people without much talent are hugely successful. When Patty Griffin records one of the best albums I've ever heard, and her record label won't even put it out, that annoys me. When Matthew Ryan gets dropped from his label, that pisses me off.

"So when I ask those questions—'Am I not pretty enough? Am I too outspoken?'—I already know the answers. The answers to all those questions are yes. I'm not bitter about that, really; I don't lose sleep over it. To be honest, I don't want to be a star, I don't want to be famous; I want to be successful enough that I can do music full-time. In twenty years, I want to be Lucinda; I don't want to be Shania Twain. Lucinda can still walk down the street, but she can sell out 2,000-seaters."

Chambers may not be a threat to Twain in the States, but the self-deprecating young woman is already a star at home in Australia. Her family's group, the Dead Ringer Band, enjoyed a #1 country single and won several Best Country Group awards. When Chambers's solo debut, *The Captain,* was named album of the year by the Country Music Association of Australia last year, Chambers accepted the trophy from Slim Dusty, the "Hank Williams of Australian country music," as she puts it.

They made quite a pair, the wrinkled patriarch in his trademark floppy hat and the young woman with her spiky dark hair and multiple piercings. It was as if Ani DiFranco had accepted a CMA award from Ralph Stanley.

In fact, the buzz over the event stirred such interest in Australia's non-country market that Chambers's album climbed into the pop Top 10 (it had already topped the country charts). Then she surprised everyone—even herself—by being named overall best female vocalist at last October's ARIA Awards, Australia's equivalent of the Grammys. It was an upset as surprising and as meaningful as Bonnie Raitt's sweep of the 1990 Grammy Awards and Alison Krauss's sweep of the 1995 CMA Awards.

It helps to remember that Australia's country music industry is tiny, analogous to the blues community in the United States. The old-timers cling to a peculiarly homegrown form of country music—the bush balladeers such as Slim Dusty, Tex Morton, Buddy Williams, and Eric Bogle, who sing about Australian events and places in the style of Jimmie Rodgers, the Carter Family, the Weavers, and Hank Williams. The newcomers mimic mainstream Nashville tastes, preferring Garth Brooks, Shania Twain, and their Australian knockoffs.

Before Chambers came along, there wasn't a real alternative-country scene in Australia, though rootsy folk-rockers such as Paul Kelly, Uncle Bill, Archie Roach, and Vika and Linda would fall under that umbrella here in the States. The key figure is Kelly, a gifted, populist roots-rocker in the vein of Bruce Springsteen, Dave Alvin and Steve Earle. Always a critics' favorite, he existed on the commercial margins until 1997's *Songs from the South: Paul Kelly's Greatest Hits* unexpectedly topped Australia's pop charts.

"He's just a very inspiring artist," Chambers says, "and a lovely guy. It's very easy to get lost in a Paul Kelly song, for he's such a good storyteller; he has a way of painting a picture like no one else. I've worked with him a lot at home, and it's amazing to watch an artist like that every night, where every song just blows you away.

"When I wrote 'I Still Pray' for this new album, I knew I wanted to do it as a duet with Paul. Also, there's a Paul Kelly tribute album in the works, and I get to sing my favorite song of his, 'Everything's Turning to White,' which I sometimes do in my live show.

"Paul's not really a country artist, but has a real folky, country feel to his songs. But if you tell people in Australia that he's country, they'll laugh at you because they think country is hats and hay bales. That's why we have our own Garth rip-offs and Faith rip-offs. Fortunately, we still have some of the original bush balladeers like Slim Dusty, who has done some amazing things with Australiana. I actually sing on his one-hundredth album."

This year, four Australian natives found themselves on the U.S. country charts. Jamie O'Neal and Sherrie Austin had both moved to the United States without any involvement in Australia's country scene. Keith Urban had enjoyed success Down Under, but he too moved to the States. Only Kasey Chambers invaded the American charts without abandoning her home.

Nothing could be more Australian than Chambers's life story. She was just three weeks old in 1976 when her father, Bill Chambers, packed up Kasey, her brother, Nash, and their mother, Diane, and took them fox hunting on the Nullarbor Plain. It was supposed to be a six-month adventure, but Bill did so well catching foxes and rabbits and selling their skins that the family went hunting seven months a year for the next ten years.

Larger than the state of Colorado, the Nullarbor stretches for miles upon miles of reddish dirt and blue bushes. It is so flat that you can see more than fifty miles in any direction, and it is so deserted that you are unlikely to see another house or vehicle in all that area.

Nullarbor is Latin for "no trees," and there is not much water either. The only towns are railroad sidings, and those have only five or six houses apiece. The summers are unbearable, but in the winter the Chambers family would turn off the dirt roads, dodging limestone caverns and giant wombat holes.

Diane and the kids would get up in the morning, gather firewood, and do several hours of home-schooling. Then Bill would get up and stretch the previous night's fox skins on pegboards to dry. After dinner, after the psychedelic, big-sky sunsets, they would all climb into the cruiser again and go searching for the nocturnal foxes. Diane would drive, and Bill would stand up through the hole in the cab roof with a spotlight and a rifle as they bounced over rocks and bushes.

"We would leave in April, which is the fall in Australia, and stay till October," Kasey recalls. "We were in a different place almost every night. Our beds were set up in a Toyota Land Cruiser, and our stuff was in a trailer. My brother and I helped shoot rabbits and turkeys. When we weren't hunting, we'd sit around the campfire and eat rabbits, turkeys, pigeons, and kangaroos. Then my dad would get out his guitar and we'd sing.

"We'd sing church hymns and Australian bush ballads by Slim Dusty, Buddy Williams, and Tex Morton. But mostly we sang American country songs by Jimmie Rodgers, the Carter Family, Emmylou Harris, and Gram Parsons. Those singers weren't real well known in Australia, but for some reason my parents loved them, and sang them all the time, so I thought everyone knew them.

"Growing up in the outback provided a good grounding for what I'm doing now," she adds. "We didn't have TV or videos or toys, so all our attention was devoted to music and day-to-day survival."

This is the Isolation-Bubble Theory of Pop Culture Development. Sometimes artists are better off being quarantined from contemporary music so they don't face the temptation of imitating what is already out there. Instead, they can come up with something so old or so new that when they finally emerge from isolation, they sound like no one else.

It worked for Prince as he grew up in the R&B-deprived environs of Minneapolis with no clues but his Sly & the Family Stone 45s. It worked for Brian Wilson as he holed up in his bedroom with his Four Freshmen records and invented a new vocal music for surfing, a sport he never tried. And it worked for the Chambers family as they sang Townes Van Zandt songs out on the Nullarbor Plain.

After ten years of this nomadic lifestyle, in 1986 the family settled back in Southend (a small town on the South Australia coast halfway between Melbourne and Adelaide) so the two children could go to a regular high school. Bill went back to fishing, but he didn't give up on the family sing-alongs. Instead of singing around a desert campfire, the parents and kids began singing in local pubs as the Dead Ringer Band. Bill played Dobro, banjo, mandolin, and guitar; Diane played bass; Kasey and Nash played rhythm acoustic guitar; and everyone sang. Eventually Nash took up the drums and studio engineering. Before long, the family was back on the road as touring musicians.

"We didn't have a record contract," Kasey remembers. "They just got itchy feet and wanted to play music. My brother had already left school, and I dropped out at fourteen. We took all our music gear, stuffed it into the same trailer we had used on the Nullarbor, and hit the road. Most nights we slept under the stars in our sleeping bags; we didn't know people stayed in motels. It was pretty much like when we were hunting."

The family's first recordings were two cassette-only releases credited to Bill Chambers: *Sea Eagle* (1987) and *Kindred Spirit* (1991). The first Dead Ringer Band release was a 1992 four-song EP, *A Matter of Time*. The Dead Ringer Band eventually released four full-length albums for Massive Records in Australia, and though they haven't been released in the United States, they are available as imports from companies such as Miles of Music.

Their 1993 debut disc, *Red Desert Sky,* is underwhelming. The arrangements are a rather clumsy imitation of 1950s American country, and the original songs are unsubtle celebrations of living in rural Australia, where if you are "Born in the Country" under a "Red Desert Sky," you can feel the "Power of the Land" as you drive down the "Road to Nowhere." The recording does offer the earliest compositions by Kasey, who was seventeen at the time.

The band had made a quantum leap forward by the time it released its sophomore album, *Home Fires,* in 1995. Diane Nash had turned the bass duties over to professionals; Bill, Nash, and Kasey had matured as both singers and songwriters; and the arrangements were in a more comfortable, Flying Burrito Brothers vein.

The eight strong originals are mixed with astute covers of songs written by Gram Parsons, Lucinda Williams, and such Australian figures as Darren Coggan and Pat Drummond. The family-penned "Australian Son" topped the country charts for seven weeks, and nineteen-year-old Kasey anticipated the character of her solo albums on the autobiographical "Gypsy Bound."

If you are only going to buy one Dead Ringer Band album, however, get 1997's *Living in the Circle.* Clearly more comfortable in the studio, producers Bill and Nash Chambers fashion a crisp, flexible sound that recalls Emmylou Harris and the Hot Band. There are superb covers of Townes Van Zandt's "If I Needed You," Maria McKee's "Am I the Only One," and the Carter Family's "No Depression." Bill shows off his honky-tonk roots on "That's What Makes a Broken Heart," and Nash emerges as a convincing singer-songwriter on "Halfway to Sydney" and "Life's Little Mysteries."

But *Living in the Circle* makes it clear that Kasey was the Dead Ringer Band's most valuable asset. At twenty-one, she had honed her voice into the dramatic instrument it is today. And her songwriting—especially on "Things Don't Come Easy," "The Last Generation," and "Already Gone"—had found the simple, emotionally naked approach that proved the perfect vehicle for her voice. Critics and fans were soon clamoring for a solo album.

Before that could happen, though, the Dead Ringer Band sought to escape its contract with Massive Records. After some tense negotiations, the settlement called for one more album, and the quartet delivered *Hopeville* in 1998. It was an album devoted entirely to covers of American country and alt-country songs by the likes of Steve Earle, Jimmie Rodgers, Rodney Crowell, John Prine, Nanci Griffith, Michelle Shocked, Fred Rose, and Lucinda Williams. Though it was done quick and cheap to get out of the contract, it features Kasey's marvelous vocals on some terrific songs. In 2000, Massive released the eighteen-song anthology *Till Now: The Best of the Dead Ringer Band*.

Between the second and third albums, an American stumbled upon the Dead Ringer Band. John Lomax III, the nephew and grandson of legendary folklorists Alan Lomax and John Avery Lomax, respectively, formerly managed Townes Van Zandt and Steve Earle. He had just started writing a country-music column for a British magazine, and in 1996 was running a record export business when Massive Records gave him some CDs by Australian country acts.

Lomax was skeptical. No overseas performer had ever made much of an artistic dent in country music, and the only Australians who had found much commercial success were Olivia Newton-John and Diana Trask. But Lomax pushed the Dead Ringer Band's *Home Fires* into the CD player of his 1986 Cadillac. Before the first song was finished, he was a convert, whooping and singing along as he barreled through the Tennessee countryside at eighty miles an hour. The moment would change his life.

"It was like the first night I heard Townes Van Zandt in 1966," he recalls. "As soon as I heard Townes, I said, 'Here's a guy who has it all.' And the Dead Ringers had it all. They had all the things Nashville has forgotten: honesty, purity, simplicity, really lovely harmonies. It was not perfect—it was rough and ragged—but it was so right.

"You could tell this was music done by people whose hearts were in the right place, who were just doing it for the music. Though it was obviously influenced by American music, they were untouched by the Nashville penchant for professionalism. It reminded me of the Carter Family. And it was so unexpected. I was expecting something dreadful, and what I heard was celestial."

Lomax signed on as the group's American manager and made the first of an eventual seven trips to Australia. He brought the group to Nashville several times, almost landing a deal with Almo Sounds and then another with Atlantic Nashville. Both of those promising prospects fell through, even as the band's conflicts with Massive grew worse.

The accumulating pressures threatened to tear the family and the band apart. Bill left the family in 1998 to live with Audrey Auld, a Tasmanian-born singer-songwriter whose debut EP, *Audrey*, he had produced earlier that year. Later that year, the new couple, credited as Bill & Audrey, released an impressive trad-country duet album, *Looking Back to See,* on

Australian label Reckless Records. Diane recovered by taking a seven-week trip through Africa with Kasey.

The Dead Ringer Band went into limbo, but gradually the pieces came back together. Bill and Diane found a way to be friends if not spouses. The focus shifted to Kasey's solo career, with Bill and Nash playing in her band and Diane handling the merchandise. Once the band was out of its Massive contract, EMI Australia signed the Dead Ringers as a group and Kasey as a solo artist. Lomax shifted his focus to a U.S. solo deal for Kasey. As he did, he passed out Dead Ringer albums to musicians, journalists, and A&R execs.

Steve Earle, one recipient, called her "the best female hillbilly singer I've heard in a long, long time." Evelyn Shriver, who had just launched a new Nashville office of Asylum Records, eventually offered Kasey a U.S. solo deal. Lucinda Williams heard the Dead Ringer Band's "Things Don't Come Easy" and said, "I knew within four lines . . . that it was a great song, and I was crying before it was over."

"Lucinda has been the biggest role model I've ever had," Chambers confesses. "I first saw her live in '89 when she came to Australia with Rosanne Cash and Mary Chapin Carpenter. My dad is a big Rosanne fan, but I'd never heard of Lucinda or Chapin. When I heard Lucinda sing the first few lines, it sounded so different that I didn't know if it was really, really good or really, really bad.

"But a few lines later, I said, 'Oh my god, this is the best thing I've ever heard.' I loved the way she got onstage and just sang. She wasn't trying to prove anything; she was just doing what she was born to do. I immediately went out, bought her album, and listened to it again and again. Before that, I had just listened to music because my dad liked it. I had liked it, too, but this was an album I had discovered on my own, so it was my own.

"My manager, John, knew her and sent her an album. She sent a note back to me saying she liked it and if I were ever in Nashville, we should catch up. Now, whenever I'm in Nashville, we go out for drinks and she takes me out to see bands. She gives me the big pep talks whenever I see her. She always says, 'Do what you do and don't let anyone sway you into doing anything that doesn't set well with you.'"

Williams sings harmony on the *Barricades and Brickwalls* track "On a Bad Day," and she took Chambers along as an opening act on a five-week tour during May and June that included the stop at Wolf Trap. And Williams's influence is all over Chambers's two solo albums.

"She got me into songwriting," Chambers says. "It wasn't until I got *Sweet Old World* that I started taking songwriting seriously. The beauty of Lucinda's songwriting is she says things in a song the same way she says them to you in conversation.

"Matthew Ryan is one of my favorite songwriters, but he's the opposite. I love his songs, but I have no idea what he's talking about. I know

Matthew quite well, and the way he writes is not the way he talks to you. But when Lucinda talks to you, it often sounds like a line out of one of her songs."

The breakthrough song for Chambers was "Cry Like a Baby." She kicks off most of her shows with this song from her first solo album, and the Wolf Trap date was no exception. The midtempo folk-rock number has the conversational lyrics of a Williams song, but the melody is sweeter and the vocal less guarded.

One moment she declares, "I'm just a kid," with a wide-eyed innocence to back it up, but the next moment she insists, "I'm not much like my generation," with a stubborn defiance. And when she adds, "I don't hide my pain to save my reputation . . . I still cry like a baby," her miraculous voice makes it a statement of both weakness and strength, implying that she is often overwhelmed by emotions but that she's brave enough to let it show in public.

"That's the song that best describes me," Chambers acknowledges. "I wrote it one night backstage at a Dead Ringer Band gig, and as soon as I wrote it, I knew I wanted it to be the first song and the first single on my first solo album. I do still cry like a baby. I have some very strong parts of my personality and some very weak sides, too."

Tears are a recurring image in Chambers's songs. "These pines . . . won't carry me home when I cry," she sings on "These Pines" (from *The Captain*). "Do I cry too much?" she asks in "Not Pretty Enough." On "The Nullarbor Song," also from the new album, she declares, "If I'm not here in the morning, I'll cry a river of tears." On "I Still Pray," the duet with Paul Kelly, she sings, "I still cry for Baby Jesus." On "Million Tears," she sings, "Take these tears, wash your skin / I'm having trouble breathing since you walked in."

"It's because I cry a lot," she admits. "It's that simple. I'm a really emotional person. I'm not a down and depressing person, and even when I do cry, it's not always because I'm sad. I cry when I hear a really good concert, not because I'm sad but because it's hitting somewhere inside me. I cry at movies. I cry the first time I play a song.

"To hold those things in is unhealthy; it's good to express those things in any way you can. If I wanted to stop it from happening, I could, but I figure, 'What the hell?' Sometimes I do the whining crying, and then I have to grab hold of myself and say, 'What are you doing, you idiot?' I hate that, when people cry to get attention or because they want something. But if you cry without expecting anything in return, because something affects you emotionally, that's fine."

"Cry Like a Baby" did become the first song and the first single on *The Captain,* which was released by EMI Australia in 1999 and Asylum/Warner Bros. in 2000. The title track (which featured backing vocals by Julie Miller) became controversial despite its insinuating melody and haunting vocal. Some feminists objected to the chorus lyrics that told a man, "If I tread upon your feet, you just say so / 'Cause you're the captain, I am no one / I tend to feel as though I owe one to you."

"I can understand why people think it's politically incorrect," Chambers says, "but it wasn't about that at all. In fact, it wasn't about wanting someone to overshadow me; it was about me not wanting to overshadow someone else.

"I wrote *The Captain* as a thank-you song to a guy. He wasn't a boyfriend at the time, though I had a four-year relationship with him later on. He was shy and always hanging around in the background. He was my best friend, and he was always coming to interviews and gigs where the spotlight was on me. I was saying, 'Thank you for coming along; someday I want to switch roles so you can be out front and I can be in the background.'"

Kasey's new American label brought her to Fan Fair in Nashville in June 2000, where she stood out like a wildflower on the well-tended lawn of mainstream country acts. This past spring, she opened a string of dates for Robert Earl Keen. In March, she did two shows at the South by Southwest Music Conference, including an outdoor set for several thousand people at Austin's Waterloo Park.

The second of those SXSW dates took place on St. Patrick's Day inside a white-canvas tent behind Yard Dog, a folk-art gallery. The tent was packed shoulder-to-shoulder and toe-to-heel with skeptical bizzers and eager fans, all eager to find out if the buzz about this young Australian had any substance. Chambers herself was giddy with excitement, but as soon as she unleashed her voice on "Cry Like a Baby," she had the crowd in the palm of her hand.

She did only five songs from *The Captain,* preferring to fill out the show with some of her favorite American songs, including Tim Carroll's "If I Could," Fred Eaglesmith's "Freight Train," Woody Guthrie's "Do Re Mi," and Ella Mae Morse's "Cow Cow Boogie." When she did Lucinda Williams's "Changed the Locks," Williams's former guitarist and producer Gurf Morlix was among those in the crowd nodding his approval.

Chambers also did her now infamous but unrecorded parody of a commercial country song: "Don't look up my dress unless you mean it," she belted out with as much twang as she could muster. "Don't put your hand upon my thigh. Before you stick that in, you better clean it. I hope I go to Texas when I die."

She also introduced two songs from *Barricades and Brickwalls,* which was in the midst of being recorded at the time. "The Nullarbor Song" was an autobiographical number about her years in the desert with her family. If that song recalled the material from *The Captain,* the new album's title track (and leadoff tune) was much different. A fierce rocker in the spirit of Williams's "Hot Blood," it is a warning to a skittish male that "iron bars and big old cars won't run me out of town / I'll be damned if you're not my man before the sun goes down."

"That track is a lot heavier than anything I've done before," Chambers agrees. "I explore a lot more styles of music on this album. On the other side of the scale is 'A Little Lonesome,' which is a lot more country than I've ever gone before. We've learned how to let the songs go where they have to go.

"The first album was about my family; this one is more about where I am right now, and what I'm becoming. I meant everything I said on the first album, but those songs were written from the viewpoint of a seventeen- to nineteen-year-old. These songs were written from the perspective of a twenty-four-year-old, so they have to be different."

The album includes another aggressive country-rocker, "Runaway Train," with howling harmonies by Buddy Miller. "Million Tears" is a moody, chamber-pop ballad with treated guitar, drum brushes, and Matthew Ryan's hushed harmonies. The album's only cover song, Gram Parsons's "Still Feelin' Blue," is a lively two-step that kicks off with a fiddle solo. "Ignorance," a hidden track at the end of the disc, is her first protest song, a critique of her own political apathy.

"I was doing an interview in L.A. after one of those high-school shootings in America," she explains, "and as the interviewer walked away, he said, 'If you're not pissed off, you're not paying attention.' And I realized that I'm not pissed off, that I'm just coasting through life, just having a good time. Part of it is living in Australia, where we don't have half the crime that the U.S. has or the hunger that Cambodia has or the disease that Africa has.

"I realized that I'm in a position where I can help or at least call attention to the problems. But I didn't want to write a song saying, 'All you people are horrible; stop doing this.' It was more about me. Why am I like this? I wanted to tell people, 'Don't be embarrassed that you're like this, because we all block things out on TV. I was like this as well, and there was a day when I woke up, so you can wake up, too.' It's not a preaching song; it's more of a confessional, 'This is what I'm doing wrong, and this is what I'm going to do about it.'

"When I first played the song for my boyfriend, I warned him, 'This is the saddest song I've ever written.' After I played it, he said, 'That's the most positive song you've ever written.'"

Barricades and Brickwalls was released in Australia in August. It was soon followed by the publication of *Red Desert Sky: The Amazing Saga of the Dead Ringer Band,* a biography by John Lomax III. Lomax, who stepped down as the group's U.S. manager in June, draws on hours of interviews with the band to describe the years of hunting on the Nullarbor, the years of scuffling in pubs, and the eventual triumph of awards and Kasey's solo album. (Though the book is unavailable outside Australia, it can be ordered from the publisher, www.allenandunwin.com.)

"There's no one else in Australia like Kasey and her family," Lomax writes, "but there are several artists with a lot of potential. Bill Chambers produced a new album, *Dusty Smiles and Heartbreak Cures,* by a sixteen-year-old singer-songwriter named Catherine Britt, who's quite promising. Audrey Auld, Bill's ex-girlfriend, is also very good. Kevin Bennett, who used to lead a band called the Flood, is a sort of a white-soul, Delbert McClinton type."

"Yeah, Kevin is great," Kasey agrees. "He reminds me of Son Volt. And Catherine could be a star because she already has the most amazing voice; it's like Patsy Cline meets Julie Miller, but very unique. Cold Chisel was a great rootsy pop band, like Mellencamp and Springsteen. Don Walker, the main songwriter in that band, has been successful on his own.

"The Finn brothers [Neil and Tim] are in the same vein as Paul Kelly, only more pop. They're very well respected, and Crowded House is one of our biggest bands ever. I did their 'Better Be Home Soon' as a B-side because I've always loved that song. Like most great songwriters from New Zealand, they have lived in Australia all their life, because there's not much of a music industry over there. It's like Canada and the U.S.

"One of my favorite songwriters is Brent Parlane, who lives in Melbourne. He, too, was born in New Zealand but has lived in Australia all his life. He writes really good songs, but now he's forty-five, and he knows he's never going to be a big star. My brother has produced a couple of his albums. He's like James Taylor and Buddy Miller and a lot of stuff in between."

For now, though, Kasey Chambers is the international ambassador of Australia's roots-music scene. She sold more than 100,000 American copies of her debut album without any help from country radio, and she'll likely do even better with her second. One recent development will undoubtedly affect Chambers's plans to promote the album in the United States this year. Chambers and her partner, Cori Hopper, announced in early December that they are expecting a child in May. Chambers says she plans to proceed with a U.S. tour in February that has already been booked.

"These new songs have been written over the past three years, and I did go through a heartbreak during that time. I was feeling very lost. I found that selling double platinum and winning an ARIA doesn't fill your heart and soul," she says. "I didn't find out what would satisfy me, but I did find out that material things wouldn't. I said, 'OK, this isn't what I'm going for. I love my career, and I do appreciate it, but it's not enough.'

"I spent my childhood living on the Nullarbor Plain and having no material things at all, but those were the happiest days of my life. I've gone from having the most simple life in the whole wide world to having the world's most complicated life. Part of that is just missing your childhood; it is the difference between being ten and being twenty-five. Even if you didn't grow up on the Nullarbor and then go into the world's most superficial business, you might feel that way."

"Southern Kind of Life," a song on *The Captain,* was inspired by the sale of the family home in Southend in 1996. With the increasing success of the Dead Ringer Band, the Chambers clan moved to Avoca Beach, an hour and a half north of Sydney on Australia's eastern coast, to be closer to the music industry. When the old house was sold, it was as if a door was being closed on their old life.

"We had been away so often and so long that I thought it wouldn't be a big deal to go back to Southend," Chambers remembers. "But as I went through and cleaned out all our stuff, I got this feeling we were losing something very important. I realized I had had a great childhood. I hadn't appreciated it at the time, because it was just my life. But when I was twenty and wrote that song, I recognized how disappointed I was that it was gone."

She pauses for a moment. "On the other hand," she points out, "I no longer have to worry about shooting a kangaroo so I can eat."

Make Me Wanna Holler

*Loretta Lynn Collaborates with Jack White to Make a
Country Album of a Whole New Stripe*

ND #51, MAY–JUNE 2004

Barry Mazor

Loretta Lynn knows exactly why she decided to go ahead and make
Van Lear Rose—an album different enough in sound from what
many would expect, given the hundred or so records she has made
before, that people will certainly be asking questions.

"At this point, I figure it won't make me or break me!" she laughs.
"And I just thought that it would be fun. It's time for fun now."

It is no secret that in the early 1980s, faced with strong pressure to
make records that were more pop than the modern honky-tonk sounds
that had been her natural setting in the '60s and '70s—the sounds of
"One's on the Way" and "Don't Come Home A-Drinkin'" and "You're
Looking at Country"—Lynn had walked away.

"Yes, I just quit recording. I said 'Take it or leave it: If you want me to
sing, it'll be country.'"

Twenty years later, the sounds that brought the "blue Kentucky girl" to
the Country Music Hall of Fame and to the White House during the
administrations of six presidents are not precisely those in the foreground.
On *Van Lear Rose,* released April 27 by Interscope, she is backed throughout—with a bit of pedal steel and fiddle on the side—by the often screaming electric guitar of producer Jack White, of White Stripes, and a rhythm
section right out of Cincinnati garage band the Greenhornes.

"Well, we decided," says White, "that no matter what the songs turned
out to be, no matter how we arranged them, I wasn't going to say 'We're
going to make a country record,' or 'We're going to make a rock record,'
or even 'We're going to combine those things.' Let's just let Loretta and
that steel guitar be country, and whatever else happens—happens.

"Loretta's voice is country as hell; there's no stopping that. Whatever is
going on musically, in any of her songs, once she starts singing you don't

even notice that anymore; it's just a backdrop for her. When she starts singing, all the rest is just a trick to get you paying attention to the stories."

Lynn most certainly did not walk away from the sort of pop that came into play here. "As far as I'm concerned," she says, "it's the countriest thing I ever heard.

"But now, that singing a song one time and it's over, that was funny to me."

As hard as it is to believe, given this album's consistent strength and appeal, and the relative unfamiliarity of the whole situation for the session participants, its thirteen tracks—all written by Lynn—were essentially captured in single performances caught in two sets of sessions at a simple eight-track studio in a big old house in East Nashville.

"This is what shocks me about the whole thing," Lynn emphasizes. "I sung those songs but one time. I'd get up to do a song, and the only thing that I'd have to do over, maybe, was if I missed a line or messed it up; then Jack would say, 'Well, let's go back and get that.' He'd take that first take. So . . . God be with us!"

"We had to do this quickly," White explains. "I didn't want to waste her time—but also to get as much real Loretta as could be done before we started overthinking it.

"That's how I usually record. If you go back and look at the albums that you love, Bob Dylan's *Nashville Skyline,* for instance, all of the best albums are done really quickly—because if you don't do it that way, then it gets into overthinking and overproducing, and that starts to ruin it."

■ ■ ■

White's emphasis on enabling spontaneity couldn't be more different from Lynn's experiences making her heyday hits with her mentor, musical partner, confessor, and, in her words, "father figure," the great Owen Bradley. He would have her run through a song three or four times to get more inside it, even when, as was often the case, she had written the thing herself.

Bradley, understandably, is still Lynn's model of a producer. The atmosphere he created for recording her was paramount, and set the standard for her permanently. (Not that the sound of those 1960s and '70s records wasn't cause for some intense discussion.)

Bradley is mainly recalled now, by ardent admirers and harsh critics alike, as a key figure in developing the lusher, string-laden, more urbane Nashville Sound associated with the records of Lynn's pal Patsy Cline, for instance. Two notable things about that are relevant here: One, that is not the sound of Lynn's recordings with Bradley; and two, she wasn't sure at first that she liked the differentiation.

"I said, 'Owen, this song "You're Lookin' at Country"? Please don't play it real, real country! Let in some strings; get some more people in on the session, which'll maybe give it a real good sound instead of some goofy old country sound, like the Fruit Jar Drinkers or something!'

"But all of a sudden I turned 'round and he was saying, 'Over there; get that Ernest Tubb lick! Over there, get that Roy Acuff lick!' And I looked at Owen and said, 'I thought we were gonna try to cut this record a little different!' And he just said, 'It's country, girl.'

"He told everybody that I was country, first and foremost. Which was right. I would have trusted anything he did."

For *Van Lear Rose* to work as well as it does, on its own terms, something approximating that kind of trust needed to get established again—though young White was obviously not going to be any sort of father figure this time. Much about the beginnings of their relationship has been told: White met Lynn after the White Stripes' version of her hit "Rated X" was brought to her attention, and they hit it off; Jack and Meg White spent some time with Lynn; they played a show together in New York last year. The beginnings of trust were there.

"We had worked that show up in New York, and I just thought he was a great kid," Lynn says. "So when Jack come to me and said he'd like to record me, I said, 'Fine; I'm fixin' to record!' And I give him that chance."

What White was feeling, however, was the responsibility of the venture—which would be, in fact, the first of Lynn's albums to be made up entirely of her own songs. (Not counting a 1968 release that pulled together her first Zero Records singles from the dawn of the 1960s, an album so obscure even she no longer has a copy.)

And this project was also something very new for White.

"I was walking into this on tiptoes, humbly asking permission to be involved," he says. "I went down and spent a day with her after she sent me some demos of songs, which were all just amazing. And I said, 'OK, let's sit down and kind of play these songs together.' But she wouldn't play guitar in front of me! So I'd ask her what key it was in, and she'd know the key and the lyrics and chord changes, and we went from there.

"Loretta had so many songs—piles and piles of songs. She first sent me ten demos, and when we went down to Nashville, in two days we recorded eight of those; all eight are on the album. Then she sent over another batch, and I picked the best of those.

"I had produced a lot of bands," White continues, "but when a band comes in, they've already had and rehearsed their songs for a long time. Here, I had to arrange these songs, put the band together, learn the song, and, in effect, turn around to the band and say, 'OK, let's arrange this now.'

"Every time we did something with Loretta, I was just astounded how well it was working. There were no problems to overcome. I don't know why—very strange. It surprised me, as excited and thrilled as I was, because I'd been, 'Hey man, jeesh; I hope this works!'"

The songwriter he has called "the greatest of the last century" at their live show and in more than one interview was not entirely without trepidation about this project, either.

"I did ask him before we went in, 'What do you think we're going to come out with?' Because I was wondering a little bit about this kind of thing myself," Lynn allows. "And he said, 'Well, what could we not come out with if you sing.' I guess that was why he had me sing just the one time; he thought it was good enough. He's a big Loretta Lynn fan, you know."

In the process of making this record, that became even more of a two-way street.

"Jack, at his age, I kind of felt, watching him clean the records up, as he got all of the talking and stuff out between the records, I seen a little Owen Bradley in this young boy.

"I wouldn't catch what he would catch." she explains. "I would just be listening to my voice, but he was listening to everything. If it would just be a tiny little guitar deal that he didn't like, out it'd come. I'd say, 'Why did you do that?' And he'd say, 'Well, here's the feel that you have for this song, and this don't need to be in there, and we'll take it out now.' So I noticed that he had an awful lot of knowledge.

"But when he ran in with these four little musicians, I thought, 'Oh, mercy!' I thought he would be bringin' a little more than just four. I was shocked, but I didn't say anything. 'Cause Owen always had six and seven. And when I walked in and there was just four of them, and they're just kids in their early twenties, I looked down and said, 'Oh, boy!' I thought maybe I was stuck out there kind of naked.

"So those four kids went in, with Jack singing the songs he wanted me to do, and put the music down—but the boys stuck around in case they needed to be there, and overdubbed some of them. Mostly I sang with the tracks. After we got going, I didn't even worry about it."

The musicians, in addition to White on electric guitar and occasional keyboards, included Greenhornes Patrick Keeler on drums and Jack Lawrence on bass—which assured that, however undefined the sound was allowed to be, there would be a strong garage-rock rhythm element to this album. These were not boys who had spent a lifetime playing straight country.

For pedal steel and Dobro, White called on Dave Fenny of the Detroit alt-country band Blanche, which had opened for the White Stripes and Lynn at the New York show. Blanche's co-leader Dan Miller adds occasional acoustic guitar and background vocals; he had been with White in the country-leaning rock band Two-Star Tabernacle, which backed R&B vet Andre Williams on a Bloodshot Records single, pre–White Stripes.

To this mix, White added the veteran and much-lauded fiddler Dirk

Powell, whom he had met while participating in the sound-track sessions for *Cold Mountain.* But the balance, based on the musicians' proclivities alone, was clear enough: Lynn was about to rock.

■ ■ ■

She was, it turns out, quite prepared to do so. Anyone who saw her duet with White on the live and electric version of "Rated X" in New York last year would not be entirely surprised. But the honky-tonk queen's interest in rocking—suggested, just barely, in such previous records as her hit "Out of My Head and Back in My Bed" or her version of Fats Domino's "Blueberry Hill"—did not begin in the last year.

The recent re-release on DVD of *Conway Twitty on the Mississippi,* a 1982 prime-time television special, gave an earlier clue. When Twitty and Jerry Lee Lewis get together for a shipboard revival of some of their rockabilly hits of a previous lifetime, Lynn is seen sitting right up front in the audience—and rocking out rather nicely.

Of her own numerous duets with Twitty, Lynn points out that the lyrics in those indelible numbers, while often talked about, were not necessarily the key thing to be paying attention to there. "I think me and Conway went for the melody and the beat," she says. "We wasn't even hardly listening to the words!"

For Lynn, in fact, those sorts of duets, including "What Your Lovin' Does To Me" and "I Can't Love You Enough," instantly bring to mind a rambunctious side of her recordings she sometimes has forgotten herself.

When her late husband Doolittle Lynn was bedridden toward the end of his life, she relates, she once put on an album of her duets with Twitty to make him feel better, as Conway and Doo were great personal friends. But as she sat by the bedside with the records playing, these songs seemed to startle her all over again.

"I asked him, 'Doo, how come you let me do them songs with Conway? They're the dirtiest songs I ever heard!'"

Doo said that they both liked them, and he knew better than to try to tangle with them both at once. It was another singer with whom Twitty once competed that, we learn now, has been number one for Loretta Lynn since the 1950s.

"I tell you, Elvis Presley was my favorite singer," she declares. "I was in the state of Washington, and they had no country music out there then. I never heard the country singers! They didn't make Washington state at that time, though they do now. I tell ya what I like of Elvis's, and I do sing that: 'Don't Be Cruel.' It might even have been a little faster than what Elvis did when I do it.

"So, you know what—and this is true: 'Have Mercy on Me, Baby' on the new record wasn't a new song. I wrote that for Elvis Presley just before he died. And I never sung the song again. But when I went in to cut this record with Jack, and with him being rock 'n' roll, I thought, well, I'll just drag 'Have Mercy on Me, Baby' out. At first I was only singing it to let him know what a fan I was of Elvis. But Jack said, 'I like that; let's cut it.'

"And I hadn't sung rock 'n' roll—but I could!"

Indeed, the very first thing anyone coming to *Van Lear Rose* will notice is that Lynn, born in 1935, can still sing rock 'n' roll (and anything else she is called on to do, for that matter) as cuttingly and as strongly as an awful lot of people born in 1955 or 1975 can only wish to.

She doesn't think that is so remarkable. She offers a pointed answer to that Ryan Adams line about starting a country band because punk rock was too hard to sing: "You know, with rock 'n' roll you can make mistakes on it, where you can't with just plain country. Plain country is the hardest thing there is to sing; I don't know how many people know that. It's got to be right. A person that loves country music can hear when a person gets off tune—and that's not always true with rock."

On "Have Mercy on Me, Baby," Lynn growls and pleads and begs. It is a cut on which the gamble of putting the young rockers and the veteran country singer together pays off in spades.

White says of the track: "The Greenhornes' rhythm section is coming out strong on that—the bass runs and stuff. That could be for Elvis, or the Yardbirds, or Loretta Lynn, all at once....And her singing at the end there, that 'Have Mercy' rave-up, well that's just insane! And she was laughing so hard."

Another along those lines is called "Mad Mrs. Leroy Brown," which incidentally (and, apparently, accidentally) serves as a sort of answer song to "Bad, Bad Leroy Brown." Lynn says she came up with the same character name but had forgotten the old Jim Croce hit.

"When she sang me 'Mad Mrs. Leroy Brown,'" White recalls, "I started playing the riff on a piano, a Ray Charles riff, because she was talking about Ray Charles all the time. And she just belted that one out."

■ ■ ■

If all of this gives a sense that this project simply hijacks a willing Lynn into a late-breaking side-trip from her own neighborhood, that would be an unfortunate misimpression. *Van Lear Rose* exhibits considerable variation: adventures into several new areas, hard country songs as good as any she has delivered in recent decades, and remarkably consistent songwriting strength.

"Every song was attacked differently," White says. "I love to do that, and tried my best to give each song its own character. Nobody should be able to say, 'On your new album, I like that track six!' They should be able to say, 'I like that song "Portland, Oregon" or "Van Lear Rose"' and remember the name and mood of the song.

"Loretta has some sort of natural, instinctive way of writing that you can't teach people—a sort of double-chorus, backwards sort of writing where she writes a chorus and then that's not enough; there has to be a second one too. And the second chorus wraps up the whole intention of the song. 'Fist City' is a good example of that."

Another such song shows up on this album. "Family Tree," in which a mother confronts "the other woman" head-on, is just the sort of feisty, in-your-face hard country song Lynn fans often associate with her most. But details of the married life that the singer lets loose at the end raise the story up a notch or two.

When asked how she learned to perfect her craft this way—to master, absolutely, the classic Nashville songwriting "turnaround" at the end of a song that recasts all that has come before—Lynn replies, "I don't know; I guess it was something I just knew. But you do have to know how to start out and end 'em!

"When I started writing songs, I had four little kids at home, so I told Doo to bring me home a songbook, and he brought that *Country Music Round Up*. I looked at that and thought, 'Well, gee whiz; this ain't no big deal, rhymin' lines. I ought to be able to do that.' 'Honky Tonk Girl' was my first, and I started just turning them out from there.

"When I write, now, I go to my bedroom. I've got a music room upstairs, but I seldom go up there, because I'd rather go to my bedroom, for some reason. I don't know why. It's more warm, I think. And I just lock my door, and I'm away from the world."

And how has forty years of experience changed the way she writes songs when she gets there?

"It don't get any easier, I'll tell you that!" she asserts. "You just have to get to know that it's going to be OK. Now, if I know what the story is, then I know the song is gonna be fine. It may not turn out like everybody else likes it, but I know I'll have my song."

Because there were only two Lynn originals on her last album, *Still Country,* released four years ago, some may have wondered if she had overcome a creative impasse or reached a new creative explosion with *Van Lear Rose,* for which she wrote about fifty songs in preparation. It wasn't that way at all, she contends; *Still Country* producer Randy Scruggs just had other songs in mind, and she had only shown him the two.

"But I've always written, always," she affirms. "Maybe I would start songs and go back in a month or two months and finish them up, or maybe I would start 'em and go back in a year and finish them. The reason I just wrote so many new ones, though, is I knew I was going in to record, and I thought I'd better get some up-to-date stuff!

"That 'Family Tree' was easy to write because the end of it, you know, where I say, 'I brought along his old bulldog Charlie, and the bills that's overdue?' That's happened many, many times! That's the only way I can do, is write from true life, or else being able to stand from the side and watch somebody else's life goin' by. That's the only way I can write a song."

■ ■ ■

A prediction: There are songs right out of that "from true life" vein in this collection that will join "Coal Miner's Daughter" and "Don't Come Home A-Drinkin'" and "One's on the Way" as indisputable keepers.

The openers are two of those: the title country ballad "Van Lear Rose" and the very different, catchy "Portland, Oregon."

Van Lear, we are reminded, is the town where Lynn's daddy would shop at the mining company store—and the Rose turns out to be the girl he brought back from there. The comic story behind the second song ("Portland, Oregon and sloe gin fizz / If that ain't love, then tell me what is," it goes) was related in Lynn's second memoir, *Still Woman Enough,* two years ago. She was teasing the sometimes wandering yet jealous Doo by means of a fake, blatant date with Ernest Tubb's guitar player Cal Smith, on the evening of a Portland golf tournament.

White calls "Van Lear Rose" the achievement he is proudest of on the record. "Portland, Oregon" (which Lynn points to as her own favorite) gets the most lavish arrangement, beginning as a sort of Hindu psychedelic concerto and resolving into a country duet with White.

"Loretta had wanted us to do a duet together, which scared me because I was afraid people would think I pushed my way into the song just to sing with her, for my own selfishness," White explains. "Originally, she sang all the lyrics, but they are written for two people, so that was the one to do, talking back and forth."

Potentially more enduring still is "Miss Being Mrs.," a from-the-heart lament full of a widow's utterly frank longing. It could work for anyone who has lost a spouse, and not quite like any other country song you could name. On the album, it appears as a stripped-down acoustic number, almost a demo, recorded live by Lynn and White alone—and is all the more touching for it. Lynn once said she had always written either out of love or loneliness; this little classic, finished right before the recording sessions, was clearly born out of both.

There are several Lynn firsts on this album. "Women's Prison," one of those "watching somebody else's life going by" songs, is a first for anybody—the first country song, or any other sort anyone seems to be aware of, that deals with the last minutes of a woman facing execution.

Lynn had played plenty of shows at men's prisons, but it occurred to her that no one ever seemed to book shows at women's prisons (which she hopes to do now), or had bothered to write a song on this subject. It shows utter empathy for the individual in the situation, pays attention to the fine, ghastly details, and makes no judgments—very much in the Merle Haggard mode. The execution takes place right in the lyric, with the organ tone hanging there at the moment of death—and then a gentle voice wafts in with "Amazing Grace." It is devastating.

It also turns out there is a bit of comedy connected to it.

The gentle voice, which sounds for the world like Lynn, is actually White, trying out the sound. They had talked about maybe having a gospel chorus do it, and thought better of it. White stuck with the subdued ending, but it wasn't the only one considered.

"It was so funny," he recalls. "Loretta said maybe we should do something at the end there where somebody yells, 'Pull the switch! Pull the switch!'"

We will leave to posterity the question of who was the gentle traditionalist and who the tough garage punk on that decision.

There is an utterly different Lynn in the song "High on a Mountain Top," which might be described as rousing pop bluegrass, somewhere between the Bryants' "Rocky Top" and sunny Ola Belle Reed folk singalongs. Don't be surprised if bluegrassers turn to it with more traditional instrumentation, and fast.

It brings to mind the curious circumstance that Lynn, despite hailing from Kentucky mining country, has been so little involved with Appalachian music per se. Having grown up in Butcher Holler hearing Bill Monroe and Roy Acuff on the Opry via a battery-operated radio, she famously turned not in the musical directions of those natives of her home area, but instead toward the sound of the other star on those broadcasts, the honky-tonk of her future partner Ernest Tubb.

"That's right," she says in retrospect. "And here I come out of Kentucky! I don't know why that happened, exactly, but you know, I do like to shock people! Maybe that's why I did what I did. And also, I was soon working one honky-tonk after the next. One night I was singin' on the bar, and I got up and walked the bar singing and playing my guitar—barefooted, because in them days I had no money to buy socks with, and pregnant!"

For those kinds of one-nighters, "Wreck on the Highway" was apparently not the right sort of material.

The life of a family that couldn't afford shoes, or maybe had to walk twelve miles to get to a doctor—a life modern audiences, even country audiences, can find difficult to truly grasp—is the stuff of the story recorded on *Van Lear Rose* as "Little Red Shoes."

The track started out as a song idea derived from a tale related in *Still Woman Enough* of a time she very nearly died as a child, and her mother stole her some shoes to warm the feet that had never known any. With all of the other songs outright Lynn compositions, White decided to keep the whole set that way, so "Little Red Shoes" is not quite a song collaboration; rather, White's tune runs in and out, strategically, as an instrumental behind Lynn's spoken telling of that painful and poignant story.

If the track brings any other recording to mind, it may be the old Lou

Reed–John Cale story and rock tone experiment "The Gift." This time, however, the tale is not bizarre, but harrowing. White's production forces the listener to pay attention to Lynn's words ever more closely.

The album concludes with a lone rewrite, an updated take on "Story of My Life," which in its shorter original form had been cut for Zero Records in the early 1960s. Lynn gets in a nice lick at the Hollywood studio that never coughed up enough cash to her for *Coal Miner's Daughter*, but mainly celebrates a life centered on her husband, her children, and her music. Every verse is punctuated with a series of inimitable, rhythmic "yeah-hay!" calls from Lynn, and the song ends with her joyfully affirmative laugh.

■ ■ ■

This unpredictable encounter between the queen of honky-tonk singing and songwriting and the young garage-rock star who simply, demonstrably gets her work has resulted in an album that arrives as a seamless whole. With its charming, adventurous variety—from bluegrass sing-alongs to screaming literature, from honky-tonk laments to growling rockabilly— inevitable comparisons will be made to the Rick Rubin–Johnny Cash collaborations. But that is too easy, and shallow. There was no one sound goal here, no one sense of what Lynn "ought to sound like." These sturdy, memorable songs have been remarkably well served by an imaginative set of arrangements.

"This is the best thing I've ever worked on, no doubt about it," White acknowledges. "It shows Loretta is still a viable songwriter, just as important as she was forty years ago. I hope that new people will become interested, through this record, in her old material, and that it will get people excited about country music who ordinarily wouldn't."

A tour with Lynn and the band from the record, including White on lead guitar, is in the works for this fall. Lynn's own band is learning the new numbers, too, to add them to their repertoire.

And Lynn is still writing away, she reports, including an album's worth of new gospel songs, as well as new songs for a Christmas record, including one about the love life of a couple of reindeer called in to substitute when Rudolph has the flu.

She is, even now, no less thrown by changing circumstances or the challenges of coming up with something "up to date" than she was when she started writing songs in her head at the age of nine.

"I've always said that you have to be different, great, or first," she reasons. "So maybe I was first—first to come to town, write my own stuff, and sing it. You know, I think that's what the whole deal has been."

Down from the Mountain

Patty Loveless Ventures Deep into the Valley of Her Homegrown Soul

ND #34, July–August 2001

Bill Friskics-Warren

Patty Loveless was eleven years old when her parents picked up and left their home in Pikeville, a small mining town in southeastern Kentucky, to rent a place a couple hundred miles west in Louisville.

It was hardly a happy move. Patty's father, John Ramey, had taken seriously ill, and needed medical attention; he had quit the mines some years earlier, but not before coal dust had settled in his lungs. Money was tight as well. All that John and his wife, Naomi, had to feed and clothe the three kids (out of seven) and one niece who still lived at home with them were his monthly black-lung and Social Security checks.

Then there was the isolation. Apart from the four grown children who had gone ahead of the rest to Louisville, the move marked the first time any member of the family had lived far from Pikeville, the place where, for generations, Rameys and Bolins (Patty's mother's kin) had raised their children, worked in the mines, and buried their dead.

As if all this wasn't enough, Patty's parents took their brood out of the countryside at a time when virtually every urban center across the United States was in turmoil. It was 1968: The nation was rife with conflicts over the Vietnam War, the Equal Rights Amendment, and civil rights (and, after the Stonewall riot the following year, gay rights).

The mix of loneliness and alienation they felt in the strange new city that would never be home to them was shattering—particularly for Patty, who by her own admission was shy and had a hard time making friends at school. Determined to lift his youngest daughter's spirits, John Ramey took $100 of the money he didn't have and bought her a small Epiphone guitar. He also paid for her to take a few lessons.

That instruction was short-lived—Patty was impatient, bent on learning chords when her teacher insisted she start with notes—but it wasn't long before she was sussing out the changes to the latest hits by Dolly Parton and Loretta Lynn. And writing songs. Some echoed what she heard on the radio, but most were inspired by the older-sounding music of her parents: the songs of Bill Monroe and Molly O'Day and Kitty Wells that Patty's mother sang while working around the house, or the Stanley Brothers and Flatt & Scruggs records her dad played on the family phonograph.

At first her folks' music struck Patty as unrelentingly sad, especially those shuddering Stanleys records, but soon enough the likes of "Rank Stranger" and "Man of Constant Sorrow" were moving her to give voice to her own misery. Nowhere did she express the feelings of isolation and estrangement she knew in Louisville more indelibly than with "Sounds of Loneliness," the lament of an old, old soul that, amazingly enough, Loveless wrote when she was just fourteen.

Harmonically reminiscent of "Amazing Grace," the song concludes and serves as the cornerstone of *Mountain Soul,* her luminous new collection of Appalachian ballads. (The recording also appears on the soundtrack to the movie *Songcatcher.*)

"Hear the sound of my heartbeat / It beats so loud, oh I can't stand it," Loveless intones to begin the third verse, wrenching the word "stand" from the back of her throat. Then, making her way to the final, dirge-like stanza, she moans, "Oh that sound, that lonely sound / It grows louder . . . and louder . . . and louder . . . and louder," as a second, third, then fourth voice joins her on successive cries, each in turn adding a new layer of harmony.

The sense of abandonment conveyed here, of being left utterly alone, is as absolute as that heard in Blind Willie Johnson's "Dark Was the Night—Cold Was the Ground" or Robert Johnson's "Stones in My Passway." What is freezing Loveless dead in her tracks, though, isn't some wall of rocks or cloak of darkness, but the throbbing loneliness echoing from the caverns of her inconsolable heart. With the fiddles of Carmella Ramsey and Deanie Richardson droning their ancient tones behind her, Loveless's plaint doesn't just sound older than the hills; it sounds as old as loneliness itself.

That sound, a barrenness that has reasserted itself at various points throughout her life, is evident in many of her records. It is there in the anguished, purling tones she trades with George Jones on the almost Wagnerian "You Don't Seem to Miss Me." In the quiet desperation of "Nothin' but the Wheel." In the tortured lover's prayer of "Don't Toss Us Away." On many of her hits, the titles alone cry out with the sounds of loneliness: "Lonely Days, Lonely Nights," "Lonely Too Long," "The Lonely Side of Town."

Of course, this is hardly the only emotion in Loveless's music; she has playful and randy streaks, among others. And her desolation is never merely forlorn or despairing, but is steeped in the resiliency she got from her parents and from the Rameys and Bolins who bred it in them.

Still, no less than the coal in the hills around Pikeville, "that lonely sound" of which Loveless sings pervades her music and is embedded there. It certainly lies at the heart of her new album, a record that, more than any of her career, finds her getting back to the roots of her raising.

■ ■ ■

"I wanted this particular record to focus on the Patty of the past," Loveless says, sitting in the shade of a towering hackberry in Nashville's Centennial Park. "I wanted people to understand a little bit more about me, and where I come from. Not only that, but about the music I do and why I do it."

Without a doubt, the loamy arrangements on *Mountain Soul*—chopping mandolins, plinking banjos, penumbral harmonies—conjure images of the looming hills and dark hollers around Loveless's native Pikeville. As does the material on the record, which includes her updates of Appalachian standards such as "Shady Grove" and the hair-raising "Man of Constant Sorrow," rendered here as "Pretty Little Miss" and "Soul of Constant Sorrow," respectively.

Much of the album is haunting, even mournful in tone; yet, perhaps paradoxically, it is precisely the sort of music that got Patty's parents, a dignified, extremely hardworking couple, through some of the roughest patches of their lives. Indeed, it offered them a measure of transcendence in a world that rarely afforded them any.

"Music, I think, gave my parents a way to escape," Loveless explains. "It gave them a connection to the rest of the world, a sense that something better was out there. It spoke to their souls.

"I remember daddy sitting and listening to the Stanley Brothers all the time. I used to say, 'Why do you listen to this music? It makes me cry.' But now I understand why. Because it's so moving, it's so soulful. It's just amazing that people can do that with their voices, to make you feel and to bring you to tears. And it's not to sadden you. It's to move you, you know? To inspire you."

As an example, Loveless cites the "old line" singing she and her father used to go hear at a small church in Louisville. An "old regular Baptist preacher" from back home near Pikeville would come up to the city once a month to give the sermon. He would also lead them in hymns, singing one line, which the congregation would echo; they would repeat the process, line by line, to the end of the song. All of the singing was a cappella, and it wasn't unusual for the worshipers to reach a fever pitch emotionally.

"He would preach hellfire and brimstone," Loveless recalls, referring to the clergyman. "I mean stomping and yelling. Then he would turn to the elders and look at them to get some kind of response, to move them. I think that the preacher knew that, somehow, through the singing, his message would go through them. It would make them get it even more.

"And that's what music is about, what it has always been about—in country, in bluegrass. The best music moves people, and there have been times that I felt that the music that influenced me so much could move mountains. Truly, that it could make you see beyond those mountains."

Several songs on *Mountain Soul* drink directly from the wellspring of old-time gospel of which Loveless speaks, notably "Rise Up Lazarus" and "Daniel Prayed," the latter buoyed by an unbounded call-and-response with Ricky Skaggs. One song, a chilling cover of Darrell Scott's "You'll Never Leave Harlan Alive," doesn't just look beyond the mountains, it finds its protagonist escaping them only to be forced to return and, ultimately, to be stuck there till he dies.

"Where the sun comes up about ten in the morning / And the sun goes down about three in the day / And you fill your cup with whatever bitter brew you're drinking / And you spend your life digging coal from the bottom of your grave." So goes the final chorus, testimony to a life that Loveless's father, who spent his days entombed in the mines just like his father and his wife's father before him, knew only too well.

"Grandpa Bolin had to go work in the mines at fourteen, as a young boy, in order to help support his family, and Grandpa Ramey, he and all his boys, including my father, worked in the mines," Loveless explains. "It was the only kind of occupation, the only good life for them back then, even though it was hard. I look back at my father, who used to go down four miles deep into the mines. He had some back problems, but daddy didn't complain. And how they used to have to bend over down in those mines. Just think about how long they were down there. They'd go down when it was dark, and when they'd come up it would be dark."

■ ■ ■

Very little of that darkness crept into Patty's early years growing up in Pikeville and nearby Elkhorn City. Her parents saw to that. "Sure, to people today, and to some people back then, we probably were poor," she admits. "But my brothers and sisters and I, we didn't know it. Mom and daddy always made sure we had school clothes, shoes. Even if they had to go borrow the money to give us a Christmas, they would do it. They would put themselves into debt.

"They would owe the company store. That's pretty much what it would come down to. Daddy would do whatever it took to make his kids happy. He always stressed, especially to his sons—I don't think he ever imagined women going into the coal mines to work, which they do—to get an education. Daddy wanted all of us to have a better life because he knew that there was something better out there."

Foremost among those things that represented "something better" in the Ramey household was music, and not just for Patty. By the time her father bought her that $100 Epiphone guitar, her brother Roger and sister Dottie had already been performing together locally as a duo called the Swinging Rameys.

"My brother was singing with my sister long before he started singing with me," Loveless says. "That's my sister Dottie, the one who passed away in '96. Man, she was great; she was wonderful. If anybody could sing like Patsy Cline, she had her down. I used to love to just sing backup with Dottie. I was the one that did harmonies.

"My sister was a big influence on me from the time I was eight years old on. I was in awe of her. Her beauty. Her character. She was a little fireball, but a really good person."

Dottie got married and quit the Swinging Rameys right about the time Patty took up the guitar. Roger, however, continued to work the local jamborees as a solo act, mostly doing covers; he sang everything from the honky-tonk of Hank Sr. and Ernest Tubb to then-current country-politan hits by Conway Twitty and Charley Pride. One day when Patty, at the time not quite thirteen, was out on the porch fooling with her guitar, he invited her to sing with him at a jamboree that night. At first she demurred, but Roger wouldn't relent, so she finally gave in.

If anything, Loveless remembers, she saw it as a chance to get out of the house. "Mama would not let me go anywhere," she begins. "It was just a small jamboree. There were maybe two hundred foldout chairs in this little old building in Louisville. This guy—I guess he always wanted to be in country music—put a band together and would host a little show every two weeks. It probably cost people a dollar to get in, and he paid us five dollars apiece."

Loveless recalls working up maybe a handful of covers to play that first night. She sang "Harper Valley P.T.A." and "You Ain't Woman Enough," and she and Roger did at least a couple of duets together: Loretta Lynn and Ernest Tubb's "Sweet Thang," and Porter Wagoner and Dolly Parton's "Jeannie's Afraid of the Dark." The folks in the audience ate it up, a response that not only soothed the crushing loneliness Patty had felt ever since her family left Pikeville, but also signaled the first stirrings of a renewed, if somewhat fleeting, sense of community.

"That's when it hit me," Loveless says. "It was like, 'Wow, this is almost like singing to my mom's family.' I mean, I was scared to death, but it was a wonderful thing. The more we did it, the more it felt like I had finally made friends. I was having such a hard time, and this guitar, and the music, it helped me to make friends."

■ ■ ■

A year or so later, Patty and Roger were down in Nashville auditioning for Porter Wagoner. "I met Patty when she was fourteen," Wagoner remembers. "She and her brother came to Nashville; they were fans of mine and Dolly's. They came by the office one day and asked if I would listen to Patty sing some, which I did. She had just written a song called 'Sounds of Loneliness.' I thought it was a great thing for her to have written a song of such depth at that age. The melody was really good on it too."

Parton recalls Patty singing "Sounds of Loneliness" around that time as well. "I was so impressed that she could write so well, being a child that young," Parton says. "I remember . . . how lonesome and haunted it sounded . . . I also remember another song that she used to sing called 'Marvin's Garden.' I tell her all the time that she should write more. I don't think people realize what a wonderful writer she is. She's shy about that . . . but she should get over [it] because she has great songs."

Wagoner says he knew back then that Patty had a future in country music. Indeed, he liked her writing so much that it wasn't too long before he cut a demo version of "Sounds of Loneliness." Nevertheless, he advised her to go back and finish high school. "I told her, 'The smartest thing you can do is go ahead and get your education. Your career is going to be there.' And I knew it would be too. I could just see that she had that longing, that drive."

Later on, Patty went out on the road a couple times with Porter and Dolly. "Dolly's room was in the back—it had a bed in the center—and once we set up all night back there, singing trios and things," Wagoner recalls. "Years later I told Patty, 'You know, I reached a real milestone in my life that night. I'm probably the only guy in the world who spent the night in a bed with Dolly Parton and Patty Loveless.'

"Of course, nothing happened," adds Wagoner, ever the wag. "We just sang till we fell asleep. We must've been a pretty sight the next morning, all sprawled out on that bed like that." Fittingly enough, a version of "Just Someone I Used to Know," one of Porter and Dolly's biggest hits from that era, appears on Loveless's new album, with Jon Randall playing Porter to Patty's Dolly.

Wagoner and Parton weren't the only Opry stars Loveless hooked up with while still a teenager. Two years after auditioning for Wagoner, she became the featured "girl singer" in the Wilburn Brothers' road show. On the strength of originals such as "Sounds of Loneliness," she signed a deal with Sure-Fire Music, the publishing company owned by the Wilburns through which Loretta Lynn, Loveless's distant cousin, once published her songs. And it was while working with the Wilburns that Patty, who then was still using the surname Ramey, met Terry Lovelace, a rock drummer with whom she moved to North Carolina and later married.

The relationship didn't just sidetrack Patty's career in country music; it nearly killed her. "It was always a dream of my dad's for me to make it in country music," she says. "But when I got into this rock 'n' roll thing, he said, 'Child, it's gonna ruin you.' And you know, he was right. It almost did."

■ ■ ■

Patty Ramey was nineteen when she left Nashville for North Carolina. "I don't know, maybe I was the wild child of the family, but I actually ran off with this drummer," she says, referring to Lovelace, whose name she took when they married (she changed it to "Loveless" after they split). Contrary to most reports, she adds, Lovelace wasn't the Wilburn Brothers' drummer, but was working in a band she sang in called the Americountry Express.

"I was living in a different world in North Carolina—totally different than what I was used to," Loveless explains. "I came from a close-knit family that was very protective. Even the Wilburn Brothers and Porter Wagoner and my brother Roger—they were very protective of me. And now to be living with this guy who was truly a rock 'n' roller; I guess I just rebelled."

Patty says that she and her mother didn't speak to each other for months after she moved in with Lovelace. She also missed her father, whose health grew progressively worse. It was a lonely time, one of lingering sadness and increasingly heavy drinking that, much like her family's move to Louisville, took Patty away from many of the people and things she loved. She still sang country music now and again, but mostly she played in after-hours rock clubs to people she calls "the walking dead."

"I'm talking about people who were getting off work at three o'clock in the morning and had nowhere else to go," Loveless says. "They didn't feel like going home, and they would come and stay at this establishment, this speakeasy, we worked at. We'd play until six o'clock in the morning, from eleven at night to six in the morning, so I guess I was becoming one of the walking dead too. Or one of the living dead. I don't know any other way to put it. I wasn't living. I was just existing."

In 1979, Patty's father died, a loss that not only hit her hard, but also triggered a downward slide from which she almost never recovered. Her drinking had gotten so out of hand that one night, after barely making it through the first set in a local club, her bandmates had to carry her back to her room, where, utterly despondent, she stopped just short of killing herself.

"I felt I'd let my family down, so I started to cut my wrists," she says. "I was crying and kicking myself in the butt at the same time, and all of a sudden my mother came to me. At that point I popped up and started going, 'All right, if your mother can live through moving away, living in a strange city, losing her daughter, who ran off, and losing the father of her children, losing her soulmate, losing her friend, losing her companion for life, what gives you the right to drink your life away? What gives you the right to take your life? She gave you life. Why should you take that from her?' And that stopped me. And finally, after that, things started to change."

■ ■ ■

For starters, Patty quit drinking and separated from Lovelace. She also started singing country music again, but apart from Emmylou Harris, she found the names and voices she heard on the radio in 1984 and '85 totally different from those she knew when she had left Nashville nearly a decade before. "I called my brother Roger, who was living in Kentucky at the time, and said, 'Who are these people?'" Loveless recalls, alluding to the likes of neo-trad heavyhitters George Strait, Reba McEntire, and the Judds.

Roger didn't just catch his sister up on the latest country hitmakers. He talked her into meeting him in Nashville to cut a demo or two, which he shopped for her with little success until the morning he wormed his way, unannounced, into the office of Tony Brown, then vice president of A&R at MCA.

According to the story he told Patty, Roger, who would manage his sister's career until 1990, got his pitch in before Brown had a chance to throw him out of his office. "Roger said, 'Look, if you don't hear this girl sing, you're going to miss out on the best girl singer in his whole town,'" Loveless begins. "Tony told him he had two minutes, so Roger played him 'I Did.' Tony listened, and then he listened and listened and kept Roger for, I think, about forty-five minutes. Then he said 'Look, can you get this girl?' I was still living in North Carolina at the time, so Roger called me up and said, 'Tony Brown wants me to fly you in. He wants to meet with you.'"

Even more serendipitous was that morning's introduction, via tape, of Loveless to Emory Gordy Jr., the former bassist for Elvis Presley, Neil Diamond, and Emmylou Harris, who would become Loveless's producer and, in 1989, her second husband. At the time, Gordy was working with Brown in the A&R department at MCA, during a period in which the label was signing up the likes of Steve Earle, Lyle Lovett, and Nanci Griffith.

Explains Loveless: "From what Emory tells me, he listened to my tape and said, 'Tony, where did you say this girl is from?' And he said, 'North Carolina.' And Emory said, 'Really? That's interesting. She sounds like she could almost be from that little area, that little town called Pikeville, in the southeast part of Kentucky.'

"Emory is one of those people—he studies," Loveless says. "And he was really tied into that particular area because he used to listen to it all the time when he was growing up in Georgia. He had gone through Pikeville in '56, when he was twelve years old, just a year or so before I was born. It was just so weird how it all came together."

It took awhile for Loveless's early records to find an audience. In fact, it wasn't until early 1988—by today's standards, a virtually unheard-of six singles into her tenure at the label—that Loveless's steel-sweetened recording of the Dallas Frazier weeper "If My Heart Had Windows," a hit for George Jones in 1967, became her first Top 10 country single.

By that time, the neo-trad fervor that greeted the mid-1980s arrival of Earle, Dwight Yoakam, and Randy Travis had cooled some. MCA's other rootsy mid-decade signees had certainly fallen out of favor with country radio. Lovett's records no longer cracked the country Top 40, and Earle and Griffith had dropped off the singles charts altogether.

Loveless, however, was just getting started. Her next seven singles, everything from the honky-tonk heartache of "The Lonely Side of Love" to the rockabilly-leaning twang of "Blue Side of Town," went Top 10. Two of them, the Buddy Holly–style "Timber, I'm Falling in Love" and the

Linda Ronstadt–like "Chains," even reached #1, in 1989 and '90, respectively. Despite her often more-rockin' sound, Loveless was lumped in with the rising class of '89 that included Clint Black, Lorrie Morgan, Alan Jackson, and future 800-pound gorilla Garth Brooks.

Most of Loveless's big hits were written by folks with strong ties to the Nashville hit mill—Kostas, Matraca Berg, Deborah Allen, and Rafe Van Hoy. But she drew from left-of-center sources as well: Her soul-on-ice cover of Lone Justice's "Don't Toss Us Away" went to #5 in 1989, and she had hits with Earle's "A Little Bit of Love" (#3, 1988) and Lucinda Williams's "The Night's Too Long" (Top 20, 1990). She also recorded "Some Morning Soon" by bluegrass singer Claire Lynch, who, along with Vince Gill, lent harmonies to many of Loveless's early hits. Regardless of the source, Loveless always showed a great ear for material—due in part, no doubt, to the unassailable taste of her parents.

■ ■ ■

But despite nonstop touring and considerable chart success, Loveless never graduated to the level of, say, Reba McEntire or the Judds. Even after "If My Heart Had Windows" went Top 10 and she finally got her own tour bus, she was still making only $450 a night playing clubs, and she was using virtually all of that to pay her band.

By 1992, after four albums and nineteen singles for MCA, Loveless finally reached the point of saying, "'If I can't make a decent living at this'—I mean, I loved the music, and the records were selling—'there has to be a change.'"

"There were a lot of people at MCA who believed in what I did, but they didn't have the power to make things happen," Loveless continues. "Some of them, their hands were tied. And those that had the power, I don't think they understood. So finally I was allowed to leave MCA. I didn't get out of my deal for free—trust me, I was so in debt to those guys. But finally I was able to walk away with my name, and with my music, and go to another label."

A whole lot more than debt followed Loveless to Epic, her new label. In the fall of 1992 she found her very career in jeopardy when she had to undergo laser surgery on her vocal cords. Remarkably, she made a full recovery and, with her husband Emory behind the board, proceeded to make her best records, including some of the finest to come out of Nashville during the 1990s. In 1993 she released *Only What I Feel*, a platinum-selling album anchored by three Top 10 singles, notably the Harlan Howard–Kostas co-write "Blame It on Your Heart," which was #1 for two weeks.

Next came *When Angels Fly*, which yielded four more Top 10 hits, including the torchy "Here I Am" and a version of Gretchen Peters's wrenching "You Don't Even Know Who I Am." Like its predecessor, the album sold more than a million copies. It also took home honors for best country album at the 1995 CMA Awards, while 1996's *Trouble with the Truth* not only won the 1996 CMA award for best country album but also garnered Loveless that year's ACM and CMA awards for best female vocalist.

"You Can Feel Bad," a surging kiss-off, and "Lonely Too Long," a morning-after ballad as sexy, and as empathetic, as Dusty Springfield's "Breakfast in Bed," were the chart-topping singles from *Trouble*. Among the record's other highlights were Loveless's renderings of songs written by Jim Lauderdale and Richard Thompson, as well as the tensive country-soul of the album's title track.

Would-be traditionalists doubtless take exception to some of these more burnished tracks, not to mention the favor they found with such venal institutions as country radio and the CMA. And then there are those who would trot out critical double-speak like "real" or "authentic" to tout Loveless's MCA sides over her less overtly hard-core recordings for Epic. Such terms, though, are never terribly helpful when discussing music that is inherently commercial—music that, no more or less than the latest records by Wilco or the Wu-Tang Clan, is made by artists who aspire to some sort of mass appeal.

More to the point, Loveless's records with Gordy at Epic constitute one of those increasingly rare convergences of artistry and popularity. Indeed, Loveless's sides for Epic are to her work at MCA what Elvis's comeback recordings are to his sessions for Sun: slicker, punchier, and more "produced," and gloriously so, just as they are better and much more authoritatively sung. Of course, at this point, we haven't even gotten to Loveless's 1997 hit recording of Lauderdale's "You Don't Seem to Miss Me," a collaboration with George Jones that approximates Orbisonian heights of obsession and is, genre notwithstanding, one of the greatest singles of the past ten years.

■ ■ ■

"You Don't Seem to Miss Me" also proved a harbinger of things to come, and, ultimately, of liberation for Loveless. Perhaps because of Jones's presence on the record, programmers in some markets deemed it, ridiculously enough, "too country" for country radio. As a result, it became Loveless's worst-performing single since "Nothin' but the Wheel" stalled at #20 on the country charts in 1993.

"It went to ten," Patty says incredulously, referring to the single's highest chart position (actually, according to *Billboard,* it only reached #14). "I think we have all worked ourselves into a situation where we have to be #1 every time out," she continues. "I think that's sad, I really do. It's just so sad that we have pushed ourselves to where if a record isn't at the top of the charts, then something must be wrong."

The whole experience of being told that a record George Jones sings on could be "too country" for anything got Loveless to thinking, and not just about radio's increasingly narrow playlists. The previous year, she witnessed the death of her sister Dottie, and her husband Emory suffered a protracted illness. Suddenly she found herself rethinking her entire career.

"I felt my myself beginning to weaken," Loveless admits. "I was losing heart, and I thought, 'I need to get away. I need to get away from the whole rat race of "Let's get a record out, let's work it. Let's get out there on the road and promote it."' It just seemed like things were going too fast, way too fast."

The upshot of all this searching was that Loveless took 1999 off, among other things to start putting down roots with her husband and to begin building a house in the mountains of northern Georgia. Meanwhile, back in 1997 and '98, she had already begun nurturing her musical roots by sprinkling songs such as "Pretty Polly" and "Some Morning Soon" into her live shows. (An unearthly version of the former, recorded as a duet with Ralph Stanley, was #1 for three weeks on *Bluegrass Unlimited* magazine's National Bluegrass Survey in 1997.)

"I found that people wanted to hear that sort of thing," Loveless says. "Then, when I was in L.A. last year, one of the guys in marketing from Sony was out there, and he happened to catch the show. After he saw how moved people were by the acoustic stuff we did—and how they gave us a standing ovation—he came backstage and said, 'Maybe we should do a whole record of this stuff.'"

No doubt this wasn't the only reason that Sony, Loveless's record label—the same imprint that wouldn't let Ricky Skaggs do a bluegrass record at the height of his mid-1980s chart run—was willing to take a chance on *Mountain Soul*. The album's unvarnished fiddles, banjos, and Dobros may be anathema to today's pop-leaning radio programmers, but at least the account execs at Sony knew they still had a potential single or two from Loveless's underrated *Strong Heart* album left to work to country radio. Although now, perhaps spurred by the success of the video for "Man of Constant Sorrow," from the *O Brother, Where Art Thou?* soundtrack, Sony is readying a video of "The Boys Are Back in Town," the opening track from *Mountain Soul,* to market to CMT as well.

■ ■ ■

Regardless of how Sony handles the release of *Mountain Soul,* the last thing anyone can say about the album is that Loveless is jumping on the *O Brother* bandwagon. She had begun reintroducing mountain and bluegrass material into her live shows before the Coen Brothers even thought of tapping T Bone Burnett to produce the *O Brother* soundtrack; more to the point, she has been singing the stuff her entire life. And vestiges of it have been there in her recordings all along.

"I've tried to put a song or two in that mountain vein on each of my albums," Loveless acknowledges, citing "Slow Healing Heart" and "Half Over You," both from her first album for MCA, as examples. Among any number of others, there is her cover of the Stanleys' "I'll Never Grow

Tired of You" from *Honky Tonk Angel,* and her rendition of Claire Lynch's "Some Morning Soon" from *On Down the Line.* More recently, she has appeared on *Big Mon* (Ricky Skaggs's 1999 all-star tribute to Bill Monroe), and Ralph Stanley's *Clinch Mountain Country.*

This is to say nothing of the undeniably Appalachian quality of Loveless's back-holler alto, a voice as indelible as those of her fellow Pikeville-area natives Dwight Yoakam, Keith Whitley, and Loretta Lynn. Much of what has been written about Loveless compares her singing to Lynn's and, to a lesser extent, to that of Dolly Parton and Patsy Cline. And, without doubt, those resemblances are there. But as with Hazel Dickens, another mountain singer, albeit one who mines a more rough-hewn style, the two dominant influences on Loveless's singing are men—Ralph Stanley and George Jones. In particular, the spine-tingling moans and wails of the former and the elongated phrasing, right down to the bent and swallowed notes, of the latter.

"Yes, that's where I got a lot of it," she blurts out when I suggest as much. "I have been listening to those two particular singers since I was a child. I think that when we're younger, we absorb so much more than we do as we get older.

"It's kind of ironic," she continues. "I don't have any children, but I've been around a lot of babies. And the one I've taken notice to mostly these days is Emory's new granddaughter, Suzanne. She's only two, and she is absorbing what I do. I'll sing, like, the old mountain stuff to her, and lately she's learning songs; she's just a little past two, but I hear her sing them while she's playing. So now when I look back on those years when I was a child, I'm thinking, my mother would sit and listen to the radio, or when she was cleaning house she would listen to the radio all the time, or she'd go around the house singing and humming."

■ ■ ■

With Loveless, it keeps coming 'round to family, or at least community, which is just another name for the extended families that she watched make room for cousins and other kin back in Pikeville. And it is that intimacy, that kinship, which sets her *Mountain Soul* apart from other similar projects, from Dolly's recent Smoky Mountain triptych to the *O Brother* soundtrack. Rather than arranging a super session or hiring a bunch of outside pickers to play on the record, Loveless made her album with the very same people—her musical family—with whom she had been performing its songs live.

Sure, there were a few ringers who came in to sing and play on the album, notably Ricky Skaggs and Travis Tritt. But even here, Loveless had recently worked with both men, and from the way they sing with her on the album, especially those scorching duets with Tritt, they might as well have been out touring with her or, for that matter, been blood relatives.

"I wanted the people that were performing with me onstage to be a part of it," Loveless says. "I thought, 'We've been playing with each other. We work with each other all the time. Now is the time to go in and cut something.'"

Besides, she adds, "Watching them work just does something to me. It sparks me and motivates me. Like when Carmella [Ramsey] and I are in the same booth singing and looking at each other, and knowing that my sound could leak onto hers, and hers onto mine. Just looking at her and watching her roll her eyes at me, or me roll my eyes at her, and then hearing the engineer come back and say, 'Man that was great.' She and I just look at each other and laugh, because we're like, 'Yeah, right.'

"Were there mistakes? Sure there were. But here we were going, 'Here it is, warts and all.' We wanted to make the record as if people were actually sitting there and watching it all take place. Not as if we were onstage, but like we were in somebody's living room—we almost were—and people were there and we were entertaining them."

Nowhere does this living-room vibe come across more than on the album's closing track, "Sounds of Loneliness," a recording so intimate it practically belies the depths of spiritual and emotional barrenness it conveys. Loveless has sung the song ever since she wrote it back in Louisville when she was fourteen. She even cut the song, with a string section, though not to her satisfaction, for MCA in 1987. But it wasn't until her manager, Ken Levitan, asked her if she had anything to contribute to the soundtrack to *Songcatcher,* a movie set in Appalachia, that she even thought of recording it again.

"I watched the movie, and I looked at Emory and said, 'You know what I think would be a good song for this? Not some old mountain song, but "Sounds of Loneliness."' And he went, 'You're right.' The movie reminded me of a traditional mountain-type thing, so we went in and we cut it that way.

"We ended up cutting the song in my basement, and it was perfect. Just absolutely perfect. Jeff White was on it. Carmella and Deanie [Richardson] sang and played fiddles. Emory played guitar. It was just so amazing.

"And it does sound sort of mountain," Loveless concludes. "I think that's the reason it was my dad's favorite tune I had written. He would always want me to sit in the kitchen and sing it to him. And when I would sing for him, he'd say, 'You know, I just love to hear you do things like this.'"

A Simple Path

Kieran Kane Follows a Straight Line to the Heart of His Songs

ND #43, JANUARY–FEBRUARY 2003

Peter Cooper

ogs on the floor, mandolin on the couch, paintings on the wall. Kieran Kane made the paintings, plays the mandolin, pets the dogs. Kane is sick today, dressed in staying-home clothes. He hasn't been painting, though he has likely been noodling around on the mandolin a bit.

That is the same mandolin—a modest, inexpensive Kentucky brand model he bought off a store rack—that has been heard all over the world. He carries it with him when he performs, and its wood has resonated in places Kane has never been. That is the mandolin that used to be on the radio.

This morning, Kane sought to cancel a career-spanning conversation. But the afternoon brought a second wind, and, anyway, he knows the talk should veer at times toward *Shadows on the Ground,* his new album, a work of which he is understandably pleased and proud.

Shadows is like other Kane records, only more so. Or less so. Maybe more so because it is less so. Known for more than two decades as a writer and player who uplifts common words and simple melodies, Kane, in *Shadows,* has brought forth his sparest and simplest effort to date. The instrumentation is acoustic; the lyrics hold great meaning but little sophistication. Two of the songs have only one chord. The arrangements and structures aren't skin and bones—they are bones.

"He's been doing this for a long time: paring it down and down to just the cleanest, most necessary, most fundamental parts of a song," says Kane's longtime friend and collaborator Kevin Welch. "I watch him as he's working, getting closer to his ideal songs and his ideal record. I see him heading purposefully toward a goal he has. Was it Matisse or Cézanne who ended up making little cardboard cutouts, who just got things simpler and simpler? Kieran reminds me of that."

For now, Kane is moving slowly toward the mandolin. He picks it up, doesn't strum or pluck it, moves it to a corner, and clears a place on the couch.

■ ■ ■

"It was right here," Kane says, looking around the room. "Right there, actually. Right in that spot. That's where Roy was standing." Roy was Roy Huskey Jr., a revered bass player who died too young. Huskey played upright bass for Emmylou Harris and a lot of other people, and his first trip to Kane's living room cemented the lineup of the O'Kanes, a band fronted by Kane and Jamie O'Hara.

"This was clearly the rocket-to-stardom country band in the mid-'80s," Kane recollects. "Accordion, mandolin, fiddle or banjo, acoustic guitar. We needed an upright bass player, and Roy said he'd come over. He showed up an hour and a half late. Had an overcoat on. Black shoes. Jeans. Roy came in, put his bass down, hit a D note, and all of us went, 'Oh my God.' He hit one note. Hadn't even played anything, and it was perfect."

The odd thing is that such base-level simplicity was at the root of something that ultimately provided mainstream country music's lustrous apex of far-out freakdom. Porter Wagoner's pseudo-psychedelic *What Ain't to Be Just Might Happen* album and Willie Nelson's long-haired, pot-smoking reinvention were a start, but the trips that went all the way into the ether occurred sometime around 1987, when the O'Kanes arrived in showcase clubs around the nation, tuned up, turned on, and roared.

The songs were unaffected, sometimes containing only two chords, and the lyrics were well whittled and mournful. "Ooh, shed a tear for the man with the bluegrass blues," Kieran Kane and Jamie O'Hara would sing, harmonizing over an all-acoustic soundscape in a manner that caused a *Country Music* magazine reviewer to write, "If the Delmore Brothers were alive today, they'd be the O'Kanes."

But then, midway through "Bluegrass Blues," things would get weird. The mountain breeze signified by brother Richard Kane's fiddle suddenly carried a whiff of patchouli. Kieran's mandolin work shifted from feathery melody to flyswatter-swift chops. Drums and bass went from stately to jazzy to something else entirely. And accordion player Jay Spell, who had been gently rocking as if on a front porch, would begin what looked like a seizure and sounded like a rapture.

"Jamie or I would walk in front of him right in the middle of what he was playing. He'd already be playing his ass off, and we'd start yelling, 'Get outside! Get outside!'" Kane remembers, sipping from a congestion-battling shot glass of Powers Irish whiskey and moving to the edge of his seat at the memory. "And Jay would go totally wild, get totally atonal. It was incredible."

Well, it *was* incredible. It was zero to sixty with a squeeze of the bellows, and for some reason it seemed to make perfect sense. "Bluegrass Blues" became, in Kane's words, "an opera," one with themes that seemed to encapsulate the entireties of past and possibility. Unprocessed instruments would suddenly sound as wild and unrestricted as any Hendrix guitar solo.

This wasn't exactly a continuation of the vaunted neotraditionalist movement that began in the early 1980s with Ricky Skaggs and continued with honky-tonk revivalists Randy Travis, Ricky Van Shelton, and others. And this wasn't just a "let's shock 'em" experience, like Patty Loveless donning a Grace Slick wig and singing "White Rabbit" or something. This was a crew of masterful musicians with unassailable knowledge of and reverence for the music that, fifteen years later, delights the *O Brother* set. This was stuff that pleased Buck Owens yet veered toward Miles Davis. It was the modern-day Delmores one minute, and the next it was what one paper later described as "the Doors of country music."

And these guys were on the radio. On country radio.

"The O'Kanes were an inspiration for me getting back into playing music," says Buddy Miller, now acknowledged as among the best roots-based singers, producers, songwriters, and musicians of our era. "I had laid it down for about six or seven years, but I remember driving in San Francisco and 'Oh Darlin'' came on the radio. It was so simple and so perfect. I think within a couple of months, Julie [his wife and an equally acclaimed songstress] and I moved to Los Angeles, and I started playing with Jim Lauderdale. It seems like an unusual thing to combine the simplest country song with free improvisation, but the Grateful Dead were running a parallel path, and it seems like this was a natural extension."

Thing is, the Dead couldn't have quite done this. The Dead could get this wild, but not this precise. They could get this emphatic, but rarely this elemental. Miller is correct that this was a parallel path, not a repaving.

A few years later, it was gone. Vanished. The O'Kanes followed their 1986 self-titled debut and 1988's glorious follow-up, *Tired of the Runnin'*, with 1990's iffy *Imagine That*, and then they dropped the whole thing altogether. The showcase clubs showcased other acts; the radio moved on to Garth and Clint and all of that; and what Steve Earle had termed "the great credibility scare of the 1980s" receded into virtual nothingness, and then to alt-country, and then to Americana, which is supposedly where Kane now fits.

"It burned too hot," Kane says of those times, of those songs, of that band. "It burned out. I guess it's well remembered, more by musicians than by civilians. I don't know that there's a legacy."

And then Kane takes another sip of Powers, coughs, clams up, and waits for the next question.

■ ■ ■

Kane was born in 1949 in Mt. Vernon, New York, which doesn't explain much of anything. He played drums and dug Bo Diddley, though a friendship with a musician named John Van Valkenburg led to an advanced study of the Carter Family, Johnny Cash, and all of that.

"He was twenty-five and I was fifteen," Kane says. "He may be the best harmony singer I've ever worked with, but he couldn't do it professionally. He was terrified to be in front of an audience, but he could sing you every Carter Family song there ever was. We'd ride around upstate New York in a car, trying to tune in WWVA out of Wheeling, West Virginia. It was the only country station you could get on the radio. We'd drive all around in his '57 Ford, trying to get a signal and listening to 'The Coffee Drinking Nighthawk' all night long. John kept his record collection in his trunk, and everything was completely scratched up. When he'd play records, you'd hear static, with Bill Monroe or the Carter Family coming from somewhere behind it."

Kane didn't take Van Valkenburg's 1957 Ford to Nashville nearly a quarter-century ago. By then he was living in California and playing in a San Fernando Valley bar, when he met Nashvillians Rafe Van Hoy and Deborah Allen, two successful music-industry folks. They liked him, he liked them, and they encouraged him to try Music City.

Kane knocked out the back seat of his Volkswagen convertible, jammed the car with possessions, and headed to Tennessee, his pregnant girlfriend in the passenger seat.

"Really, Deborah Allen got me a publishing deal with MCA before I moved," he said. "But I never signed it. I was so excited about it, and they were going to give me $50 a week, which was great. But three weeks after I came to Nashville, they said, 'We've been playing these songs for people, and we think on this one here you need to rewrite the second verse, and [on] this one here we were thinking maybe you ought to write a bridge.' I went, 'Yeah, well, I'm finished with those songs. You guys said you liked 'em, and you were going to sign me based on them. Now you want changes. I can't do that. I don't know how to do that.' So I never signed the contract."

Destitute songwriters who stand on principle don't normally last too long in Nashville. But Van Hoy took him around to other publishers, and Don Gant at Tree Publishing offered a little money and the promise he would get Kane some studio work playing guitar on demo records. Kane signed a deal with Tree. The VW arrived in Nashville with one fewer cylinders than it started out with, but its driver had a leg up on a career in music.

Back then, Tree's lineup of song scribes included some honest-to-goodness legends as well as promising upstarts. Bobby Braddock ("D-I-V-O-R-C-E"), Sonny Throckmorton ("Middle Age Crazy"), Curly Putman ("Green, Green Grass of Home"), and others were there, playing mentor to young guns such as Kane, Kevin Welch, and Jamie O'Hara.

"It was a pretty wild crowd, but Kieran was a little more tame than the rest of us," Braddock recalls. "He had a young family and no money and a lot of talent."

He also had a song he had written with older brother Richard, one called "Play Another Slow Song." Johnny Duncan kept the words, ditched the melody in favor of a recitation ("Don't worry, they've been making Muzak out of my songs for years," Braddock told him upon hearing the playback), and had a Top 10 hit with that one.

He had also begun playing demo and master recording sessions, contributing the melodic hook to Hank Williams Jr.'s "Texas Women," a song produced by notorious Nashville kingpin Jimmy Bowen. Beloved by some for modernizing Nashville recording processes, Bowen was reviled by others for his brusque personality and his Steinbrenner-esque hiring and firing practices.

Kane won a songwriting award for "Slow Song," and he attempted to parlay the recognition into a record deal. A possibility at Mercury with Tom T. Hall producer Jerry Kennedy didn't pan out, and Kane called Bowen's office at Elektra in hopes of improving his situation.

"I said, 'I've got a deal on Mercury Records, but I don't want to record for them; I want to work with Jimmy Bowen,'" Kane recounts. "I actually had no deal. I was just saying this, but I guess it appealed to Bowen's ego on some level.

"He signed me, and initially I was very happy about it. I've got a record deal, and, more importantly, I've probably gotten a $20,000 advance. The album had four or five singles. The first, 'You're the Best,' did quite well, and each one after that kept doing worse and worse. And the record just isn't very good."

Elektra's Nashville division was eventually folded into Warner Bros., and things got sketchy enough that Kane asked for his own release. Today, fans still approach Kane with his debut LP. He sometimes autographs it "Don't play this for anyone. Thanks. Kieran Kane."

While it didn't make him a star, Kane's time at Elektra/Warner Bros. included a lesson that some artists would find debilitating, but he found rather freeing. With Bowen's permission, Kane watched as one of the label's radio promoters worked to convince FM stations to drop a single by one artist (Gail Davies) in order to get more airplay for another (Conway Twitty).

"He was going, 'I don't want any more adds on Gail's record, because

I need Conway Twitty to be #1 next week," Kane says. "He was sitting there killing one of his own singles.

"I watched him do this, and it was incredibly liberating. I realized [that] I don't really have anything to do with this. If my records are not going to do well because somebody from my own record label is sitting in my office saying, 'Don't add it,' I might as well do the things I love."

By 1984, Kane had no intention of finding a record deal. This was fine with Nashville labels, which considered him a headstrong artist whose string of songwriting credits (Alabama's "Gonna Have a Party" chief among them) was fraying.

"I found myself so many times finishing a song and going, 'I don't really like it, but maybe the Oak Ridge Boys would cut it,'" he says. "I was sick of having that feeling about my work.

"And that's when Jamie O'Hara and I started working together. We'd both reached a similar point. We'd both learned the craft of how to write songs, so now the thing was to write things you like, but still working within the form of a country song."

The two began making demos in Kane's attic, with Richard Kane supplying some electric guitar and fiddle. Braddock remembers O'Hara coming into work, explaining a bit of what was happening. "Jamie told me one day, 'Kieran and I have been holed up in his attic writing these songs, and they're a bit different. Not really elaborate. A lot of them don't even rhyme.' That was the first I heard of the O'Kanes."

The demos involved a good deal of adding and then subtracting elements. The intended effect was a distillation, an essence. "We were trying to find a way to make it incredibly simple, yet still interesting," Kane says.

Working on a demo for "Daddies Need to Grow Up Too" (an unfortunately maudlin title for an unflinchingly honest song), Kane asked Richard to overdub a harmonica over a fiddle. The result sounded like an accordion, and the result was quite pleasant. That is how Jay Spell entered the picture. Roy Yaeger came in to play drums, Roy Huskey Jr. was the upright-bass man, and Kane's West Nashville house was the rehearsal hall. The band played on Tuesdays at a club called Bogey's, though some nights the only audience members were Kevin Welch and fabled songwriter Harlan Howard.

"When Kieran and Jamie got together, they were on a different mission," Welch said. "It was fascinating when they started making those demos. Those guys were minimalists, and this was stripped-down, groove stuff. They'd write a song with, like, one riff that went on the whole time. Maybe a chord change for one second, but then back to the riff. It was very deliberate writing. And nobody in Nashville was paying attention at first. They were totally overlooked."

Just who they were is up for debate. The songs were co-written by

O'Hara and Kane, who also did the lead and harmony singing. But the sound was undeniably a group effort that couldn't be replicated by session musicians. When Columbia Records' Rick Blackburn heard the demos and signed the band, O'Hara and Kane became the visible members.

"It was based on our songs and our harmonies and that front thing of the guitar and mandolin, but it was also based on this band," Kane says. "As far as the record company was concerned, Jamie and I were the O'Kanes, and I believe at some point we started to believe that ourselves. It was always sort of fuzzy, and that finally started becoming a problem."

Whatever and whoever the O'Kanes were, they weren't permanent. The first album was a surprise hit; the second album was a free-form masterpiece of live-in-the-studio musicianship and remarkable songwriting; and the third album was a compromised effort featuring an outside producer (the first two had been produced by Kane and O'Hara) and a bevy of studio musicians.

"We had six singles, and I don't think there was a moment over two years when we weren't on the radio," Kane says. "But then it all just went sour. For me, I do my best to enjoy that moment as it comes along and then to go, 'Well, it's done. It was fun.'"

Beyond the O'Kanes, "the great credibility scare of the 1980s" was done as well. The country-music world awaited its next savior, and he would soon appear in the cowboy-hatted form of Garth Brooks. Kane and O'Hara's old pal Welch was signed to Reprise at the time, and he watched the whole thing crumble for those who dreamed of a commercial country world that would include Earle, the O'Kanes, Foster & Lloyd, Nanci Griffith, Lyle Lovett, and others of that ilk.

"We all knew it was going to be brief," Welch said. "I don't think any of us realized just how brief it was going to be."

■ ■ ■

Kane's split with O'Hara was amicable. The two remain friends, though they don't record or write together anymore. The albums are out of print; all that remains commercially available of the O'Kanes is a ridiculously constructed Lucky Dog Records compilation called *The Only Years* (no "Can't Stop My Heart from Loving You," no "Daddies Need to Grow Up Too," no liner notes, no mention that Jay Spell, Richard Kane, or any of the others were ever in the band at all).

Writing alone again, Kane took his lyrics from bare-bones to trim, and the expansive jams of the O'Kanes were replaced with a tighter weave. Kane's octave mandolin (like a mandolin on steroids) took the place of Spell's accordion as the soundscape's defining feature, and song subjects shifted from the O'Kanes' atmospheric amalgams to reflections on Kane's life.

"I think he's such a wonderful writer," Braddock said. "There's actually a similarity in the way he writes and the way Alan Jackson writes. They both cut through a lot of the veneer, and it's something that's done in the language of the common, everyday person yet still really says something."

Problem is, the common, everyday person doesn't hear too much of Kane's work unless Alan Jackson chooses to record one of his songs (as he did in 1998). Kane's first post-O'Kanes solo album, 1993's *Find My Way Home,* illustrated the oddity of the situation. With the O'Kanes, Kane had hit records that sounded too rooted, too artsy, and too dark for the commercial market. As a solo artist, and with *Find My Way Home* in particular, he wrote well-crafted, accessible songs that should have been hits, but weren't.

"That whole Atlantic record [*Find My Way Home*] has been a bit of a shock," Kane says. "The record company spent a lot of money, something like $750,000. They made an expensive video and everything. Rick Blackburn had moved to Atlantic as the head of the label, and I think he signed me as his 'maverick.' Nothing really happened, and I've never gotten a royalty statement from Atlantic. Ever.

"No more than two years after the Atlantic thing, I was playing a cafe in Oslo, and a guy came up and asked me if I had a record coming out," Kane continued. "I told him I didn't have a label now, and he said, 'Oh, I imported your last record, and if you had a new one coming out, I would buy some.'"

In fact, the Norwegian importer said he would buy 1,000, at $8 apiece. "I said, 'I'll make you a record.' And I went home and made *Dead Rekoning.*" (It is a fine album; don't ask about the spelling.) "Right around that time, Kevin Welch was trying to figure out what he was going to do because he was through with his major-label deal. He and [drummer and *Find My Way Home* co-producer] Harry Stinson and I sat down over a bottle of scotch at my kitchen table one night. We finally said, 'Let's just start a record company. How hard can it be?'"

Turns out, it isn't hard to start a record company. It is, however, hard to make a living from a self-started, independent record company's proceeds.

Stinson, Welch, Kane, fiddler Tammy Rogers, and guitar slinger Michael Henderson ended up buying into what became Dead Reckoning Records. Except for Stinson, the owners all put out albums on the label, and they all toured together, performing on one another's songs in one big friendly band that played with synergy and soul. Soon after *Dead Rekoning* was released in 1995, the Americana music movement coalesced. All things once again seemed possible, and Kane's debut as an indie artist was another critical success.

Though lacking the sheen of *Find My Way Home,* the album was full of subtle pleasures, from the percussion of "Cool Me Down" (played on a metal folding chair by Stinson), to the fiddle-accordion interplay of

Rogers and Fats Kaplin on "Bell Ringing in an Empty Sky," to Kane's own tough-nosed, soulful performance on "Find Somebody New." The album marked DR001 seemed a sure signifier of success.

"At first we had these thoughts of 'Tammy'll handle the publicity, and Michael will be the A&R guy, and Harry will . . .' and I set up an office in a room in my house. I hired J. D. May [a former Tree employee, now executive director of the Americana Music Association] to do the booking."

It didn't quite work out that way. The tours were marvelous, and the label released albums of quality. But the "close-knit team of world-class musicians performing various mundane, workaday chores" thing didn't go smoothly. Soon, Kane says, it was he, Welch, and May doing the lion's share of the work. Sales did not match inspiration, and there was no massive corporation to write off the losses at year's end.

The upside was complete, unquestioned creative freedom and the ability to record and release albums whenever the urge arose. Kane's songs may be heard on 1998's *Six Months, No Sun,* 2000's *The Blue Chair* and *11/12/13* (a duo set with Welch), and on the collective *A Night of Reckoning* disc released in 1996. Taken chronologically, each album finds Kane honing his craft, writing with restraint, singing in his crisp, unadorned baritone, and providing atypical rhythmic work on guitar and mandolin.

"He's like the rhythm god," Welch said. "Kieran is the best rhythm player I've ever known, and a lot of people don't realize that. He joined my band, the Overtones, for a while in the 1990s, and we were making a record for Kelly Willis [her 1993 self-titled album]. I told the producers, 'You need to get Kieran's mandolin up in the mix. Put him up there where the drums are.' They did, and the groove just went crazy."

■ ■ ■

After *The Blue Chair* made its run, May left to head the AMA and Kane and Welch were back at the home office, answering phones and handling the paperwork.

"Around then, I got really, really sick," says Kane. "Then I didn't have much time to do the business, and we kept pulling back. We had some good records out, but we were running up a lot of debt, and we couldn't turn in any sales."

Kane's illness is nothing he prefers to elaborate on. Suffice it to say that he feared for his life, and that he no longer fears for his life. He did, however, fear for what he had built at Dead Reckoning Records. The original owners were all still involved, but all except Kane and Welch now held smaller shares.

"Everything was falling apart," he says. "We had no money to do any more records, and we had no distribution. Kevin and I talked, and we thought, 'What we really need is someone to license the catalogue so we don't have to think about it.' That's when Compendia came charging out of the woods and said, 'We'd like to license your catalogue.'"

Problem solved, emergency averted. By May 2002, Compendia Music Group, an independent record company (home to Joan Osborne, among others), was in charge of getting Dead Reckoning albums back in stores. Kane and Welch were once again free to pursue creativity and to ignore most of the business-oriented minutiae. But Kane wasn't able to sigh in relief.

"I had a strange year," he says. "My son was very ill. He called me last February when I was in New York, and he told me he had Hodgkin's disease. So I wasn't giving a shit about anything at all, except getting him well. And there's nothing I can do about that, so it's pretty frustrating. Then Compendia called me in May about doing a new record, and the last thing I wanted to think about was doing a record."

So he didn't think about it much. He simply culled eleven songs—nine that he had co-written, plus a Carter Family song and the same arrangement of "Handsome Molly" that he used to sing with John Van Valkenburg—and pulled together a core group of musicians to record them.

"First of all, for some reason, these songs I'd written seemed very life affirming, and they seemed to tell a story together," he says. "So that began to make sense to me."

Shadows on the Ground was recorded at Nashville's Moraine Studio in a room so small that the musicians had to enter and exit single file. "I'd always wanted to make a record where everybody's in a room together, and we sing and play, and whatever we do at that moment in time is what's on the record," Kane says. "No fixes. Nothing changed or altered in any way. Honest to God, the whole thing took maybe two-and-a-half days, including mixing. I didn't even have to do a photo shoot: I just gave them one of my paintings and said, 'Use that.'

"And for me, in some ways this is the most important record I've ever done. It's the furthest thing from a tossed-off record. To me, it's jazz. It's a totally feel thing, all the way through. I like the first impression, and I always have. It's the only way you'll always hear things you've never heard before when you listen to the record. Because this way, nothing is planned."

Dedicated to Kane's son Lucas, *Shadows on the Ground* makes no reference to lymphatic cancer, to disease, or to anything that would bind the songs to a particular experience.

"There's death, but death as just another part of life, which I believe it is," Kane says. "I'm not afraid of death. I've actually thought I was a goner, and it turned out I wasn't. But my reaction to that was, 'Life is highly overrated.'"

Thus, on the title track: "Truth is always truth, stone is always stone / We all live and die, but not alone / We go by different roads / We go by different names / Shadows on the ground, all look the same."

Lucas is, it seems, getting better. At twenty-three he is set to return in

January to his studies as a film major at Nashville's Watkins College of Art & Design. Checkups and CAT scans will continue, and cancer doctors aren't ever quick to use the word "cured." They have, however, used the word "miraculous."

As for Lucas's dad, he still gets out into the ether every now and again in duo shows with Welch. The *11/12/13* album documented the beginnings of what has developed into an improvisational set that sometimes summons a bit of that O'Kanes spirit.

"It's evolved into a totally different creature," Welch said. "We'll walk offstage sometimes and go, 'Jesus Christ, where did that come from?'"

And so Kane continues on in his own peculiar way, skinning back words and sounds on albums, then giving in to whimsical (though always musical) impulses onstage. If that leaves an impression, then so be it, but don't bet on Kane to ego-surf through music-history books for validation of his own importance.

"My son was taking a speech class in college, and I asked him, 'What'd you do the speech on?' He said, 'Well, that everything I have of worth— the clothes I'm wearing, the fact that I'm going to school . . . everything in my life is based on the fact that my dad has written a song at some point.'"

The whiskey glass is on the table as Kane settles back into his seat. "That, to me, was a legacy. Not having played mandolin on the radio."

Horse of a Different Color

Or How Paul Burch Went Off-Broadway
and Joined the Ballclub

ND #18, November–December 1998

Jim Ridley

When Paul Burch was growing up, the single record that made the most impact on him wasn't what is thought of as roots music. It wasn't an archival folk recording smelling of dust and shellac, though, as a kid, Burch had access to those and loved them. Of all things, the album that shaped his idea of long-playing greatness was the two-record soundtrack to the movie *American Graffiti*.

"Really," says Burch, leaning forward in a rocking chair in the living room of his East Nashville apartment. His eyes widen as he talks; his hands measure the air. "An amazing record, just one great song after another. Every song has a totally different feel, and I didn't know until I got older all those singles represented the sound of different cities—Chicago, Philadelphia. I just loved that one record could contain so many different colors."

The connection between color and music comes up often at Burch's place. Stuck to his refrigerator door is a color wheel. Linked to each shade is the color-coded name of a different artist, from Vic Chesnutt to Jesse McReynolds. That is the musical and emotional spectrum he wants on his next album. "I like that Bob Dylan sounds different every record," he says, rummaging around for Klondike Bars in a kitchen painted the royalest blue and the lemoniest yellow you have ever seen.

His upstairs apartment, which includes a tiny studio (keyboard, mixing board, reel-to-reel) in a narrow room with a map of the United States, is painted in a scheme that would make Pedro Almodovar pale. The living room would be red if he hadn't run out of paint. All that survives of the effort is a jagged crimson streak that parallels the ceiling. Guitars and mandolins appear in every corner, like ficus plants. These are the comforts of home.

Indeed, that may be the great charm of Burch's music: that it seems as natural a part of daily life as color. The son of painters and writers, Burch plays a joyous, lilting brand of hillbilly swing that is rambunctious yet relaxed. In its own way, it is as full of different shades and different regions as the *American Graffiti* soundtrack.

Wire to Wire, his latest CD for Checkered Past Records (both of Burch's albums appeared in France on the Dixie Frog label several months in advance of their U.S. release), crackles with the resulting voltage from Texas swing and Bakersfield country and even Merseybeat pop all zapping into the same transformer. Recorded with his sterling band, the WPA Ballclub, the album even has some of the freewheeling, almost primordial looseness of another of Burch's favorite records, Bob Dylan and The Band's *The Basement Tapes,* which, like *Wire to Wire,* was recorded by a bunch of buddies cooped up in a small room. But it never sounds consciously retro. The album has the immediacy of old music when it was recorded live and new fifty years ago.

■ ■ ■

Paul William Burch Jr. was born in Washington, D.C., to parents who loved art and literature and folk music. He spent his early years living on the Arthur Godfrey farm, an artists' compound just outside the D.C. area. The farm frequently drew visitors such as Les McCann and Linda Ronstadt, and whenever possible his parents supplemented the influences around him with trips to the Smithsonian Institution's enormous archives of American music and folklore. Among his first discoveries was the Stanley Brothers' "Little Birdie," but he was just as entranced by his parents' stash of Dylan and Beatles LPs.

Burch keeps a memento from these years in a stack of records by an old portable turntable in his apartment studio. He reaches into a box of musty vinyl—again, that smell of dust and shellac!—and withdraws a 78 acetate so weather-beaten and worn you fear a stereo needle would shave it into ribbons. "It doesn't have many plays left in it," he cautions, and gingerly lowers the needle to the surface.

It issues a burst of tinny static, the white noise of an age before television, and then a man's nasal tenor pierces the crackly fog. He sings as if he would have only this one chance to speak his mind, and he lashes out at a faithless lover, returning again and again to a single accusation: "You sold me down the river to a sea of misery." The intensity of the performance is chilling. The fragility of the acetate makes it seem downright heroic.

"I found this in the attic at the Arthur Godfrey farm," Burch says, rubbing his hands above it as if to warm them. "There's no record of who did it. But I learned it just so it wouldn't be lost."

Burch's parents split up when he was young. Miraculously, though, the divorce left him with two loving, supportive families: He is equally close to his natural mother, a painter, and to his father and stepmother, both teachers. "They all wanted me to feel happy and secure," he says. When his mother left the farm to join the arts community in D.C., Burch went to live with his father and stepmother in Oxford, Mississippi. He then moved with them to West Lafayette, Indiana, where his father taught at Purdue University.

Burch had learned to play drums along to Beatles records and later to old R&B sides, but he didn't take up guitar until he was about twenty-one. Even then, the old rockabilly and blues he liked—as well as Elvis Costello and the Clash—didn't have many fans in Indiana in the early 1980s.

One exception was Jay McDowell, a kid a few grades below Burch in one of the high school classes his stepmother taught. To help McDowell overcome his fear of writing, Burch's mom had assigned him to keep a music journal, and he gratefully filled pages with observations on Gene Vincent and other rockabilly idols. "She kept saying, 'He likes the same music you do,'" Burch says. They became friends, drifted apart for a time after high school, then became reacquainted in a jam session at a house Burch was renting. "We were playing 'Be-Bop-A-Lula,'" Burch recalls, "and Jay came downstairs, picked up a guitar, and played the solo note for note." They later became bandmates, learning old rockabilly and blues tunes off a Sun Records box set.

After attending Purdue—and serving a stint in a psychedelic band called the Atomic Clock—Burch moved to Boston to play music professionally when he was twenty-four. Not only did the city have a strong folk history itself, but it also offered close proximity to the legendary folk clubs of New York, where Burch's heroes had strolled as giants among men.

"I'd take the train in and carry my guitar all the way to the clubs in the Village," Burch remembers. "I actually got to play." How was it—romantic? Exhilarating? "Empty," he says ruefully.

Burch stayed in Boston for four years, during which time he played in a folk combo called the Bag Boys. But he longed to play genuine country music with actual lap steel guitarists and fiddlers, and he was sick of the pretentious Berklee music-school crowd—the kind of people, he observes, "who went around acting like they were on a first-name basis with 'Miles' and 'Diz.'" Some of his friends from Indiana had moved to Nashville, and when Burch found out Bill Monroe played weekly gigs at nearby Hendersonville's Bell Cove Club, he decided to move there in 1994.

"My dream was always to have that old hillbilly sound," Burch explains. "Until I moved [to Nashville], I couldn't find anyone who could play like that." Almost immediately he hooked up with a group of musicians. A year later, he had been featured in *Billboard* as part of a revolution on the streets of Music City.

■ ■ ■

Frankly, Burch is a little sick of talking about Lower Broadway. "It was such a small part of my life," he says, with the mildest hint of exasperation.

"It was only a few months, not the biggest event in my whole career." And yet those few months on Lower Broadway left an unshakable, lasting impact on everyone involved.

By the early 1990s, apart from the Grand Ole Opry and a few dive bars and hotel-lounge outposts, Nashvillians had largely forgotten what live country music sounded like. In 1994, the year Burch moved to Nashville, that was changing. A downtown revitalization effort had led to the restoration of the Ryman Auditorium, the Opry's most famous home, which would again host weekly bluegrass shows. But where would audiences go afterward?

That summer, just after the Ryman reopened, a gaunt scarecrow of a singer named Greg Garing began playing hillbilly music in the upstairs room of Tootsie's Orchid Lounge. For a decade prior to his appearances at Tootsie's, Garing had served an apprenticeship in stone country music, including a stint as a fiddler with bluegrass great Jimmy Martin. At Tootsie's he started putting together a band that could recapture the great lost sound of 1940s country. That was the initial spark that set off the explosion.

Not long after Burch moved to town, his friend Jay McDowell, now a Nashvillian, invited him to see an act playing three doors down from Tootsie's at Robert's Western Wear. One Monday night in August, Burch packed his guitar and went down to Lower Broad.

Word was just getting out that you could actually see honest-to-god honky-tonk music being played on Lower Broadway. When Burch showed up at Robert's, a dilapidated boot shop and bar with a tiny stage in the front window, Garing and a bandmate, bassist Preston Rumbaugh, who now plays with Dale Watson, were hanging out. Dos Cojones, a duo made up of singer Chuck Mead and drummer Shaw Wilson, was onstage. As the night got looser, Mead invited Burch and Garing up to sing some of their own songs. That was when things got strange.

Burch wound up playing drums onstage with Mead and Rumbaugh. They had just started jamming when a voice bellowed from the back of the room, "Twenty-five dollars for every Hank song!" The voice belonged to Music Row million-seller John Michael Montgomery, who had parked his entourage at one of Robert's rickety tables.

The bandmates took the challenge. "Chuck kept saying, 'C'mon, what's another one?' and I'd count off 'My Bucket's Got a Hole in It,'" Burch recalls. Montgomery watched goggle-eyed. At the end of the night, Platinum Boy owed the band a whopping $650—which they graciously whittled down to $600, the most the ATM would disburse.

No sooner had Burch gotten offstage than he ended up talking at length to Garing. "He kept going on and on about how I should come down to Tootsie's and how his guitar player just couldn't get the right sound," Burch recalls. "Of course, he was sitting right next to his guitar player, Justin Thompson, who, I'm pretty sure, was paying his rent at the time."

Thompson, for his part, says Burch was a "tone-deaf" guitarist and Garing was just giving Thompson a hard time because he was thinking about leaving the group. At any rate, come that Friday, Burch was installed in Garing's band. In the meantime, the Montgomery story had spread like wildfire, and the place was mobbed.

"I was so excited after leaving Tootsie's that night I ran out of gas," Burch remembers. He was driving to Alabama to see his parents, he explains, and he was so jubilant he forgot to even glance at his fuel gauge. "I was just singing all the way to Alabama," he says with a cackle. "A kid on his way to the Rolling Stones show in Birmingham had to give me a lift."

With Burch as designated bandleader, Garing was soon packing Tootsie's on weekends, and Mead and Wilson's band, BR5-49, was starting to draw crowds at Robert's. For a while, Burch recalls, the attention and the celebrity parade were fun—except maybe for the time that, in the space of one song, Lucinda Williams managed to carve grooves in his prized Martin guitar with her long fingerpicks.

The biggest thrill was the night Marianne Faithfull breezed into Tootsie's. She wanted to sing Arthur Alexander covers, and Burch obliged, even coaxing her into dueting on her own numbers. But the triumph was dampened, he says, when Garing got all the credit for the evening. "That's when it all started to bother me," Burch says.

The band members hadn't been friends from the beginning, but they liked the attention. Plus, Burch loved the opportunity to play. Burch credits Garing with schooling the band in the finer points of playing hillbilly music. "Because Greg had played with all the old cats, he was good at showing you how it worked—'The guitar does this, the bass does this,'" Burch says. "And he and I got to be close in a really short time. He could rely on me, and that gave me the confidence to sing."

But Garing, a large and restless talent, was being courted heavily by labels and publishers, and the prospect of getting trapped as a Hank Williams imitator pleased him no more than it did Bocephus. Furthermore, tensions increased within the band. Burch says Garing's early band members resented his stepping forward to sing his own songs, while Thompson says Burch "was too big for his britches." By February 1995, just seven crazed months after he had started playing at Tootsie's, Burch quit the band.

Garing soon left to pursue a Zeppelinesque rock project. He now lives in New York, where he released a solo folk-electronica record called *Alone* and runs a hootenanny called the Alphabet City Opry that is reminiscent of Lower Broad. The band splintered.

Shortly thereafter, according to Burch, he received a call from his former bandmates, who wanted to put the band back together. "They thought we could make a pile of cash," he explains. He reluctantly agreed to a rehearsal at his place. The only trouble was, his place was right above

Garing's, and Garing was certain to think his whole band was conspiring against him.

Just a few bars into "Steel Guitar Rag," the room below erupted in curses and broom-banging. Garing stomped upstairs and unloosed a torrent of abuse upon his former band, then stormed off. A moment of uneasy silence passed. "Kenny Vaughan, the guitarist, said, 'Does he have a gun?'" Burch recalls. "Justin Thompson said, 'Yeah, but it doesn't work.'"

The reason Burch doesn't enjoy talking about this period now, he says, "is because the whole episode was a mess of missed opportunities, pettiness, greed, and dumb luck on everybody's part."

Even today, opinions vary wildly about the entire episode. Burch's supporters say he put up with a lot of erratic behavior and self-aggrandizing from Garing, while Garing's supporters, such as Justin Thompson, say Burch tried to take over his band and his sound. Garing himself declined comment through an intermediary. The only details anyone agrees on are the delight and excitement at the beginning and the sour feelings at the end.

■ ■ ■

The strongest voice of encouragement Burch says he received in Garing's band was from lap steel player Paul Niehaus, who had become one of Burch's closest friends in Nashville. Niehaus, a veteran of rootsy Nashville bands such as the Dusters, got the Tootsie's gig because Garing insisted on lap steel, not pedal steel. "Lap steel was how the old cats did it," Burch explains. "There's a huge difference between it and pedal steel—it has that 1940s sound, which is what we wanted." The late Owen Bradley once heard Niehaus playing on a Garing session and compared him to Jerry Byrd, Ernest Tubb's revered steel player.

When Garing's band disintegrated, Burch and Niehaus stayed together, playing as a duo. They had been particularly close, and Burch trusted Niehaus as a musician and friend. "Paul was like a canary in a coal mine," Burch observes. "He was watching out for me because he's always trying to help people out. He'd let me know if he had a bad feeling about something, and he was usually right."

If Lower Broad's aftermath had taught him anything, Burch says, it was to make music with people whose company he enjoyed. "Vic Chesnutt has this great quote on the liner notes of, I think, *West of Rome*," he says. "It says, 'So-and-so played his guitar part and split.' And I know exactly what he's saying! You make the best music playing with people you really like, not people who are out the door the minute they've played their part."

That aesthetic was what initially attracted Burch to Lambchop, the sprawling Salvation Army band of a country outfit he performs with when he is not leading the WPA Ballclub. The only band in Nashville with a kickball team, Lambchop had been playing for years under the name Poster Child, until some suits representing an Illinois band with a similar name threatened legal action. Their practices involved lots of food and beer, and they were open to pretty much anyone who dropped by.

When Burch moved to Nashville, he had noticed that Lambchop singer-guitarist-songwriter Kurt Wagner and reed man Jonathan Marx would come to see him whenever he performed at Springwater, the rough-hewn West End dive that played host to Tom House, John Allingham, Ann Tiley & Ricky Lee, and the long-running Saturday-night Working Stiff Jamboree. His friend and frequent singing partner Deanna Varagona convinced him to come to a practice. It didn't click immediately.

"I was very quiet, they were very quiet, and I didn't think they wanted me back," Burch explains. "Then Deanna called me a few weeks later and said, 'Why haven't you come around?'" As the Tootsie's scene and its aftermath got increasingly weird, Burch took solace in Lambchop's camaraderie. Burch now plays percussion and vibes with the group, whose recent recordings (including a stint backing up Vic Chesnutt on his upcoming Capricorn album) have taken a decidedly R&B turn.

That suits Burch fine. Apart from the WPA Ballclub—which contains several Lambchop members, including Niehaus, bassist Dennis Crouch, and vocalist Varagona, who lives in Chicago—Burch and Niehaus have a side band, the Smoky Bacon Combo, which covers classic Stax and Crescent City soul instrumentals in the basement of Guido's, a local pizza joint.

Burch's love of R&B is most evident, however, in the songs for his next record. The early demos he has made in his home studio are a departure from the breezy, rambling swing of *Wire to Wire*. Where that album has a deceptively low-tech sound—Burch proudly claims that every song is written in a different key—the new songs are fleshed out, in some cases with chicken-scratch guitar licks, funky drums, and the rolling throb of a Hammond B3 organ.

As on *Wire to Wire* and in the most indelible moments from Burch's first LP, 1997's *Pan-American Flash*—which was partially recorded with members of Garing's band, under circumstances that somehow produced even more hard feelings—the tracks don't just sound timeless; they sound unmoored in time, as if they had drifted across decades and caught different currents of sound.

"We need to make the kind of cool pop records we heard when we were growing up," Burch observes. "You move away from the model; you go through life; you come back to the model. You internalize what you like, and it lives within you. You do new things by not trying to run away from what you love."

The key to getting those sounds, Burch believes, is working with people he enjoys. Besides Niehaus, Crouch, and Varagona, his WPA bandmates include George Bradfute, a brilliant guitarist and producer who has played with everyone from Webb Wilder to Collin Wade Monk, and Larry Atamanuik, the drummer who put the pep in Emmylou Harris's Nash Ramblers on her *At the Ryman* live album. Bradfute isn't some hotshot session man called in for an hour; he lives near Burch in the same East Nashville neighborhood that was ravaged by tornadoes last April.

Burch says one of the things he has learned since making *Pan-American Flash* is to keep the recording sessions as loose and informal as possible. For one recording date, Burch enlisted his friend Joy Lynn White—a marvelous vocalist in her own right, whom Burch hopes to produce someday—to transport several pounds of barbecue across the state from the Cozy Corner, a renowned Memphis BBQ hangout. White delivered the meat, although several ounces had mysteriously disappeared in transit. What the session lost in eating time, Burch says, it gained in cheer and fellowship—which is apparent in the music.

"I never say 'my bass player' or 'my drummer,' I say 'the drummer in the WPA.' That's not my idea of making music," Burch says. "Dennis Crouch grew up in a family of western-swing players. George makes his own guitars and is a hero to every guitar player in town. Paul taught himself lap steel with mentors who never left the old sound behind, and he did what few people ever do, get his own sound on steel. Deanna flies six hundred miles to sing with both bands [the WPA and Lambchop] on a regular basis. And Larry is acknowledged as the man who was the missing piece in the WPA and plays with us for very little and misses maybe one gig out of forty."

For a seven-month period four years ago, Burch got a taste of what country music is like as an industry. It was professional, and it was nothing personal, and it wasn't what he wanted. He walked away, and he is now making the most vibrant music of his career, with bands of outsiders.

"The WPA Ballclub is really perfect the way it is now; it's just what I wanted," he says. Ask him how so, and he laughs. "Even if they weren't in the band," he explains, "those guys would be over here eating barbecue."

Coal Miner's Sister

Hazel Dickens's Long Journey from Appalachia to America Is Also the Story of Women's Awakenings in Bluegrass Music

ND #20, MARCH–APRIL 1999

Bill Friskics-Warren

> People said that hearing Delia Byrd sing was like hearing heart-break in a whole new key. Her voice could make you sweat, make you move, make you want to lift your hands and pull justice out of the air.
>
> DOROTHY ALLISON, *Cavedweller*

These lines, taken from Allison's latest novel, describe a fictional rock 'n' roller in the Janis Joplin mold. But they could just as easily be about Hazel Dickens, a singer whose piercing, rough-hewn wail, an ache as raw as a wound laid bare, can evoke a woman in childbirth, a mother ravaged by grief, or the prophet Jeremiah crying out in the wilderness. At its most lovelorn, Dickens's voice is also perhaps the purest embodiment of Hank Williams's lonesome whippoorwill.

Take "Forsaken Lover," the obscure Woody Guthrie plaint that opens *Heart of a Singer,* an album of duo and trio recordings that Dickens made late last year for Rounder Records with Carol Elizabeth Jones and Ginny Hawker. "I will tell the sad, sad story / I'm gonna tell a story true / 'Bout an old, forsaken lover / And his heart broke sad and true," moans Dickens to the strains of a resolutely strummed guitar. Guthrie's lines are conventional enough; what isn't conventional is the way Dickens holds onto the word "old" for a full measure so that it hangs in the air like mist in a mountain holler. By the time Jones, Hawker, and the fiddle player add their doleful harmonies, it sounds as if the whole valley is weeping.

Dickens's gift for conveying such close-to-the-bone emotion, for "putting you there," as Hawker likes to say, has been the hallmark of her forty-year career, one that looms as large as that of any bluegrass or old-time singer to emerge since the folk revival of the 1950s. Dickens hasn't enjoyed the commercial success many of her peers have; she isn't the virtuoso that other pickers are, either. But by teaming with longtime partner Alice Gerrard to become the first women to front their own bluegrass band, Dickens has created a legacy that is undeniable. Her songs of struggle and liberation, from the coal miners' lament "Black Lung" to the proto-feminist broadside "Don't Put Her Down, You Helped Put Her There," are as hard-hitting and direct as any ever written.

Heart of a Singer, Dickens's first album of new recordings in eleven years, came about as most sing-alongs and picking parties do—by happenstance. Dickens, Jones, and Hawker first sang together at Mike Seeger and Alexia Smith's wedding in 1995. But it wasn't until they gathered again at the 1996 Folk Alliance in Washington, D.C., that they first considered recording as a trio—and even that was somewhat by accident.

"I was wandering through the lobby, and there the two of them sat," Jones recalls, referring to Dickens and Hawker, "so I ran and got my guitar, and we had a big old time." The rest of the week, Hawker says, the three women sang together every chance they could. "Soon we noticed that every time we sat down, a crowd gathered, and I think [Rounder Records president] Ken Irwin noticed it too. At least that was when he first mentioned the idea of making a record to me."

"The blend and the feeling was just so intense," recalls Irwin, who, with Ronnie Freeland, co-produced the album with the trio. "It was just something I had to document."

For her part, Dickens had reservations about the project—not about Jones or Hawker, with whom she loves singing, but about the way her vocal style can at times slow down the recording process. "Get me out on the porch, and I'll sing all day long," Dickens says, sitting in the living room of her one-bedroom co-op apartment in Washington, just outside Georgetown. "But I don't like recording all that much. I'm just not that quick in the studio. A lot of it is because I'm particular, but part of it is my intonation. Sometimes I'll hit a take right on. Other times it'll take me awhile."

Dickens's experience isn't unusual for someone who grew up singing in church and at home without musical accompaniment, settings in which she wasn't tied to a particular melody line or harmony pattern, and where feeling took precedence over how a song might be written. To some extent, the same is true of the duo format she favored during her twenty-some-odd years with Gerrard. There, often singing high tenor à la Ralph Stanley or Ira Louvin, Dickens could move freely around her partner's loamy lead, which carried the melody.

"Working within a trio setting is so much more confining," she says. "You can't just sing anything you want to sing. A lot of times I'm apt to go off on a tangent. It'll sound really good to me, but maybe when I do, when I try to experiment, my pitch will become a problem. It's too bad, because it just gets in the way of a great adventure."

Despite the lack of harmonic freedom the *Heart of a Singer* sessions at times afforded Dickens, the album has more than its share of epiphanies. Not the least of which are Dickens's gale-force lead on "Love Me or Leave Me Alone," her soaring tenor on "Old River" (a duet with Hawker), and the way the trio tears through the Molly O'Day barn burner "Coming Down from God."

Jones, who also records for Rounder with her husband, James Leva, as Jones & Leva, believes that the three women, all of whom grew up in Appalachia, share "the same aesthetic in a very primal sort of way."

"We were all brought up with singing; we've all taught singing," echoes Hawker, who has released albums with her husband, New Lost City Rambler Tracy Schwarz, and with Kay Justice. "It made for a very rich mixture."

Doubtless some of this rapport also had to do with the fact that Jones and Hawker were singing with the woman they regard as a musical hero. Gushes Jones: "When I was learning to play music and listening to records, Hazel & Alice were everything that I dreamed I could be—their singing, their forceful presence, and their songwriting, which was so far beyond what the normal person could hope to achieve in their wildest dreams."

Jones's experience is little different from that of numerous women who were convinced by the example Hazel & Alice set that there was a place for them in the male-dominated world of bluegrass. Lynn Morris, Kate Brislin, Alison Krauss, Laurie Lewis, and Claire Lynch, as well as several men, including former Johnson Mountain Boy Dudley Connell and Dry Branch Fire Squad leader Ron Thomason, cite the duo as an inspiration for their music or careers.

Hazel & Alice's reach extends to country music as well. Their arrangement of the Carter Family's "Hello Stranger" was the blueprint for Emmylou Harris's version of the song, while their rendition of "The Sweetest Gift (A Mother's Smile)" induced Naomi Judd to start singing with her daughter Wynonna. The ragged-but-right music of the neo-hillbilly band Freakwater would be almost inconceivable were it not for the do-it-yourself harmonies of Hazel & Alice.

Come All You Coal Miners

Dickens's far-reaching influence is all the more amazing when you consider her hardscrabble beginnings. A child of the Depression, she grew up one of eleven children in the coal-fields of Mercer County, West Virginia. Her father, a Primitive Baptist preacher and a powerful singer in his own right, hauled timber to feed his family. Dickens's brothers worked in the mines; one of her sisters cleaned house for the bosses at the mines; and her mother slaved over a scrub board and stove iron all day. Diversions, needless to say, were few.

"We didn't have a lot of outside influence—in fact, none that I can remember," Dickens recalls. "We were lucky every now and then to have an old radio so we could hear the Grand Ole Opry. Until I left home at sixteen, I probably had only been out of the county, or maybe over to Virginia. Apart from that, I don't remember going anywhere other than to a relative's house. And that was just a few miles away.

"So everywhere I'd go, it was all the same music. If you went to the church, and we only went to the Primitive Baptist church, unaccompanied singing was all you heard. You also heard old-time music, and whatever string music might be on the radio, and of course what they played on the Opry, which back then was all very old-timey."

Perhaps to escape her harsh surroundings—the squalor was one thing, but she also saw black lung eat two of her brothers alive—Dickens left home during the early 1950s to work in the factories of Baltimore. There she made everything from beer cans and paper cups to electrical components. Factory life and the hillbilly ghetto in which she lived were hardly better than the misery she had known in West Virginia. What they did offer, though, was exposure to a much larger world.

Dickens had help exploring her new surroundings from Mike Seeger, whom she met through her brother Robert, a patient at the tuberculosis sanitarium where Seeger, a conscientious objector to the draft, was doing his community-service hours. Seeger and Dickens played music together almost from the start. Seeger also introduced Dickens to the local picking-party circuit, a scene that brought together urban folkies and the mountain folk who had migrated to the city.

"There was a small folk-song community in Baltimore," Seeger recalls, "a meeting of working-class bluegrass people, like Hazel and her brothers, who were reared in old-time music, and urban folk-music people, who were often liberal politically. It was a unique time. This didn't happen much in Washington, and it didn't happen much in other places. It happened with the Almanac Singers [in New York City], but this was bluegrass, and this was the '50s, the middle of the McCarthy era. It was also just after the *Brown* [*vs. Board of Education*] decision.

"Hazel struck me as being a little bit shy, but still assertive," Seeger adds, recalling his first meeting with Dickens. "I don't know if I should say tense or not, but she was a little on guard." To hear Dickens tell it, more than merely circumspect, she was much like any other hillbilly transplant, as raw as anyone "from right behind the plow or right out of the coal mines."

"I was still a country girl," she says. "In fact, I felt very strange going anywhere with Mike because back home I had to have an escort when I went out, somebody in the family. I couldn't just say, 'I'm going out on a date.' My father would have slapped me over; he'da took the belt to me. So I was a lot more country for a long time—still am—than most people ever thought.

"I would go to these sings, and there would be people sitting around," Dickens continues. "I'd never seen people sit on the floor cross-legged. I had no frame of reference. Everyone I knew generally sat in a chair. Today, I can figure things out pretty quickly, but for a long time I went through such bewilderment that I didn't know if I was gonna lose my mind or what."

Compounding her feelings of alienation and homesickness was the fact that Dickens was, for all practical purposes, the only woman active in Baltimore's bluegrass scene. Were it not for her friendship with Alyse Taubman, a social worker who also "played a little fiddle," the culture shock Dickens experienced might have sent her packing back to West Virginia. Several of the wrenching songs she later wrote about Mercer County suggest as much. "West Virginia, oh my home / West Virginia's where I belong / In the dead of the night / In the still and the quiet / I slip away like a bird in flight / Back to those hills, the place that I call home," she sings on "West Virginia My Home." Cradled by John Baker's mournful harmonies, Dickens's craggy alto is the sound of longing itself.

"Alyse was trying to save me from I don't know what, maybe the factories," says Dickens of Taubman's efforts on her behalf. "She said she had to get me out of those sweatboxes. She was really good at what she did, and didn't realize that I was a subject, and I don't know that I was, but her support—and friendship, one of the closest I've ever had—was just what I needed."

Seeger agrees that Dickens's adjustment to city life was due in large part to the way Taubman fostered within her a growing consciousness and feeling of worth and empowerment—that, and to the singer's undeniable pluck. In Dickens, Seeger observes, "you had a remarkable person coming out of a family that was just totally destroyed by industrialization, surviving all that and reacting to it with the very best that could come out of that experience."

Who's That Knocking?

Dickens played in a number of local bands as the 1950s wore on, several of them with Seeger. She also gigged in bars as a solo act, singing the latest Kitty Wells and Jean Shepard hits as well as covers of some of the better-known songs of her old-time heroes, Wilma Lee Cooper and Molly O'Day. Dickens didn't find her own voice as an artist, though, until Seeger and others introduced her to Alice Gerrard, who was dating another of their picking pals, Jeremy Foster.

"It wasn't by accident that Hazel and Alice met," Seeger recalls. "Hazel, Alice's soon-to-be-husband Jeremy, and I used to play with a guy named Bob Baker. And it was kind of like an agreement between us that they should meet. I think we got together at Bob's house the first time, in

'56 or '57. But it was a little while before Hazel and Alice actually started playing together."

Dickens remembers her first meeting with Gerrard as having taken place at a music party at the home of Taubman and her husband, Willie Foshag. Gerrard doesn't recall their initial meeting at all, except that Foster once said to her, "There is this little girl with an incredible, big voice that you've got to meet."

However and wherever they met, Hazel & Alice seemed an unlikely pair. Looking back now, though, their collaboration in many ways typified the cultural cross-pollination, the convergence of urban lefties and mountain folk, that made the Baltimore music scene during the 1950s so special. "There was this huge influx of people from further south who had come up to this northernmost Southern city," notes Gerrard, a college-educated, classically trained musician from an upper-middle-class home.

"There were bars and country-music parks all over the place," she continues, alluding to the likes of New River Ranch and Sunset Park, where Bill Monroe, Flatt & Scruggs, and the Louvin Brothers often played. "Harry Smith's *Anthology [of American Folk Music]* also came out [in 1952], and that was big with all of us. So there was this attempt on the part of those of us who didn't necessarily grow up with the music to make contact with some of the people that were playing this kind of music. Some of the country people became mentors, like Hazel did with me; there was that kind of a relationship, as well as a friendship, which was forged around the music."

Hazel & Alice played together at jam sessions and other social gatherings for several years before they gave their first public performance. The occasion was the Galax Fiddler's Convention in 1962. "We were doing very sparse stuff, like Molly O'Day, which is banjo and guitar, and Carter Family songs, autoharp and guitar," Dickens says. "We were very surprised at how well we were received, because we came up against some real competition."

Not long after that, at a music party in Virginia, Dickens remembers David Grisman and Peter Siegel suggesting that she and Gerrard cut an album. Grisman and Siegel, who were just starting their own record label, offered to help the women make a demo tape, which they eventually did in *Bluegrass Unlimited* magazine founder Pete Kuykendall's basement.

"It was very raw, not very polished at all," laughs Dickens about the duo's demo recordings. "We didn't know how to polish anything. We didn't know what that word meant."

There is some confusion about how extensively the duo shopped the tape. Dickens recalls a rejection letter from Vanguard saying that Doc Watson met the label's quota of folk heroes; but in the end, Moses Asch of Folkways Records advanced them enough money to pursue the project.

Hazel & Alice recorded their debut, *Who's That Knocking,* in Pierce Hall of the First Unitarian Church in Washington, over two days toward the end of 1964 (not long after an auto accident claimed the life of Alice's husband, Jeremy Foster). The LP mostly featured bluegrass covers and boasted such stalwart pickers as Grisman on mandolin, Blue Grass Boy Lamar Grier on banjo, and the late Chubby Wise, then an alum of Monroe's band, on fiddle. Rounding out the lineup were Dickens on upright bass and Gerrard, who has since become an accomplished fiddle and banjo player, on acoustic guitar.

Who's That Knocking, released by Folkways in 1965, not only contained great playing and the duo's bold, forceful harmonies, but also was among the earliest bluegrass records made by women. The female-led string bands that preceded Hazel & Alice, such as the Coon Creek Girls, were strictly old-time musicians. And while West Coast honky-tonker Rose Maddox made a terrific bluegrass album in 1962, it was a one-off project from someone who generally worked outside the bluegrass fold. By contrast, Hazel & Alice were expressly a bluegrass act; they not only fronted their own band, but also sang the same material, and sang it in the same tenor-and-lead style as many of the bluegrass men.

Somewhat remarkably, neither Hazel nor Alice remembers encountering much animosity in bluegrass circles, which at the time could not have been more of a boys' club. Dickens suspects that some of this might have been because the duo didn't pursue slots on some of the bigger bluegrass festivals. "If we had tried to compete for the same jobs as the Stanley Brothers or Bill [Monroe], we might have run into some trouble," she says. "If we'da had an agent and really gone at it, I think there would have been a lot of people who wouldn't have hired us.

"As it was, we were booked on some of the festivals that Bill and the other male acts were booked on. I'm not sure if they looked at us as a novelty, or if they took us seriously. But I do know that as soon as we started singing, they had to take us seriously. Because we certainly weren't square, and we weren't singing stuff that they weren't singing. So there were a lot of them, especially down through the years, that gave us respect."

Foremost among them was the father of bluegrass himself, Bill Monroe. "Bill was extremely supportive," remembers Gerrard. "Hazel and I were in awe of him, but he was also a friend who would come to Washington and stay at the house. Once when he and Peter Rowan were there, kinda messing around and singing, Bill just out of the blue said, 'Here, I want you to have this song.' It meant a lot to us. I don't think he'd even published it at the time."

The song in question, "The One I Love Is Gone," first appeared on Hazel & Alice's second and final Folkways LP, *Won't You Come and Sing for Me.* It might even have become a bluegrass standard were it not for the prevalence of minor keys the duo used in their arrangement of the song, hardly the sort of thing that appeals to most latter-day bluegrassers.

Finding Their Voices

Hazel & Alice recorded *Won't You Come and Sing for Me* not long after releasing *Who's That Knocking*. Like its predecessor, the record was very much in a bluegrass vein, even to the point of featuring most of the musicians who played on the duo's debut. Inexplicably, though, the album stayed in the can until 1973, just as Rounder was about to release the landmark *Hazel & Alice* LP, a record that encompassed country, folk, and old-time music as well as bluegrass. (Smithsonian/Folkways reissued the duo's two Folkways albums on a single CD, *Pioneering Women of Bluegrass,* in 1996.)

In the meantime, the two women toured extensively, singing in clubs and at festivals and rallies, as well as taking part in singer-activist Anne Romaine's Southern Grassroots Revival Project. From the late 1960s until they called it quits in 1976, Hazel & Alice were regulars on Romaine's traveling multi-act shows. The experience proved to be something of an awakening for the duo, not only inspiring them politically, but also helping them find their voices as songwriters.

"In my opinion," says Gerrard, "that was one of the major, significant crossroads, getting us more conscious of ourselves—of our role—and of a lot of political issues. It provided a forum and an encouraging, supportive place where we could begin to explore our own music in terms of our songwriting, and in terms of arranging with just the two of us."

Mike Seeger, who also went on some of the Grassroots Revival tours, and for a time was married to Gerrard, believes this was also when Dickens's songs took a political turn, addressing themes that previously had been latent in her writing. "[Romaine's support] helped encourage Hazel to put her strong working-class identity to work in her songwriting," Seeger says. "Alice had some of that to start with. But I think that going around to the coal camps and talking to people greatly empowered Hazel to express the feelings she always had anyway. The voltage was always there; it just needed to have the amperage to flow."

Dickens, who had grown up amid the political unrest of coal miner strikes and picket lines, agrees. "I didn't have a very large vocabulary, and I also had not gone very far in school, so there were all these things that I felt that I couldn't articulate. I had always objected to man's inhumanity to man, to people treating people badly. And after I got away from where I grew up, I always hated seeing poor people. I'd get on the bus and see a little girl shivering, and [I'd] immediately want to go buy her a coat or give her something else that I had."

Perhaps foremost among Dickens's social justice concerns was the exploitation of workers. "My one brother would come home from the mines, and he'd be so tired that he'd sit down in the chair and give me a nickel to wash the coal dust off his face and his ears and his neck," she recalls. "When you watch that, it's got to rub in. I wrote 'Black Lung' after watching my oldest brother die of the disease. He had stomach cancer that had eaten clear through to the bed. They just put padding under him and sent him home from the hospital to die.

"Then I watched one of my sisters die, and it was the same thing—lung and breast cancer. And another brother that died of lung cancer. I had seen so much that I finally said, 'Shoot, I may as well start trying to put some of this into song because I know there are other people who might relate to it and might have been in the same situation.'"

Filmmakers Barbara Kopple and John Sayles certainly recognized as much. Kopple included four Dickens originals, including "Black Lung" and the solidarity anthem "They'll Never Keep Us Down," in her 1976 Oscar-winning documentary, *Harlan County, U.S.A.* Ten years later, Sayles—who had first heard Dickens in Kopple's picture—cast the singer in *Matewan,* his movie about the 1920 massacre of striking coal miners in West Virginia. Dickens's part was just a cameo, but her performance, singing a cappella at a miner's graveside, was one of the film's most riveting scenes, no doubt because Dickens, rather than acting, was reliving a nightmare she had known back home in Mercer County.

"The scene took place on one of those great misty, rainy West Virginia days up on a hill above a holler," Sayles recalls. "As we were setting up for it, with the gravestones flapping in the wind because they weren't real gravestones, Hazel was saying that a bunch of her relatives, including her brothers, had died of black lung, and that she'd sung at and been to so many funerals in similar situations. I think that, and just the power of her voice, really lent something to the scene and to the actors, and even to the crew, who are usually so busy with their jobs that they don't tune in that much to what's happening on-screen. So it was almost a moment of reality, whereas film is so much artifice until you actually play it. It was like being at a real funeral."

Several years earlier, Hazel & Alice likewise found audiences responsive to the strong women's perspective they expressed on their 1973 Rounder debut. In fact, Dickens's "Don't Put Her Down, You Helped Put Her There" so resonated with the incipient women's movement that the duo found themselves adopted by feminists almost everywhere they went.

"That just sort of happened like that," remembers Dickens. "I'm not sure why, because we certainly didn't know anything about the women's movement. We were writing about our own experience. They were things we needed to say. It's stuff that had probably been milling around in our heads for some time, and definitely in my experience.

"At first, I was very scared to write about stuff like that," she continues, referring to sexism and the oppression of women. "I can remember the first time I sang 'Don't Put Her Down, You Helped Put Her There.' I was at a party standing in the middle of all these men. It was here in Washington. Bob Siggins was playing banjo, and when I got done, everyone just looked at each other, and Bob said, 'That's a nice song, but I won't be able to sing it.' And I said, 'Of course you can. You can sing that song.'

"Someone else had a [negative] reaction to it when we were in Canada," says Dickens. "But Bob Dylan was at that same gathering, the Mariposa Festival, and he liked it. He even wanted to know who I was. So people had different reactions. Dudley Connell, he'll sing it with me. Ralph Rinzler was the same way. He'd say, 'You gotta sing that song.' Ralph was a real supporter of that stuff."

Pioneering Women

Shortly after Hazel & Alice recorded their second album for Rounder, *Hazel Dickens and Alice Gerrard* (1976), the duo split up. "There were a number of issues, but it really boiled down to my wanting to do something else," Gerrard explains. "So it was my idea, and it wasn't received well by anybody, including Rounder. And it was kind of bad timing; we had just finished recording our second LP for Rounder."

"People thought that [it was my doing]," says Dickens, "because I went out on my own. But that's not the way it was. Rounder wanted me to keep making records, but at first I was scared to go out on my own, because I very much relied on being with Alice."

"Unfortunately," says Gerrard, "for quite a long time the breakup damaged our friendship, but we've got it back on track lately. I feel very close to Hazel and her family. We've known each other for such a very long time. In some ways, we're like sisters who fight, but who'll always be close because of our shared experience."

After she and Dickens went their separate ways—the duo has, on occasion, reunited for festivals and special events—Gerrard went on to record with the Harmony Sisters, a trio that released a pair of fetching albums for the Flying Fish label. Gerrard also recorded with several old-time musicians, including legendary fiddler Tommy Jarrell, and made a film, with Stacy Conway and Les Blank, about Jarrell's life and music called *Sprout Wings and Fly.* And shortly before moving to Durham, North Carolina, in 1987, she founded the *Old-Time Herald,* a respected mountain-music quarterly. Gerrard also released her solo debut, *Pieces of my Heart,* on the Copper Creek label in 1994.

Besides her contributions to *Harlan County, U.S.A.* and *Matewan,* Dickens continued to record for Rounder, releasing a series of powerful albums, including *Hard Hitting Songs for Hard Hit People* (1980) and *It's Hard to Tell the Singer from the Song* (1987). Both records found Dickens indulging in her passion for vintage honky-tonk much more than she had in her recordings with Gerrard. In fact, several of Dickens's more recent originals, such as "Old Callused Hands" and "A Few Old Memories," betray the influence of George Jones, a photo of whom, appropriately, hangs alongside a rendering of activist Mother Jones on Dickens's living-room wall.

The soft-spoken, acid-tongued daughter of Appalachia hasn't sung on many picket lines lately, limiting her schedule as she has throughout much of the 1990s. However, after being back in the studio with Jones and Hawker, Dickens says she is ready to make another solo album, news that doubtless will please Rounder's Ken Irwin, who has been bugging her to do so for years.

Dickens also has emerged as something of a matriarch, a source of inspiration and a role model for many of the contemporary bluegrass scene's younger stars, such as Lynn Morris, whose recording of Dickens's "Mama's Hands" was #1 on the National Bluegrass Survey for six months in 1995. Her influence is also apparent in alt-country bands such as Hazeldine, whose 1998 disc *Orphans* opens with a cover of "Mining Camp Blues" based on Hazel & Alice's version of the song on their 1973 Rounder album.

"I was first drawn to traditional bluegrass music—the first-generation stuff, Bill Monroe, Flatt & Scruggs, Jimmy Martin, the Stanley Brothers," says Morris. "It was like nothing I'd ever heard. But very little of it reflected the perspective of women, and that's where Hazel comes in so strongly. You gotta admire her grit, and her refusal to sidestep an issue. She gets involved. She has more nerve than anybody to tell the truth in a song. And her singing—it's raw, it's powerful, it's from another planet in terms of what I grew up listening to in West Texas.

"I'd never heard anything like that in my entire life," Morris continues, referring to the first time she heard Dickens sing. "When I was growing up, people were trying to get away from the old Depression days. If things were considered country or primitive, they were to be put behind you as well. I had no idea there was this other world of raw emotion in music."

"Hazel has always aimed for the higher goal—to sing and to write about the human condition," says Hawker. "And that cuts across all cultures. You don't have to be from southern West Virginia to feel the songs she writes and to feel the songs she sings. I sang 'West Virginia My Home' one time for a group of college kids, and after it was over, one of the young women was in tears and said, 'I'm from New Jersey. I wanna go home.'"

Jones agrees with the assessments by Hawker and Morris. "I think one of the great challenges in writing is to write about things that are about the deepest emotional content without being sentimental," she observes. "You have to avoid clichés. You have to avoid oversimplifying things, or magnifying things. Either way is deadly, and that's what I admire so much about Hazel: She's writing about matters of the heart, but she does it in such a way that it's never sentimental and it's never overstated. 'Mama's Hands' is a really good example of that.

"But there's another side of her writing, too, which was so important to me as a teenager: the spunky 'I don't give a shit' kind of songs, the 'You can do right by me or you can get out' songs. Those songs are so Hazel. And she doesn't just write that way, she talks that way."

Indeed, as Dickens herself declares in one of her best-known originals, "It's hard to tell the singer from the song."

Quicksilver Girl

Gillian Welch Leaves Much Unspoken, Trusting Her Music

ND #35, SEPTEMBER–OCTOBER 2001

Grant Alden

Shortly after the lunch rush ends, Gillian Welch comes to breakfast, leaving David Rawlings home to sleep off the long drive from New York. She enters dripping wet—it is, briefly, monsoon season—and smiling. Nobody gives her a second glance, though the Pancake Pantry is one of the few places in Nashville where one might glimpse Garth Brooks or Buddy Miller, where heads turn like owls at the scent of fame or, sometimes, talent.

Regardless, this is unmistakably her moment, that rare instant in one's career when concealed doors open suddenly and one must hunt among the horns for a halo. Not that it shows. Central to the success of the *O Brother* soundtrack (on which she wrote, sang, and earned an associate producer's credit) and with a key role in *Down from the Mountain,* the new film documenting the concert reprising the soundtrack, Welch is perfectly poised to cash in, if not sell out.

And perhaps she will, only it will most assuredly be on her terms.

Which are these: She will write songs and make records, and the songs that fit on her records will be released on the label she and Rawlings have just launched, Acony. And though one may easily find bizzers around Nashville who doubt the wisdom of those choices, her third and newest release, *Time (The Revelator),* is an extraordinary artistic achievement. And that is her answer.

Those words gurgle like the clichés they are, but the music brooks no argument against their use. The ten songs of *Time (The Revelator)* weave together in intricate, subtle, revealing patterns, the words and ideas recirculating throughout, culminating in the fourteen-minute-and-forty-second epic closer, "I Dream a Highway." They have made one of the finest albums released in this or any other year.

■ ■ ■

Time (The Revelator) is explicitly a folk album, provided one understands folk music to be a continuum, not an archive. Provided one understands folk music to encompass everything from old-time fiddle tunes to rock to country to blues to bluegrass, and whatever else litters the landscape that might be of use. Welch and Rawlings have gathered together fragments from across the rich history of American music and reset them as small, subtle jewels adorning their own keenly observed, carefully constructed language. At the same time, they have moved past the Appalachian murder ballads ("Caleb Meyer," etc.) of previous albums and into fresh territory that seems uniquely their own.

In this new world, they link Elvis Presley to the John Henry myth ("Elvis Presley Blues"), quote Steve Miller with an attacking banjo ("My First Lover"), and draw upon the resonances of Blind Willie Johnson's sanctified blues classic "John the Revelator" for the title song (during which Welch quite gracefully sings the word "fuck").

It makes no difference whether the bracingly honest "My First Lover" is autobiographical, but certainly one of the album's core issues—the relationship between fame, art, and a musician's life—strikes close to home. Amidst the images dominating "April the 14th Part 1" (which include the sinking of the *Titanic,* the onset of the Oklahoma Dust Bowl, and Abraham Lincoln's assassination) appears an Idaho punk band playing a gig that won't even put gas in their van. "But I watched them walk through the bottomland," Welch sings, "and wished I played in a rock and roll band."

Sure enough, the next song is the almost joyous "I Want to Sing That Rock and Roll," a live track common to the *Down from the Mountain* soundtrack, which Welch has said grew from Carter Stanley's comments on a live album recorded during the depths of country's late-1950s rock 'n' roll depression. Which in turn is followed by "Elvis Presley Blues." Playing with the chords of fame.

Two songs later (in "Everything Is Free"), she sings, "I could get a tip jar, gas up the car, try to make a little change down at the bar. Or I can get a straight job, I've done it before, never minded working hard, it's who I'm working for."

All of which is rather more speculation than she would be comfortable with. "I want everybody to come to it the way they want to come to it," Welch says, plates aside, sipping coffee. "Because it's funny, this word thing. Different words have power for different people. I want people to have their own attachments."

To that end, they have chosen not to print the lyrics to *Time (The Revelator),* and we are left to puzzle things out for ourselves. "I have no idea what this stuff looks like written," she says. "I think it would feel really different. You just have to hear it. Really, I just think there'd be a big discrepancy between what it looks like on the printed page and what it sounds like."

An early-career encounter with *Newsweek* taught Welch to keep some distance from the printed page. While she is unfailingly gracious, she reveals nothing by accident. In fact, she seems to have acquired much of the poise and grace of her two presumed role models, Carol Burnett (from whom she may also have learned that wonderful laugh) and Emmylou Harris. Not that there seem to be secrets lurking; simply that the creative process is inescapably private.

Nevertheless, she is willing to provide a few clues. "'Revelator' was the starting point," she offers. "That really was the first song written for the record. Or, rather, when that song got written, I think both of us thought, 'OK, we've started our new record.' Every song that got written after that, the question was, 'Is this part of the record?' And then it was usually a pretty easy yes or no."

■ ■ ■

Welch and Rawlings have long stood together at the microphone with a quiet, careful tension. Though their music is still painted in muted tones, they have added brighter, sharper hues to this album (the cover is even a color photograph). It is all a matter of degree, of course, but her vocals seem to have a new assurance, and the freshness of discovery charges their vocal and instrumental interplay.

"We're pretty detail-oriented because we have to be," says Welch. "Since there's not a sweeping variation in instrumentation—you're not going to get the song with the accordion and then the song with the horns—everything needs to be assembled so that the variation that is intended, and is there, is displayed correctly.

"We've come to realize, even constructing set lists, [that] our palette is a little more constricted than some people's. And so we have to take a certain amount of care in the presentation. So, yeah, we're pretty careful about sequence and what sits next to what. Plus, those little tiny connections that happen from song to song, they actually build up. They start to pile up, and then they create this other thing."

All of which reflects their maturation as artists. Of 1996's Grammy-nominated debut, *Revival,* she says, "I see that, now in hindsight, as a collection of songs. Less of an album project and more of a collection of songs. Which is fine, and very appropriate for a first record."

But her second album, 1998's *Hell Among the Yearlings,* revealed more focus on creating a cohesive work, to the extent that no less than three copies of the album circulated—with different songs, different versions of songs, and different sequences—prior to the formal version being made available to consumers.

"Yeah, the second album was an attempt to make an album," she agrees. "And this was also more cohesively conceived, in a way. The songs sort of presented themselves and identified themselves as being part of this record. They're just the ones that had to be on there."

Some of which has to do with her writing process. "All the stuff was getting written all together. I tend to write a lot of songs simultaneously," she says. "And I don't finish 'em . . . I finish a whole batch in one week. But what that means is there are numerous months where I have nothing to show."

In the end, Rawlings helped her to focus by propping two banjos against the glass door of her old writing room. "Oh, she could have gotten out if she wanted to," he says cheerfully over the phone.

Well, banjos aren't exactly bass amps.

"No, but they're scarier than bass amps when they're looking at you like that."

Anyway, it worked. She sighs. "There are songs kicking around that should be slapped on tape and given to my publisher. I don't know, twenty songs that I just need to record."

■ ■ ■

Pronouns become awkward when speaking of Gillian Welch and David Rawlings, for though it is her name and face appearing on the album covers, they are partners in Acony, they write together, they share a home, and they receive equal billing in performance. A fully integrated creative team. "We're a band," she offers with a tinkling laugh, "a little band."

This, too, is of their particular design. Rawlings politely declined to be photographed for the cover of this magazine. "That would be the same reason that I wasn't on the record cover," he explains, gently. "Which, you know, it's not complicated to me, but it might be really complicated to try to explain, and it might look really bad in print. I'll explain it to you sometime if you want, but not . . ."

Though he is effusive in person, Rawlings would prefer not to be interviewed, though not for any of the usual reasons: "I say a lot of stuff, but it takes so damn long. I say so much nonsense getting around to the two sentences that I mean, that it just ends up being, like, fourteen paragraphs of crap . . . I don't believe anything I say until I get to those two sentences."

But he knows people talk. "It bothers me because sometimes people think it's not OK."

There is such a tradition of exploitation in the music industry that it is assumed you are being exploited.

"Yes! I would agree with that. And it's really funny because now it's so obvious. I don't like being on the back [cover of the new album], but I'll take it because it's a beautiful picture. I'm more interested in the picture than the fact that I'm in it."

But, no, he'll not be producing others, not just yet. "Oh, goodness. I don't think so. I don't know how there would be time to do that," he answers softly.

▪ ▪ ▪

Welch calls back a month later. Yeah, some demos got cut, she says, rushing to more urgent matters: "We cut a record with our friend [Texas songwriter] Mark Ambrose. We talked him into coming here for two days, so we cut a record with him."

This is all possible because the Country Music Foundation has (temporarily) given Welch and Rawlings the keys to RCA's famed Studio B, one of those places where the old magic happened. Evidently, it still does.

"Bob Moore was there the day they handed us the keys," Welch says with barely restrained joy. She had met the venerated A-Team bass player one night at the Station Inn. "He was driving by, saw the door open, so he stopped and came in. He showed us how they set up. 'Thank you for the starting place, sir!'

"He said, 'Well, the vocalist was always there, always there facing that corner.' And sure enough, we moved around the room, but by god there's a good spot, and we just stood there. And then there's another corner where you see pictures of the Everly Brothers set up, facing each other around the mike. We did some stuff over there, too, in the Everlys' corner. It was like the Elvis setup, and the Everlys' setup.

"The first thing I made Dave and Matt Andrews, the engineer who we worked with on the O Brother thing, [do], the first week we were in there, I said, 'OK, I don't care how many times you gotta climb up that ladder, you're hooking up that echo chamber.'

"It's been quite a long time since there's been an analog setup in there. Long enough that there was a lot of garbage in the cable troughs in the control room. We cleaned up the place a fair amount. How many control rooms can you pull up stuff and find rhinestones in the cable troughs? Who's wearing rhinestones in the control room?" She is nearly giggling.

They chose Studio B over an earlier plan to record at home ("it was too much to ask a professional engineer to work in that environment") because it was so clearly a place of business. "Studio B has such a history of being a place where you go to work," she says. "That is a workin' room. There's very little documentation from in there, because they were working too hard. And you feel it when you go in there. You just went in, and you worked. The lounge is like a break room at a factory or something, with a Formica table and a couple chairs."

Rawlings, who flew solo in the producer's chair for the first time (well schooled by T Bone Burnett, who produced Welch's first two albums), remembers pre-production with slightly less glee. But then, he was climbing the rickety ladder. "There was a lot to be done," he says carefully, adding a short laugh. "There were a number of weeks of twelve-hour days that had nothing to do with making music."

In the intimacy of that studio—just Welch, Rawlings, and engineer Andrews—the ambitious (yes, cinematic) "I Dream a Highway" came to life. "That was an interesting sort of final cathartic moment," she remembers. "That's largely the first take. And we'd only played it that one time. I'd always had it in my head that that would literally be the last thing we cut for the record. But it wasn't. I did 'Ruination Day' after that. I don't think it means anything. It just got to where we had to do that one because it was going to be such a large chunk of the record. If for some reason it didn't work . . .

"We'd spent the whole day with [John] Hartford at his place, and were just beat. We were very wrecked. Took a break, got some dinner, came in and did that. And that was the whole night."

■ ■ ■

Prevailing wisdom in the South, most recently expressed in *Down from the Mountain* by Ralph Stanley—whose music was to prove central to Welch's creative wakening—argues that country music is a Southern thing, that it flourishes only in the mountains and valleys and deltas south of the Mason-Dixon Line. Born to it, or not.

This, of course, would negate the work of Canadians Hank Snow and Shania Twain, of Australians Keith Urban and Kasey Chambers, of songwriters Fred Rose and Tompall Glaser. While one or two of those might be better off forgotten, it seems fair to argue that country music would be vastly poorer were its exponents restricted to residents of the South.

No, the issue isn't so much geography as it is class. Country has long been the music of the working class, and the working class has chased jobs across this continent since the first Europeans landed (see: Detroit, Bakersfield, etc.). With the rise of Garth and Trisha, country moved from those working-class roots to suburban townhouses and prospered, however briefly. And abandoned its core audience.

Here is an ugly story. An acquaintance briefly worked for WSM-AM, home of the Grand Ole Opry, the station whose present motto is "Too Country and Proud of It." Sure enough, a traditional country crowd showed up for a remote promotion, producing more than a little awkwardness. Their trucks weren't pretty, they didn't buy anything, they weren't easy to look at, and it was hardly the sort of audience one might sell to advertisers.

That is country music's real identity battle, though it is probably all over but the shouting. The extension of that argument frames country music's historic pendulum, ever swinging from pop (Vernon Dalhart) to traditional (Jimmie Rodgers) sounds.

Welch works in the thick of the dispute. She was born in New York and raised in Los Angeles, a child of certain kinds of privilege; her parents did music for *The Carol Burnett Show*, and so she did not come innocently to the footlights. This is a peculiar pedigree for a country musician. She finished a degree in photography at the University of California–Santa Cruz before heading to Boston's Berklee College of Music, where she met David Rawlings. At the time, his band (like many in Boston in the early 1990s) sounded rather like the Pixies.

"By that time I had decided that I would really like to try to make my living playing music, and I thought I would do whatever I could to make that seem more likely," Welch laughs. And sighs. "I didn't really know much of anything about reading music or any sort of professional skills. And so I went to school for two years.

"And then after being there, it was like, well, nope, really all you have to do is be musical and try to express yourself, and other musicians will understand. You don't need to speak in terms of music theory or whatever. But I didn't know that until I went there. And then, of course, I also met David there, so I'm awfully glad that I did do it."

Together, Welch and Rawlings discovered and developed their extraordinary, writerly voice for country music. It is no accident that Emmylou Harris recorded "Orphan Girl," nor that the Nashville Bluegrass Band (on 1998's *American Beauty*) cut "Red Clay Halo," the fourth track on Welch's new album. But despite the title of her debut, she and Rawlings are not a revival act seeking to replicate country music's halcyon days.

"Somebody asked me if we struggled, if we walked the line between commerciality and our own thing," she says, choosing carefully. "No, we don't deal with that at all! But that issue, of modernity versus traditionalism, conservation, yeah, we deal with that a lot. For instance, for three years now we've been lucky enough to play Ralph Stanley's festival. That's a really heavy gig for us. That's a difficult gig for me.

"That's one of the proving grounds for us, personally, of that exact issue. Are we modern, and yet do these people—who are some of the staunchest traditional music fans I've ever seen—do they like us? Because the majority of people up there are playing only Stanley Brothers songs that are forty or fifty years old. And then I get up there, and I'm playing new songs that they've never heard before? You know, what does that mean? So that's a big deal for us. The fact is, we keep getting asked back. So that's good."

Not just asked back. Ralph Stanley chose to sing two duets with her on his new *Clinch Mountain Sweethearts* album. Other recent side projects have been similarly significant: Her contribution to the *Songcatcher* soundtrack is arresting, as is her cut on *Avalon Blues,* the new Mississippi John Hurt tribute. ("I have the lowest guitar," she says proudly. "But Beck beat us on tape hiss.")

And she still sings that rock 'n' roll. For years Rawlings has fronted a garage trio called the Esquires, in which Welch plays bass. "No one's going to hire me and Dave to play New Year's Eve," she says merrily. "We hate New Year's Eve parties; we just wanna play. Thus, the Esquires were born."

She even admits the possibilities of an Esquires album emerging—sort of. "Well, we started compiling a best-of-the-Esquires from our live tapes," she says. "I don't think the Esquires could possibly make a studio album, so there might be a best-of-the-Esquires live album at some point. But we're really dubious about the market for it."

Point is, Welch and Rawlings are working musicians, vastly curious (you should see Rawlings's guitar collection), consumed with the process of creation and not its consequences. It is, in part, the tension between wishing to be accepted by Ralph Stanley's audience and the need to create fresh work that makes their work so compelling.

"It's not something I think about consciously that much," she says, "but, clearly, making the record in RCA Studio B, it's all around us. It's the world I live in because I'm a songwriter. I write new songs; I love old music."

■ ■ ■

Welch first met the late John Hartford while a student in Santa Cruz. "I went up to him after a show, probably in '86," she remembers, "and I talked to him for a little while and got him to autograph one of his records in his beautiful longhand. I still have that.

"We have the same booking agent, so we did some shows with him, right about the time our first record was coming out. We'd been out to his house because, basically, you can't know John and be a musician and have him not have said, 'Come out to the house and play.'"

So when T Bone Burnett begin to create the *O Brother* soundtrack (Welch happened to have the *Odyssey* on her nightstand when he called), Welch and Rawlings immediately thought of the friend they had called to fact-check the name of a fiddle tune whose title became the name of their second album, *Hell Among the Yearlings.*

"T Bone just kind of, who knows why, but every now and again on the *O Brother* sessions, he would leave and say to me, 'You produce this one,'" Welch says. "And one of those was a session with John. So John Hartford was the first thing I ever produced. It basically consisted of, 'Oh, that seemed like a good one. Did you like that one, John?' That was fun."

The May 2000 concert at the Ryman Auditorium, which became the *Down from the Mountain* documentary, was also fun. Until Welch arrived the day of the show, she had no idea she would be singing "Indian War Whoop" with Hartford. "He didn't think he could hit that note, so I was the stunt war whooper," she laughs. "With his sense of humor, of course there was no rehearsal. There's no form. There's form, but it's improvisational, so he could go wherever he wanted, and I just had to follow. He was playing with me!"

That, of course, was the original point of the *O Brother* music. Money came after, and without warning. "My life isn't different," Welch says. "I've met some more erudite folks, some people I really, really like, like the

Coen brothers. Great to meet them; every time I talk to them it's a great spot in my day.

"This little light has been shined on our little community. We just went and played Carnegie Hall, and it was crazy. But it's all the same people that I've known, our little world. They plunked us at Carnegie Hall. So it feels the same; we're just getting a little more attention right now. And everyone's just maybe dressing slightly better."

Despite the soundtrack's multiplatinum sales, the artists on *O Brother* haven't stumbled upon a pot of gold. "Nothing's really changed monetarily," she says. "You know how far behind the record industry is; ask me a year from now. There might be a little windfall, but no one made crazy deals, because no one knew it was going to be a big hit. There were a lot of artists, and the pie is being split a million billion ways.

"I was just happy that they were putting out the record. I remember when we were putting it together, there were a couple months when I was afraid that at any moment someone would come to me and say, 'Well, they've decided that there has to be a Shania Twain song on here.'"

Indeed, Welch's primary memories of the process are artistic. "Singing with Alison [Krauss] was the great surprise of the *O Brother* thing," she says. "We'd never sung together before, and I wouldn't have guessed that we would have a good, natural blend. I know she's a badass and how great she was, but there's nothing you can do about a blend. You either blend with someone or you don't.

"And then the three of us [adding Emmylou Harris], that was great, too. I would do more stuff that way. I think Emmy is so excited to get to sing the low part. She always is asked to sing way up high, because she can, and there's nobody better. But it's really entertaining for her. And then when Alison and I did 'I'll Fly Away,' Alison's on the baritone, which is funny."

■ ■ ■

There is nothing funny about starting your own record label, a business every bit as prone to failure as restaurants, antique stores, and magazines. Given that the first two albums Welch and Rawlings made had combined sales of roughly 200,000 in the United States, it is a fair guess they could have attracted another label when Almo Sounds, the label started by A&M co-founders Herb Alpert and Jerry Moss, closed its doors.

Instead, they launched Acony, naming their label after the mountain flower she sang of on "Acony Bell," a tune from her debut album. (It is an Indian word more commonly spelled "oconee"; the flower, she says in her press material, is a sign of better things to come.) A handful of former Almo staffers work on marketing their records; they have sworn to sign no other artists, and believe the trade-offs to be worth the trouble.

"If there have been a few more decisions on my plate, they have been made so much more rapidly that it's balanced out," she says. "That appears to be what's happening. I'm a little more involved, but it's all moving quicker."

And it seems to have been an easy decision. "There was no one out there that excited me," she says in regard to considering other label options, picking her words even more carefully than usual. "The first time around, Jerry Moss excited me. I don't know how else to put it. He's legendary, he's a gentleman, he's personable, he cares about the music. All that stuff. You look at him: Is he a label exec? No. He's a record man. He makes records. And I saw no replacement.

"And he was a gentleman enough to retire and send me on my way with my records. How often does that happen? So, given that opportunity, OK, I'm going somewhere and I'm taking my records with me, there are some companies that I have a sort of nostalgic attachment to. There are labels that I look at their name, and I've got a lot of records in my collection that have their name on them. But none of those people work there anymore, and they don't function that way anymore.

"And this is the kicker to the whole thing: One of the main reasons we started our own label was for the stability. Believe it or not, me starting my own label seemed like a better bet for long-term stability, which is really important to me. I don't have time to every two years be getting into contract negotiations. I can't be moving around and doing that. I hate the record business; I just want to make records. So, because I hate the record business, I started my own label.

"What? I'm supposed to hang around in the majors long enough to get screwed? And then do it? No, because I barely have time to write and tour and make records as it is. I don't have nearly the time to make the records that I would like to. I wish I had five more records out there in the world already. I don't, but I'm working on it."

Go Your Own Way

Ryan Adams Stakes a Claim to Solo Territory While Whiskeytown's Fate Hangs in the Wind

ND #29, SEPTEMBER–OCTOBER 2000

David Menconi

There are plenty of clubs where you can go see bands around Raleigh, North Carolina. There is the Brewery, over by the NC State campus, where the Backsliders made their live record a few years back. Or Humble Pie in the downtown warehouse district. Or the Lakeside Lounge, home to the best jukebox in town.

But the heart of the scene beats in a modest bungalow a few miles east of downtown, at Lakeside co-proprietor Van Alston's house. Drop in at any hour of the day or night, and there is no telling who might be trading songs around the kitchen table—visiting out-of-town luminaries such as Alejandro Escovedo and Eric "Roscoe" Ambel, accomplished local songwriters such as Kenny Roby and Chip Robinson, or a choice assortment of various Chicas and Yayhoos.

Chez Alston is also the closest thing Whiskeytown's Ryan Adams has to a home address in Raleigh nowadays; he generally stays there whenever he visits his former hometown. On a comfortable evening last October, Adams and Alston were entertaining a few visitors in the living room. There was some talk about the baseball game on the television (game six of the National League Championship Series), and Adams's upcoming first-ever solo tour.

But most of the conversation centered on the PBS *Sessions at West 54th* Gram Parsons tribute program, which had just been recorded in New York City. The show featured an A-list lineup organized by Emmylou Harris and including Victoria Williams, Chris Hillman, Wilco, Gillian Welch and David Rawlings, and Whiskeytown. In fact, it opened with Harris and Adams dueting on "Return of the Grievous Angel." It is hard to imagine a bigger honor than singing one of the late Parsons's signature songs with his original duet partner.

Adams had a cassette of the recording with him at Alston's house and asked if anybody wanted to hear it. Silly question. So Alston turned down the sound on the baseball game, and Adams cued up the tape. Halfway through the song, the unanimous opinion around the room was that it sounded great. Adams, however, merely shrugged.

"Well, it gets better," Adams said. "She was real nervous at first."

Emmylou Harris, that is.

It is never easy to tell just when Adams is putting you on. The only hint he gave was to arch an eyebrow as everyone else in the room fell over laughing.

■ ■ ■

The next night, Adams took the stage at Local 506 in neighboring Chapel Hill for the opening date of his solo tour. In contrast to his previous show at the same club—an unannounced December 1998 show that included an expanded Whiskeytown lineup, with Adams playing almost every song on piano—this was bare-bones stark. Adams walked out all alone, took a seat, and started in on a slow heartbeat of a riff on his acoustic guitar. Then he began to snarl some of the most heart-stabbing lyrics he has ever written:

> Make me a list of all the
> Things that I don't
> Want to know; keep me sane.
> Make me a wish that I
> Never have to know ·
> What it is you do
> When I have to go.
> 'Cause I know a thing or two.
> My birthday, it keeps falling on
> The day before yours does . . .

The crowd had been chattery at first, but was struck dumb halfway through the first verse. It didn't matter that they had never heard this song before, only that Adams's performance was utterly transforming. The rage in his voice built line by line before ebbing like a wave crashing onto rocks at the end of the verse.

Afterward, everyone looked around as they clapped, blinking, as if coming out from under a spell—which happened repeatedly that night. Adams played mostly new songs, with similar results for almost all of them. He drew the loudest applause for "Hey There Mrs. Lovely," a heartbreaking song that was just, well, lovely.

"Yeah, it figures you'd like that one," he muttered afterward. "I fuckin' HATE that song."

■ ■ ■

It has been five years since I interviewed Adams for the very first issue of this magazine. He had shown up with some quotes about his band Whiskeytown that he had scribbled onto the back of a restaurant receipt. (Among them: "There's something about the way we play when we are under-confident that is essential to what we expect from ourselves.")

He is twenty-five now, and has grown up a bit since then. He is less self-conscious and more sober, even though he no longer has to lie about his age to get into bars. As the above anecdotes illustrate, however, Adams remains as brash as ever, and he can still back up the talk. And as the saying goes, it ain't bragging if you can do it, especially under pressure.

In the past year, Adams has become a single man in many ways, sundered from his girlfriend, his record label, and possibly his band. Adams and his girlfriend split up earlier this year, prompting his recent move from New York City to Nashville. And he became a record-label free agent after Outpost Records was dissolved in the Universal-PolyGram merger. That threw the still-unreleased third Whiskeytown album (which had been tentatively titled *Pneumonia*) into a protracted limbo from which it may never emerge, and also put the band itself on hold.

Because he writes songs the way most people breathe, Adams has continued writing and recording through it all, amassing enough material for a half-dozen albums since Whiskeytown was last heard from on 1997's *Strangers Almanac*. But because of the music industry's glacial pace, most people have missed out on hearing the past three years' worth of Adams's phases and stages. Fourteen of those songs are finally surfacing with the September 5 release of Adams's first solo album, *Heartbreaker,* a one-off deal with Bloodshot Records.

Whiskeytown has always been a rather fluid entity, with members coming and going. Given that Adams's primary bandmates are also busy with side projects—fiddle player Caitlin Cary with Tres Chicas and a solo EP of her own (*Waltzie* on Yep Roc Records), multi-instrumentalist Mike Daly with Alejandro Escovedo and others—the obvious question is whether Whiskeytown exists as anything more than a name by now.

"Well, I'm excited for *Pneumonia* to come out," Adams says. "But I can't guarantee there will be a Whiskeytown then. I want *Pneumonia* to be a brilliant last record."

A brilliant last record? Is this it for Whiskeytown, then?

"Yeah, definitely. I don't want to do it anymore. I always said I didn't want to be thirty years old and still 'Ryan of Whiskeytown.' And there's only so much bad luck a band can maintain until you take it as a sign. I'm onto different stuff now anyway.

"It's not like we sat down and said, 'OK, this is it.' But . . . this is pretty much it. I don't see what validity we'd have at this point, anyway. We kind of did what we set out to do, and closing out the Whiskeytown chapter now would be better than going on. A lot of people already don't like seeing Whiskeytown anymore, because we got too 'professional.' They're mad nobody's puking anymore."

Whether this really is it for Whiskeytown remains to be seen. But pulling the plug now would make a certain amount of sense, given the band's ongoing personnel volatility. There was the fall 1997 blowup that expelled three-fifths of the lineup, including guitarist Phil Wandscher; the spring 1998 implosion in which ex-Firehose guitarist Ed Crawford and bassist Jenni Snyder departed; and the summer 1998 regrouping, when Backsliders Brad Rice and Danny Kurtz and Superchunk's Jon Wurster signed on just in time for Whiskeytown to take an opening-act slot on the John Fogerty tour.

Adams actually cites the Fogerty tour, on which Whiskeytown had to contend with crowds ranging from indifferent to hostile, as the beginning of the end.

"I think Whiskeytown's egg timer got set for me on that Fogerty tour, which I was basically pushed into," he says. "Whatever democracy did exist was that everybody else really wanted to go out, and I didn't. But we did that tour, and that's when the sound and the morale of the band kinda got lost.

"And can I say something else about all this? I never for one second intended to be the front man for Whiskeytown. I always wanted it to be more like the Eagles, this shared bigger band, so the identity wasn't just me, and it became me when Phil left. I did not fire ten band members. A lot of people who left this band did so for super-personal reasons that had nothing to do with me. Some I did fire, mostly because I was the only one with the balls to do it.

"Anyway," Adams concludes, "morale changes, and none of us even live in the same city anymore. When you have to fly somewhere to have a band meeting, your band is gay, and you should break up."

■ ■ ■

Most people who didn't like *Strangers Almanac* objected to the slick sound of Jim Scott's production. Those people shouldn't have any such complaints about *Heartbreaker,* which is certainly the loosest record Adams has ever put out. It commences on a playful note with an in-the-studio interlude straight out of *High Fidelity*—a record-geek argument between Adams and David Rawlings concerning which Morrissey album contains the song "Suedehead." After making a $5 bet (which he subsequently won), Adams starts to count the next song off . . .

. . . But has to stop because, he declares, "Eth's got a mouthful o' cookies" (that would be producer-drummer Ethan Johns). Finally, Adams hollers "Left for dead!" in a perfect faux–*Monty Python* accent, and they are off and running on "To Be Young (Is to Be Sad, Is to Be High)."

"That lead-in is not an edit; it's exactly what happened directly before we went into that song," Johns recalls. "They were full-fly into this argument, so I thought I had a few minutes for a quick snack. Then when Ryan started to count off and stopped, it was because I had a soda in my hand and a mouthful of cookies. When I heard that later, it was so funny I didn't want to cut it off."

"To Be Young" swings hard, setting Rawlings's cutting lead guitar under a dry, top-dead-center vocal that is completely devoid of reverb. The sound is Bob Dylan circa 1965, with Adams's voice conjuring up a sly brew of Dylan's sneer, Mick Jagger's yowl, and John Lennon's croon.

As the credits note, *Heartbreaker* took a grand total of fourteen days to make. Johns estimates that two-thirds of the record was just him and Adams playing live in the studio together, with minimal overdubs afterward. Rawlings and Gillian Welch appear on several tracks, and Emmylou Harris duets with Adams on "Oh My Sweet Carolina," his love letter to his old home state.

Maybe the most remarkable song is "Damn, Sam (I Love a Woman That Rains)," which Adams made up on the spot. It is full of the sort of absurdist imagery usually associated with existentialist Texas singer-songwriters, such as Adams's declaration that he is "as calm as a fruit stand in New York, and maybe as strange."

"We were in the middle of cutting something else, and he got that look," Johns says. "Just froze, and started playing that riff. Five minutes later, he came out of his little reverie and said, 'Check this out.' You can hear the take starting up at the beginning of the cut because he started playing before I could get to the tape machine and whack 'Record.' That was the first time he ever played it out loud, and it actually sums up this record perfectly. To me, that's the heart of the record. It made the whole thing make sense because it was completely dictated by Ryan's headspace at the time."

Most of *Heartbreaker* is in a subdued key. It is ostensibly a sad record about falling out of love, and plenty of the album's songs are indeed quite melancholy. "Call Me on Your Way Back Home," for example— "'Cause I miss you / I just want to die without you."

But the funny thing is that, if you just listen to the record's sound and mood rather than the words, it doesn't sound downcast at all. Instead, Adams sounds as if he is having the time of his life.

"Maybe I've gotten so used to all this adult pain that I actually like it," he says. "I don't know. I'm always saying that Christina Aguilera song 'What a Girl Wants' is actually really sad if you think about it, 'cause she's talking about how nobody really gets what they need from anybody else unless they ask or unless they're lucky. Why is it when you're good to someone who loves you, they say they must be lucky? That kind of says something about the shit we are as people.

"So maybe I'm the reverse. Maybe I just admit we're all full of shit up front, and then try to have some fun with that."

One of the most notable aspects of *Heartbreaker* is what isn't on it—virtually none of the songs from last year's solo tour. Originally, those songs were to go on Adams's first solo album during Whiskeytown's hiatus. But recording was put off for several months, and when that happens, the inevitable result is that Adams moves on to his next set of songs. That leaves Mark Williams, who signed Adams to Outpost Records and is negotiating his next major-label deal, wondering what to do with Adams's huge and growing backlog of unreleased songs.

"I encouraged Ryan to do this solo record as a way to keep busy and get something out there during this period," Williams says. "So of course he went and wrote a whole new batch of songs that weren't even around for that solo tour last fall. Most of this record, he wrote the week before with a whole different flavor—and those other songs went by the wayside."

Adams says he plans to resurrect those earlier songs as his second solo album, *Destroyer,* which is already partially recorded. But he writes so fast that it is hard to imagine he won't be off to yet another set of songs when it comes time to do another record.

Chances are good, then, that *Destroyer* will join the ranks of other "lost" Ryan Adams/Whiskeytown recordings. The list includes *Forever Valentine,* a 1997 Chris Stamey–produced album the band made as a Christmas present for Williams; *Fucker,* a set of songs written and recorded with ex-Replacements bassist Tommy Stinson; *SnoKobra,* Adams's hard-rock alter ego; and scores of four-track recordings he has made over the past few years.

Adams talks of putting out those tapes someday as a double-CD set called *Exile on Franklin Street* (Franklin being the main drag in Chapel Hill) or *Four-Track Mind* (a title that has actually already been used by jazz saxophonist Seamus Blake).

At the moment, the lost record that looms largest is Whiskeytown's aforementioned *Pneumonia.* It is a solid record with some fine individual songs that rank among Whiskeytown's best, but the album lacks the overall cohesiveness of *Strangers Almanac.* It was recorded over a period of months in 1998–1999, in three distinct phases. There are experimental tracks, not all of them successful; piano-based pop songs along the lines of Randy Newman's; and country-flavored songs of a piece with *Strangers.*

Johns also produced *Pneumonia,* with a mix by Scott Litt. Numerous outside players were also involved, including Tommy Stinson, James Iha, and Joe Henry bassist Jennifer Condos. They recorded more than thirty songs, the majority of which few outsiders have heard. So whatever finally emerges might be completely different from the advance copies that went into limited circulation before Outpost folded.

"I've decided I want *Pneumonia* taken back to its original mix and concept," says Adams. "We did some stuff to it that was pretty unholy with the mixing, trying to turn an arty record into something that would be more accepted. If I get my way, there will be eighteen songs on it, four of which nobody's ever heard."

When that might happen is anybody's guess. Getting another long-term deal has taken much longer than anyone expected. "Every time I think I've got this solved, something else happens and it doesn't work," sighs Mark Williams. "*Pneumonia* will come out as soon as we can put it out in the proper way and do it justice. Had I known it was going to take this long, I don't know what we would've done differently. But we've come this far, and now Ryan's got the solo record. So the plan is to let him focus on that for the rest of this year, then hopefully get the third Whiskeytown album in early spring of 2001.

"Of course, Ryan will have written another two albums' worth of great material by then."

■ ■ ■

Everyone involved with Adams cites his fall 1999 solo tour as a turning point. Van Alston, who served as tour manager (and subsequently co-wrote two songs on *Heartbreaker*), remembers, "When we went out for the first few shows, he was always worried: 'How am I doing? What's it sound like?' By the end, it was, 'I'm gonna kick everybody's ass tonight.' I wouldn't call it a leap of confidence, because he always had a lot of it. But just getting out there and doing it really proved to him that he could."

Last year's other big public event was the *Sessions at West 54th* taping in New York City, where Adams bonded with the people who would become his circle of music friends in Nashville—especially Emmylou Harris, Gillian Welch, and David Rawlings.

"That was the most time we'd ever spent with him," recalls Welch. "After the show, we ended up playing music until 4 or 5 a.m. He seemed kinda burnt on Manhattan, and when we retired to his neighborhood bar and played for a while, he kept saying, 'Nobody ever does this up here, just plays for fun.'"

At the time, Adams was looking to make a change after spending two years in New York. Since he had recently hooked up with a new Nashville-based manager, Frank Callari (who also handles Lucinda Williams, the Mavericks, and Kim Richey), all signs seemed to point toward Tennessee. So he picked up and headed for Nashville, moving into a house with his Whiskeytown bandmate Brad Rice.

Leaving New York behind proved to be more difficult than anticipated, however. Adams found himself surprised at how much he missed the city. Less surprising was how much he missed his girlfriend.

"Being away from my girlfriend and New York, both those really changed me," Adams says. "I mean, I was just numb with shock at how upset I was. I had no idea how attached I'd grown to New York City itself. Once you start haunting those streets, it changes you. I'd always read in books that New York either spits you up and shoots you right back where you came from, or puts the hook in you. It put the hook in me."

Both aspects of the move found their way onto *Heartbreaker*. With contributions from many of Adams's new neighbors, the album is his Nashville coming-out party. And if *Heartbreaker* sounds like *The Freewheelin' Ryan Adams,* it has its Suzi Rotolo figure in the person of Adams's ex-girlfriend.

"On this record, there are so many songs concerning her and us," Adams says. "I thought if I was gonna put it all on the table, I'd actually put one song with her name on it."

That would be "AMY," spelled in capital letters on the track listing and easily the lushest-sounding song on the album. Its chorus is as simple and sentimental as anything Adams has ever written: "Oh, I love you, Amy / Do you still love me?"

Adams says this isn't the first song he has written about the person he calls "my Anita Pallenberg, the coolest and most beautiful woman I've ever met. . . . I've always been pretty forthcoming about her on-record. 'Everything I Do' [from *Strangers Almanac*], that's her. And everybody's favorite Whiskeytown song, 'Avenues' [also on *Strangers*], is about me wishing I could be with her in New York: 'The cab is here but can't take me to your house.' That's because I was in Raleigh.

"When I first got up to New York, I was such a newbie she had to explain to me how avenues go one way and streets go the opposite way. If I remembered that, I could get around. So that song is about how it doesn't matter where the fuck I go, I'm still going in her direction."

Still, Adams did move away, which he says seemed like the right thing to do at the time. Along with his band's ongoing business problems, Adams and his ex both endured separate family-related traumas last year (which he declines to talk about in detail). The couple's relationship was a casualty, but Adams seems to hope that is not the last word. As with his musical career at the moment, everything is up in the air.

"It's hard to describe the nature of the relationship at this point," Adams says, choosing his words carefully. "Last year we were both going through so much turmoil and were so exhausted from our own lives, we couldn't really be there to support each other. So we went our separate ways. Then things got better for her and me, and we kinda started to mend. We were as adult as we could be about it.

"So . . . I don't know. We'll see."

World Wide Open

Jay Farrar

ND #36, November–December 2001

Peter Blackstock

Sebastopol: A small semi-urban community located on the western edge of the Santa Rosa plain in Northern California. It is 50 miles north of San Francisco, and about 15 miles from the Russian River. The city, incorporated in 1902, currently has a population of about 7,900 people.

WEB SITE FOR THE CITY OF SEBASTOPOL

Sevastopol: The largest non-freezing commercial and fishing Black Sea port of Ukraine. Located in the southwestern part of the Crimean Peninsula, on the site of the ancient Greek colony Khersonesus. The city itself and the Black Sea Fleet, based in Sevastopol, have occupied a prominent place in Russian and Soviet history. Its population is 390,100."

WEB SITE FOR THE CITY OF SEVASTOPOL

Vestapol: An open-D guitar tuning, "favored by blues and slide guitarists as well as many folksingers and modern fingerstylists."

WEB SITE FOR *Acoustic Guitar* MAGAZINE

Tracing the trail in Jay Farrar's thoughts, from experiments in guitar tuning to a bucolic little burg just north of the Bay Area, sheds a little light not only on the title of his new album, *Sebastopol,* but also on his nonlinear approach to music in general.

"Vestapol is a guitar tuning; originally I was thinking of using *Vestapol*" as the album's title, Farrar attempts to explain. "Because Vestapol comes from 'Sevastopol,' which was an early blues song, I guess named after a city in Russia." (Actually now in the Ukraine, after it and several other Russian states regained their sovereignty in the wake of the Soviet Union's demise a decade ago.)

"That's what piqued my interest, that whole concept of a blues song about a city in Russia. But anyway, from there it just went to *Sebastopol*. It just sounded better. And at this point, maybe there's a linguist or some blues authority that would know if there may be a connection between the two, Sebastopol and Sevastopol."

Turns out it is more of a historical matter, actually a mildly interesting one, if veering onto yet another entirely unrelated tangent. "The name of Sebastopol first came into use in the late 1850s as a result of a prolonged and lively fistfight in the newly formed town, which was likened to the long British siege of the Russian seaport of Sevastopol during the then-raging Crimean War," reports the City of Sebastopol Web site. "Britain, France, Sardinia and Turkey fought Russia in this war, one of the first wars to be directly reported by journalists and photographers. . . . Evidently, many Americans in the West sympathized more for the Russian than for the British cause, as there were at one time four other Sebastopols in California."

None of the songs on *Sebastopol,* Farrar's first solo release after four albums with Uncle Tupelo in the first half of the 1990s and three with Son Volt in the latter half, have anything to do with Northern California or the Crimean Peninsula—though they might relate in more general terms to the earth as a whole as it stretches between those opposite edges of the globe. "The world is gonna burn up four billion years from now / If it doesn't happen anytime soon," he observes on the opening track, "Feel Free." On the album's first single, "Voodoo Candle," Farrar sings of being "Caught between two worlds." Later, on "Direction," he watches as "The world spins around, in step with the best intentions / It's what we're here for / So dear to die for."

All of which is surely a too-careful exercise in seeking to tie together a thread that doesn't really exist on *Sebastopol*. It is not, by any stretch, a concept album; rather, it is simply a collection of exemplary songwriting, clearly Farrar's best suite of material since Son Volt's 1995 debut *Trace*. Stylistically, it is as broad-ranging an album as Farrar has done to date, planting traditional-style folk ballads next to off-kilter rhythmic rockers, gorgeous pop melodies next to spacey instrumental sketches.

Nevertheless, if there is any semblance of a theme running through the album's lyrical references and veiled images, it would probably be this: a concern for the state of the world. It extends to the album's closing track, "Vitamins," which advises, "Break it apart and take it down / You're just mad at the world"; and even to an outtake that didn't make the record (but may surface on an ensuing EP), titled "Different Kind of Madness," which yields an intriguing, ultimately uplifting refrain: "It's not the end of the world / You can't even see it from here."

Then again, what Farrar is saying in his songs often takes a back seat to how those songs sound. And that applies not just to the melodies behind the words, but to the words themselves.

More than perhaps any songwriter since Michael Stipe—who peppered R.E.M.'s early records with what became known as "Stipean" references to catacombs, moral kiosks, Cuyahoga, and Philomath—Farrar allows the rhythm and tone of the vowels and syllables he chooses to help shape his lyrics, a kind of sonic diction device.

"Yeah, certainly that is taken into account," Farrar acknowledges. "Sometimes just the sound of the words is as important as the literal meaning." (Recall his previous statement that he drifted from Vestapol to Sebastopol because "it just sounded better.")

This was not so much the case in the beginning, when Uncle Tupelo's early albums focused on dark blue-collar realities and relied on a commoner, more straightforward approach to language.

A shift became apparent in the first verse of "Slate," the opening cut on Uncle Tupelo's final album; the word "farcical" jumped far enough out of left field that one Tupelo fan Web site featuring transcriptions of the band's tunes cites the lyric as "so far so good." Elsewhere, the names of such tunes as "Chickamauga" and the album's title track, "Anodyne," seemed to employ words that cast a mood or tone as much as they define content.

Farrar's tenure with Son Volt found him venturing further in that direction; words such as "anesthetize," "caryatid," and "countenance" imbued his tunes with an increasingly, well, Farrar-esque feel. A line from the song "Medicine Hat" seems to capture the essence of this development: "There will be catchwords filled with infection."

The catchwords continue on *Sebastopol*. Among the arcane terms and phrases that pop up along the way: "Esperanto," "glycerin," "stevedores," "parabolic louver lighting," and "sanguinary vitamins."

■ ■ ■

As much of a signature as the sound of the words, however, is the way they are sung. If there is one particular quality that has tended to draw listeners to the music Farrar has made over the years, it is his voice. His strength is not a matter of histrionics, though he can convey considerable emotional power at times; nor is it related to range, though he sometimes hits high notes that are beyond the reach of most male singers who prefer to forsake falsetto. Rather, it is a simple sense of melodic expression, which resonates with an impact that is difficult to describe or convey in words.

A couple of his friends and colleagues give it a try. "The thing about Jay's voice is, it's like he opens his mouth, and it's just pure fucking tone," says John Agnello, who co-produced *Sebastopol* with Farrar. "And it's beautiful tone, it's really pleasing. There aren't many guys who can elicit that kind of feeling.

233

"There's a bar in Hoboken [New Jersey] that I sometimes go to with friends, and *No Depression* [Uncle Tupelo's debut album] is in the jukebox, and I'll punch up 'Whiskey Bottle,' and it'll just come on in the middle of the night, and it's just—it gives me chicken skin to this day."

Superchunk drummer Jon Wurster, who played on six of the seventeen *Sebastopol* tracks, confesses, "One of the things while we were recording—and not to sound like a total ass-kiss—but I almost pinched myself a couple times, just like, 'God, I'm actually playing here, and that voice is there, in the other room.' . . . His voice is so distinct, and almost timeless. It could be from any era of rock; it wouldn't be out of place in any era, really."

The distinctive nature of Farrar's voice also affords an enviable advantage as his recording career progresses. It provides an anchor for his body of work, allowing his music to stretch out in different stylistic directions while remaining stamped with his personal imprint.

Never has that been more apparent than on *Sebastopol,* which finds Farrar expanding his horizons by using a broad range of instrumentation and experimenting with unusual rhythm structures. "I hear it as a continuation of his oeuvre," Wurster observes, "but I think it's obviously a little more out there in terms of instrumentation."

Largely that stems from Farrar's decision to approach *Sebastopol* specifically as a solo album rather than as a band project. "I think the basic process may have been different, in that I didn't specifically write the songs to be re-created in a live context, or with specific people in mind," he says. "I just wanted to let them evolve as they may, just put whatever instrumentation seemed to fit the song.

"With Son Volt, we were primarily interested in always trying to record as much live as possible, knowing that we'd be re-creating it in a live context. But with this, it was more of a building process, just building the songs from the ground up."

Thus, he began with bare-bones demos featuring only voice and acoustic guitar. Even at that stage, Farrar had already been tinkering with the typical approach to songwriting. "Most of these songs were written in a slack key or in alternate tunings that I either looked up or made up," he writes in the press bio for *Sebastopol.*

That in itself was not necessarily new. "I have been doing it since Uncle Tupelo, but it sort of reached the point where I was using alternate tunings on almost every song," he explains. "Which, on the early records, it would just be one or two songs on the record.

"Some of the tunings I'd been using to write songs before, but some of them, I'd basically just experiment until I found a tuning I liked. And others were completely by accident—just picking up the guitar after it had been banging around the case and found its own tuning."

Farrar has since adapted the songs back to standard tunings for the sake of streamlining operations onstage. "Otherwise I'd have to be like Sonic

Youth when they used to have about fifteen or twenty guitars," he jokes. He has also stripped things down in general for the live setting, with former Blood Oranges guitarist Mark Spencer his only accompanying musician. "I'm more drawn to the idea of just presenting the songs in kind of basic form, just playing them on acoustic, which is very close to the situation in which they were written," he says.

In the studio, though, the next step was figuring out who would help shape the sound surrounding the skeletons of the songs. Farrar turned first to Agnello, who had mixed three songs on Son Volt's last record, *Wide Swing Tremolo.* As a producer, Agnello has manned albums by Buffalo Tom, Steve Wynn, Varnaline, and more than a dozen indie-rock bands of varying renown; as an engineer, his resume is so extensive that he is almost assuredly the only person with credits on albums by both Patti Smith and Patty Smyth.

None of which was really of much concern to Farrar, who says simply, "I was primarily impressed with what he had done with the *Wide Swing Tremolo* stuff." For his part, Agnello had been a fan of Farrar's music since Uncle Tupelo's early days, and had even lobbied to work on *Anodyne,* Tupelo's 1993 swan song (which ended up being produced by Brian Paulson).

■ ■ ■

They convened in April 2000 in Millstadt, Illinois, a town of 2,500 about forty-five minutes from Farrar's current residence in St. Louis (but very near his original hometown of Belleville). Over the past few years, Farrar has been in the process of converting Son Volt's rehearsal space into a studio. "It's kind of an old factory building, and upstairs there are batting cages, which you definitely have to work around," Farrar says.

Wide Swing Tremolo was recorded there with more of a makeshift setup, but a multitrack analog machine and other equipment were installed permanently just prior to the *Sebastopol* sessions. "We actually turned it into a functioning studio," Agnello says.

They discussed the possibility of recording at a more professional facility—Agnello frequently works at Water Music in Hoboken, and *Sebastopol* was later mixed there—but "it was fairly apparent that he wanted to be around home. With him just having his son at that point—he was probably a year old—I respected his not wanting to be away from home. It didn't matter whether we were in a real studio or not; he really wanted to be home."

Avoiding the noise from the batting cages meant adhering to a decidedly nocturnal schedule. "It was really challenging because of the hours we were working—from nine o'clock at night till about six every morning," Agnello says. "When we'd walk in, you would hear the clankering above us, and dust would fall. So we had to cover the gear every morning. We were making this record in the trenches. It was pretty funny."

The sweltering Midwest heat also began to take its toll as April gave way to May and June, Agnello recalls. "There was one night toward the end of the recording where it was just starting to get warm in Millstadt, and the space had no ventilation. And we looked at each other and went, 'We've gotta get some air conditioning going.' So we looked around the walls, and picked out a spot, and the next day just basically carved a hole in the wall and shoved an air conditioner into it. I remember both of us with little hacksaws cutting this pressboard wall to try to fit this air conditioner into it.

"The night before, I was sorting out a couple tracks of vocals that we had, and I remember hitting 'Stop,' and it was three in the morning, and I could hear snoring. I'm sitting there in no shirt and underwear because it was, like, 110 degrees in this space. And I look down, and behind this huge rack of gear, Jay's just sleeping. Because it was so hot, he just lost it. There were, like, a lot of really funny nights like that."

All of those things ended up having an influence on the character of the album, Agnello contends. "It was basically two and a half months of a whole new environment where it was like, 'Let's challenge ourselves to do it this way.' But also, along with that were these crazy late-night journeys. Like, at four in the morning, we'd both be exhausted, and we'd walk down to the gas & grab and go get snacks and coffee.

"We'd have all these moments where we'd just talk. And if we were doing a record normally in a real studio somewhere, we might not have that kind of situation. There were a couple of nights when there were blackouts, where we ended up at a local bar sipping beer until they got the power back on. And stuff like that just added to the whole vibe of the record, and how we communicated with each other."

Superchunk drummer Wurster affirms he also caught that vibe during his sessions with Farrar and Agnello. "That's what the record really reminds me of, is just the three of us in this space at four in the morning, recording this stuff," he says. "It was almost like you were the only people on earth; it's like nothing else really exists."

■ ■ ■

Agnello and Farrar got the basic tracks down in a couple of primary sessions featuring two different drummers—the first with Wurster, the second with Matt Pence of Denton, Texas, band Centro-Matic. "I got to know him when Centro-Matic came over to record some songs at the same rehearsal space," Farrar says. "I think they were living here at the time, and they were working with a mutual friend. Matt's drumming struck me as being powerful and unique; it reminded me of Levon Helm." (Interestingly, Wurster later comments that he thinks Pence "almost plays like John Bonham, I think.")

Farrar's ties to Wurster go back a bit further. Wurster remembers wearing out Uncle Tupelo's second album *Still Feel Gone* in the early 1990s, and exchanging postcards with Jeff Tweedy about a Superchunk show Tweedy and Farrar had attended in Athens, Georgia, while they were recording their *March 16–20, 1992* album. "I remember I called Jay kinda out of the blue when we were considering Brian Paulson for our *Foolish* record, which came out in '94, because he [Paulson] had just done *Anodyne*," Wurster says.

"And then a good friend of mine who was a guitar tech for us [Dewitt Burton] ended up being Son Volt's longtime guitar tech for years. So, I eventually met him through Dewitt. But I never really got to know him that well; you know, he's so quiet, it's hard to get to know him period, I think. But he was always real friendly and cordial."

Shortly before Farrar finalized plans to record in Millstadt, "I got an e-mail from him saying, 'I'm putting this solo record together. Would you wanna play some drums on it?'" Wurster continues. "And I was just thrilled because he's probably my favorite songwriter of the last ten years or so. So it was just a major honor to be asked to do that."

Among the other well-known musicians listed in the credits on *Sebastopol* are Gillian Welch and David Rawlings, who appear on a seemingly age-old country-folk original called "Barstow." (Welch provides harmony vocals, while Rawlings adds acoustic-guitar and lap-steel accents.) "Basically it just seemed to lend itself to what they might be able to contribute," Farrar says of the song.

"Son Volt was the first tour that we ever did, right when our first record came out," Welch says, explaining how they first got to know Farrar in 1996. More recently, "He sent us a cassette of 'Barstow,' and I really loved the song. We went up there [to Millstadt], and it was pretty freeform; he just said, 'Well, what do you wanna do?' And I said, 'Well, I'll sing,' and he asked David if he'd play lap steel.

"I'm really proud to be on that song. In fact, Dave sang 'Barstow' in our show the other night! I hope Jay doesn't mind. He did a really lovely version of it."

Among the other musicians on the record are bassist Tom Ray, formerly of the Bottle Rockets; Farrar's brother Wade, who plays stand-up bass on one track; St. Louis saxophonist Lou Winer; and Portland slide guitarist Kelly Joe Phelps.

But the real ringer was Flaming Lips multi-instrumentalist Steven Drozd, who came up one weekend from Oklahoma City to help flesh things out. "It just kind of came about from John [Agnello] asking me what I'd been listening to," Farrar says. "And I told him I thought the Flaming Lips' *Soft Bulletin* record was interesting, that I liked Steven's playing a lot."

Drozd's contributions ended up being essential to the finished product. The dramatic string swells and atmospheric sonic washes flowing from his keyboards appear on five of the album's best songs and create a direct connection between Farrar's record and *The Soft Bulletin,* the Lips' groundbreaking 1999 release. Drozd's playing has developed the same sort of signature quality that Farrar's voice provides, and the mingling of those two presences on *Sebastopol* is frequently breathtaking.

"When we talked about finishing these songs, he was the guy," says Agnello, who had known Drozd for years and worked with him briefly on a previous project. "His stuff made it into, like, a Panavision movie. And I don't really know anybody else specifically who could come in and actually do what he did."

■ ■ ■

The record was finished by the summer of 2000, but by then, the big question was who would put it out. Warner Bros., increasingly disenchanted with Son Volt's declining record sales (the band's second and third albums combined didn't sell as much as their debut), was not expressing confidence. "People changed positions at Warner Bros., and at that point I knew I was gonna be looking for a different home," he says. "They didn't want to do either a Son Volt or a Jay Farrar record."

One of those people who changed positions was Joe McEwen, who had originally signed Uncle Tupelo to Sire for *Anodyne* and had remained the A&R representative for both Son Volt and Uncle Tupelo during his tenure at Warner Bros. McEwen resurfaced at Artemis Records in early 2001, and Farrar soon followed him there.

"It seemed like that was the natural direction to go," he says. "Joe has good instincts, and we have a good relationship, and I considered that important. . . . There was some interest from some other labels, but primarily I felt that it was a natural progression to just keep working with Joe."

The progression apparently seemed just as natural to McEwen. "He called me over the summer [of 2000] at home when he was working on this record, and I was no longer at Warner Bros.," McEwen recalls. "He invited me to come to the studio; they were working in Hoboken at that point. I thought it was encouraging because it wasn't Son Volt, even though the voice is unmistakable, but I thought he was trying some interesting things."

The fact that Farrar had made a solo album instead of a Son Volt album came as no surprise to McEwen. "We had talked about it at Warner Bros. before," he says. "We started to make some plans about how we would do it and who we might work with. So I knew that he was gonna do it solo."

Farrar isn't necessarily ruling out future work with his Son Volt bandmates Dave Boquist, Jim Boquist, and Mike Heidorn, but he says, matter-of-factly, "After five years of touring and recording, it just seemed like it was time for a change. They're a good group of guys, and we're all on good terms, and the possibility is there for us to do something in the future. But it probably won't be on the same scale, even if it does happen."

Asked whether he sees any similarities between Farrar's decision to leave Uncle Tupelo in 1994 and his split from Son Volt in 2000, McEwen says he views the two situations differently. "Back then, you had two guys who were very strong personalities, and there just wasn't room in one band for them anymore," he says of Tupelo's dissolution. "Which was a shame. I can remember so well when I heard about it, and meeting them, and trying to get them to talk; but by that point, there was no reconciling.

"But this was just something where Son Volt really was his band, and he was the voice of the band; there wasn't another songwriter. And I think he wanted to try some different things."

Farrar, however, acknowledges that perhaps there are some cycles becoming apparent in his need for change to spark the creative process. "I guess I'm starting to see some similarities," he says, "in that, you know, it seems to be a five-year plan."

■ ■ ■

The irony of this latest cycle in Farrar's career evolution is that while Son Volt appears to be going by the wayside, there is actually some new activity for Uncle Tupelo on the horizon. Farrar and Tweedy have tentative plans to hash out the contents of an upcoming Uncle Tupelo anthology to be released sometime next year on Sony Legacy.

The anthology project is largely the result of a recent legal settlement with Rockville Records, which released Uncle Tupelo's first three records. Farrar and Tweedy won back the ownership of those records; Sony Legacy expects to eventually reissue each of the discs separately in addition to the anthology, which will also contain some previously unreleased material. "We will be both contributing ideas and probably deciding whether to remix some stuff or not, and just deciding what songs will go on it," Farrar confirms.

Asked whether there were some leftover tracks from the sessions for those three records, he replies, "It has been brought to our attention that there are some. I know that I had certainly forgotten about that, but we will have to go back and listen to them to see if they're up to par."

There is also the possibility of including some live tracks, most likely from the band's widely bootlegged farewell show at St. Louis venue Mississippi Nights in May 1994.

Don't expect a reunion gig to follow suit, although enough time has passed to heal old wounds—with a little assistance from Roger McGuinn, who helped bring the two together in New York in April 1997.

"I was kinda responsible for them talking to each other for the first time in years," McGuinn admitted in a September 1997 interview. "We did a taping up in the VH1 studio with Wilco, and then I said, 'You know, Son

Volt's playing downtown tonight,' and they said, 'Yeah, we know.' And I said, 'How do you guys get along?' And they said, 'Well, you know, kinda like you and David Crosby used to get along.'

"And I said, 'Oh, OK. Well, I'm gonna go down and see Son Volt tonight.' And they said, 'Well, yeah, I think we're gonna go down there too.' So they did, and it was fun. I think everybody got along OK."

Outside the Wall

*The Jayhawks Glide beyond Americana in Relentless
Pursuit of a Great Pop Record*

ND #27, MAY–JUNE 2000

Erik Flannigan

Before Uncle Tupelo joined the major-label ranks by signing with Sire/Reprise for their 1993 swan song, producer and label impresario Rick Rubin—a man instrumental in launching the careers of the Beastie Boys and Public Enemy—signed a roots band from Minneapolis to his Warner-distributed label, Def American. There, the Jayhawks—at that time, Mark Olson, Gary Louris, Marc Perlman and Ken Callahan—found themselves unlikely labelmates of artists such as Danzig and Slayer.

While it would be a bit much to credit Rubin with an essential role in the evolution of alternative country, his signing of the Jayhawks to a major-label deal should be recognized as a significant signpost. The band's 1992 label debut, *Hollywood Town Hall,* earned considerable praise and established Olson and Louris as a songwriting tandem with a glimmering future.

Three years and a couple of drummers later, the Jayhawks returned with *Tomorrow the Green Grass,* which earned Olson and Louris still more accolades and a minor hit with "Blue." But the partnership was not fated to continue: Olson decided it was time to leave the band he, Louris, and Perlman had formed ten years earlier and make music with his new love, Victoria Williams.

Olson and Williams moved to Joshua Tree, California, and, along with fiddler Mike "Razz" Russell, began making records as the Original Harmony Ridge Creek Dippers. Louris, Perlman, new drummer Tim O'Reagan, and keyboardist Karen Grotberg elected to carry on.

In many ways, though, it is only with the release of their new album, *Smile,* that the Jayhawks feel fully reborn. The years between yielded some serious soul searching, a remarkable album overshadowed by the death of a label, and a decision to make a career record with the man behind *The Wall*.

Don't Leave Me Now

In late 1995, after completing several months of touring behind *Tomorrow the Green Grass*, Gary Louris and Mark Olson convened to begin the songwriting process for the band's next album. "He played me his and I played him mine," says Louris. "And as usual he was very supportive. It was never, 'I don't like this shit; we should be doing my stuff.' It was, 'That's great. I like that.'"

But after the second or third such session, Olson left early and went for a long drive. When he returned, he told his songwriting partner of ten years that he was walking away. "He'd obviously driven around thinking about it," Louris recalls four years later without a hint of ill will or hurt feelings. "He wanted the control back that he had at the beginning of the band, and other reasons.

"The bottom line is I have a ton of respect for him. When the band was starting back up, I was very defensive about the whole thing, and mis-quoted in many ways. I want to set the record straight by saying that what he and I had was magical and very important. We're not a better band without him, we're a different band. . . . There are many nights when I miss having Mark there. On the other hand, I'm really loving what we're doing right now. You have to move on."

And so they did, but not before Louris reexamined just where he stood. "When Mark walked out the door and tears were shed and words were spoken, I spent a couple days saying, 'This is a crossroads. Here's the chance I have to do something else.' I started thinking if there were other bands I could join, other people I wanted to work with. It's kinda like when you get a divorce: All of a sudden you think about those people you could have dated, and you now can.

"But when the fantasies you may have entertained become reality, you realize they were better left as fantasy. And the reality was that I loved everybody in the band and that we wanted to continue. Another fantasy was to have more control, more room for my songs. When that reality came, it was also tough because I realized how much I had relied on him."

Olson's departure marked the end of a chapter for the Jayhawks, but it wasn't precisely the beginning of the next one. That had actually come earlier, when drummer Tim O'Reagan joined the band after the release of *Tomorrow the Green Grass*, which was the first album to feature keyboardist Grotberg.

"My first reaction [to Olson's departure] was to carry on," bassist Perl-man said from the road in the midst of Columbia's *Smile* promotional tour in March. "We had finally put together a band of musicians that I enjoyed playing with, in Tim and Karen. We had had good drummers, but I clicked with Tim.

"I knew that I had to give Gary some time. Maybe I pushed us back, and Tim did too. The one thing that did disappoint me was that I felt like we had the quintessential Jayhawks record in the making if Mark hadn't left."

"It was a marriage that lasted longer than most real marriages," Louris says. "We were together a long time: ten years. That's more than a lot of my favorite bands put together. So it's not like it came prematurely. The problem was everybody had too many ideas, and there wasn't enough room. When he did leave, it was scary, but something kept us going. We looked at the alternative of just stopping, and that didn't seem quite right.

"To this day I think Mark is disappointed we used the name. We tried to change it, and for one reason or another it didn't happen. There are many times I've felt bad about it, but now I feel like it's keeping the memory alive. We represent the Jayhawks. We still play Jayhawks songs, but it is a different Jayhawks; I think Mark has probably come to terms with that. As long as he knows that we're not pretending he wasn't here. Hopefully, by keeping the Jayhawks name around, it also reminds people of what he's done with us in the past with great older records, and maybe it will make people more aware of the Original Harmony Ridge Creek Dippers."

Show Must Go On

Resolved to carry on as the Jayhawks (Six Green Olives was one of several half-serious alternatives that were thankfully rejected), the band began demoing new songs in Minneapolis, and eventually spent the spring and summer of 1996 recording *Sound of Lies* with producer Brian Paulson. While Louris assumed primary songwriting duties after Olson's departure, the album featured songwriting contributions from all four members, including O'Reagan's "Bottomless Cup" and the Perlman-Louris tune "Trouble," the third of three majestic pop gems that open *Sound of Lies* and a song that marked Perlman's most significant writing contribution to date.

"The chorus, 'It's better than being alone,' was Gary's," Perlman recalls. "He came up with that years ago, and I spent almost ten years trying to write a song around it, and failing miserably. And at the point when I was so frustrated with myself that I was gonna quit the music business, it just came to me. I called Gary up frantically and said, 'I've finally got it.' He said, 'Bullshit. You've said that ten times already.' But something inspired me."

"Trouble," along with "The Man Who Loved Life" and "Think About It," established from the outset that *Sound of Lies* was something new. Elaborate three-part harmonies and crescendos and wide-screen arrangements mark all three, distinguishing the album, and the post-Olson band, as reaching for something more majestic and emotional with its songs while still remaining true to its roots.

"'Blue' was going in the direction of something that's kind of majestic," Louris answers when asked about the origin of those grand vistas, though he gives much of the credit for the sonic shift to Perlman. "He's attracted to the big pop stuff, whether it is [Golden Smog's] 'Nowhere Bound' or [Soul Asylum's] 'Promises Broken,' both of which have that multi-part '70s pop feel."

"I appreciate Gary saying that," Perlman responds, "but it wasn't like I was the only one who felt that way. At the time when he was left to be the main songwriter, there was a lot of pressure, and he was thinking about the songs and writing really good ones. Not being a songwriter, I took it upon myself to work on the arrangement aspects and production—to think about the things that weren't there in the songwriting. But I wasn't really all that good at it. I had ideas, but I didn't have enough experience in the studio to put that into practice."

Given the striking layered arrangements on *Sound of Lies,* Perlman's self-deprecating recollection is hard to fathom, as is the fact that Louris recorded no demos for the album. "For *Sound of Lies* I purposely went in unprepared," Louris says, "and took a make-the-songs-come-together-in-the-studio approach, à la Dylan. But then I realized I wasn't Dylan and that our music takes more planning."

Is There Anybody Out There?

However it came to be, *Sound of Lies* was a remarkable achievement for the band, and would have been for any band that had just lost a primary singer and songwriter. Trouble is, a lot of folks, even those who might have called themselves Jayhawks fans just a few years earlier, not only didn't hear it, but may not have known it was ever released. The band's label, American Recordings (formerly Def American), folded its tent within weeks of the album's release, effectively burying *Sound of Lies* before it had received any mainstream exposure, says Louris. "We made a video, which we weren't allowed to put out. We were told we couldn't do interviews. I think they put out a single but didn't do anything for it. I'm not saying it would have gone anywhere. Who knows?"

Given that "Blue" had been something of a minor hit, a ready-made audience for *Sound of Lies* was at least theoretically ignored, and the band didn't help matters when they elected not to mount a substantial tour in support of the album. "We waited it out," Louris concedes. "It's hard enough to tour anyway; to tour with nobody to help you is a waste of time. Though, in retrospect, maybe we should have toured a little bit more anyway. We didn't realize we were going to sit out a year."

After American shuttered, ending its distribution deal with Warner Bros., Rubin took the imprint and a few of its remaining bands, including the Jayhawks, to Columbia. *Sound of Lies* was eventually re-released on that label, but Columbia elected not to work the record—which by then was two years old—anew, instead encouraging the band to make its label debut a fresh start.

The Jayhawks may have spent the better part of three years out of the spotlight, but they didn't lay idle. The band played several shows in 1997 and a dozen or so gigs in 1998; during that stretch, they added guitarist Kraig Johnson—an old pal from Minneapolis band Run Westy Run who had teamed with Louris and Perlman in Golden Smog—to the lineup. All the while, they were writing and demoing songs in their own Minneapolis studio and learning a bit of studio craft in the process.

By late 1998, with more than an album's worth of demos complete, the band started shopping for a producer. One unlikely name bandied about at the time was the Dust Brothers, though Louris says that notion was short-lived. "[We talked to] John King. He agreed to do three songs, but he was so in demand, and he never really committed to a time. The same with Tom Rothrock and Rob Schnapf, because I liked the Elliott Smith record. But again, we were kind of low priority. The other guys that were available didn't seem quite right. We started producing the record ourselves, but we just disagree too much. We need somebody to arbitrate."

Enter Bob Ezrin—producer of Lou Reed's *Berlin,* Alice Cooper's *School's Out,* and Pink Floyd's *The Wall*—who came as an unlikely recommendation through the band's Columbia A&R person at the time. The band sent him some demos; he replied with a three-page letter that laid out in candid detail what he liked and what he didn't.

"His bottom line was: 'I love the band. I love their sound. They can sing. They can play. I love what this could be. Are these guys willing to do some hard work?'" says Louris. "We said yes."

"I agreed to go to Minneapolis, at least to talk to them," Ezrin recounts, "because somebody felt so strongly that this was something I should do, and I believe in that sort of serendipity. I got there, met the band, and fell in love because they are such wonderful people, so genuine and so committed to doing great stuff. At the same time they were kinda beaten up. So I felt for them on two levels: They were so committed to doing something great and hanging on against all odds at the same time. I got the sense that it was a mission, that I had to do this. If I didn't take this on and do a good job, a great band might disappear.

"So I said, 'Because we're on a mission, we don't record until we have great material, whatever that takes.' We went through a lot of stuff to even get past the process of pre-production. I mean, there was a point at which Rick Rubin didn't want me to produce the album. That's OK; everybody's entitled to their opinion. But with this band, I had a feeling they needed somebody like me who would focus in on the material and on the production values—the vibe, the sound, the ethos of the record—and not treat it like I was just throwing five people in a studio and doing a quick project. That would be death for them. So we started. Gary handed me sixty-five pieces of material that he'd been working on, and we started whittling them down."

Another appeal for Ezrin was what he calls the "boy–girl sound," the dynamic between Gary and keyboardist Karen Grotberg, whose vocals are a big part of the sound of *Smile.* "I loved the dynamic," he says. "I loved the fact that here was a band that could sing about life and pain from both points of view. I was getting sick of male singer-songwriters, angst-ridden, tunnel-visioned self-proclaimers. What I liked about Gary was he was really looking at things from different points of view, and he created little mini-dramas. Karen got to play a great role. She gets best supporting actress for my money." (With the completion of the album, Grotberg left the band to raise her baby daughter. Former Dag keyboardist Jen Gunderman has capably filled her shoes.)

Ezrin says two tracks in particular from the demos caught his fancy: "What Led Me to This Town," a song the band had originally written for the soundtrack to a Vince Vaughan film; and "A Break in the Clouds," an older song that went through a major overhaul for *Smile.*

Perlman, who has written two educational primers on movies for eighth graders, explains the band's cinematic foray: "Gary and I are both film nuts, and we had always wanted to get involved in writing [music] for film. We were sent the script for a movie called *Cool Dry Place,* and I wanted to take advantage of it. I thought it was something we should prove to people we were capable of. So we read a little bit of it, and I said we're gonna make this really powerful song out of three simple chords. We went from there and wrote it in the back of the bus very quickly.

"Once Gary gets a little germ, he's a master of melodies. 'Break in the Clouds' was another one; that's an old song of Gary's, something he'd written way back in the early days of the Jayhawks when it was a country song, a two-stepper. He was never satisfied with 'Break in the Clouds' that way, and he always wanted to make it into a soul song. 'What Led Me to This Town' inspired him to move it in a new direction. We got together and batted around some ideas, and Karen, Tim, and I all threw words at him. 'Break In the Clouds' is his 'Trouble'—a song Gary had been trying to finish for years, and it finally came together. There's nothing more beautiful than a song you thought was never gonna happen and all of a sudden it clicks."

But what became of *Cool Dry Place?* "Straight to video," Perlman laughs. "Mike Mills [of R.E.M.] was in charge of the underscore, and he recommended us. Then he and a lot of the production staff left. We rip on it because they didn't use our songs, but we've never seen it. Which is fine, because the songs became the linchpins for this record. But Gary's gotten really good at it. I'd hire him to make a soundtrack for my movie."

Another Brick in the Wall, Part 1

Presented with so much music and committed to getting the best out of the band, Ezrin began pushing back during pre-production. "He was instrumental in cracking the whip as far as writing," Louris says. "He thought I was a lazy songwriter. He said, 'I bet I know what kind of songwriter you are. I bet you're an inspired songwriter, which means you write when you're inspired. But you really don't want to go back and do the nuts-and-bolts, wringing-your-hands-pacing-the-floor kind of craftsmanship that's necessary."

"It's not that he's lazy," Ezrin counters. "I think Gary's problem comes from a reluctance to make a commitment. And a lot of that stems from being in a band where somebody else was the front guy and he had to play second fiddle, then splitting up and becoming the front guy and feeling self-conscious about that. [Even] having people tell him, whether it was labels or producers he was working with, that he just wasn't quite good enough.

"[It's about] not letting yourself off the hook, believing that you've got to keep going until something gets great. And then when it's great, you lock it in, set it in stone. I thought Gary was a noncommittal writer and that he did not tend to go back and refine, because refinement requires decision making and commitment. But to be fair, every songwriter I've ever worked with has some of that problem. The hardest thing about writing is to develop that discipline to go back and play with your creation and refine it until your creation is relevant to the rest of the world."

"Gary is an interesting combination of obsessiveness and insecurity sometimes," Ezrin posits later in the conversation, "where he gets onto something and will not get off of it. And then there are times when he cannot make a decision, because he's not really sure. But he is so honest about that and so completely willing to explore anything. And he, I think, has found in his relationship with me somebody who respects him. He knows the level of respect I have for him and for his ability, so he knows that when I talk to him that way, it's always from a foundation of admiration and approval. It wasn't about my standards; it was about the standard he set by his best work."

"Bob is not such an amateur psychologist," Perlman observes with a snicker.

Another Brick in the Wall, Part 2

Depending on whom you ask, producer or band, Ezrin was either very familiar or somewhat familiar with the band's history. Ezrin says he knew the band's "Americana-ish" past, and was a little surprised by the lush pop direction of the demos he heard. Louris recalls an incident at Ezrin's Santa Monica home that helped illustrate the legacy now under Ezrin's stewardship.

"We were in his guest-house, and all of a sudden his manager faxed over some English magazine which had picked the top 100 albums of the '90s. They included *Hollywood Town Hall, Tomorrow the Green Grass,* and *Sound of Lies.* Bob was impressed because he didn't know the kind of Americana background we had. He said we have to make sure we don't turn our backs on our audience. And I was happy to hear that because we would like more people to hear us and buy our records, but not at the expense of the people who've been loyal to us for so long.

"Yes, these records are different than earlier records, but we're not starting from scratch, and we're not doing anything different than most of my heroes—which is, they challenged their audience. For that 10 percent who want *Hollywood Town Hall* again, they may be disappointed. I think there are a lot of people like me who like Americana music, but that's only one part of their music. They like a lot of different things.

"I'm attracted to beautiful-sounding stuff. I didn't grow up listening to Americana music; that was something I listened to when I was twenty-seven or twenty-eight years old. It was the last piece of the puzzle for me. [I was into] British punk rock, power pop, and art rock. I'm pretty well-rounded in English and American pop music—from Cole Porter to Chemical Brothers, I've listened to and absorbed a little bit.

"The folk-Americana thing is not something I built my music around. It's something that was added on top. I liked the soulfulness of traditional music, and I loved when that was put together with pop and took away some of the cheesiness. One of the highest compliments paid to us recently by a good musical friend was 'You guys are a soul band.' We have some of that in us. Tim's drumming is soulful, and Marc's always been one of the best bass players I've ever seen, and very underappreciated."

"Even when we were supposedly alt-country," adds Perlman, "to us it was the soul aspect of country music. If you look at Gram Parsons, the best stuff was 'Dark End of the Street.' Soul music was our common ground. Tim comes from a soul and R&B background. He's an amazing soul singer. He can do Marvin Gaye like you wouldn't believe."

Perlman's own influences inform the kind of lush grandeur of *Sound of Lies* and now *Smile.* "I'm a huge proponent of strings and piano," he says. "The most nerve-wracking thing for us was to figure out how to do that without it sounding cheesy. We've all got our little thing: Gary's got Genesis. I've got Elton, up through *Goodbye Yellow Brick Road.* Those records were so innovatively produced and [were] the template for how great pop records should be made. Especially the little things that people don't think about, like where the drums go. All of sudden there are no drums until the end, just fills. Bob kinda comes from that era. We looked at the way to do the drums in the way that Gus Dudgeon worked, going for great fills and not worrying so much about the drummer being a metronome. Tim played fills like Nigel Olsson did on 'Don't Let the Sun Go Down on Me.'"

"The very last drum fill that comes in toward the end of 'Mr. Wilson,' I just live for that," adds Gary. "That was my attempt at a 'Nothing Compares 2 U' kind of thing."

Another Brick in the Wall, Part 3

At its core, the album Ezrin and the band ended up making is a classic Jayhawks record. It just might not sound like it at first. Sure to raise a few eyebrows is the use of drum loops as the rhythm track on songs such as "Somewhere in Ohio" and "Queen of the World."

"I felt like it was important to bring the sound of the band into the twenty-first century," Ezrin offers. "The writing is essentially great folk music. But if you framed great folk music in a more modern presentation package and opened up the spectrum sonically, and you weren't completely limited to five or six core instruments, you could really create drama in a folk context. Folk music is either not dramatic enough or melodramatic, because somebody's shouting at you and banging on an acoustic guitar. Occasionally you get that person who's just in the zone, but they are rare."

Gary concedes Ezrin's perspective to a degree, though he doesn't see the use of loops as a departure so much as an accurate reflection of a band that doesn't want to be pigeonholed. "Way before Bob we've been playing with drum machines," he says. "I think we have to let loose and have a little fun, not worry about rules that we may be putting on ourselves and blaming on others. We're pretty funky dudes, whether it's the real beats like the Meters or drum machines.

"One thing that we wanted on this record was more sex to the band. More movement. We have a lot of songs where people just stand there. We wanted a few songs where people might actually move a bit. That's where these kinds of songs came from, [though] 'Ohio' was something that he [Ezrin] directed us to do. Perlman had a three-chord progression—G, B, E minor—and basically not much else. Bob said it would be cool if we made a modern folk song. We succeeded at a very crucial point, where Bob felt we were about three songs short of making a great record. And I think in that time we wrote 'Somewhere in Ohio,' we reworked 'Queen of the World,' and I wrote 'Mr. Wilson.'"

Louris finishes his thought with an intriguing addendum: "We had a lot of great songs that didn't make the record, and I hope that those come out. I'd like the demos to come out at some point."

In the Flesh?

Gary's comment is, to some degree, a delayed reaction to a question posed the week before in Austin, when the band performed at the South by Southwest Music Festival. The question was about "Someone Will," a song the Jayhawks performed in 1998 that shares the music and verses of "I'm Gonna Make You Love Me"—though, crucially, not the chorus. The song's melancholy chorus (which simply repeated the words of the title) was rewritten and replaced with the more upbeat sentiment of "I'm gonna make you love me," which both retitled the song and made it the album's best choice as a single.

In Austin, Gary responded to the initial question about "Someone Will" with customary candor. "Our producer and record label loved the first half of the song, and they thought it was the single, but the chorus wasn't big enough. So we went through this big battle. I wrote with a lot of different people and ended up working with this guy named Taylor Rose from Nashville. In some ways, I like it better, and in other ways, I like the old way. It's a more subtle song the old way."

Later that day, Louris acknowledged that the question had made him wistful toward "Someone Will." "I didn't want to change it, but I ended up with a version that I love also," he said, clearly feeling both sides. "We need to make a statement on this record. We've been gone a long time. I don't think there's anything wrong with trying to get on the radio. . . . People who don't want to be heard on the radio are either too concerned with how cool they are [or] they are insecure."

His next comment proved even more confessional: "I'm embarrassed we haven't had a hit yet. It seems like [since] we've been together this long, we ought to have one. I don't want to be a cult band. I have no interest in that."

A week later, Perlman is quick to offer his take on the question, the song, and what changing it means or ultimately doesn't mean. "It has nothing to do with selling out. It has nothing to do with the label ordering us to do anything. We wrote fifty or sixty songs for this record, and a lot of them are amazingly beautiful. A lot of the songs that I co-wrote didn't make this record for the reason that they weren't written for a record like this. At the time we were working on them by ourselves in our own studio, we were envisioning the *Sound of Lies* thing taken another step into the moody atmospheric thing. It came down to whether this was going to be a career record, or a personal, artistic record we release ourselves. And when the opportunity came to us to make a record where we were gonna reach a lot of people, we geared the record toward that.

"It's not that we did what suited them; I wanted to make a dance record. I wanted to make a record that people could shake their asses to. I love moody atmospheric stuff, and there's a record for that. Those demos could easily be on that record or B-sides or a retrospective or soundtracks, just not this record.

"We had one major rule, and that was we're gonna make the best and most cohesive record possible. And once [we made] the decision, we refocused ourselves and went that way. Songs like 'Somewhere in Ohio,' 'Queen of the World,' and 'I'm Gonna Make You Love Me' were geared for this record and written for this record with the sole purpose of being good pop songs and having cool rhythms. We're not doing it because it's hip and cool and we're gonna sell a bunch of records."

Happiest Days of Our Lives

"This record is very uplifting," Louris says a week after Austin, "but it's not like we're the New Christy Minstrels. We still have our edges and certain baggage we carry around." And he is right. The Jayhawks are still the Jayhawks.

"I'm proud of every single song on every single record that this band has put out, even from our first record that no one has," Perlman declares with unwavering conviction at the end of the interview. "We've never made a bad record. How many bands can say that that have been around this long?"

And it's not over yet. "I'm excited to get out there and work it as hard as we did in 1992 and say, with a good record label and a great record and a great band, that we gave it a shot." Louris concludes. "When I look at my kid someday, I'll say, 'The old man gave it a shot.' If it didn't take, a least I can't blame anybody but myself. We know we have an audience. We know we can play. The issue is more to leave behind some kind of musical legacy."

In through the Out Door

Two Years of Turbulence Cast Wilco in a New Light, Spinning Off Satellites

ND #39, May–June 2002

Paul Cantin

The story of what happened to Wilco in the past couple of years isn't always a happy tale, but it does have a happy ending. So let's start there.

After countless delays, a split from their record company, and the departure of two key members, Wilco finally, officially released its embattled new album, *Yankee Hotel Foxtrot,* on April 23. In the lag between the completion of the record in April 2001 and its release, the current lineup of the group—singer-guitarist-songwriter Jeff Tweedy, bassist John Stirratt, keyboardist-guitarist Leroy Bach, and drummer Glenn Kotche—has already recorded a new Wilco album. They also served as the backing band for R.E.M. sideman Scott McCaughey's forthcoming Minus 5 album.

On the very day *Yankee Hotel Foxtrot* arrived in stores, former Wilco guitarist-keyboardist-songwriter Jay Bennett released his own record, *The Palace at 4 AM,* recorded with longtime pal Edward Burch. Where *Yankee Hotel Foxtrot* is challenging and experimental, Bennett and Burch's assured effort is full of sweet melody, heartfelt lyrics, and classic pop-rock stylings.

Former drummer Ken Coomer has regrouped at his Nashville base, where he has become an in-demand sideman and session player (he has cut tracks with Emmylou Harris and Steve Earle lately) and has begun working as a producer. He is also prepping for another album with the roots-rock semi-supergroup Swag.

All three camps claim they are happy with how things have turned out.

Tweedy says of Wilco's present configuration: "The band that I was most comfortable with, and the people that I am most comfortable with making music, are in my band now."

Says Bennett of his burgeoning solo career: "I am having the time of my life. I don't know if you can tell, but I just am . . . this is kind of maybe what I thought my life was going to be like."

And Coomer says he has been relishing his time away from the touring demands of Wilco. "I wondered how I would adjust to being off the road, and it is wonderful. For the first time, I feel like I have a home," he says. "It has been sort of falling into place. I want to do it all."

So perhaps all's well that ends well. But that is not the same as saying all has been well with Wilco.

■ ■ ■

It is appropriate that a work as mercurial as *Yankee Hotel Foxtrot* really has no precise starting point. During the 2000 tour promoting the second volume of *Mermaid Avenue,* their Woody Guthrie–related collaboration with Billy Bragg, Wilco had been working some new songs into their sets. According to fan-created online set-list databases, "Reservations," "Kamera," "Ashes of American Flags," and "I'm the Man Who Loves You" were road-tested at various dates. At solo shows, Tweedy had offered up acoustic versions of those last two, plus "War on War" and "Heavy Metal Drummer." With most of the songs in sketch form, Wilco had been gathering at their Chicago loft-studio by late 2000 to begin tentative work on recording. But the border was indistinct between demoing the material and actually making an album.

"With this band, demos were the album," says Coomer. "The great thing about having your own studio is the clock isn't running. We'd hole up there and mess around and try stuff."

Adds Bennett: "It was all demos. It was all album. It was all just making music." He says the only agenda was to use Wilco's open-ended studio time to their advantage and to try anything. "There is everything from round-table discussion of what a tune should be like, to absolute and complete spontaneity of people grabbing the nearest instrument."

Tweedy says the advantages of owning their own recording space were obvious, but the process also had its pitfalls; given so much free time to create, a band can lose what he calls "a sense of compass." "It can become really fragmented and chaotic, so loosely defined. You can lose sight of it," Tweedy says. "But you have the luxury to let songs evolve. We definitely gave almost every song on the record more than one chance to become something different."

As the new songs began to take shape, Tweedy's notion of what the album should sound like began to coalesce. The abstract lyrics would be echoed in a more free-form style of music that would mark a distinct departure from the orchestrated pop sound of 1999's *Summerteeth* and the roots-rock flavor of their earlier records.

"I didn't think I had the desire or ability to make that same record again. There were ideas I had about space and things like that," Tweedy says, adding that the alt-country label had become "reductive and limiting" some time ago.

"The second *Mermaid* record had a certain staid quality: traditional, a little more conventional," says Stirratt. "The one idea we had was [that the new record] shouldn't sound like anything we had ever heard before. We should not be afraid to set our sights that high."

As the new year dawned, Wilco was making faltering progress on a new album that carried the working title *Here Comes Everybody*. But in January, Coomer says he was blindsided by a call from manager Tony Margherita: The "everybody" in the album's working title wouldn't include him.

■ ■ ■

Coomer has had plenty of time to adjust to life after Wilco, but the confusion and pain of his ouster from the group he was a part of from the start is still evident in his voice.

"I didn't hear from anyone except John [Stirratt] for two weeks," Coomer said from his Nashville home. "At that point, you have already gone through the emotions."

At the time of our interview in January, Coomer had still not spoken to Tweedy or Bennett, and said unspecified issues between himself and Wilco inhibited his ability to comment on the record about aspects of what had happened. (When asked if Wilco had been required to settle up with Coomer both financially and legally, Tweedy declined comment.)

Coomer does say that he had no indication his job was on the line, and that the band hadn't given him any signal he was in jeopardy.

"The way it was handled was ridiculous to me. There was no reason given," says Coomer, who joined Uncle Tupelo circa 1993 and appeared on their swan-song album *Anodyne,* then stayed aboard for the creation of Wilco.

Coomer says the album that would become *Yankee Hotel Foxtrot* was "five-eighths" completed when he was sent packing. Tweedy counters that the decision came while the band was still in the early experimental phase, and that work on the album hadn't begun in earnest.

"I really didn't feel like Ken and I in particular, and Ken with the band as well, had the same chemistry that we needed to make music that I was proud of," Tweedy says, adding that he was the one who hatched the notion of finding a new drummer, but that the other group members endorsed it. Bennett agrees he seconded the idea.

"There's some material in the band that Ken was not accomplishing. That can be attributed to a lot of things in Ken. Out of respect for him, I won't go into much detail," Bennett says. "You couldn't fill in his weakness without taking away his greatness. The things where he was being weak were the areas where we needed him to be strong. If we tried to change him, we would have wrecked his greatness as well."

Some of the songs that proved to be the most challenging—"Ashes of American Flags," "Radio Cure," "Poor Places," and "Kamera"—were built on unconventional musical ideas that were initiated by Bennett.

"Ken could always wrap his head around a three-chord Jeff Tweedy song, in the time it took to record it," Bennett says. "I wanted to see those compositions of mine on the record. I thought they were important. I felt they represented a stage in growth for the band."

Just as Bennett is prepared to plead guilty to making unusual musical demands on his friend and bandmate, Tweedy pleads no contest to the harsh manner in which the news was delivered to Coomer.

"I wish I had called him and talked to him personally. I didn't make the decision [to split with Coomer] by myself. I instigated it, but I certainly had no lack of support from members of the band, and I felt it was a little unfair at the time to be made the mouthpiece for such a hard decision," he says.

For Stirratt, the hardest issue is this: When does the group's devotion to a particular sound for a particular record become more important than nearly a decade-long relationship with Coomer? "That is the question of the day, frankly. It is a choice: How [far] at the forefront do you put this vision?"

Stirratt adds that there may have been issues surrounding the split with Coomer that weren't directly related to the band's new direction, and he cites his own choice to relocate to Chicago from New Orleans as contributing to his improved rapport with Wilco. (Coomer had remained in Nashville.)

"I guess I made a conscious decision to move and . . . communication can be so weird," Stirratt says. "I just wanted to establish myself there. That can really help working relationships."

Tweedy himself points out the irony of his neglecting to see how difficult it would be for Coomer to get the news from manager Margherita. After all, Margherita was the one who gave Tweedy the news that Uncle Tupelo was over when Jay Farrar decided to leave the band in the spring of 1994.

"I can only hope that time will heal that wound. I would hope that at some point in the future, Ken and I can be friends," he says.

Says Stirratt, of the way Coomer received the news: "It was pretty hideous. I am pretty embarrassed about that, quite frankly."

To add to what must have been an already stressful situation, the day the split with Coomer went down, photographer Sam Jones arrived at Wilco's loft, cameras in tow; he had previously arranged to begin shooting a film about the making of the new album.

"I came expecting the first real sessions. And when I got there, Jeff took me aside and said, 'Ken isn't in the band,'" says Jones. "I never saw Ken. His drum set was still there when I got there. It had just happened."

• • •

While the mood was initially somber, progress on the new album changed almost immediately with the entry of Glenn Kotche, who had worked with Tweedy on some extracurricular projects. Kotche had helped Tweedy record the soundtrack to the Ethan Hawke–directed film *Chelsea Walls,* and had also performed on an as-yet-unreleased collaborative album with Tweedy and musician Jim O'Rourke. Anyone who has seen Kotche in action with Wilco's new lineup knows he is a very different kind of drummer, with a proficiency for the kinds of off-kilter rhythms and percussion woven throughout the new album.

"When Glenn came in, he had an amazing amount of enthusiasm for the material that wasn't there before," says Tweedy. "The record really sped up. There was an energy that we were lacking. We were also getting bogged down in a lot of things that were counterproductive. Like trying really hard to make someone play something they are really not hearing, or intuitively hearing. Or maybe asking them to play something they don't like."

When asked for his view of the band's new direction, Coomer hadn't yet heard the finished album, but offers: "Sometimes you can be too arty for your own good, and sometimes I think you shoot yourself in the foot."

Adds Bennett: "Glenn is a great drummer. Absolutely. No doubt about it. . . . Not the same soul as Ken Coomer . . . [but] he came in and did what needed to be done."

If Coomer's departure signaled a changing of the guard for Wilco, their record label, Reprise, was also undergoing a cabinet shuffle that would have a profound impact on the group. Since Uncle Tupelo signed with Sire/Reprise for 1993's *Anodyne,* music executive Joe McEwen had served as Tweedy's liaison between artist and record company. And even today, he remains one of Wilco's biggest supporters.

"I just thought they were really talented and had a vision that wasn't a Top 40 vision. They just had the potential to be a great American band," says McEwen, who left Reprise in 2000 and first resurfaced at Artemis, but is now working with RCA.

Wilco was assigned a new A&R rep, Mio Vukovic, to oversee the making and the release of the group's next album. Vukovic did not return repeated phone calls for his account of what happened.

"I think [Reprise] wanted this to be Wilco's breakout record," says Bennett. "We made the mistake of letting them in on what we were doing a little earlier than we should have."

Jones's documentary cameras captured the anything-goes approach to the developing album. He says his film, now titled *I Am Trying to Break Your Heart* (the name of the album's opening track), will feature one sequence where Tweedy and Bennett cue up seven radically distinct takes of "Kamera" and discuss each version, with footage intercut showing brief clips of the making of each rendition [that sequence ultimately was left on the cutting-room floor]. Jones says another sequence shows "Poor Places" going from "a little acoustic number to a noise thing."

"There are songs that went everywhere. They got super straight, super fucked-up, somewhere in the middle," says Bennett. "Some are linear, like that song 'Reservations': started with acoustic guitar and vocal and gradually added stuff to it. Others got very dense and then got thinned out and then dense and then thinned out."

The finished version of "Ashes of American Flags" is based on a home demo Bennett says he recorded on his own, with his drum track recorded on a single microphone. "Pot Kettle Black" shifts gears from a noisy, atonal intro to energetically strummed verses, down to a drum–machine–electric-piano treatment and onto a string-drenched finale. "Heavy Metal Drummer" avoids the raunchy treatment implied by its title in favor of a beatbox rhythm. The tuneful "I'm the Man Who Loves You" takes a hard left turn with an abrasive electric-guitar hook and an out-of-nowhere, wheezy horn break.

The initial music the band sent the label was never intended to represent what the finished album would sound like. It was a work in progress, but Tweedy says there was an increasing repugnance for Wilco's apparent new direction. "I think they got progressively disheartened," he says of the label's response. "The reactions got progressively colder."

In hindsight, Bennett says it shouldn't be a wonder that the label would gradually develop an aversion; the sound got weirder as the sessions dragged on. The more melodic songs got dropped from the album, and some midtempo tunes got, in Bennett's words, "fucked with."

Still, says Tweedy, "Nothing was ever presented as: This is what it is going to look like when we're done. 'This is where it is now' is as much as we would ever tell them. And next time you hear it, expect it to be different."

While Bennett embraced and even initiated some of the record's more experimental features, he says he has some sympathy for Reprise's position, in that the early versions of the songs may have raised hopes that the new album had the potential to be more commercial.

"[The label] gets a new set of new rough mixes, and the three up-tempo catchy songs are gone, and the two midtempo catchy songs are now a barrel of noise; that is going to upset you," Bennett reasons. "I didn't fully agree with dropping the catchy, up-tempo numbers, because I have this rule: I think albums are important, the sequence is important, lyrical statements are important. But in my mind, there is a trump card. It's called a good, fucking catchy song."

By March, the group had posted a message on its Web site announcing it had recorded twenty songs for an album that would now be called *Yankee Hotel Foxtrot,* which was targeted for release in July. (Among the songs recorded but not slated for inclusion on the album were "Cars Can't

Escape," "Magazine Called Sunset," "Hummingbird" and "Shakin' Sugar"; the last of those ended up on Bennett and Burch's album.) By late March, Wilco had gone into Chicago's CRC recording studio to finish the record. Tweedy's pal Jim O'Rourke (Gastr Del Sol, Tortoise, Sonic Youth) was called in to help mix the disc.

"The last couple of weeks of mixing with Jim brought the songs back into focus," says Tweedy. "The things that ended up not being mixed or finished sound more like *Summerteeth* and *Being There*. They were denser, and that was something we really wanted to avoid. . . . I would think, when I look back, it was the most exciting time, being able to focus on it in a more condensed amount of time."

As final choices were being made about which songs to include on the album, Tweedy began to pick up on a current running through the record. Despite the unconventional setting, the songs formed around his distinctive take on patriotism.

"There is some vague notion that I was writing songs about my perception of America, you know? I wanted to write things that were more accurate, without being flag-wavingly patriotic, but trying to embrace the things right in front of me, that I can appreciate. . . . I wanted to be more interior about looking at my environment . . . really trying to focus on the really small things in front of me."

Wilco forwarded the first six mixed songs to Reprise, and that initial batch was met with vague concern. "The only specific comment I heard about anything musical was the vocals sounded masked. I'm not sure I have any idea what that means," says Tweedy.

Nonetheless, the band sent back word that it would complete mixing and then address Reprise's concerns. When the full eleven songs were completed and sent off to Reprise, this time their efforts were countered with two weeks of icy silence. When the company did get back in touch, it was with a generic request that *Yankee Hotel Foxtrot* be altered. Tweedy retorted the band wasn't interested in making changes.

McEwen, for one, was delighted with the results, and had he still been in a position to do something, the story may well have turned out different. "I had nothing to do with *Yankee Hotel Foxtrot*—unfortunately, because I love it. I think Jeff is an incredibly gifted artist, and [is] continuing to grow before our eyes," he says. "Different personalities [at Reprise] could have made it work, but not the ones who were there then."

■ ■ ■

On July 3, 2001, Jones's documentary cameras were set up to film an interview with Wilco manager Tony Margherita. Just as they were about to begin, Margherita received a call from Reprise. As Jones's crew rolled, Reprise and Wilco divorced via telephone.

"He [Margherita] saw us filming it, and he just let it go. Half of it was he was involved in the phone call, and the other half was, hey, this is what

I signed on for. For whatever reason, he just kind of continued the phone call. We didn't need the other side of the phone call to understand what was going on," says Jones.

Although Vukovic was overseeing Wilco for Reprise, a source working with the band confirms that veteran record producer David Kahne, who was then serving as head of A&R at the label, ultimately had a hand in the final decision to let Wilco go. Last August, the *Chicago Tribune* reported that Kahne gave *Yankee Hotel Foxtrot* the final thumbs-down during the transition between the departure of longtime Reprise president Howie Klein and the arrival of the company's new boss, Tom Whalley.

With Reprise bailing on *Yankee Hotel Foxtrot,* some may have seen an excuse to push the panic button. Tweedy saw an opportunity.

"Sometimes I can try and imagine what [the label's rationale] was. But mostly, I am just appreciative," he says. "Don't ask too many questions: That was what I felt at the time. Once they said that [the band could leave Reprise], we basically moved very quickly to help that along."

In fact, Tweedy says their contract had provisions that if Reprise refused to release the record, Wilco would be free at a later date to release the disc through alternate means, while still potentially remaining signed to the company. In short, there were limits on Reprise's ability to keep *Yankee Hotel Foxtrot* under wraps. Tweedy confirms the group was ultimately able to buy back the unreleased album for about $50,000, and Wilco was released from its contract.

A devil's advocate might wonder if the Reprise execs had a point. They were, in theory, expected to help the band sell an album with seemingly limited commercial appeal. Their view, evidently, was that *Yankee Hotel Foxtrot* wouldn't have a fighting chance without the inclusion of a more likely radio song or a revised, more mainstream sound. But Wilco's decision to stand their ground was informed by experience.

When the group completed their 1999 album, *Summerteeth,* Reprise insisted there wasn't a song suitable for radio consumption. The band obliged by returning to the studio and coming up with the tuneful "I Can't Stand It," which failed to significantly buoy the album's commercial fortunes (despite receiving the mixing ministrations of—guess who?— David Kahne). With *Being There* in 1996, Tweedy says there were suggestions that "Monday" didn't stand a chance at radio unless the track's horn section was removed. And while McEwen says he has no memory of the incident, both Tweedy and Coomer recall a label request for the fiddle to be removed from "Casino Queen" on the band's 1995 debut, *A.M.,* in the name of securing airplay.

In short, there was evidence that Wilco had been down this road with Reprise before, with little to show for their efforts. So perhaps the hard line taken against sweetening *Yankee Hotel Foxtrot* was understandable, given the futility of previous conflicts and concessions. But Tweedy says he is reluctant to be seen as a champion of artistic integrity in the face of rapacious corporate values.

"I understand the story that can be told out of this is good. I mean, the man hassling the little guy," he acknowledges. "But I don't want to sound like we did anything noble. We just did what you are supposed to do. I look at it as, I want to be fulfilled making a record, and after I finish making it, will I stand by it?"

So now Wilco was a free agent with a completed yet unreleased album on its hands. But just as the divorce from Reprise was being announced in August, word got out that Wilco and Jay Bennett were now estranged.

■ ■ ■

During the final stages of the making of *Yankee Hotel Foxtrot,* Bennett was consumed by an awful, familiar feeling. It was the same sensation he had felt back in adolescence when he had quit playing Little League.

"When I was twelve, I was going to be a pro baseball player. That was it," Bennett recalls. "Then one year I got a different coach . . . and he wouldn't play me and didn't respect me." Bennett says that impertinence transformed him from someone who wanted to go to practice every day into someone who prayed for rain. "I fell out of sports the same way I fell out of Wilco," he says. "The last month in the studio with Wilco, I had the I-hope-it-rains feeling."

A measure of Bennett's unease with Wilco can be taken by the creative flourishing that followed. He quickly removed his mountain of gear from the group's loft, built a studio in his Chicago-area home (dubbed Pieholden Suite Sound), hooked up with longtime friend Edward Burch, and began making music at a furious pace.

"I called Ed up, crying, the day after I left Wilco," says Bennett. "My number one choice was to take what we have always done sitting on the couch, and do it sitting on top of the world. . . . I knew pretty quickly after Wilco, the next morning, that that is what I wanted to do."

In a manner that might confound the folks at Reprise, Bennett and Burch's album, *The Palace at 4 AM (Part 1),* sounds like the more-commercial Wilco record the label was hoping for. An eighteen-track, work-in-progress version Bennett passed along in February moves from gorgeously understated folk-rockers such as "Puzzle Heart" and "Like a Photograph," to the wide-screen pop of "Whispers or Screams" and "Talk to Me," to the disarming roots-rock of "Junior." "Drinkin' on Your Dime" and "Venus Stopped the Train" (the latter is one of two compositions co-credited to Tweedy) are dreamy, Beatlesque soundscapes, but the chilling "No Church Tonite" and the consoling "Little White Cottage" (both based on lyrics mined from the Woody Guthrie archives) are plainspoken and direct.

Bennett is blessed with a husky baritone that is nonetheless expressive, and he finds a nice foil in Burch's voice. There is a breadth and ambition to the record at odds with the genre-driven mentality of modern music, but that may well be due to the sheer volume of material Bennett and Burch have amassed.

Aside from the songs earmarked for *The Palace at 4 AM (Part 1)*, Bennett says he and Burch have already completed enough material for two more albums, and he hopes to issue it all before the end of 2002. [Bennett and Burch eventually released an acoustic version of the album, titled *Palace 1919*.] "I have a musical life to explore," he says, "and I would be doing myself an incredible disservice to not explore."

Bennett describes the break with Wilco as a mutual "no-contest divorce" that was executed about two or three weeks after work was completed on *Yankee Hotel Foxtrot*. (Tweedy apologetically declined to discuss specifics of Bennett's departure from the band, but dates it to the period when a separation from Reprise was being negotiated.) Filmmaker Sam Jones, whose documentary camera was trained on Tweedy and Bennett throughout the making of the record, says he saw no behind-the-scenes melodrama. "They seemed healthier to me, relationship-wise, than other bands. [Bennett's departure] did come as a bit of surprise."

To chart his contribution to Wilco, Bennett says one only need mark the difference between the straightforward, roots-rock sound of their 1995 debut, *A.M.* (which was made before Bennett joined as a touring member of the group), and the expansive, more experimental sound of what followed.

Asked what he brought to the table, Bennett replies: "A lot. Just a ton. The studio savvy. Engineering capabilities. Some kind of technical knowledge that nobody else in the band has. Multi-instrumental talents. Emphasis on harmony.

"I'd be lying if I said it didn't get to me that, every once in a while, Jeff would get credit for something everybody knew was my idea. But I think that people saw what happened to this band when I joined."

"I will say this," asserts Coomer. "If you don't think Jay was an integral part of how that band evolved—he was."

The months that have passed since his split from Wilco have given Bennett some insight into what caused the fracture. He now reckons his partnership with Tweedy was based on symbiotic learning. By the time *Yankee Hotel Foxtrot* was finished, that process had exhausted itself, leading to strained relations.

"I was enjoying Jeff's company less and less," he says. "One of Jeff's great skills is learning things from other people, and probably something about his personality that is irksome to me is, he could be accused of using people up—I wish I had a better phrase for that.

"When the learning dynamic left our relationship, we didn't understand what a huge percentage of our relationship that was. And not just musical learning. A lot of emotional learning as well."

Stirratt says Bennett's role within the band transformed during the making of *Yankee Hotel Foxtrot* from a deeply involved musical contributor to embracing the technical, engineering side. "He was placing himself in this other arena that I don't think anyone else wanted him to be in, frankly," he says. "I have seen articles where [Jay] talked about his love for the road, which is bunk, as far as I'm concerned. There is one guy in the band who disliked touring more than anyone else. His dream is more about staying home, recording bands, and making records."

Tweedy dates his own feelings about a need for a change to the brief solo acoustic tour he undertook in March 2001, just as the final work was being completed on *Yankee Hotel Foxtrot*. The solo shows—Tweedy's first outside the Chicago area—were done "to remind myself about what my responsibilities were to make a song happen by myself, to stay in touch with the songs.

"After that, some part of me, down deep, subconsciously started not tolerating things feeling less than that. . . . There had to be a way to have a band that could play more with one mind. That led to some of the revelations about my relationship with Ken as a musician—not as a person—and as well with Jay."

Bennett says he now sees the departure of Coomer, too, as key to the transformation of his relationship with Tweedy.

"Ken Coomer was the heart of Wilco, and we kicked him out. And we were fucking idiots for doing that," Bennett says. "I don't think we understood how much the heart of the band he was. . . . I think we saw the musical side of what we were doing. I don't think we saw the emotional side of what we were doing. I don't think Jeff and I saw what it would do to our relationship."

With Coomer gone and Kotche in his place, relations between Tweedy and Bennett were knocked out of orbit. Kotche appeared to be, in Bennett's words, "very enamored" with Tweedy, but as the new guy, he was distant from other band members. (Requests were made to talk to Kotche for this article, but he was not available.) "I don't think Glenn walked into the band knowing how much of a band it was," says Bennett. "He thought [Wilco] was the Jeff Tweedy Show."

So, is Wilco actually the Jeff Tweedy Show? It depends on whom you ask.

Bennett: "Leaving Wilco is leaving Jeff Tweedy. I didn't leave 'the band,' because without me, there isn't almost a band to leave, in the latter days."

Coomer: "It was definitely a band in some ways. In other ways, I can't really speak about it. . . . I find it comical that it is still a group, with John [Stirratt] being the only other original member. I think it is funny."

McEwen: "He may have hid behind the name Wilco, but it is as much [Tweedy's] band as Tom Petty & the Heartbreakers is Tom Petty."

Stirratt: "I am pretty tired of trying to convince anyone else about it. . . . I couldn't be in a band where I took orders. This is the most egalitarian group that I have ever been in."

Tweedy: "I feel I have tried to make it as much of a democracy as I can. I have always really wanted to have a band that was invested in what we were doing, and I don't think I have ever squashed anyone's ideas.

"Right now, I feel the band has become more what I wanted the band to be like my whole life—the collaborative spirit. And also, maybe some of the things are more clearly defined internally than they have ever been."

■ ■ ■

When word of Wilco's free-agency leaked out, they were besieged by around thirty offers from labels of all sizes, even hip-hop specialists Tommy Boy. There was no shortage of companies willing to pick up what Reprise had kicked to the curb—including, in a bizarre twist, Reprise itself. Sources with the band confirm that even after Reprise let the band go, the label then got in line to pitch Tweedy on returning to the fold. To no one's surprise, Wilco declined the company's overtures.

It shouldn't be a surprise that Wilco would be a hot commodity. They had amassed a substantial following, earned critical accolades, and even received a couple of Grammy nominations. They sold records in numbers that generated profits for the label (if not Lamborghinis for the band members): *A.M., Being There,* and *Summerteeth* have tallied around a half million combined on Soundscan, while the two *Mermaid Avenue* collaborations with Billy Bragg (on Elektra) add another 350,000 or so.

"I think there are a lot of people in the business who love it when a label like Reprise lets go of a band," says Tweedy. "I think there are people at other record companies who like the idea of showing the big guy how wrong they were."

After taking a couple of meetings, though, Tweedy decided that trying to build a personal relationship with a record company was not necessarily the way to go. The group was content to wait and see if any of the companies would sign off on the group's wish list. "Put their friendship in writing, and then we can hopefully work out a relationship," explains Tweedy.

Bolstering Wilco's patience was this unexpected revelation: Perhaps modern musicians don't need a record label in order to make music. Shortly after the split with Reprise, the band began streaming *Yankee Hotel Foxtrot* through its Web site, and a pirated copy of the disc leaked out through the Internet in the MP3 format, allowing resourceful (or larcenous?) fans the chance to download and burn their own copies. Tweedy says the group seriously considered continuing with that model: simply recording songs, releasing them through the Internet, and making a living as a touring act, without the mediation of the record company.

"We don't need to define ourselves by having a record deal, or even making records. . . . That's not the reason we exist as a band, to make a piece of plastic every year and a half," he says. "The best bargaining tool we had was being willing to wait until someone was willing to put into writing almost everything, or everything, we were really concerned about." Wilco ultimately signed with Nonesuch Records—which, ironically, falls within the same Warner/Elektra/Atlantic conglomerate that houses Reprise.

Nonesuch is an intriguing place for Wilco to land. A long-established oasis for acclaimed outsider artists in world, jazz, and classical forms—their roster includes the Buena Vista Social Club stable, Laurie Anderson, Bill Frisell, and Philip Glass—Nonesuch has been making a concerted effort as of late to bring aboard artists in (by the label's standards) more mainstream genres. Besides Wilco, other recent recruits have included Emmylou Harris, Sam Phillips, and the Magnetic Fields.

The new album was road-tested well before the Nonesuch deal fell into place. Wilco had already booked a tour for September in anticipation of the now-scrubbed Reprise release for *Yankee Hotel Foxtrot.* One week before the sortie was to kick off, events in New York City, Washington, and Pennsylvania forced citizens from all walks of life to reevaluate their plans. But Wilco opted to push on. Tweedy was quoted at the time as saying it was important to keep playing because he felt the group's music was a part of the fabric of the fans' lives; he now professes embarrassment at how his remarks came across.

"I really just meant [what was important was] people going out and seeing music. I really did feel that: Here is a rare opportunity to play music in an environment when people are aware and thinking about [the fact that] they are standing in a room with a bunch of other human beings, rather than just: I'm going to see Wilco tonight," Tweedy says. "I think for a lot of people, it was their first time being out of the house. The only real chance to be weak or cowardly was to stay home and not go play music."

Says Stirratt: "I wasn't up for [the tour], but we started to hear from fans. People were really going to be disappointed if we canceled it. It became a beautiful thing. . . . People remembered why art is so important in this world."

At the same time, some of the lyrics from the new material took on a new resonance against the backdrop of September 11. Stirratt says that date was one of the potential release targets Reprise had considered for *Yankee Hotel Foxtrot,* but the full force of its seemingly prescient nature didn't hit home until the group was rehearsing the song "Jesus, Etc.," which includes the lyrics "Tall buildings shake / Voices escape singing sad, sad songs." The self-evident military motif of "War on War" includes Tweedy peppily crooning "You have to lose / You have to learn how to die." "Pot Kettle Black" seems to caution against hypocrisy and to consider a reevaluation of one's own culpability: "Tied in a knot / But I'm not / Gonna get caught / Calling the pot kettle black." Perhaps most eerily prescient was "Ashes of American Flags," with its concluding lyric: "I would like to salute the ashes of American flags / And all the fallen leaves filling up shopping bags."

"When we play that song, people kind of cheer or hoot whenever that line comes up. I am not sure it is that much of a flag-waving patriotic song or lyric," says Tweedy. "I would be more inclined to say the America I love is the one that burned flags in the 1960s, and had a conscience.

"It seemed to be something very dangerous to write about at the time. It turns out it has become something a lot more relevant."

■ ■ ■

Sam Jones has lately been hunkered down for twelve-hour days combing through eighty hours of black-and-white footage documenting Wilco's odyssey creating *Yankee Hotel Foxtrot.* It includes interviews with band members (both current and departed), record execs, associates, and management; intimate footage of Tweedy at home with his family or working up acoustic versions of songs for the album; rehearsals, studio sessions, backstage stuff; and a number of live concert performances (both Tweedy solo and the full band in Milwaukee, Minneapolis, Chicago, San Francisco, and Los Angeles).

Jones, a commercial director and professional photographer, had originally hoped to make his feature-directing debut with a reverse on VH1's *Classic Albums* series: Rather than re-creating the making of a great album, he would have his cameras there to capture it now. What he ended up with is something more akin to Francis Ford Coppola's auto-industry indictment, *Tucker: A Man and His Dream.*

"The story is kind of heroic. They didn't cave in. They didn't say, we'll do what you want if you think you can sell more records," Jones says during a break. The plan now is to have a 100-minute theatrical version of *I Am Trying to Break Your Heart* ready by late summer or early fall (a full year after *Yankee Hotel Foxtrot* was originally due for release), with a DVD to follow, featuring footage left out of the film.

After the distressing time Wilco had making *Yankee Hotel Foxtrot,* anxiety reigns among some of the group's fans. With changes in lineup and musical direction, the fear is maybe the salad days are at an end. But the reality is, the short-term result will be even more music.

Aside from Bennett and Burch's multiple albums of material already prepared and awaiting release, Wilco has been busy during the lull before the release of *Yankee Hotel Foxtrot.*

"Actually, we made a record last week," Tweedy says offhandedly. "We recorded four new songs and a bunch of instrumental pieces that kind of make up a record that we are carrying around and calling our record now."

Those February sessions were conducted at the band Tortoise's Chicago studio Soma, says Stirratt, and further sessions are planned for July. "For the first time in years, we did pre-production. We thought about sequence and recording songs in sequence. It just makes a lot of sense," he says, adding the methodology was sweet relief after the protracted genesis of *Yankee Hotel Foxtrot*. "I don't want to spend a year and a half on a record ever again."

Tweedy says Wilco's plan is to "keep making records all year, and keep doing it in short bursts," while giving themselves limited windows to complete their work—"saying we are going to make a record by the end of this week, and if that means it is one song that is thirty minutes long, we are going to do it."

And that is just the tip of the iceberg. The Minus 5 album featuring Wilco is anticipated by summer on Mammoth (its working title is *Down with Wilco*). The record Tweedy made with Kotche and O'Rourke was released in 2003 by the Drag City label under the title *Loose Fur*. Tweedy says there is still a distant possibility a soundtrack album to Jones's movie (featuring outtakes and live material) could see daylight, too. And Rykodisc has scheduled Tweedy and Kotche's *Chelsea Walls* soundtrack for April 23, coinciding with the release of both *Yankee Hotel Foxtrot* and Bennett and Burch's *The Palace at 4 AM*.

Coomer says he'll continue making music as a member of Swag and as a session player, sideman, and producer. At SXSW he played gigs with Kevin Salem, Florence Dore, and others, and he recently produced a session in Nashville for singer-songwriter Joshua Bennett (with Faces keyboardist Ian McLagan and Sheryl Crow guitarist Peter Stroud sitting in). Stirratt's side project, Autumn Defense, has a new album nearly completed. If fans are looking for a comforting analogy, the reconfiguration of Wilco will result in the creation of more music—just as the rupture of Uncle Tupelo spawned Wilco and Son Volt.

Bennett says his lingering concern is that fans recognize *Yankee Hotel Foxtrot* as not "compromised by some emotional split in the band," but rather the last testament of a vital, passionate group of musicians.

"Goddammit! We were all in there heart and soul until the last note of that record," he says. "Put it this way: [Jones's documentary] does not look like *Let It Be*. It is not a bunch of guys going, 'I hate you.' It is people joyfully making music together."

Tweedy's hope is that the future will see the new Wilco continue that fundamental pursuit. "It is not about making the greatest record ever made or a record that is better than the last one, or even making the greatest song. It is about continuing to have stuff come out of us," he says.

"The goal is to kind of make as many records as we can find the time to make, in the course of touring this record and the next year, just to remind ourselves that that is really what we do: We just make stuff up."

Rocking Tall

Determination and Southern Inspiration Fuel the Drive-By Truckers' Long Haul to the Outskirts of Stardom

ND #45, JULY–AUGUST 2003

Grant Alden

The Drive-By Truckers don't much care to have their picture made. It's not the camera they object to, for few musicians are immune to the imagined comforts of fame. It's just that they don't like to be told where to stand, what to wear, or when to put down their beer. And they don't pose.

Pretty much, they just don't like to be told.

Still, theirs is not the petulance often mistaken for an entitlement of stardom; they're nice enough guys, no matter what they say. And barely famous. Instead, this intransigence is the secret of their survival and, yes, of their success. There aren't a whole lot of people these five guys listen to who aren't in the band. Even then, it's a fight.

A long, hard fight. They're old for van warriors, all but Jason Isbell, the new guy, who's barely dry. By now, any sensible man would have quit and found something to do besides sleep in strange beds and stand in the smoke and chase the phantom dreams of rock. Except that art is not a sensible enterprise.

And so, instead of doing what they've been told, the Drive-By Truckers have laboriously fashioned themselves into a potent and important band, even though the whole notion of a rock band itself now seems anachronistic. A classic rocking band, featuring three first-rate and highly competitive songwriters. And they did it their way, in the finest punk-rock tradition.

The Truckers' fourth album appeared two years ago, the double-disc *Southern Rock Opera,* initially released on their own Soul Dump imprint. As imperfect as it was audacious, it received such notices that, a year later, Lost Highway picked up the record (it clocked in at #22 on the prestigious *Village Voice* Pazz & Jop poll for 2002). Early this spring, Lost Highway turned around and sold the Truckers' follow-up back to the band's management. So it was that *Decoration Day,* their fifth and finest album, came to be released June 17 on New West Records.

All of which more or less explains the photographer *Entertainment Weekly* sent down from New York. He's an older guy, sings fragments of jazz while he shoots, and doesn't tell the band what to do. The Truckers, who live around Athens, Georgia, and Muscle Shoals, Alabama, drove up to meet him in Nashville. It isn't exactly their favorite city, and the weather sucks today, but it's just barely late enough in the afternoon that you can order a dollar beer without feeling like a full-blown drunk.

An earlier lineup of the Truckers played here at the Springwater, but nobody recognizes them, and nobody pays the photographer much mind. The band is dressed no differently from the college students playing pool, or the out-of-work working folk who sit astride their stools with familiar ease, or the two kids hunched over acoustic guitars on the small stage in the back room, trying to teach each other a song.

Eventually, after Jason has put up the high score on the bar's trivia machine, the band ambles outside and stands more or less where it is asked. Once the kids have left the stage, the Truckers frolic some with the pink fringe that serves as a backdrop.

And then the photographer's done and it's back to the hotel until a couple guys from their management office show up with a repaired laptop and a credit card that takes everybody to La Hacienda for dinner and a few more bottles of beer.

■ ■ ■

After fits and starts and gut-wrenching songs placed variously amid four previous outings, *Decoration Day* is the Drive-By Truckers' first great album. It is, at last, the sound of a band with a firm grasp on its own possibilities, and lives up to most of the brags made on behalf of *Southern Rock Opera.* All three songwriters hit what they aim at, and the band plays with fresh confidence, a little polish, and a touch more patience.

Maturity, even.

Mind you, there's no sonic revolution here. They are nothing more nor less than a rock band at work in that old classic form; it is the songs they are playing that are new, and demand attention.

It is still a hard record (they don't make easy ones), once you get past the peculiar joy of sprawling guitars and take in the lyrics. Can't help but be a hard record, centering as it seems to on disintegrating relationships. It opens with front man Patterson Hood's "The Deeper In," about the love of a brother and sister, their four children, and the seven years in a Michigan prison it cost them. Not the stuff of hit singles, that. Fifteen songs later, the record closes with guitarist Mike Cooley's exquisitely rendered "Loaded Gun in the Closet," a study of marital accommodation as notable for its subtlety as it is for the fact that two guns are carefully placed in the house early in the song, and nobody dies. A lot of characters have died on previous Drive-By Truckers albums.

Some of the album's maturity seems to come from the steady hands of the band's newest (and, at twenty-four, youngest) member, Jason Isbell. He had played a little bit with Hood's dad, and was hanging around the house where *Southern Rock Opera* was recorded, fresh out of college and hunting work. Isbell and Hood had already struck up a friendship when guitarist Rob Malone left the band.

"When whatever happened with the last guy happened," Isbell says, "I was just in the right place at the right time. They were playing a house party at that same house that night, and the next day they were doing a photo shoot, and then the day after that they were going on the road."

He went with them, learning the songs in the van and onstage. Though the title track—a classic and true feud story—came from Isbell's pen two days after he joined the band, it is his other songwriting contribution that cements *Decoration Day* as an exceptional work. He wrote "Outfit"—a father's advice to his son—for his dad, including a couplet that neatly summarizes the band's ethos: "Have fun but stay clear of the needle / Call home on your sister's birthday."

"Jason's an old soul," Hood says. "Jason is older than me in so many ways."

He also adds considerable versatility to the band. "David Lindley's his favorite guitar player," Hood smiles. "I'm so lucky because I've got Cooley, who grew up on Carl Perkins and bluegrass, and Jason. Jason's [also] a good piano player, and he plays banjo and mandolin and Dobro. So it isn't three guitars all the time."

■ ■ ■

Southern Rock Opera landed the Truckers a management deal with Vector, a Nashville firm whose clients include the current iteration of Lynyrd Skynyrd (loosely the subject of the *Opera*), as well as Emmylou Harris, Lyle Lovett, Patty Griffin, and John Hiatt. And it brought them to the attention of Lost Highway, the Universal boutique that has sold seven million copies of the *O Brother, Where Art Thou?* soundtrack, and made Johnny Cash's *American IV* a gold record.

Lost Highway sold a little over 20,000 copies of *Southern Rock Opera*, but that's probably not what ended their relationship.

Cooley, sprawling in a stray hotel room, offers his typically caustic summation: "It went exactly like I thought it would. We got a lot of free liquor; we drank it. We made a record, they told us they wouldn't fuck with us, they fucked with us, and we left. It went exactly like I thought it would. No surprise to me."

Lost Highway, naturally, offers a more measured answer. "We found ourselves in different musical directions," e-mailed Frank Callari, senior vice president of A&R and artist development for the label at the time.

"We think they're an incredibly talented band, and we wish them all the luck."

In the end, it doesn't much matter. Lost Highway gave the band enough money to go to Dave Barbe's Athens studio (where they had recorded before) and get the job done right. It took all of two weeks, maybe, plus overdubs and such.

"We made the record we wanted, had no interference, never even saw anybody," Hood says. "They didn't hear a note of it until it was mastered. They were a little cranky about the fact that we mastered it before we sent it to them. We were supposed to send it to them before we mastered it, but . . . we made the record we wanted to make, and if it's not the record they wanted, then at least they were nice enough to let us go. Whatever."

The transition to a new label went quickly, especially given that a major corporation and attorneys were involved. "We asked on Monday, and they dropped us on Friday," Hood says. Simple as that. Presumably it helped that the band's management had the financial resources to buy the album back from the label.

Originally scheduled for a May release on Lost Highway (the label had already pressed advance copies of the disc, some of which ended up on eBay), *Decoration Day* wasn't homeless for long.

"I work with a lot of Athens-based musicians," explains Peter Jesperson, now senior vice president in charge of A&R at New West Records. "I think I originally knew Patterson as the sound guy at the High Hat. I know that Jack Logan had given me a cassette before they ever had an actual CD out, probably in 1995 or '96. I fell in love with 'Nine Bullets.'"

That was really the only reason Jesperson broke his own informal rule—the kind one develops when there's a toddler at home—against going out one Friday night. "They walked onstage [at the Troubadour], and it was one of those magical performances," he remembers. "I batted my eye, and the next thing I knew it was one o'clock and they had just put on an astonishing rock 'n' roll show. I floated on out of there.

"I came into the office Monday morning and went into [label president] Cameron [Strang]'s office and just spewed for five minutes about how great a show it had been. He kind of smiled and said, 'Well, it looks like their album could be available to us.'"

■ ■ ■

Hood and bassist Earl Hicks had plotted the *Southern Rock Opera* on a road trip from Athens back home to Alabama, almost before the Drive-By Truckers existed (and long before Hicks joined the band). Hood's vision for the album was—and is—linked to a screenplay he has been rewriting since 1985. The opening song, "Days of Graduation," was borrowed from that still-evolving work. "The scene that song talks about, the car crash, is the end of the last scene in the film, the horrible rite of passage," he says. "But it's based on a two-week period right before high school graduation.

"I've got other ideas, but it's the one I've decided to finish first, if nothing else because I think it'd be the cheapest one to film and the one I could probably learn how to make a movie on the easiest. I don't really want to make the same mistake there that I made in the band." He laughs.

In some ways, Hood approaches the Truckers as if he were a film director getting the best from his shifting cast. It explains the sometimes cinematic ambition of their work. The *Decoration Day* track "Sink Hole" was, he says, inspired by the Academy Award–winning short film *The Accountant*. He and Hicks have also discussed making a documentary about the legendary musicians of Muscle Shoals, before it's too late; it was Eddie Hinton's death, Hicks says, that really spurred them.

Southern Rock Opera didn't start to become a real possibility until Cooley, not as prolific a writer as Hood (who says he has written 3,000 songs), brought in his ideas. "Honestly, without exception, Cooley's written my favorite song on every record," says Hood. "To me, 'Zip City' is absolutely my favorite song on *Southern Rock Opera*. And I think the most important line on the whole record is the line at the end of 'Shut Up and Get On the Plane': 'Living in fear is just another way of dying before your time.' That sums up the record in one line. That's everything that's really important to know about that record, forgetting all that bullshit about dualities."

By any measure, the whole notion of a two-disc rock opera dealing with the legacy of Lynyrd Skynyrd was a drunkard's dream waiting for daylight. The idea that an obscure independent band who preferred to release albums on their own label—with nary a trust fund in sight—might do so was, well, an invitation to fail, and in a fairly public way.

"We were taking on a really ambitious project without any money or any budget," Hood admits. "We had such clear-cut ideas of what we wanted, and it was all stuff that we really had no business trying to achieve on what we had to work with. It's pretty miraculous. We pretty much made the record that we were trying to make, but it was not pretty making it." He can laugh, now.

"It had already been six years [in planning]," he continues. "It got to the point to where I honestly think that's what kept us from breaking up. What actually saw the record through to getting finished was that we had talked about it for so long and had so many people tell us we were crazy, that pure stubbornness . . . if we dropped the ball now, we're going to have to live that down, and we couldn't accept that kind of failure. And so, God damn it, we're going to make this record, even if it kills us and we kill each other in the process."

Nothing went right. "It was not a fun time. Everybody was having all kinds of bad personal shit go down. We'd been on the road so much, and we cut the damn thing three different times.

"The first time, we knew we were demoing it, so we knew that wasn't it. But the second time, we thought we were cutting it, and we took a week and a half off from touring to go down and cut it in this house that we got access to down in Auburn [Alabama]. Then we took back off on the road for three more months straight. Hell, if I went home, that meant I had to face the music there!

"Things for the band were just at the very beginning of kind of looking like it was all coming together, so it wasn't the time to let up. It was the time to throw another log on the fire and just see, because I'm not getting any younger. So we did that other three months on the road, and during that time spent a lot of time playing some of those songs, and saw 'em really take on another level. So then we went back to cut it again. In the meantime, we went through another bass player. Every time we cut it was with a different bass player.

"So that's when Earl, who had produced two of our records before that, came forward and said, 'Fuck it, man, I'm just gonna play bass.' I didn't really question him. I knew he'd never really played in a band before, or really ever played bass before. But Earl's one of those guys, if he says he's going to do it, you just kind of take for granted that he's going to do it, and so he did."

In fact, Hicks says, bass was his first electric instrument. "I hadn't played it in a couple years," he admits, but his job installing studio gear had given him some insights toward "those old-school Southern bass players and rhythm sections. I gained a new perspective on how you should play bass, on the role of the bass in the context of a song, how not to step on lyrics, working with the drums."

"He still essentially produced that record," Hood insists. ("The band produced it," Hicks answers.) "He actually refused a credit for it because, he said, 'I'm a member of the band now; it'd be cheesy.' But essentially he produced the record. He recorded it and tracked it. Plus he was playing bass. He'd been in the band for two weeks and was still learning the songs and learning how to deal with us, which is a very different relationship as a member of the band from being your producer."

The last thing any of them expected was to end up on a major label. "We had no business being there in the first place," Hood says, without rancor. "We were so frustrated having the *Rock Opera* get the press it got, and we couldn't get it in stores. We could not get distribution. And the deal Lost Highway offered us was the best option we had to rectify that."

■ ■ ■

It is tempting to overlook the quality that has most allowed the Drive-By Truckers to survive as a self-managed, self-booked touring band most of these long years. It is the full-throated, unmediated bellow of mob joy most commonly heard at a football game won in the final minute, or at the prospect of a hard-fought arena-rock encore.

Difficult though it is to admit, there are far more guys wanting to stand hard against the stage pumping their fists and spilling cups of beer on their dates (if they have dates) than there are careful listeners standing back by the soundboard, arms crossed, contemplating the nuanced eloquence of plain-spoken lyrics, nodding in time to the rhythm section of Hicks and drummer Brad Morgan.

"I've always been drawn to the smart writers," Hood nods. "I've always loved Elvis Costello or Richard Thompson or whoever, people who wrote really great lyrics. But at the same time, there's a side of me that loves big, dumb rock. And particularly when done smartly."

Southern Rock Opera gave the band an opportunity to grapple with substantive and terrifying issues, to argue for the reappraisal of a great American rock band, and to discover just how close their reach came to their grasp. It gave critics a chance to revisit Southern rock, to wrestle with the impact of the American South, and to show how open-minded they were (or weren't) about the legacy of George Wallace.

It was a beautiful mess. Not quite the masterpiece some proclaimed, surely not even everything the Truckers had hoped it would be, *Southern Rock Opera* featured a handful of gripping songs and served notice that, like the Bottle Rockets and surprisingly few others, the Drive-By Truckers would write about and for the working man and woman. We all are welcome to come along, so long as we don't spill beer on the soundboard.

The central issue in their music is class. They write, without romance, about the poor and the barely working and the marginal. It's about giving voice to those whose votes are not counted (because they rarely bother to vote), whose stories rarely interest a mass audience (the exploitation of *Jerry Springer* notwithstanding, for it is only an index of their desperation to be noticed).

"We're writing songs about these people 'cause we think they're interesting," Cooley says. "And some of 'em, yeah, it's to pay tribute to a certain degree. But at the same time, they're interesting people. They're who we find interesting, so we write about 'em. Some of 'em are people we've known, and, as far as the new record's concerned, I guess a few of 'em are people we know really well, or have known.

"But they're worth writing about; they're worth telling stories [about]. They were enough like us to where, if I check out, I would hope somebody would write something about me. Maybe they will."

"All my favorite musics have a very strong sense of place," Hood says. "You didn't have to listen to Tom T. Hall long to figure out he's from eastern Kentucky. And I love that. The early R.E.M. records were all about Athens, Georgia, and when I first moved to Athens, it was a thrill, driving around and seeing places that I'd heard sung about."

The working class has long been a great rootless mob, moving across Europe to the United States, restlessly hunting jobs and stability on this continent ever since. "I know more Southerners in Chicago than I do in Atlanta," notes Hood. Doubtless that has much to do with the ferocity with which otherwise unspectacular pieces of land are defended in songs such as Hood's "Sink Hole."

"I come from a family farm," Cooley says. "At least one side of my family. What that land means is, it is almost sacred. We all went out and did our thing, became whatever we became, and then a few times a year we go back there, and we're on that land, and you feel grounded again. You feel like no matter how much you enjoy your life outside of there, there's a place you can go to and everything still makes sense. To a certain degree.

"And that's what you're taking away if you do away with the idea of self-sufficiency, that idea of a family having its own place. And making 'em think that's not cool is a lot of what has happened. Go to the city, find your fortune is a fine thing, you know?" He pauses. "But when you leave, where are you going to go? Where are you going to go where it makes sense?"

Southern Rock Opera features cover art by the illustrator Wes Freed, whose raw style comes straight from the world of homemade under- ground comics and is far from politically correct. Like the band's name, its cover artwork has often created mixed messages. "I know a lot of people had real problems with the artwork, particularly on *Gangstabilly* [illustrat- ed by Jim Stacy]," Hood acknowledges. "But to me, that was the kid in those songs. That was Cooley at twelve, and that was the kinda kid who wanted to be Steve McQueen. He's leaning up against a shitty old car that he really wishes was a muscle car, and the girl ain't too hot, but she's warm, and it's someone else. All that rang true to me."

■ ■ ■

None of their albums would have been made—indeed, the Drive-By Truckers would not exist—if Patterson Hood weren't the kind of stub- born visionary the South seems specially suited to nurture. Over the years, he has booked and managed the band, and it is largely (though not exclu- sively) his vision that has guided it. Not one of the band's three singers has the kind of voice that would recommend they join you for a night of karaoke, much less compete on *American Idol*. And while they can all sure- ly play, nobody in the band is yet a candidate for Nashville session work.

It is one of the myriad beauties of rock 'n' roll that their imperfections meld into such a compelling band. But it hasn't been easy.

"At first I thought, gosh, man, he can't play for shit, can't sing," David Hood says. David was and is the bass player in the Swampers, the Muscle Shoals studio band whose work rivals the Wrecking Crew from the West Coast and Nashville's A-Team. He is also Patterson's father. "I thought, do something else. I've always been impressed with his writing, but they have worked at it so hard and so long that I'm very impressed every time I hear 'em now. But before I was impressed with the band, I was impressed with the ideas in the songs and the albums."

"I have tried to give up the rock habit," Patterson says. "I really, really did. But just never for very long and never with any success. Really and truly it's the only thing I've ever found that I'm worth a shit at. I'm a lousy waiter, I'm a worse cook, and I did enough construction to finance the making of a record to know that I absolutely didn't want to do that for a living. I'm just not really much good for anything else."

Hood's first wife went to high school with Isbell's mother; Cooley, who has been making music with Hood in various configurations for almost twenty years, went to high school with Isbell's stepmother. Muscle Shoals, Alabama, is a small community.

Hood and Cooley had gone to adjacent high schools; they finally met in 1985 when Hood needed a place to stay and some guy he knew needed a roommate. "It wasn't even anyone that either of us really liked," he remembers. "In fact, I think the other guy ended up being the worst roommate in the world.

"[We] more or less started playing together immediately. We were broke, sitting around playing [guitar], and it just clicked. The next thing you knew, we had Adam's House Cat [their first band]. In those days, we fought. We fought," Hood says, almost with glee, certainly with pride. "We fought hard, and we fought every day. Every night was a bloodbath because we didn't agree on anything."

Hood carries their unreleased album around on his hard drive, calls it *Town Burned Down,* and dates it November 25, 1990, when he burns a copy, curious to see what some guy from Seattle will make of his early work.

"What Adam's House Cat had done in the '80s sounded very comparable to a lot of what happened and became really big in the '90s," he says. "There's not really a big piss bit of difference between what we were doing and what Pearl Jam was doing. We were just doing it a few years earlier."

Well, maybe. Hood and Cooley (who sang only in the background at this point, and hadn't yet begun to contribute his own songs) both had gruff vocal styles, roughened now by another dozen years of smoke. *Town Burned Down* seems, from this distance, to owe more to the heartland rock of Springsteen, Mellencamp, and Seger than to the metal-punk fusion that became, however temporarily, grunge. (No surprise, then, that Hood says Springsteen's *Darkness on the Edge of Town* was "the record that got me through high school, pretty much.")

From the opening track, "Lookout Mountain" (which contemplates suicide: "No more worries about paying taxes, what to eat, what to wear ... who will pay my credit card bills, who will pay for my mistakes"), *Town Burned Down* reveals the same mix of grim rural pride and claustrophobia that would evolve into the Truckers' best work. One of the Adam's House Cat songs, "Buttholeville," survives as the penultimate track to the Truckers' 1998 debut, *Gangstabilly,* while "Lookout Mountain" is the second track on the live disc *Alabama Ass Whuppin'.*

The band broke up. Hood and Cooley soldiered on for a year or so as a duo called Virgil Caine, then tried to put another band together (the deftly named Horsepussy), and ended up not speaking for a year.

"When Adam's House Cat was over, everybody thought it was time for me to—'All right, you had your run of it, didn't work, time to buckle down,'" Hood says with a little twinkle. "I was like, 'No, it ain't over yet. It ain't over 'til I say it's over.'"

Cooley went back to painting houses, and Hood moved to Athens, hoping to start another band. He waited tables, mixed sound at a club called the High Hat, and played solo gigs whenever somebody canceled or an opening act was needed. Hicks moved there about a year later.

■ ■ ■

"Nobody's my age in Athens, Georgia," says Hood with an easy, raspy laugh. "When I moved to Athens nine years ago, I was the oldest person I knew there. But that's worked to my advantage a lot because I'm meaner than they are.

"I think a lot of what [the band's] gotten to do is based on the fact that we are still doing something that pretty much everyone [else] out there doing is ten to fifteen years younger. We're just meaner about it than they are. We don't have the next ten years to fiddle-fart around. So we go in there and take names."

("Yeah, right," David Hood says. "He'd like to think he's mean. I like to think I'm mean, but I'm not.")

By his mid-1990s arrival in Athens, Hood says, "my writing was kind of going into a rut, and I'd gotten really disillusioned." The change of scenery worked. "I met a couple of new friends in Athens who were really hard-core into Loretta Lynn and old country stuff. It was almost the story that you, I'm sure, hear all the damn time. It was almost like I had an epiphany from it. I'd had a great-uncle who was always watching *Hee-Haw*. I didn't want to watch *Hee-Haw*.

"At thirty, thirty-one, thirty-two, whatever I was then, it was like, God, this is great. And then you hear a writer like Tom T. Hall. All the sudden I started writing all these songs. Pretty much the *Pizza Deliverance* record was written in a real short period of time right there. I actually wrote it before *Gangstabilly*. At the last minute we ended up cutting this new batch of songs instead, so we cut our second record first. We've never done anything the smart way."

The *Gangstabilly* lineup was assembled specifically for that first recording session, and evolved from there. Hood had been playing with a guy named Chris Quillen, but two weeks before they went into the studio, Quillen died in a car wreck. "We were all still kinda thrown for a loop on that, or the Alabama half of the band who knew him and was close to him was," Hood recalls. "The other half of the band had never met him.

"So it was like this band kinda started on a weird note. At the same time, I've always felt like Chris was a part of the stuff that we've done. It would've been interesting to see how the last several years would have panned out if he would have been around. He was an amazing player."

Two of the five tracks they recorded on June 10, 1996, "Nine Bullets" and "Bulldozers and Dirt," became the band's first 45; revised, they became the opening tracks for 1999's *Pizza Deliverance,* which included "Margo and Harold" from that original session.

And in contrast to the response to Adam's House Cat, audiences seemed to like what they heard. "Not many people in the beginning," Hood says. "The first batch of people that heard it, some of 'em kind of stuck to it. And every show, and every town, it seems to be when we come back, more people come. And it's always been that way."

Only Hood and Cooley remain from the original lineup. Not all of them were ready for what Hood had in mind. "We all quit our day jobs around the time *Pizza Deliverance* came out," Hood says. "It was kind of like, if we're going to do this thing, let's fucking do it. Let's get in the van and go. And that's when we had some personnel changes because some of the people who were in the original lineup weren't really able to make that leap. And I respect 'em for that."

Membership in the band was fairly flexible. Matt Lane (of the Possibilities) played drums on the first two records before giving way to Brad Morgan; pedal-steel player John Neff (of the Star Room Boys) appeared as needed; Hicks produced and filled in on stray instruments; Rob Malone played guitar and bass.

Their first records were a little rough, partly by intent, mostly as a concession to cost. "The vocals were too buried under all that guitar," Hood acknowledges. "A lot of which is because we cut our first three records live. So there was all that bleed; so to turn the vocals up was also turning up the cymbals and guitars. We cut *Pizza Deliverance* in my living room and *Alabama Ass Whuppin'* in a buncha clubs, so we had the technical limitations of the way we did it.

"True, I guess we could have done the vocals not live, might've been an option, but at the time it didn't seem like one. For some reason, that was what we wanted to do. Maybe I read one too many Neil Young interviews growing up, or something."

Gangstabilly was recorded in the then-new studio built by ex–Sugar guitarist David Barbe and his partners. Hood paid for their time by helping build the studio. Hicks became a producer for their next record largely by default. After years of mixing live sound and installing studio equipment, he took what seemed a logical step when his friend needed help.

"We had the songs for *Pizza Deliverance* and wanted to cut 'em and had no money whatsoever to do it with," Hood says. "[Hicks] had a pretty good job at that time, and it gave him access to a pretty good rate on some gear. He took out a loan, bought the gear, and recorded *Pizza Deliverance* for us. And then recorded the live record, and I think did an amazing job on both of those, particularly considering that it's not like it was any incredible gear. It's pretty much the bare minimum you could record a band with. The same gear's what we used on *Southern Rock Opera.*"

■ ■ ■

Important as it is, making art is an essentially selfish enterprise. It is a compulsion that demands arrogance and ego and singular focus, for without an abundance of those qualities, one would not presume to share anything more than a firm handshake with the rest of the world.

Art will eat everything you have, especially your kin, even if you're no good at it. And even though its impulse is to reveal some portion of yourself to strangers, the simple desire to create art separates you from all others.

"Dreams are given to you when you're young enough / To dream them before they can do you any harm," Cooley sings on "Sounds Better in the Song." If there is one idea central to *Decoration Day,* it arrives in the previous stanza: "And 'Lord knows, I can't change' / Sounds better in the song / Than it does with hell to pay."

"There were points a couple years ago, when everything around me was just falling apart . . ." Hood says. "If you have any sense at all left, you have to look in the mirror and ask yourself, 'Why am I doing this? Is this really worth it?' And really, the only answer I could come up with is yeah. This is it. This is what I gotta fuckin' do. And I can't quit now. If I quit now, I might as well roll over and die."

There is a fierceness and a certainty about the Truckers these days that seems newly arrived. Although they seem always to have believed their work was good and valid and worth doing (had they not believed, we would not be here thinking about it, for they would have quit and vanished), only recently have enough people come to share their enthusiasm to make anything like success seem possible. Now they're in a bit of a hurry.

"I'm not twenty-two anymore," Hood nods, "and the rest of 'em aren't that far behind me, except for Jason. He's bought us a lot of time; he's taken about ten years off of each of us, I think, just from how he is."

Nevertheless, their lives are about to change; the dynamics within the band are about to shift. Hood plans to marry for the third time next spring and talks seriously of starting a family. Cooley has been married for five years (he and his wife have been together almost ten years, all told), and will have his first child right about the time *Decoration Day* is officially released. Isbell will have been married for less than two months by then (his wife, Shonna Tucker, plays stand-up bass on one track).

Hood knows how he wants the Drive-By Truckers not to end. "I know I'm not going to be able to continue what we're doing right now forever," he says. "If everything I see in my head could go even slightly right, I'd like it to be something that we can do off and on from time to time for the rest of my life.

"I can't imagine a point in time when I wouldn't genuinely be thrilled to get to play with these guys and get to do what we do, or whatever version of it we can do by that time. Even if it's a matter of every couple years getting together and doing a little tour and making a record and then going on to whatever we're having to do to feed our families.

"It would make me very happy if we could get this thing to a point to where there was actually enough of a market for that to where when we did do it, it would make us a little bit of money. And it wouldn't be having to mortgage something in order to go do it."

Meanwhile, there's a new bar in town to check out, a show to be played in Knoxville, a noon checkout to reckon with, and more records to be finished. Hood's been helping Isbell produce a solo album (David Hood even plays bass on one track), and the Truckers have already cut or demoed—time will tell which—eight songs for their next album (working title: *The Dirty South*).

Oh yeah, and at least a couple of films to be made.

"Neither one of us are ever really short of ideas," Hicks says. "We're short on time to make 'em happen."

"Yeah, I've gotten everything I want," Cooley cracks, "I just haven't gotten everything I need."

A Life of Quiet Inspiration

Sam Beam Turns Wood and Wire into Iron & Wine

ND #50, MARCH–APRIL 2004

William Bowers

Sam Beam makes morning music. Recording under the name Iron & Wine, he has fashioned a somewhat haphazard yet coherent discography, any assemblage of which can hold its own with a rise-and-shine classic such as *Charlie Parker with Strings* or Doc and Merle Watson's *Two Days in November.* His oeuvre won't send you on an odyssey through the big-eyed solicitors outside the corner store in hopes of organizing a reunion tour with Old Milwaukee and the Tallboys. It might sooner inspire you to sober up and settle down, perhaps even, as one of Mississippi writer Barry Hannah's characters once aspired, to "quit fucking around and be a Christian."

Beam's 2002 debut LP, *The Creek Drank the Cradle,* opened with a reference to morning's "rusty gears," a metaphor that workaholics and alcoholics can readily fathom. The album is commonly referred to as a masterwork of whisper-folk, the kind of platter you can spin without waking the house's remaining droolers on those dawns when you are the first sod out of bed and you just know that NPR is going to piss you off. That opening song also contains a very un-hell-raising notion: "We gladly run in circles / But the shape we meant to make is gone." A confession of mundaneness yanking the steering column out of someone's hands? How can such sentiment kick off an album on Sub Pop, the label Nirvana broke?

Well, Sub Pop has softened significantly; its current flagship would probably be the coo-able, barely American dream-pop of Albuquerque's the Shins. Meanwhile the Fruit Bats write lite pastoralia, Beachwood Sparks aims to outstone the Byrds, and even Modest Mouse front man Isaac Brock has embarked on a banjo-and-bare-bones solo trip. The Seattle label has taken steps toward Southern-ification, signing Texas yahoos the Baptist Generals and mid-Florida porch-poets Holopaw. Iron & Wine remains the roster's most "rustic" item, however, what with Beam's slide overdubs and lo-fi production conjuring the textures of Depression-era 78s.

Beam swears that the scrapey sound of his initial releases is the result of his doing the best he could with a "shitty recording setup," a four-track-and-computer compromise. Yet one can't help but think that the hushed-ness erupts from Beam's temperament, or at least his predicament, as a married father of two. He is a rather subdued fellow, and he has admitted that he sneaks into his "hole" to write and record. "Dad-rock" is much maligned by hipsters hankering for the diluted responsibilities of eternal puberty, but that term is an ageist qualifier of contemporary work by McCartney or Costello. Beam's fatherly dimensions are more expansive, and probably have much to do with how his music seems to fend off the night-time-is-the-right-time oblivion espoused in most neu-blues and post-folk.

A friend of mine who just became a pappy calls Iron & Wine's *The Sea & the Rhythm* EP his "iced Elysium." Another, whose wife is expecting, reports that the out-of-print *Calling Your Boys* seven-inch has been hog-ging his turntable. Once, a girl, despite my deficiencies, proposed that she and I stage some matrimony and pool our cash in an attempt to score an intimate Iron & Wine "wedding" performance. When the good folks at UPS left my copy of Beam's new album, *Our Endless Numbered Days,* under my muffler-hoarding neighbor's patriotic doormat, I paused to imagine what a better world this might be if Sub Pop just abandoned the profit motive and sent Iron & Wine albums to every address within feder-al jurisdiction.

■ ■ ■

The son of "yeah, we love Jesus" parents, Beam hails from the gub'mint towns of Columbia, South Carolina; Richmond, Virginia; and Tallahassee, Florida. He currently resides in tropical, metropolitan Miami, where he teaches cinematography and screenwriting at Miami International Uni-versity of Art & Design. He often sounds more excited about the possibil-ity of a future career in filmmaking than he does about his present gig as a songwriter, which came to pass as a result of some random and acquain-tance-directed mail-outs of his household sessions (a launch saga similar to that of Athens, Georgia, bedroom-rocker Jack Logan).

Beam insists that he sees himself as, well, Sam Beam, Family Man, and not as the commodity Iron & Wine. Thus he is blasé about having stum-bled into a spot others would give their lucky elbow to attain. He comes across as sincere and plainspoken enough to not be pulling a disingenuous Dylan when he answers most questions about his music with a pause fol-lowed by, "I don't really think about it."

On Sub Pop's high profile, its groupthink, and its kindler, gentler ten-dencies, Beam offers, after a pause: "I don't really think about it. There's definitely a vibe, but it never really feels like we imagine the '60s. But I have made really good friends. We don't feed off each other, musically, necessarily, but I meet some really nice people. It feels good. And yeah, it'd be different if I was touring with, say, Mudhoney rather than the Shins, who are great guys and can really drink, but I don't see us as making 'pussy music.'"

After the Sub Pop signing, and the initial release's garnering of critical praise, a few Beam strays rose to prominence in the obsessive indie world via EPs and compilations. Beam recorded a cover of the Flaming Lips' "Waitin' for a Superman" (for a *Yeti* magazine compilation) in his plaintive idiom, practically reducing the song to its heartbreakingly delusional lyrics and rivaling the impact of the relatively orchestral original. He worked similar reductive magic on a cover of digital-emo duo the Postal Service's "Such Great Heights" (which hopefully gave some dance kids an opportunity to catch their breath) for an EP of the same name, and on a rapt version of the Marshall Tucker Band's "Ab's Song" (for the new *Starbucks Sweethearts* compilation). His greatest departure thus far is a fleshy "realization" of "Sleeping Diagonally" by melodic-to-mathematic instrumental band Six Parts Seven, included on that band's recent remix album, *Lost Notes from Forgotten*. Even his visit to KCRW made the rounds through his growing fan base.

Somewhere along the way, though, collections of Beam's private, unpolished tapings got shadow-distributed as both tangible bootlegs and as pieces of Internet-hijacked intellectual property, boasting invasive titles such as *Home Recordings*. Beam is flummoxed by his own black market: "Oh shit, man. There's so much stuff out there. It's funny because before I had a contract, I had no idea of making money. I just spread my music around. Now, obviously, I'd like to feed my children, like anybody else."

Money, though isn't Beam's sticking point. Quality is. Aware that today's busy downloader privileges the "rarity" as an artist's central keeper or defining kernel, Beam views such material as his secret stepchildren: "It doesn't bother me that people burn and trade the albums that are out as much it does that they burn and trade stuff that's not out. Versions of some songs that I've found out were on the Internet, I wasn't finished with them. It was disappointing to me because they were given to a few really close friends, so it was kind of like a betrayal. Not that I ever told them. It's a two-way street. On the one hand, people discover your music through the Internet; on the other, I'd like to have some control."

He laughs, as if catching his seriousness about this non-career. "Whatever. It doesn't matter, in the end."

■ ■ ■

Iron & Wine's 2004 album, due out March 23 on Sub Pop, contains a mix of never-before-heard tunes and older ones with retooled arrangements. It sounds entirely different from its predecessors, mostly because of its polished—OK, pristine—production at the hands of Sub Pop's star knobsman Brian Deck in an actual studio in Chicago.

Beam says Deck got him to listen to and appreciate the clearer versions of his songs: "On previous recordings I was just compensating; it's so easy just to wash everything. This time, clarity seemed more important. I don't know if I'm going to go to the studio again. I did it for the experience. I didn't really know what to expect."

Beam discovered that he had been spoiled by the sleep-on-it pace of home recording. "I tell you this, though, that time clock is a pain in the ass," he adds. "That's the thing about the studio I really don't want to deal with again—being under the gun, having to rush."

Perhaps that rush is why this batch doesn't sound as welcoming as *The Creek Drank the Cradle,* and takes a while to settle into its groove. (And maybe the album's title, *Our Endless Numbered Days,* refers as much to the boundaries of professional recording as it does to those of mortality.) Whereas *Creek* seems breezily strummed, *Endless* (especially at its beginning) feels anxiously plucked, as if certain tracks are meant to suggest a clock's portentous timekeeping. Even the overt blues of "Free Until They Cut Me Down" plays as if its Tupperware has been over-burped.

Another huge difference in the execution of this record is that Beam brought his touring band with him to the studio. Jonathan Bradley, E. J. Holowicki, Jeff McGriff, and Patrick McKinney all play on the record, while sister Sarah adds some backing vocals. But their contributions largely maintain a transparency, right down to the library-volume drumming. Leave it to Beam, whose four-piece live show I once saw get drowned out completely by murmuring townies, to do a full-band record that is actually quieter than his lonesome work.

"Arriving at this sound for these songs took us a long time," he says. "When we first went out as a band, it was really loud and kind of dumb. Well, not dumb—the guys I was playing with were really talented, and the flairs and all were still there, but we just weren't quite sure how to make it Iron & Wine."

Left to fend for himself against the silence, Beam now reeks of the 1960s and '70s. The starker approach makes apparent how his vocals evoke such feminine fellas as Cat Stevens and James Taylor, and his fretwork (aside from, say, the detectable traces of Lindsey Buckingham) signals patterns from tunes by Nico, Cat Power, and Roberta Flack. The album's multiple allusions to dead patriarchs, the trippy banshees of "Cinder and Smoke," Sarah's assistance, and the stunningly beautiful woman-centered closing track are enough to provoke the listener into thinking that Beam consciously went yonic. He swears the album's girl power is adventitious, after a pause: "I hadn't really thought about it. I guess, in a house with my wife and my two girls . . . no wonder I made a women's record."

Beam maintains that the studio pinpointed his strong points (melody and imagistic lyrics), and he is right. *Endless* will still fare well years from now, yet I fear that its subtleties may test the maturity of Beam's college-age audience. Are we ready for love songs that aren't trying to be seductive, or for compositions so provincially delicate that their having been recorded in a northern ubermunicipality seems impossible? *Endless* is centered on physical aftermaths, as opposed to the emotional fallouts of *Creek:* "ashes" and "teeth" are in its "grass." On *Creek,* the characters were trying to brush off the lint from their religious upbringings, but God is frequently invoked as a kind of balm in the new songs.

"The tone is different," Beam concedes. "There are not as many typical love songs."

My cocky faux-detachment from religion, nature, and family won't let me follow Beam into some of these tunes' territories. The chorus of "Fever Dream," for example: "I want your flowers like babies want God's love." Beam subverts my straight reading: "That is, like, the most noncommittal love song ever."

Beam reports that his own spiritual doubts haven't changed, but confesses that the new album is softer on religion. It is also more opaque. "On Your Wings" is built around the humble refrain "God give us love in the time that we have," but it also indicts the creator's beneficence via rumors of war, and potentially meaningless megadeath, before it busts into a (fittingly) muted stomp: "God, there are guns growing out of our bones / God, every road takes us farther from home / All these men that you made, how we wither in the shade of your trees / On your wings we are carried to the sea." Ahem, paging Mr. Zimmerman: You have, yawn, yet another worthy new descendant.

"Passing Afternoon" (the one I dubbed "stunningly beautiful" a few paragraphs back) could play as a solemn testament to the vitamin power of disciplined faith: "And she's chosen to believe in the hymns her mother sings / Sunday pulls its children from their piles of fallen leaves." This joint could be used to evacuate the old tear ducts; I fear the citizen so hard-core that he or she can't be moved by the blossoming, understated piano that caps it. Beam says of its genesis: "That one's based on a friend whose optimistic religious views kind of counter their huge life problems."

Even his more abstruse songs cast a spell. Beam taps some blearily picaresque vein, triggering memories in many listeners, who flash back to host interior short-film festivals. (Since you asked: When I listen to Iron & Wine, I'm always transported—in the slo-mo, grainy black-and-white of our media brainwashings—to a childhood afternoon when my mom was visiting her boyfriend at his junkyard. My sister and I devised a game: She would hide among the cars, and I would try to hit her with handfuls of rocks. We had so much fun, and were so adrift in kid heaven, that we failed to notice how many hoods we had dented, vinyl tops we had knicked, and windshields we had cracked. Mom punished us with due aggression, but the boyfriend just gazed at the wounded cars and wept.)

Beam credits his natural filmic tendencies. His knack for scene setting "comes from habit, and inclination. That's the way I engage myself. I'd rather portray than pass judgment. I'd rather describe a scenario than analyze or take a side." He is a gifted observer. We joke about dreaming up a consummate Florida image. I suggest a shopping cart filled with dead palm fronds; he suggests we add a pom-pom.

Another of the album's gems, "Sodom, South Georgia," juggles huge myths and connotations. No, there is no Sodom in the Peach State, only a Sodom Cemetery, in Rockdale. Perhaps this song's funeral is set there, or perhaps the title is a pun on the biblical "cities of the plain" and the Georgia cities with "Plains" in their names, or maybe Beam is referring to the missing half of *The Cotton Patch Bible* (a translation of the New Testament set in Georgia, with Atlanta as Jerusalem's smog-in). The song is magnetically recalcitrant, almost gleefully unknowable. What's with all those nonlinear similes ("slept like a bucket of snow"), and what do the "Sunday"s and "Christmas"es and the "acre of bones" mean? And what is one to make of the chorus: "All dead white boys say God is good"?

Beam isn't telling, understandably. "That character means that line literally. About his father. Or the glory of the grave. Or it could be racist. It's difficult for me to explain. Maybe it's irresponsible."

Beam laughs. To anyone in need of some Old Testament action in Georgia, I recommend the town of Locust Grove, even though its only plague is the strip-mall aesthetic of every interstate exit.

■ ■ ■

This is the part of the article in which we ruminate on this week's hypotheses regarding the infamous *No Depression* parenthetical, "Whatever That Is." Since you asked: I'll go ahead and out myself as a "rurban," that type of pea-splitting country boy who has cultivated a smidgen of sophisto-slang and ordered a pair of European loafers, but who feels doomed that he will have to drop the shtick when he reaches Jesus' expiration date, only to take up the "professional Southerner" pose. I've filled Mead notebooks with sketches for the perfect Nudie suit.

Beam isn't very forthcoming when put on the spot by some press boob to guesstimate his role in the alt-country canon. After a pause: "I don't really think about it." Which didn't strike me as a coy copout, unlike when he lent me the harm's-length elucidation, "Different songs are about different characters."

How does he feel about how "Southern music" gets the privilege of being a diaspora ranging from anonymous cotton-gospel to "Ashokan Farewell" to Bubba Sparxxx, while "alt-country" is considered a ghetto? And what of the double standards to which many critics hold acts such as

Iron & Wine, decrying their albums' "sameyness" in the face of dozens of monochromatic genres? What about how Beam and only a few other artists even mention birds or landscapes in their material?

Beam: "I tour two weeks every four or five months, and I'm not out to get trashed or laid. It's so rare that I consider myself part of the music world, or a trend."

He finally yields his opinion that alt-country image making strikes him as "kitsch." And who couldn't agree that the old-timey "agrarian" mimicry is as silly or dangerous an escapist fantasy as gangsta rap or the *Wonderful World of Disney*? The cultural critic Daniel Harris aptly points out that the trick of Cracker Barrel–type plastalgia is that it gets us "purists" to buy products by "alluding to a time before consumerism." But wait: Beam's releases are packaged with "olden" atmospherics, and he sports that full Pentecostal/prospector beard, yet we know that he knows what year he is in, and that he has a cell phone, and that he is featured on a Starbucks sampler.

When faced with what is obviously a problem only for us teeth-gnashing, woolgathering music typists, Beam appeals again to his happenstance ethic: "I just record. I just play. I just write songs about what I'm interested in. I'm proud of the new album."

■ ■ ■

The last seven things I almost know about Iron & Wine: Those of you weaned on Jimmie Dale Gilmore might not hear enough voice in Sam Beam's voice. He reads to keep up with the current poetry scene. He admits that he occasionally desires a good "rocking out." He has a weakness for holiness snake-handling church bands, but lately listens to a lot of African music. His crib in Miami boasts a yard. The authenticity myth is a waste of time. The industrious trot of "Love and Some Verses" is irresistible.

Author Notes

GRANT ALDEN is art director, co-editor, co-publisher, and co-founder of *No Depression*.

PETER BLACKSTOCK is co-editor, co-publisher, and co-founder of *No Depression*.

WILLIAM BOWERS has been published in *Open City, Oxford American, Magnet, Esquire,* and Pitchforkmedia.com. He has appeared in four anthologies, including Da Capo's *Best Music Writing 2004.* His book *All We Read Is Freaks* was published in 2004.

Canadian correspondent PAUL CANTIN is a Toronto-based writer. His first *No Depression* piece was a 1998 profile of the Sadies in *ND* #17. Since then, he has written about Dan Penn, Ron Sexsmith, Beth Orton, Stompin' Tom Connors, and others.

Senior editor DAVID CANTWELL is the author of *George Strait: An Illustrated Musical History* and the co-author of *Heartaches by the Number: Country Music's 500 Greatest Singles.*

PETER COOPER is a music critic at the Nashville *Tennessean.* His contributions to *ND* have included profiles of Lonesome Bob, Cowboy Jack Clement, and Eric Taylor.

JOHN T. DAVIS is a journalist, author, and music historian living in Austin, Texas. He is the author of *Austin City Limits: 25 Years of American Music,* and the co-author of a forthcoming autobiography of honky-tonk singer Johnny Bush.

ERIK FLANNIGAN is a music critic and Internet executive based in Los Angeles. He is a former editor at *Ice* and *Backstreets.*

Senior editor BILL FRISKICS-WARREN is music editor of the *Nashville Scene* and has contributed to the *New York Times, Washington Post, Oxford American,* and *Village Voice.* He is the co-author of *Heartaches by the Number: Country Music's 500 Greatest Singles.* His book on pop music and the urge for transcendence will be published in the fall of 2005.

Senior editor GEOFFREY HIMES has written about music full-time since 1977 for the *Washington Post, Rolling Stone,* National Public Radio, *Crawdaddy, Country Music, Bluegrass Unlimited, Sing Out, Downbeat, Jazz Times,* and many others. His songs have been recorded by the Kinsey Report, Steve Key, Billy Kemp, Edge City, and others.

Contributing editor SILAS HOUSE is the author of the novels *Clay's Quilt, A Parchment of Leaves,* and *The Coal Tattoo.* He has written about Buddy Miller, Kelly Willis, Delbert McClinton, and others for *ND.* He is a professor at Eastern Kentucky University and with Spalding University's MFA in Writing program.

BILL C. MALONE is professor emeritus at Tulane University and is the author of *Country Music U.S.A., Singing Cowboys and Musical Mountaineers,* and, most recently, *Southern Culture and the Roots of Country Music.*

Senior editor BARRY MAZOR has been writing about American music since the 1970s. He is also a contributor to the *Wall Street Journal, Washington Post, Village Voice, Nashville Scene,* and *Country Music Today.*

Senior editor DON MCLEESE is an associate professor of journalism at the University of Iowa. He was formerly the pop-music critic at the *Chicago Sun-Times* and the *Austin American-Statesman.*

Contributing editor DAVID MENCONI is the music critic at the *Raleigh (NC) News & Observer.*

JIM RIDLEY writes about film for the *Nashville Scene.* His writing has also appeared in *Cinema Scope, Variety, Psychotronic,* and *Shock Cinema.*

Contributing editor LLOYD SACHS is a pop-culture columnist and editorial writer for the *Chicago Sun-Times.*